Linguistic perspectives
on literature

Linguistic perspectives on literature

edited by
Marvin K. L. Ching
Michael C. Haley
Ronald F. Lunsford

Routledge & Kegan Paul
London, Boston and Henley

First published in 1980
by Routledge & Kegan Paul Ltd
39 Store Street,
London WC1E 7DD.
Broadway House,
Newtown Road,
Henley-on-Thames,
Oxon RG9 1EN and
9 Park Street,
Boston, Mass. 02108, USA
Set in Press Roman 10/11 by
Hope Services, Abingdon
and printed in Great Britain by
Redwood Burn Ltd
Trowbridge & Esher

British Library Cataloguing in Publication Data

Linguistic perspectives on literature.

1. Literature 2. Discourse analysis
I. Ching, Marvin K   II. Haley, Michael C
III. Lunsford, Ronald F
801'.4   PN54   79-42950

ISBN 0 7100 0382 X
ISBN 0 7100 0383 8 Pbk

To   Kellogg Hunt and Peter Menzel, who fascinated us
     with the world of linguistics

Contents

About the editors

Marvin K. L. Ching is presently Assistant Professor of English at Memphis State University. His teaching duties include courses in literature and linguistics. In the spring and summer of 1977, he taught graduate seminars in linguistic applications to literature. His doctoral dissertation was a linguistic analysis of the oxymoron. Papers and publications include: 'A Review of Pollin, *Poe, the Creator of Words*,' with John Lasley Dameron in *Mississippi Quarterly*, December 1976; 'A Literary and Linguistic Analysis of Compact Verbal Paradox,' in *College Composition and Communication*, December 1975; 'Releasing Students for Writing about Slang', in *Wordsmith*, vol. 1, 1979, pp. 33–41; 'The Relationship Among the Diverse Senses of a Pun,' read at South Atlantic Modern Language Association and Southeastern Conference on Linguistics, November, 1976; 'Interpreting Meaningful Nonsense,' Tennessee Conference on Linguistics, March, 1977; 'The Relationship among the Diverse Senses of a Pun,' *The Southeastern Conference on Linguistics Bulletin*, 2, No. 3 (Fall 1978), pp. 1–8; 'Dialectal Variations of the Dozens in Tennessee,' *The Tennessee Folklore Society Bulletin*, 45, No. 2 (June 1979), pp. 68–78.

Michael Cabot Haley is presently Assistant Professor of Language and Literature at North Central College in Naperville, Ill. His teaching duties include both linguistics and literature. His doctoral dissertation was a psycholinguistic model of figurative language. Papers include: 'Romantic Imagery and the Modern Psyche' with Ronald F. Lunsford at a meeting of The Popular Culture Association in the South, Birmingham, Alabama, October, 1974; 'Spatial subcategorization in the Semantics of Metaphor,' Tennessee Conference on Linguistics, March, 1977; 'Concrete Abstraction: The Linguistic Universe of Metaphor,' at SAMLA and SECOL, November, 1977. He has also received awards for his verse from Poets and Patrons, Inc., of Chicago.

Ronald F. Lunsford is presently Assistant Professor of English at Clemson University where he supervises, and teaches rhetoric to, graduate assistants in English. His other teaching duties include graduate level linguistics and undergraduate literature. His doctoral dissertation was a linguistic approach to rhetoric. Papers include 'Romantic Imagery and the Modern Psyche,' with Michael Cabot Haley at a meeting of the Popular Culture Association in the South, Birmingham, Alabama, October, 1974; and 'Cognitive Linguistics and the Concept of Literary Style,' at Tennessee Conference on Linguistics, March 1977. For the summer of 1977 he was awarded a seminar grant from the National Endowment for the Humanities to study linguistic approaches to rhetoric.

All three editors studied linguistics and literature together under the direction of Kellogg W. Hunt and Peter Menzel during their doctoral studies at Florida State University. Prior to that, Mr Ching received his M.A. in literature from the University of Hawaii; Mr Haley received his M.A. in creative writing from the University of Alabama; Mr Lunsford received his M.A. in literature from the University of North Carolina at Chapel Hill.

About the contributors

Derek Bickerton teaches in the Department of Linguistics at the University of Hawaii. His major area of specialization is pidgin and creole languages, but he is also interested in the relation between syntax and semantics—hence his interest in metaphor. Besides his principal publication *Dynamics of a Creole System* (London: Cambridge University Press, 1975), he has published numerous articles in such journals as *Language, Foundations of Language*, and *Lingua*. He is also author of several novels, the latest of which, *King of the Sea*, will be published later this year by Random House.

Michael J. Reddy has authored other papers on metaphor and figurative language, such as 'Formal Referential Models of Poetic Structure,' *Papers from the Ninth Regional Meeting of the Chicago Linguistic Society*, ed. C. Corum, *et al*. (Chicago: Department of Linguistics, 1973), pp. 493-518, and 'Multiguity: A Characteristic of Poetic Language,' *Publications of the Arkansas Philological Association*, I, No. 2 (1975), pp. 42-8.

Robert J. Matthews, assistant professor of Philosophy at Cook College, Rutgers University, specializes in aesthetics, philosophy of language, and philosophy of science (especially philosophy of psychology). His work has appeared in numerous scholarly journals, including *Synthese, Foundations of Language, Journal of Philosophy, Journal of Aesthetics and Art Criticism*, and *Diacritics*. He was an Andrew W. Mellon Faculty Fellow in the Humanities at Harvard University during 1977-78.

Tanya Reinhart received her doctoral degree in linguistics from the Massachusetts Institute of Technology and has taught in the Department of Poetics and Comparative Literature at Tel Aviv University. Interested in both theoretical linguistics and the theory of literature, she has published articles in those areas in *Linguistic Inquiry, Papers from the Eleventh Regional Meetings, Chicago Linguistic Society*, and *PTL: A Journal for Descriptive Poetics and Theory*.

Teun A. van Dijk teaches Theory of Literature at the University of Amsterdam. His major interests are theory of literature, theory of narrative, text grammar, text logic, pragmatics and cognitive psychology. Among his publications are an introduction (in Dutch) to a text-grammatical theory of literature, a book of collected Dutch articles on theory of literature, his thesis *Some Aspects of Text Grammars* (The Hague: Mouton, 1972), *Beiträge zur generativen Poetik* (Munich: Bayerischer Schulbuch Verlag, 1972), *Kontekst en Kommunikatie* (University of Amsterdam, mimeo, 1973); he edits *Pragmatics of Language and Literature* (Amsterdam: North Holland, in press) and, together with János S. Petöfi, *Grammars and Descriptions* (Berlin–New York: De Gruyter, in press).

Joseph Williams is professor of English and Linguistics at the University of Chicago. His current interests lie in stylistics and Elizabethan social history.

Thomas G. Pavel is Professor of Linguistics at the University of Ottawa. Pavel specializes in the interaction of linguistics and literary studies. His publications include literary and linguistic papers, as well as a study in literary semiotics, *La Syntaxe Narrative des Tragédies de Corneille* (Paris: Klincksieck, 1976); an essay on language and existence, *Inflexions de Voix* (Presses de l'Université de Montréal, 1976); and a collection of philosophical stories; *Le Miroir Persan* (Paris: Denoel & Montreal: Quinze, 1977). Together with John Woods, he edited a special issue of *Poetics* dedicated to *Formal Semantics and Literary Theory* (1-2/1979).

George L. Dillon teaches in the Department of English and Linguistics, Indiana University-Purdue University at Fort Wayne, Indiana. His most recent book is *Language Processing and the Reading of Literature: Toward a Model of Comprehension* (Bloomington & London: Indiana University Press, 1978).

H. G. Widdowson, who is now professor of Education at the University of London, has lectured in many parts of the world on stylistics, applied linguistics and discourse analysis. The substance of his paper was incorporated in one of the chapters of his book *Stylistics and the Teaching of Literature* (London: Longman, 1975). He is editor of the new journal *Applied Linguistics*, published by Oxford University Press, whose first date of issue is Spring 1980. Some of his other publications from Oxford University Press include *Teaching Language as Communication* (1978) and *Explorations in Applied Linguistics* (1979). He has also served as editor and contributor for *English in Focus*, a series of specialist English textbooks also published by Oxford University Press.

Irene R. Fairley is associate professor of English and linguistics at Northeastern University in Boston. She received her master's and doctoral degrees from Harvard University and has served as a reader consultant for *Publications of the Modern Language Association of America, Computers and the Humanities*, and *Language and Style*. Writer of numerous published articles on a variety of subjects, she is also the author of a book, *e. e. cummings and Ungrammar: A Study of Syntactic Deviance in His Poems* (New York: Watermill Publishers, 1975).

Samuel Jay Keyser is Head of the Department of Linguistics at the University of Massachusetts. He edits *Linguistic Inquiry*, the *Linguistic Inquiry Monograph Series*, and the book series *Current Studies in Linguistics* (MIT Press). His research is in the history and structure of English and in literary theory; several articles on prosody have appeared in *College English*. His latest book, co-authored with Paul Postal, is *Beginning English Grammar* (Harper & Row, 1976).

Shivendra Kishore Verma is professor and Head in the Department of Linguistics and Contemporary English at the Central Institute of English and Foreign Languages, Hyderabad, India. He is interested in Hindi linguistics, syntactic analysis, and contrastive linguistics (Hindi–English).

He has published a number of books and articles: *Current trends in linguistics and the teaching of Hindi as a second language* (Central Hindi Institute, Agra, 1973); *Introductions to the teaching of English*, vol. 1 (Oxford University Press, Delhi, 1974); 'Toward a linguistic analysis of registral features,' *Acta linguistica*, 19 (1969) (Budapest); 'Word order in Hindi,' *Archiv orientalni*, 38 (1970); 'Allosentence: a study of universals in linguistic theory,' *Indogermanische Forsungen*, 75 (1970); 'The present perfect', *English teaching forum*, 10, 4 (1972); 'Certain theoretical aspects of contrastive analysis,' *ITL*, 18 (1972, Institute of Applied Linguistics, Louvain, Belgium); 'The semantics of Caahiye', *Foundations of language*, 11 (1974).

Michael Hancher teaches English at the University of Minnesota and is editor of *Centrum*.

L. G. Heller is professor of classical languages and Hebrew at the City College of new York. Besides writing a number of books and articles in well-known linguistic journals, he has served at various times as editor of *Word, American Speech*, and *Challenge*, as the etymology editor of *The Random House Dictionary of the English Language* and as editorial consultant in etymology for other publishers of dictionaries, including Holt, Rinehart & Winston.

Acknowledgments

The editors and publishers wish to acknowledge with thanks permission to reprint the following material: Faber & Faber Ltd and Harcourt Brace Jovanovich Inc. for extracts from 'The Lovesong of J. Alfred Prufrock' by T. S. Eliot, from *Collected Poems 1909-1962*; Faber & Faber Ltd and Harcourt Brace Jovanovich Inc. for an extract from 'The Dry Salvages' from *Four Quartets* by T. S. Eliot; John Murray and Random House Inc. for an extract from *The Exploits of Sherlock Holmes* by Adrian Conan Doyle and John Dickson Carr; Jonathan Cape Ltd, Holt, Rinehart & Winston Inc. and the Estate of Robert Frost for 'Stopping by Woods on a Snowy Evening' by Robert Frost, from *The Poetry of Robert Frost* edited by Edward Connery Lathem, Copyright 1923, © 1969 by Holt, Rinehart & Winston. Copyright 1951 by Robert Frost; 'a like a', Copyright 1946 by E. E. Cummings. Reprinted from his volume, *Complete Poems 1913-1962* by permission of Harcourt Brace Jovanovich Inc. and McGibbon & Kee Ltd/ Granada Publishing Ltd; 'me up at does' © 1963 by Marion Morehouse Cummings. Reprinted from E. E. Cummings, *Complete Poems 1913-1962* by permission of Harcourt Brace Jovanovich, Inc. and McGibbon & Kee Ltd/Granada Publishing Ltd; The Houghton Library, Harvard University and the state of Marion Morehouse Cummings for permission to reproduce four manuscript versions of 'when god lets my body be' by E. E. Cummings; McGibbon & Kee Ltd/Granada Publishing Ltd and The Liveright Corporation for permission to reprint 'All in green went my love riding', 'Tumbling hair' and 'when god lets my body be', by E. E. Cummings and an extract from 'voices to voices, lip to lip' by E. E. Cummings; Faber & Faber Ltd for permission to quote from *The Collected Poems of Wallace Stevens*; Grateful acknowledgement is made to Alfred A. Knopf for permission to quote from *The Collected Poems of Wallace Stevens* by Wallace Stevens. Copyright 1954 by Wallace Stevens; Faber & Faber Ltd and Random House Inc. for an extract from 'The Managers' from *Collected Poems* by W. H. Auden; Jonathan Cape Ltd and the Wesleyan University Press for permission to quote from 'Leisure', from *The Complete Poems of W. H. Davies*.

PART I

The theoretical relation between linguistics and literary studies: an introduction by the editors

The light shed upon the competence and creativity of the human mind by recent linguistic theory reminds us once again that language is much more than the incidental medium of literature; it is also a shaping and finishing instrument, a primary building material, a part of the conceptual foundation. Whether these connections are considered self-evident or hypothetical, they strongly suggest that the relationship between current linguistic and literary studies is one of the most exciting possibilities ever considered, or reconsidered, in the world of letters.

Indeed, just in the last twenty years since the publication of Chomsky's *Syntactic Structures*, there has been a plethora of linguistic applications to literature which explore this possibility. Hundreds of articles, scores of dissertations, dozens of books and anthologies, and several new journals have appeared, not to mention the numerous professional conferences and academic seminars, all of which have taken up the question of what the developing linguistic methodologies have to offer literary analysis. This exploding enthusiasm emboldened Donald Freeman, the editor of one such anthology, to remark, 'A good critic is perforce a good linguist.'[1]

There was an understandably negative reaction in some formidable quarters to this small and unsuccessful *coup d'etat*. A spirit of detente among critics toward the discipline of linguistics was one thing; surrender of their own discipline was quite another. Gradually, the small school of devout 'linguistic critics' began to acquire the suspicious smell of Swift's Grand Academy of Lagado, and many students of literature resented being expected to put in their time there cranking the giant generative/transformational frame to see what new fragments of insight might turn up. Even among those who did put in their time there and discovered for their work some new theoretical objects to substitute precisely for some old literary terms, there are many who have come to feel that the opportunity to discuss literature with language scientists is an insufficient reward for carrying such heavy objects around on their backs all the time.

However, with the advanced refinement of generative theory and the advent of a number of more pragmatic language models, the time has come for a new phase of linguistic investigation of literature. This book is dedicated to the belief that such an investigation will produce, not only the most provocative possible test situation for the present state of linguistic theory, but a revolutionary kind of insight into the nature of literature, language, and man himself.

The final proof of this claim must await thorough elaboration of the research to which the papers anthologized here are often only seminal. But in order that the issues implicit in this claim might be crystallized for on-going discussion, we, the editors, offer this introduction and position statement on what we believe the ideal of linguistic analysis should be.

This statement should not be taken as an editorial policy reflecting our criteria for selection of the articles, for indeed, not all of them espouse our position, even implicitly. Integral to our position is the necessity for methodological eclecticism, both in the fields of linguistics and literary criticism. Many of the papers have therefore been selected precisely because they represent postures somewhat at variance from our own. We feel that this variation is a healthy sign, for any movement among scholars to study so complex and multifaceted a phenomenon as literature without such a variety of approaches could not be considered a serious movement or one that was realistic about the subject of its inquiry. In no other field than literature—with the possible exception of philosophy—has linguistic thought encountered such a challenging difficulty in defining its own prerogatives and limitations. But transcending this difficulty is a unifying commitment among increasing numbers of linguists to the importance of investigating literature through the features of its language. Linguists of the last twenty years have been vitally concerned with the principles of language creativity; it is therefore virtually inevitable that this interest would lead them into literature where those principles are fully exploited.

Thus our fundamental thesis is that the creative principles of human language are centrally, not peripherally, located in the semantics and aesthetics of human literature and that the ordinary linguistic competence now being formalized in language theory offers powerful and unique perspectives on the extraordinary imaginative interplay between writer, text, and reader now dominating the concerns in literary theory. This thesis will be discussed at length under Section I below.

The ambitious idealism of this thesis is not the original claim made by linguistic analysts of literature, nor is it a claim that would gain the assent of all such analysts today. For this reason Section II below will attempt to outline our thesis against a broader theoretical landscape, including the history and status quo of the relationship between the disciplines of linguistics and literature as it has been conceived by others to be.

The diversity of views about the relationship between the two disciplines derives in part from a deeper diversification within linguistic theory itself. Thus, Section III below will survey current trends in the development and interaction of competing linguistic models where these concern literary analysis.

As indicated earlier, we believe that this diversification of linguistic models in literary analysis is a healthy sign. But a more elaborate argument for the necessity of methodological eclecticism will be presented in Section IV.

I Linguistics, literature, and literary theories

Toward a 'pure' linguistics of literature

Most people have at least known of someone who has tried to get a particular kind of job but failed because 'prior experience' with that kind of job was a necessary entrance credential. Under such absurd conditions, we might well ask how anyone could hope to gain the necessary experience.

To a certain extent, and for motives vindicated by its success, the world of letters has been isolated by the same sort of closed-shop, elitist conditions. But our long successful tradition in the study of literary history, conventions, mythology, genre, aesthetics, etc. ought not lead us to believe that prior experience in that tradition is the absolute prerequisite for entrance into the meaning and delight of literature. We must be reminded from time to time that it is not primarily because we may be experts in the various categories of traditional literary scholarship that the great truths of abiding literature speak to us so plainly and universally; it is rather because we are human beings, a species most significantly distinguished by the compulsive power to conceptualize, reshape, and communicate the experience of life through language.

In a pure idealistic sense, linguistic analysis ought to offer a formal reminder of this limited perspective. Thus the articles anthologized here are linguistic not just in the sense that they exhibit a certain virtuoso with syntactic and semantic theory, but because most of them operate from the assumption that our ordinary competence with language is a primary stone in the foundation of our competence with literature. This assumption in no way entails that we think language is all there is to literature or that linguistic competence is the only ingredient of literary competence. To be sure, full literary competence must also involve critical sensitivity and appreciation, virtues which are acquired through a full range of experience with human emotions and literary conventions.[2] What the assumption does entail is that the technical analysis of how literature activates our sensitivity and appreciation should not forever neglect the study of how it utilizes our ordinary linguistic competence to do so.

However, there is a strong current tendency, even among some 'linguistic' critics, to underplay the role of language in literature and to assign linguistic competence too modest a function in the reading of literature. Jonathan Culler's words present a good example of this tendency:[3]

> To read a text as literature is not to make one's mind a *tabula rasa* and approach it without preconceptions; one must bring to it an implicit understanding of the operations of literary discourse which tells one what to look for.
>
> Anyone lacking this knowledge, anyone wholly unacquainted with literature and unfamiliar with the conventions by which fictions are read would, for example, be quite baffled if presented with a poem. His knowledge of the language would enable him to understand phrases and sentences, but he would not know, quite literally, what to *make* of this strange concatenation of phrases.

Those of us who have tried to teach poetry to naive or unwilling students will surely have to agree with much of what Culler has to say. How much the student gets out of a poem is often the direct function of how much he brings to it. It is unreasonable to expect our students fully to understand or appreciate a great poem—even a relatively simple one—until they have some notion of what to look for and enjoy.

But one small question about Culler's truism arises and leads on to another: How do students find out what to look for and enjoy in poetry? Presumably—if Culler and those for whom he speaks are to have their way—the students must gain the required knowledge of literary conventions from some 'theory of literary discourse' (p. 113). In other words, our students need their teachers (as most of us are relieved to be reminded).

We shall for the time being overlook the uncomfortable possibility that pounding formulaic literary conventions into the heads of students represents at best the necessary evil of a short-cut in sophomore literature (for we must suspect, down deep inside, that our brilliance in the classroom will never substitute for the students' learning about literature from their persistent reading of literary texts); we shall overlook this unnerving possibility because it is at this point that a second question rears its head: If students must be taught what to look for in poetry before they can understand anything central to the work they are reading, they must hope that their teachers do indeed know what to point out; how do those teachers find out this privileged information? Presumably, from their own teachers. And they?

It seems inescapable, though it is not in fashion to admit it, that literary texts themselves must at some point represent a primal source for our understanding of literature. The texts themselves must show us what to look for through their own devices of foregrounding and pointing—else how could the first teacher of the first piece of literature have decided what to teach with any confidence whatsoever that his teaching had something to do with what is central to the text?

To those at the other extreme, who have decided with Stanley Fish that 'the objectivity of the text is an illusion,'[4] what is central to the text can only be determined by those who are students of intellectual history, who may put themselves in the supposed precise position of the readers for whom the text was originally intended. For others, reader subjectivity becomes the end of criticism, so that the reader is freed to see anything his unconscious associations, fantasies, or feelings lead him to see in the text.[5] But to those like Murray Schwartz,[6] who wish to allow for both the creative, synthesizing nature of the reader's mind AND the objective artistry of the text itself, is there no alternative mediating solipsistic phenomenology on the one hand and authoritarian methodology on the other?

Although the linguistic analysis of literature cannot presume to represent a holistic approach mediating these two extremes, it is equipped to deal rather sanely with many dimensions of literature traditionally related both to the objectivity of the text and the creativity of the reader. Specifically, it is equipped to deal with the language of the text without ignoring the reader's vital role in constructing and reconstructing the multiguous meaning and effect either initiated or permitted by the language of the text. Modern linguistic theory finds itself in this ideal position with respect to literature by reason of its increasingly successful effort to capture scientific generalizations about language through the means of objective formalizations on the intuitive, creative competence of ordinary speakers and listeners. It is therefore a happy medium through which the proper balance between the formalistic and phenomenological approaches to literature might be prefigured.

A more detailed explanation regarding the adaptability of linguistic theory to the study of creativity in readership will be offered under the next subheading in this section. The present task is to clarify and limit the claim that a 'pure' linguistics, based on 'ordinary' language competence can produce worthwhile insights into the formal properties of the 'extraordinary' discourse of literature.

By way of limitation, note again that the claim does not entail the belief that the linguistic approach to literature can replace traditional criticism. Partially fostered by the overambitious claims of some linguists, this misconception is widespread. Helen Vendler's remarks are typical:[7]

> If linguistics can add to our comprehension of literature, someone
> trained in linguistics should be able to point out to us, in poems
> we already know well, significant features we have missed because
> of our amateurish ignorance of the workings of language. Attempts
> in this line . . . adopt a complacent tone implying that the authors
> have come to give a great light to the people who walk in darkness.

In contrast to early linguistic analysts of literature, we agree with
Vendler's challenge that linguists must 'add to our comprehension of
literature' by pointing out 'significant features' that have not been
noted in traditional criticism. But our position is that these features
have been appropriately omitted, not 'missed,' by traditional analyses.
Most linguists are not interested in explaining to literary critics what
they may not know about the 'workings of language', rather, they are
interested in formalizing what almost any native speaker already knows
intuitively about language, in the hope that such formalizations may
allow observations (about the importance of language in literature)
which might never have otherwise been made, let alone made explicit.
Thus, linguists do not generally think of non-linguists as 'people who
walk in darkness'; rather, they operate from the stubborn belief that
some of the 'great light' of literature is already accessible to almost any
literate human being, and they think it is the duty of the linguistic
critic, not to 'bring the light,' but to describe how our response to
this light is causally related to its formal, objective properties. It is not,
then, what traditional critics are 'ignorant' of that linguists wish to contribute; it is rather what, by virtue of their differing tools, perspectives
and objectives, the traditional critics have in the main quite properly
ignored.

We say 'in the main' because we recognize that modern linguists
have no exclusive claim to the analysis of the formal properties of language in literature. As Vendler goes on to note, there have been many
'non-linguists,' critics like 'Richards, Spitzer, Burke, Blackmur, Empson,
and others, whose sense of linguistic patterning is formidably acute'
(p. 457). It may indeed be the case that modern linguistics has failed
so far to give us critics 'comparable in literary subtlety' to these men.
But that is surely no indictment against modern linguistic methods.
In fact, if Vendler's examples of good non-linguistic critics are ex-
ceptional even in part because of their acute sense of linguistic patterning,
then we should think that their example recommends to us any linguistic method which might sharpen our own sense of such patterning.
The developing power of current linguistic theory to do this for 'ordinary language' has not been seriously denied; its power to do this for
'literary language' has not been adequately tested.[8]

Of course, there is good reason to proceed with this testing of linguistic models only if we suspect that the well-documented success

of such models in the analysis of ordinary discourse implies their potential for success in the analysis of literary discourse. Thus we are back
to our central claim, which many do not share: The operations of
ordinary linguistic competence are vital to the meaning and delight
of literature. To many others, this seems to be a trivial presumption.
It might seem to be almost like saying, 'You have to be able to read
the words in order to understand literature; therefore reading theory is
vital to literary criticism.'

Reading theory may indeed have something to contribute to literary
studies (see next subsection), but it is not analogous to linguistic theory
in this respect. Reading is clearly a secondarily acquired skill, restricted
to a minority of the earth's population; linguistic competence universally
characterizes the human condition and seems to have much deeper
roots in the very structure of the human mind.[9] According to Whorf
and others, it is almost impossible to understand the categories of
human culture and thought apart from an understanding of the categories of human language. Furthermore, the sort of competence which
is the target for description in much modern linguistic theory is the
sort which is apparently responsible for the infinite productivity and
effability of human language.[10] Linguistic models which have manifest
powers to deal seriously with such significant phenomena ought to have
manifest importance to the study of literature, for it would be difficult
to discover a list of concerns more crucial to literature than those which
are the concerns of man himself as seen through the universal features
of his linguistic competence: rationality, creativity, and the need to
characterize his experience by communicating it.

Of course, the rationality, creativity, characterizations of experience,
and need to communicate are not 'ordinary' competencies in the case
of a literary artist. But we believe that the extraordinary dimensions
of a work of literary art are often the result of the artist's novel selection and manipulation of what is common to ordinary experience. In
the same way, it is possible that at least some of the artist's artistry
might be formally and critically accessible through the analysis of how
his language selects and manipulates the features of ordinary language.
When these features are understood through the powerful models of
modern language theory, new insights about the way language functions
in the poet's vision, or about the way it functions in the reconstruction
of that vision by an ordinary reader, may well be gained for the first
time in literary research.

A linguistic analysis of literature which maintains this emphasis
ought never be viewed in competition with the more established schools
of criticism. It is not to the linguist, but to himself that the established
critic must turn, as an example of someone whose intuitions have
been schooled by a broad and lengthy reading of literature so that he
understands and appreciates the subtleties of genre, literary period,

characterization, myth, etc. Likewise, it is not to the critic, as has often been claimed,[11] but to himself that the linguist must turn, as an example of someone whose intuitions have been shaped by his formal under-standing of ordinary linguistic competence. Consequently, the estab-lished critic makes observations about a literary work which tend mainly, though not exclusively, to explain and evaluate its impact upon the established world of letters; the linguistic analyst makes observa-tions about the same work which tend mainly to explain only those linguistic origins of its impact upon any serious and intelligent reader. Language analysis has the virtuous potential, then, of touching upon some of the linguistic foundation stones of great literature's universal meaningfulness and appeal; but to the extent that it possesses this virtue, it may be less critically holistic than the observations of a trained litterateur. Of course, if the linguistic critic is also a litterateur, he may shuttle productively back and forth between the two roles, just as a traditional critic may do if he is also a linguist, trained or other-wise. But the two roles are neither the same nor in any necessary competition with one another. They ought instead to co-operate, but their co-operation must be defined as a function of the overlap between the interests and responses of a litterateur and those of any intelligent reader. For good reason, as we argue in the next subsection, this overlap is not to be considered complete. It is an overlap that occurs only at the inter-section between the shape of human culture and the shape of human language.

Not every approach to literature which seems to be linguistic es-pouses this focal emphasis upon the ordinary linguistic competence as a source of its observations. One of the best ways to illustrate what this focus implies is to examine one study which, because it lacks that focus, comes into an unnecessary and unsuccessful competition with estab-lished criticism. Consider a passage from Derek Bickerton's 'Prole-gomena to a Linguistic Theory of Metaphor':[12]

> If, in reading a poem, we encounter lexemes such as *moon, rose,* or *autumn*, we are likely . . . to give them values such as 'unattainable beauty', 'perfect beauty', and 'ripeness and/or decay', rather than 'satellite of earth', 'species of flower', and 'third season of the year.' But we would in no circumstance do this while reading an almanac or a horticultural catalogue.

Bickerton's paper is interesting and has been included in this collection. What he has said in this passage is no doubt true for experienced readers, but despite its linguistic orientation, it is not the 'pure' linguis-tic truth. Furthermore, the linguist, as such, is not in as formidable a position from which to affirm this truth as a traditional literary critic is. The reason for saying this becomes clear when we ask ourselves *why* we assign meanings like 'unattainable beauty' to the word *moon* in a poem but not in an almanac. Presumably, it is because we know that poets generally use words in this special way, whereas writers of almanacs generally do not. But what is the source of this observation? How do we know that poets use words in this special way? For most critics, it is almost enough to answer that it is because we have read other poems. For the synchronic linguist, this answer is never enough; he wants to know how we learned to perceive such figurative meanings from the 'other poems' to begin with. He wants to know how much of the poetic meaning can be understood not by reference to poetic tradition, but by reference to poetry's foundations in language.

The linguist is haunted by the suspicion that there must have been a *first* poem sometime, somewhere, which caused some fellow (who perhaps had never read anything but an almanac before) suddenly to see the moon as an image of unattainable beauty. The linguist also knows enough about the subtle metaphoric creativity of human language in general to believe that the first poem in particular probably got the fellow in question to see the moon in that way without explaining the whole thing to him, either. The linguist wants to know how the first poem performed that 'miracle,' and he is obsessed with the stubborn hope that he can explain it (without explaining it away) by reference to the poet's manipulation of common linguistic principles (otherwise, how could that first reader have understood it?). The linguist thinks he can do this without finding the manuscript of that first poem, too, because he finds poets doing exactly the same sort of thing today, not just with the moon, but with all kinds of images one would never expect them to use, even from having read all their other poems.

And each time he rediscovers this first principle of language at work in a new poem, the linguist is haunted again by the notion of that hypothetical 'first poem,' probably because he remembers that in his own reading experience there was indeed a first poem, one that opened his mind (unschooled in the learned tradition of literary scholarship though it was). He is not so foolish as to think for a moment that this adolescent enthusiasm with a first poem constituted a full and mature appreciation of poetic art; but the way in which the language of his first poem opened his imagination, lightened his heart, or reorganized his way of looking at the world, is not a phenomenon he proposes to forget in his advanced study of poetry. He is all the more determined to carry out this study through the intricate analysis of poetic language because he sees that dimension of poetry (which is the only one that could have produced the important effect he wishes to explain) so often ignored or treated cursorily by a tradition of literary scholarship whose main concerns quite properly lie elsewhere. True, the trained critic in that tradition is our best consultant for the poet's use of myth and symbol; the linguist's special target is the creative system by which myth and symbol are constructed and interpreted from the principles of language productivity.

In this view of the case, it is partially misleading to say that the traditional and linguistic critics converge upon the same objective from different perspectives; it is more accurate to say that they diverge upon different objectives from the same object. The critic relates the literary object to his formal knowledge of cumulative literary experience; the linguist relates the same object to his formal knowledge of noncumulative linguistic competence. To test this division of emphases, we need only be reminded that the successful critical tradition as we know it would have been impossible without a body of literature upon which to operate, but that the linguistic analysis of literature would, ideally speaking, operate upon the first piece of literature ever produced. In this sense only, we think the linguistic analysis of literature should be thought of in the tradition of the formalist school of critical thought (except that linguists should realize that their formalizations about literary language are not thorough treatments of literature, as the formalists evidently failed to realize). In another sense, however, linguistic theory has new developments that promise to reach beyond the formal analysis of the propositional structure of the text to account for other kinds of competence involved in the reader's reconstruction of literary meaning and effect. These are discussed in the following sections.

The aim of this subsection has been simply to clarify and limit what we mean by the claim that as a 'pure' approach, linguistics has much to offer literary analysis. The proof of that claim, we believe, begins with the kind of papers here anthologized and awaits elaboration by subsequent research in this direction.

For that reason, we make no apology for the bold idealism of this claim. It is indeed idealistic to believe that any primary insight, let alone a thorough treatment, could be realized by considering a literary work as an example of the creativity implicit in and extended from human language rather than from a well-developed literary culture. However, by virtue of the considerable advances made by linguistic theory in the last twenty years toward understanding the magnitude of human linguistic competence and its integral role in the shaping of human thought and culture, linguists can ill afford to abandon this idealism in the face of scepticism from those who know little or nothing about these accomplishments. For it is this idealism that has made those accomplishments possible in the study of language; and it is precisely this idealism that has never been adequately tested in the study of literature, man's supreme use of language. We call for a clear articulation by linguists regarding their peculiar hopes and aims and a pursuit of those hopes and aims with a boldness that dares to be vulnerable in the quest for greater knowledge.

As we shall see in Section II, however, many linguists interested in literature have not been so bold or clear. Part of the reason, we believe, is the disparity that exists between the linguistic notion of 'ideal speaker/listener' and the literary critical notion of the 'ideal reader.' We shall now turn to this issue.

Toward a linguistic theory of readership

The most serious obstacle and yet, ironically, the most inviting provocation for linguists entering the world of letters is the new emphasis in contemporary critical theory on the notion of 'the ideal reader.' According to Robert DeMaria, this 'emphasis upon readers and the act of reading' has become so strong that it has sometimes resulted in the 'exclusion' or even 'the avowed extinction of authors and literary objects.'[13] For the linguist, then, this development is both a stepping stone and a stumbling-block: the focus on reader epistemology invites the linguist's application of interpretative and pragmatic semantics to literary problems, but the movement away from textual ontology threatens to subvert the linguist's original posture of formal and scientific objectivity in the study of the language itself.

Nevertheless, the impetus behind this new interest in reader response is ultimately supportive of what we have defined as the linguist's prerogative with literature. That impetus seems to move critical theory away from narrow formalism, a partial model based solely upon the text, and to move it toward a broad phenomenology, a more holistic model based upon the dynamics of text/reader interaction. This movement therefore gives momentum to the modern linguistic investigation of literature because—although the linguist is part formalist in the sense that he is ultimately interested in the structure of the language itself—he is also part phenomenologist in the sense that his means of investigating language structure is precisely his generalizations about the innate, creative competence of the speaker or hearer of that language. From this particular linguistic perspective, then, the movement in critical theory toward more concern for 'the reader' is very healthy, as long as it does not go too far—that is, as long as the study of the way texts and readers *interac*t does not deteriorate into the study of the way readers merely *act*.

Such a deterioration would destroy the generative linguist's hopes for citizenship in the federation of literary scholars, for it would demand that he abandon his own heritage of competence-based grammar and operate under the alien banner of performance-bound scientism. But we believe that this deterioration would also spell the end of that federation itself, for it would substitute the study of literacy for what ought to remain the study of literature.

This caution on our part should not be interpreted as hostility toward the study of literacy or its relevance to the study of literature. It should only be taken as our insistence that the two are ultimately distinct, though not disjunct, endeavors. One therefore cannot neatly replace the other, any more than the linguistic analysis of literature for which we have argued can replace traditional literary criticism. The precondition of this pluralist stance, for which we shall argue more fully in Section IV, is that the proponents of alternative models should be willing to cooperate as vigorously as they are justified in competing. This precondition can be satisfied if all parties concerned will anchor the arguments for the supremacy of their various approaches to convincing declarations of accuracy in their self-imposed limitations. Indeed, if critics, linguists, and psychologists would predicate their contentions about literature on carefully-focussed perspectives rather than ambitiously-stretched claims, interdisciplinary discussions might be carried out with great benefit to all.

But it is difficult to carry on a discussion with someone who misapprehends the scope of what either he or his conversant is trying to do. Such misapprehension has apparently occurred on both sides of the debate regarding how linguistic theory relates to the developing theories of readership in literary studies and in psychology. As George Dillon points out, for example, some early generative stylists took 'the term *generative* psychologically—to assume that the model of surface structure, transformations, and deep structure was a direct replica of sentence production and perception.'[14] Dillon reminds us that Chomsky had warned against this misconception and that subsequent psycholinguistic research has confirmed that transformational generative grammar cannot seriously be used as a model of the actual psychological process through which we understand sentences. Processing is simply a matter exceeding the scope of generative grammar; it belongs to a broader psycholinguistic theory of sentence and text perception.[15]

However, the fact that generative grammar is not a psychological model of sentence processing in no way indicates—as Dillon seems to conclude (p. xvii)—that it is irrelevant to the study of text/reader interaction. We could argue that generative grammar is indeed relevant to a theory of readership in fundamentally the same way in which a theory of readership is relevant to a theory of literature.

A theory of readership will serve in literary studies only insofar as it helps us to understand and appreciate the meaning and artistry of the successful literary text. We see no direct value—for literary studies—in the question, 'What do readers do when they read?' That question, taken for its own sake, is the primary concern of the psycholinguist. The only question regarding readership which might concern the contemporary student of literature is, 'What is there in the text that makes it so eminently readable, so evocative of meaning and delight?' A student serious about this question would do well to borrow the findings of psycholinguistics about the reading process as a useful set of tips for the research he is carrying out on the literary text in question.

In addition, that student would also do well to consider the findings of generative grammar regarding the semantic principles of propositional structure. There has been no effort on the part of generative grammarians to formulate these findings in a theory which is itself psychologically real, nor are the components of generative theory arranged in psychological chronology so as to reflect the actual mentalistic process of sentence production or perception. But generative theory need not purport to represent the cognitive *processes* of text/reader interaction in order to capture the rational *laws* of that interaction. Generative grammar purports to represent the logical principles (not the psychological mechanics) of the relation between propositional language structures and predictable semantic effects. Just as the logician is interested in the underlying relations of the syllogism as these may be reconstructed from an enthymeme (which presents these relations in a varied rhetorical order), so the generative linguist is interested in the underlying relations of the proposition as these may be reconstructed from a sentence (which presents these relations in a varied perceptual order). The logician need not claim that the sequence of major premise, minor premise, and conclusion conforms to the actual rhetorical order by which people present or understand arguments; nor need the linguist claim that the sequence of deep structure, transformation, and surface structure conforms to the actual psychological order by which people produce or process sentences. Thus generative grammar makes no claim to capture the chronology of events in the brain; nor does formal logic. Neither is irrelevant, for all that, to an understanding of the abstract principles by which human reason governs discourse.

Generative grammar rests its claim of relevancy to those principles on the grounds that it can systematically (though the 'system' is theoretical and arbitrary) relate meaning to structure. Because such structures clearly exist in the text and because such meaning clearly exists in the reader, it is equally clear that generative grammar is vitally relevant to text/reader interaction.

In fact, it is probably more relevant to a literary theory of readership than a purely psychological model of reading would be. Limited to the cognitive process of reading, the pure psychological model is really concerned with the action of the reader; it is concerned with the function of the text only in so far as this is necessary to understand the psychology of the reader's reaction. Applied in its pure form to literature, such a theory would tend to founder in the affective fallacy. Generative theory, on the other hand, reverses this emphasis: It is concerned with the reader's power to act (competence) only in so far as this is necessary to understand the nature and function of language. It is therefore trained upon the language text, but focuses upon it through the lens of reader reaction; for this reason, its insights are into what may be appropriately called text/reader interaction, not merely reader reaction.

However, the usefulness of generative grammar in the language component for a theory of readership in no way implies its completeness for such a use. It is, in fact, deliberately and grossly incomplete as a language model of reading, for it deals only with the sort of language competence which is narrowly conceived as the ability to interpret the formal propositions of the text. It is now widely acknowledged that the native ability of the language user extends far beyond this kind of competence—far beyond the sentence-bound proposition to linguistic relationships that hold between sentences and text, text and context. If linguistics is to offer an adequate model of language for use within the larger theory of literary readership, it must move to account for these additional dimensions in reader competence.

Several new developments discussed more fully in Section III promise to offer compelling answers to this need. Most notably, speech-act theory provides pragmatic possibilities for studying the dynamic and creative interplay of readers, not only with the larger elements of the text itself, but also with the persona of authorship projected in the text. Although not the thrust of this collection, speech-act theory is admirably represented in its relevance to sensitive criticism by Michael Hancher's practical use of it in the analysis of poetry and by Van Dijk's forward-looking application of it to a theory of metaphoric discourse (both of these papers are anthologized here). This work will no doubt prove crucial in the full elaboration of the reader's role in reconstructing hidden dimensions of the text. As we may see in the work of Marcia Eaton[16] for example, speech act theory can serve this function by explaining how readers predictably construct—from linguistic principles and textual cues—sound interpretations about important meaning that is not in the text as an explicit proposition.

The linguistic theory of readership projected so far in this discussion, then, would consist of at least two components: (1) the generative-transformational core, stipulating the logical truth conditions and principles of meaning amalgamation from formal propositions; this component, without reference to the actual psychological processes of perception and meaning selection, would elaborate all possible semantic effects which constitute the range of meaningful choices the reader constructs either consciously or unconsciously from discrete, explicit, sentential units; (2) the pragmatic overlay, stipulating the formal rules of textual and contextual induction and deduction from implicit linguistic relationships; this component, again without any necessary empirical basis in psychology, would elaborate the range of possible hidden meanings or other meanings arising from relationships larger than discrete, explicit sentences; it would also furnish a competence-based code of author-reader co-operation for selecting preferred meanings from the above ranges of formal and pragmatic possibilities.

Such a two-part linguistic model of reader competence itself would represent only one component in a holistic theory of literacy. As we envision the entire package, the linguistic component ought to be accompanied at least by a model of secondarily-acquired 'literary competence,' in which the cumulative knowledge of conventions such as plot, myth, symbol, etc. would furnish 'scripts' or 'cognitive screens,' representing the anticipations of an experienced reader. All of these components might well be ordered with respect to one another along lines dictated by findings from cognitive psychology and psycho-linguistic processing theory. But a purely linguistic model of reader competence, it seems to us, could be one very important element for any complete formal theory of readers' interaction with literary texts.

Thus before linguistic theory can make its observations about language competence fully useful to literary studies, it must define for itself just what sort of ideal 'reader's competence' it should assume as its perspective in literary studies. We have already suggested that, for the purposes of the pure linguistic analysis of literature, it should assume, as its focus on the text, only the ideal ability to read explicit sentential propositions along with implicit textual implicatures. Perhaps this suggestion can be clarified and supported in part by returning to DeMaria's discussion of what is meant by the notion of an ideal reader.

DeMaria (pp. 463-74) argues that the sort of 'ideal reader' an analyst assumes for the purposes of his analysis will determine the form of his literary criticism. He illustrates this principle by contrasting the critical writings of Northrop Frye and Dr Johnson, among others. What DeMaria shows concerning their different underlying assumptions about the ideal reader will serve the point we wish to reiterate.

DeMaria says the quest of Frye's ideal reader is carried out in the 'landscape' of 'all literature,' so that 'the outline of the journey corresponds to the overall mythos of literature' (p. 469). It seems clear that cumulative literary exerience is a necessary part of the competence of this assumed reader; for as Frye himself writes:[17]

> In the greatest moments of Dante and Shakespeare, in, say, *The Tempest* or the climax of the *Purgatorio*, we have a feeling of converging significance, the feeling that here we are close to seeing what our whole literary experience has been about . . .

It is this grasp Frye's reader has upon the mythology of 'our whole literary experience' which, in part, makes him into what DeMaria calls a 'Promethean reader.'

But Johnson's assumed reader is no Promethean man at all, even though he is no less heroic than Prometheus. The point is that he is no litterateur, for he is a reader 'uncorrupted by literary prejudices' who rejects 'the cant of those who judge by principles rather than perception' (p. 463). He is, in fact, a 'common reader,' an 'ordinary man,' an idealized version of the common man, to be sure, one who represents the archetype of all that was best in the eighteenth-century man of reason, but a common, ordinary man nonetheless. In sharp contrast to Frye's mythical traveler who feels in the individual masterpiece a 'converging' of the 'whole literary experience,' Johnson's ordinary reader understands and appreciates the work of art by referring 'finally to nature, and general nature is found in the understanding of the abstract common man' (p. 464).

The choice presented by these two alternative readers would be relatively simple for those who behave as if the most recent good idea in a particular discipline ought to furnish the guidepost for anyone working within that discipline. But the matter is not that simple. Even if we were to grant the essential 'recency' of Frye's quite sane perspective, we should have to remember that literary critical theory is not an empirical science like bibliography; its findings do not accumulate, though our bibliographical understanding of source and tradition, etc. may indeed. Therefore, the student of literature who opts for an 'old' critical perspective is not likely to be 'out of date' (especially if he gets it from the likes of a Johnson) in the same way a student of the planets would be 'out of date' if he showed a preference for Aristotle's astronomy. The study of literature is not like the study of the planets; Aristotle's geocentric notions about the universe are gone, for the most part, but his ideas about poetics are as good as they ever were. This attitude about the history of human ideas is implicit within Frye's posture itself.

So our purpose is not to solve the debate between Samuel Johnson and Northrop Frye about how to read literature. They probably agree more than disagree, for each perspective is, for its particular objectives, quite valid.

It is clearly the case that Frye's is valid. As we have already suggested, it is unreasonable to expect students to fully understand and appreciate a great piece of literature until they have read a lot of other literature. The long successful tradition of letters which has given us men like T. S. Eliot would have been impossible without a vast body of literature from which to draw, just as the important study of cumulative literary mythology which has given us men like Frye would have been impossible without a vast body of literature on which to operate. It may even be the case that the peculiar aesthetic of twentieth-century literature is so built up from literary tradition that it—more than any other century of letters—requires a learned reader. In our time, poems are indeed made out of other poems.

But we sincerely hope that modern literary art has not become so derived as to make Culler correct in saying that anyone unacquainted with literature would be totally 'baffled' by poetry, even after persistent reading. For even though we may still be baffled in some sense by *The Waste Land*, even after we have studied the footnotes, our bewilderment may be an important part of the poem's ultimate implications. Even poems in the learned tradition are made out of something more basic than other poems; they are also made out of language. This may be true in more than the obvious sense, for the modern poets themselves are often fond of telling us that the sounds, the words, the sentences, and the language-text structures are more than merely a way of saying things in verse; they are also a way of *seeing* things. When language is granted the status of a means of 'seeing' in literature, the importance of ordinary linguistic competience is promoted as well, as far as a theory of readership is concerned. Though we may allow that poets are the masters and 'makers' of their language, the ordinary principles of linguistic creativity remain the only common ground for the poets' first rendezvous with ordinary non-poets. For reasons argued above, something must be granted *a priori* status in reader competence; as linguists, we think there is good reason for believing that human beings are born with innate linguistic propensities which, though 'ordinary' in the sense of being common to man, may be manipulated and extended by the poets among us in constructions of such universal genius that even the non-poets among us perceive the opportunity to retrace the design. As the man who could never execute the blueprint of St Peter's in Rome nonetheless may draw upon his own innate sense of order and symmetry to understand and thrill at something of what Michelangelo means to the world, so we believe that the ordinary reader must draw upon his native grasp of the creative principles buried in human language to experience, at those 'greatest moments of Dante and Shakespeare,' a 'converging significance,' the certainty that he is close to seeing—perhaps not what 'our whole literary experience has been about'—but at least what our whole *human* experience has been about. On all accounts, such moments are inseparable from what Frye himself calls 'the feeling that we have moved into the still center of the order of words' (pp. 117-18).

Probably the greatest moment of all that a reader can experience results from his being able to see in a masterpiece a converging of both literary and human experience. For this reason, we believe the kinds of ideal readership assumed by Johnson and Frye are both valid, especially since they may furnish us with a principle for delineating the unique perspectives of the linguistic analyst and the traditional literary critic.

As it is most desirable to have both kinds of reading competence collaborating in one idealized reader, so we feel that the linguistic and traditional perspectives on literature might beneficially collaborate in one overall theory of criticism.

It should be obvious that we feel linguistics is more suited to the Johnsonian perspective. Its contemporary basis for observations, as we have repeated throughout, is the ordinary linguistic competence. The similarity of this presumption to Johnson's notion of readership is no accident, really, since the philosophical orientation of linguists in the generative tradition is closely akin to that of eighteenth century rationalism.

It might be objected that the Promethean Reader of critics like Frye already incorporates this kind of 'ordinary competence' within its model of 'literary competence.' This is partially true, but it does not negate the utility of linguistic formalization of ordinary competence as well. Again, the distinction is a matter of emphasis. Because the 'learned tradition' of readership is uniquely suited to the important study of literary conventions, that is likely to be its emphasis; because the linguistic perspective on readership is best suited to the important study of how the literary vision is extended from principles of creativity implicit in the language of readers and writers, that is likely to be its emphasis. A theory of criticism weighted too heavily by either emphasis is likely to become too elitist on the one hand or too formulaic and simplistic on the other. Either event would remove the ideal reader too far from man himself.

And it is, after all, man himself from whom literature comes and for whom it is intended. If the linguistic excursion into literature serves no other function than to issue a compelling new kind of formal reminder to this effect, it shall have made a vital point. In making that point, linguists must remember that they are not best equipped to discuss all of man's competencies with literature, for there are many others to be explained besides linguistic creativity. But that competence is surely one without which there would be no writing or reading of literature at all.

II History and status quo of the linguistic investigation of literature

The sole expressed aim of many early transformational linguists who were interested in literature was to contribute formal, empirical, and quantitative data in support of established critical opinion.[18] The difficulty many traditional critics had in accepting these contributions of support was simply that they could not understand why 'established critical opinion' needed any more 'establishing,' especially since the linguists were offering mainly sophisticated quantitative data for only the most commonplace, self-evident critical insights. These early efforts may be forgiven on the grounds that they were really attempting to develop methods rather than results in any far-reaching sense. Nevertheless, there were results, and McLain has offered the only fair evaluation of these: 'It is as if a scientist were to provide the final, irrefutable evidence that 100°F is warmer than 3°F' (p. 235).

Furthermore, these early studies failed to convince traditional critics that, if linguists were allowed into the world of letters, they would forever remain content to offer flank support for their critical generals. For with the offers of supporting data came demands that critics cease giving out allegedly subjective and impressionistic opinions without raw linguistic data to back them up. Especially with the decline of strict textual formalism as the dominant school, these linguistic demands came to be received with growing disdain. In short, critics were not made any happier about threats against the independence of their perspective by the linguists' eagerness to give up their own.

Give up their own perspective, many linguists did nevertheless. They seemed to be afraid of what critics would think of them if they openly explored, with respect to literature, what was their essential idealism with respect to language, viz., that ordinary linguistic intuition is a primal source of formal observations on the language of literature. They refused to acknowledge the latent motives in the linguistic analysis of literature, to formalize those linguistic operations by which great writers make at least some of the novelty and vitality of literature accessible to almost anyone who has a competent grasp of the language. This would have sounded too much like a non-elitist approach on the one hand and too much like a pure linguistic approach on the other. These linguists did not want to be non-elite purists; they wanted to be applied elitists. But the truly elite refused to apply their methods, because traditional critics were mainly and properly interested in what could be said about a text as an example of the literary, not the linguistic, universals of human culture.

However, many linguists hold philosophical reasons for rejecting the notion of 'pure' synchronic analysis, as defined above, even as an ideal. Riffaterre has put it this way:[19]

A purely linguistic analysis of literature will yield only linguistic elements; it will describe those elements of a sequence which happen to have stylistic value along with neutral ones . . . .

For similar reasons, Freeman agrees:

It is equally important that the linguist bring to his task a sympathy with and awareness of the formal and aesthetic nature of his subject.

It is impossible to present all of the 'facts' about a literary text; the
linguist who would study style must have some idea of what kind of
facts are likely to be significant before he begins his analysis (pp.
109-10).

It would be difficult to take exception with either of these statements.
One would surely hope that the linguistic analyst of literature would
begin his work with some awareness of the 'aesthetic nature' or the
'value' of his subject. The question is, from what sort of competence
study does this aesthetic awareness of value arise?

Freeman argues that it arises from a 'critical intelligence'[20] which
must inform the linguistic analyst. We must wonder exactly what
Freeman means by this. Is it necessary to have training in literary
criticism in order to possess a critical intelligence? If so, we must also
wonder how this requirement will be co-ordinated with Freeman's
designation of linguistic analysis as a 'precritical activity.' Does this
mean it is necessary to do linguistic analysis before one can do criticism?
His later comment that a 'good critic is perforce a good linguist' seems
to indicate that his answer would be yes. Thus Freeman would seem to
argue that a linguist must be something of a critic and a critic must
be something of a linguist before either can formalize anything worthwhile about literature.

Since training in critical theory ought to help one be a better critic,
and since training in linguistic theory ought to help one be a better
linguist, it follows that some sort of interdisciplinary specialist (or
generalist) might be better qualified than either linguists or critics to
make comments about literature. Naturally enough, neither critics nor
linguists have liked this implication.

Nevertheless, William O. Hendricks has answered what he took to
be Freeman's tacit call for such a hybrid specialist by proposing a
'hyphen discipline' called STYLOLINGUISTICS (p. 9). In 'hyphen' or
'hybrid' disciplines, such as psycholinguistics, Hendricks explains, there
is no significant overlap of the primary concerns of each discipline,
but only a co-ordinated study of the inter-relationship of the areas
common to both. The stylolinguist would thus delimit as his field the
correlation between the literary critic's findings and the linguist's
analysis of language. He would study the results that can be obtained
by co-ordinating the investigation of language structure, which takes
the sentence as its formal unit of analysis, with the investigation of
literary structure, a superstructure, which is built upon but is distinct
from language structure.

Hendricks implies that his proposal will end the war between linguists and critics since, under these provisions, 'The linguist does not
have to be a critic, the critic does not have to be a linguist; only the
stylolinguist has to be knowledgeable in both fields' (p. 10).

It remains to be seen whether or not such a hybrid discipline will in fact germinate. But we suspect that, even if it does, it will not end the war between critics and linguists; it will probably only create a rather unstable DMZ. Hendricks's proposal seems to grant linguists independence from critical theory and to grant critics independence from linguistic theory only if both are content to leave the analysis of that fascinating relationship between language and literature to the stylolinguist. But linguists and critics cannot be so content. As McLain reminds us, no critical theory which ignores the artist's use of language is a complete theory; nor is any linguistic theory complete whose principles cannot be used in any way to account for the function of language in literary art (p. 250). Moreover, McLain disagrees with the establishment of a third discipline because its creation makes the two disciplines in themselves appear irreconcilable. Both literary critics and linguists must face the questions raised by each other for an adequate theory of language and an adequate theory of literature.

We suspect an interpenetration of the two disciplines will continue. By virtue of their necessary interest in the language of poetry, for example, critics will probably continue to make linguistic excursions into literature which violate the claims of linguists to precise formalization; linguists, on the other hand, by virtue of their necessary interest in the poetry of language, will continue to make literary excursions which violate the claims of critics to subtle appreciation. The presence, in this already disputed territory, of a third party, staking his own claims to it as a stylolinguist, will not end the dispute.

Further, it is not necessary to create a hyphen discipline in order to carry on interdisciplinary discussions toward ending the dispute and establishing co-operation. Progress toward this end may be achieved if all claimants to the disputed territory will state precisely what their objectives are, what sort of 'rights' to this no-man's land they hope to procure for themselves. In that spirit, we have offered the (perhaps overly precise) suggestion that linguists, as such, have the clearer claim, though not an exclusive claim, to the analysis of how literature incorporates and extends the general principles of linguistic creativity into its own particular semantics and aesthetics of language. The critic seems to have the stronger claim to virtually everything else in the description of literature.

McLain offers further suggestions illuminating how the dispute arose and might yet be settled. The source of the problem, he explains, comes from the initial attempts to analyze literature through linguistic tools: the inordinate claims of past linguistic analyses of literature; the failure of the results to be more illuminating than the product of conventional literary scholarship; and the limitations and problems with linguistic theory itself, which cause problems for literary study. The classical linguistic concepts of past analyses—the rigid separation between semantics and syntax; the meaning-preserving hypothesis; the restriction of the unit of analysis to the level of the sentence; and the relegation of literary language to deviant structures caused by violation of linguistic rules—were not suitable to explain the contribution of form to content; the structure of discourse in a text, which is more than the concatenation of separate sentences; and the necessary and sufficient conditions in the production of literary utterances. Even the category called 'natural' or 'ordinary' or 'non-deviant' language failed to illuminate the very disparate kinds of non-poetic language: telephone conversations, mathematical treatises, and legal briefs, for example. The concept of deviancy of language—the breaking of the rules of ordinary language—led to an interesting attempt at analysis of the poetry of e. e. cummings and Dylan Thomas, but could not cope with literary texts which do not seem to go beyond one's ordinary linguistic competence.

However, McLain asserts, these limitations in theory have been overcome by the new theories—those in generative semantics, the philosophy of language, and text grammars—which provide a more viable linguistic framework for literary analysis. Because McLain believes that linguistic theory has made significant recent progress toward settling its problems in theory, due in part to the influence of literary criticism, he is optimistic about the status of linguistic analysis in the world of letters. We close this section by sharing his optimism, although a closer examination of the internal debates in linguistic theory (Section III below), leads to another solution (Section IV below), a solution very different from McLain's.

III History, current trends, and future in linguistic theory

Somewhat arbitrarily, we begin our survey of linguistic theory with the developments in generative-transformational grammar. But there are at least two reasons for doing this. The first is pragmatic, arising from the fact that the articles anthologized in this collection are written from the perspective of that theoretical model, or from the perspective of models which have developed from it or following it.

The second reason has to do with the idealism discussed above. Transformational grammar was the first effort, at least in the history of modern American grammar, to adopt the objective of formalizing the intuitions of ordinary linguistic competence. In many ways, Chomsky's model of transformational grammar was indebted to the accomplishments of Bloomfieldian Structuralism which dominated the linguistic scene prior to his publications. Structuralism has by no means passed away and might indeed offer the linguistic analyst some unique tools for studying the structure of literature, as is demonstrated by the French linguistic/critical schools. But it must be seen as a tool, for the simple reason that its rigorously empirical approach forbids its user from adopting any *perspective* at all about his data, other than what may be called a scientific induction from it. Since these data are all empirical rather than intuitive, structuralism is essentially a performance model, a way of formalizing the patterns of those utterances which already happen to exist. In contrast, generative grammar is a competence model, a way of formalizing, not just the patterns of given utterances, but the principles governing our understanding of the potentially utterable. Since it attempts to account for the laws of language productivity and intelligibility, this kind of grammar offers more than a tool for literary analysis; it offers, in point of fact, a unique perspective, a way of seeing how the aesthetic creativity of the literary artist depends in part upon and interacts with the rational creativity of an ordinary reader.

We may get some insight into this difference between structuralists and transformationalists by examining Mary Louise Pratt's rejection of the structuralists' attempts to define literature in the 'non-honorific' sense. According to Pratt:[21]

> ... the very notion of literature is a normative one ... critics who
> try to define literature without reference to human values and
> preferences easily end up presupposing values and preferences—
> inevitably their own.

If Pratt is right, that is, if we are making a judgment in the very act of calling something 'literature,' structuralism, which by its own definition makes no judgments concerning its data, is unsuited to the study of literature as literature; a linguistic model, however, which can deal with linguistic creativity as well as language structure need not assume such a restricted role.

While transformational theory offers this definite advantage, it is not without its drawbacks, the most obvious of which is the lack of agreement among its practitioners. Within what is generally known as transformational grammar, there are two main schools: the transformationalists (known as the Extended Standard Theoreticians) and the generative semanticists. Two key issues help to define these two camps: the competence/performance distinction and the transformation-meaning-preserving hypothesis.

The early transformational model is a competence grammar. That is, it is an effort to describe, in a rigorously formal though non-empirical way, what an 'ideal' native speaker/hearer knows intuitively about his language. Since its 'given' is an ideal language user, and since its 'to prove' is the structure of linguistic intuition, Chomsky had to distinguish competence from mere performance, which is thought of as the body of empirical facts about actual language use. This distinction was rooted in the transformationalists' philosophical predisposition toward rationalism as opposed to behaviorism. That is, the transformationalist was interested in treating language as a rational system, one which displays universal linguistic principles, rather than simply as patterns of animal vocal behavior displayed by humans when they need to communicate.

For this reason, transformational grammar could not pretend to be a holistic model for human communication. There were many performance variables relevant to communication which it deliberately left out of its descriptions—social, biological, psychological factors, along with facts or beliefs about the world, all of which figure prominently in the communicative behavior of human beings. Chomsky justified these exclusions on the grounds that he was not studying communicative behavior; he was instead studying one of its aspects—propositional linguistic structure, the formal rational properties of which might be placed along side of 'extralinguistic' performance criteria from behavioral studies in one integrated communication theory.

This limitation on transformational theory has two important manifestations for the student who considers using this model in literary analysis: (a) as a sentence grammar, it is primarily limited to the propositional content (as opposed to implicational content) of a given utterance; (b) because of this, it must draw an idealistic distinction between linguistic and extralinguistic meaning, excluding from its formal analysis any phenomenon it considers to be merely a fact or belief about the world taken from the general culture.

Charles J. Fillmore's Case Grammar evolved, adhering to the two limitations named above, but attempting to capture the underlying semantics of sentences through a semantically-based grammar (as opposed to a syntactically-based, transformational model). Fillmore derived the syntactic relations from the semantic relations of the various nouns in a sentence to the verbs in that sentence.

The generative semanticists, on the other hand, have accepted neither of the above constraints on linguistic theory, and to that extent, the trend among these scholars has been away from the competence/performance distinction, away from the exclusive treatment of language as a rational system and more toward the treatment of language as communicative behavior. Thus we have the appearance of Lakoff's 'pragmatic' (as opposed to Katz's formal) semantics; this pragmatic approach to meaning requires that facts and beliefs about the world, as well as the social and psychological and perhaps even biological states of the speaker and hearer, must be fed into the grammar. In this tradition, a number of interesting models have appeared, formalizing some rules of 'conversational implicature,' 'speech-act criteria,' and for the application of these to literature, the so-called 'text grammars.'

It does indeed appear from these studies that some of the matters ignored as 'performance variables' by the transformationalists are worth studying and that they can be formalized under principles whose operation is as constant and predictable as those which the Chomskian model focuses upon. An example from speech act theory should serve to illustrate the point. The speaker uttering the following to a healthy individual who is not busy and who knows where the garbage should be taken is not asking for information:

1 Can you take the garbage out.

The addressee, and indeed all individuals competent in the language, will immediately know that this is a request for assistance, not a question, because the sincerity condition for asking a question is not met; that is, the speaker already knows that this person *can* take the garbage out.[22]

The early transformationalists would have relegated such knowledge to the realm of linguistic performance. However, any native speaker knows, without reference to context, that sentence 2 below and sentence 1 *can* be interchangeable.

2 Please take the garbage out.

The speaker makes this determination not from his knowledge of the world or from his knowledge of any particular context, but from his knowledge of how his language operates. Therefore, it would seem to reflect a type of linguistic competence. According to Pratt, such formalizable phenomena should be treated by a complete grammar. She reasons:

> If, as Chomsky claimed, the goal of linguistics is to describe what
> a speaker knows about his language that enables him to produce
> and understand new utterances (his competence), such a description
> must specify not only our knowledge of grammatical rules but also
> our ability to handle possible linguistic structures appropriately in
> specific contexts (p. 84).

In light of Pratt's observation, one might want to argue that factors previously labeled as performance matters should now be called competence matters. However, the transformationalists argue, with good reason, that sentences 3 and 4 below are synonymous in a way that sentences 1 and 2 are not.

3 A truck hit the bicycle.

4. The bicycle was hit by a truck.

As we will argue in Section 4, the speech act theorists' distinction between what a sentence says (locution) and what a sentence does (illocution) is an important distinction to make in talking about literature. In order that this distinction might be preserved, the synonymy of sentences 1 and 2 (illocutionary synonymy) ought to be distinguished from the synonymy of sentences 3 and 4 (locutionary synonymy); both kinds of synonymy arise from linguistic competence, but from two different kinds of linguistic competence.

The synonymy exhibited by such sentences as 3 and 4 leads us to the second issue debated by transformationalists and generative semantic theoreticians: the meaning-preserving- hypothesis. The early transformationalists (Standard Theorists) accepted the Katz-Postal hypothesis that transformations did not change meaning.[23] Such sentences as 3 and 4 were derived from a common deep structure represented by Figure 1 below.[24]

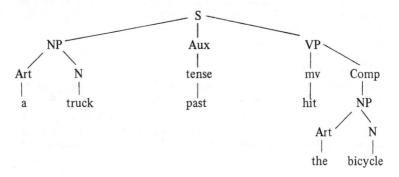

Figure 1

The generative semanticists rejected such an approach; operating on Pascal's dictum that 'words differently arranged have different meanings,'[25] they maintained that the difference in focus in pairs such as 3 and 4 is meaningful and that that difference must be represented by the underlying structures.

At this point the essential difference between the transformationalist theory (as enunciated by Chomsky[26]) and the generative semantic theory begins to crystallize. Whereas neither school maintained that such sentences as 3 and 4 have exactly the same meaning, the transformationalists did grant them a level of synonymy by positing two levels of meaning: propositional meaning, that meaning which can be represented in an underlying structure and pragmatic meaning, the subtle context-induced meaning which is added to propositional meaning. Both schools maintained that transformations did not change meaning; but they defined meaning differently. The transformationalists' definition of meaning as propositional meaning allowed them to represent such sentences as 3 and 4 by a common deep structure (see Figure 1). The generative semanticists' definition of meaning as the combination of propositional and pragmatic meanings caused them to say that these sentences must have different underlying structures.

The next stage in the debate saw the generative semanticists offer evidence (sentences 5 and 6 below) that transformations could not be depended on not to alter the basic content (propositional meaning) of an assertion.

5 Many arrows didn't hit the target.
6 The target was not hit by many arrows.

Adherents of the transformational theory countered that the change in meaning brought about by the passive transformation in such cases was effected by a special set of circumstances, i.e. the change in order of the negative and the quantifier 'many'; nevertheless, they were forced to abandon the Katz-Postal hypothesis. This led to the birth of the Extended Standard Theory which provided for a specified set of transformations to change meaning.

This controversy has some vital implications for any theory of literary style. The early transformationalists had a useful tool for talking about style.[27] Since transformations did not change the essential meaning, any differences in surface sentence structure could be labeled stylistic. The generative semanticists complicated the issue for stylists in asserting that any two different surface structures have different meanings. They are willing to allow that two different surface structures may be synonymous *in context*; but the determination of this synonymy will be dependent upon a separate component, supposedly some type of pragmatic contextual component. The Extended Standard theory still has a syntactic, non-contextual framework for talking about stylistic difference. However, with the introduction of the complexities illustrated by sentences 5 and 6, the Extended Standard theory will need some additional component to separate transformations which effect content changes from those which effect stylistic changes. Thus, in a sense, the Extended Standard theory and the generative semantics theory face the same dilemma.

It is just possible that we might gain some insight into how to solve this dilemma through the findings of speech act theorists. That is, their distinctions between locutionary and illocutionary force may be in some sense parallel to the problematic distinction between style and content. At the very least, speech act theory, with its distinction between what a sentence says and what it may be used to do, ought to furnish salient insights into the semantic and aesthetic effects of literary style.

IV   Theoretical and methodological eclecticism

When a scientific study of a subject has more than one theory to explain the phenomena of the field—such as the properties and behavior of light in physics, for example—investigation of the subject does not stop. In lieu of one analysis, some phenomena of light may be interpreted more convincingly by the corpuscular or particle theory, and others explained more clearly by the wave theory. Confusing, perhaps; but certainly scientists understand more about optical behavior than past generations. Increasing knowledge in this field has led to a recognition that the two models in quantum theory, though conflicting, are valid ways of explaining light behavior. The same principle can be applied to the study of literature through a variety of approaches, including a variety of linguistic models.

We suggested earlier that this sort of eclecticism is possible only when all parties concerned declare self-imposed limitations on their individual pursuits. These declarations may sometimes be tacit, as for example, when syntacticians merely stay out of the way of literary biographers by preoccupying themselves with the convoluted poetry of an e. e. cummings. But when the concerns of two different scholars appear to overlap in the study of the same phenomenon, either one theory will perish, or both will perish, or each will very carefully have to delineate which *aspects* of the phenomenon it intends to investigate.

In this spirit, we have cautioned the linguist as follows: Because literature is more than language and literary competence more than linguistic competence, you must acknowledge that your formalizations about literary language, while they may codify certain primary insights into the nature of literature, are not thorough treatments of literature. But in the same spirit we have warned the traditional critic: Do not think that linguistic criticism need claim to do everything that needs to be done with a literary text in order to uphold its claim to do something unique and important.

It seems to us that many of the debates which break out between various academic disciplines often arise from the failure to heed such cautions. Consider, as an example parallel to the war between critics and linguists, the debate that goes on and on between philosophical rationalists and behavioral psychologists. The former attack the latter for their reduction of human behavior to stimulus/response patterning; yet no one seriously doubts that human beings do respond to stimuli in rather predictable fashion. Whence, then, the great debate? Is it not because the rationalists take the behaviorists' claim to be that ALL human behavior is the inevitable response to some external stimulus? Why must conditioning theory be offered (or taken) either to explain precisely everything or positively nothing about human behavior? Why can we not use this model to deal with phenomena which seem to be matched to its design features and for other phenomena use other models? In literary studies, the same question might be asked about the linguistic or the traditional critical approach.

Unfortunately, this is not the question with which the linguistic approach to literature has been evaluated by most of its critics. The evaluation has too often proceeded on the grounds that linguistic theory must move to provide a holistic approach to literature or it must be abandoned as an analytical perspective. The consequence, or perhaps in some cases the cause, of this attitude has been the failure among some linguists to limit themselves to the synchronic principles of language in their study of literature. In other cases, the cause has been a non-eclectic, non-pluralist approach among proponents of more established literary critical theories.

On the other hand, many traditional critics have been reluctant to sanction, let alone investigate for themselves, the developing linguistic models because existing models are being 'replaced' by new models so rapidly that a scholar who stops to explore the literary utility of one is in perpetual danger of being called 'outmoded' by another. This is most unfortunate. If linguists expect literary critics to show an eclectic acceptance of linguistic models, they must set that example first among themselves.

The continual development of new alternatives for linguistic description is of course healthy, and any scholar who wishes to explore their utility for literary analysis will benefit from keeping abreast of these developments. But evaluations like McLain's, which imply that any linguist wishing to carry on this sort of exploration must adopt, as his own, the most recent models of linguistic theory, are patently unfair (p. 231). McLain attacks those linguistic critics with a Chomskian orientation on the basis that their theories are being 'rebutted' by generative semanticists and text grammarians. While generative semantics and text grammar indeed offer exciting alternatives to the Chomskian model, these alternatives do not have to be considered as mutually exclusive. The reason they do not, as we have already seen, is that they have differing emphases, if not altogether differing goals. The student who wishes to investigate the use of linguistics in literature is therefore best advised to consider these competing models as 'choices' which may be made on the basis of what he wants his own emphasis to be.

In this spirit, we have included here examples of literary analysis utilizing various linguistic models—transformational grammar, case grammar, generative semantics, text grammar, and speech act theory. Studies of literature must stand upon their own value, not upon their subscription to any doctrinaire presumptions about the correct or even about the most 'powerful' model. In the evaluation of any model, we must be guided by the reminder that no model can be dismissed as 'incorrect' unless it fails to accomplish its stated objectives. To the extent that its stated objectives are incomplete, even a correct model may be called theoretically 'inadequate,' but this does not preclude its utility for every practical objective. In fact, the usefulness of a given model depends in part upon how carefully it limits its own objectives, not upon how ambitiously it may stretch its own claims. If its stated objectives are worthwhile and if it fulfills these objectives as stated, then its value is established.

However, an eclectic acceptance of the value of these studies does not require—in fact, it forbids—that we take them at their frequent claim to formalize *all* the vectors of human communication in a single model. To set forth the principles of language, along with all the variables affecting language use, in a monolithic system of description is an ambitious undertaking to say the least. It seems to be motivated by a non-eclectic presumption that if our description of human communication is to be unified, our descriptive model must be unitary. McLain seems to have assumed this posture in his suggestion that only the pragmatic models are useful in literary studies.

Even if such a unitary model could be created, there is serious question for the student of literature whether or not it should be done. Such a monolithic model might have the effect of obscuring important distinctions 'between meaning in a strict sense, and pragmatically determined connotations and implicatures.'[28] The reason this collapse of the two kinds of meaning might be harmful is that it would prohibit an analysis of the subtle connections literary artists often build between the two.

For example, what is the 'meaning' of this sentence?

That door is open again.

Surely this sentence has some meaning regardless of its context. But if we know that the sentence is spoken in an agitated tone of voice by a hospital patient who is shivering in his bed, then we apprehend, not a totally different, but a distinctly additional meaning. A hospital nurse hearing this utterance under these circumstances would understand that the speaker wants the door closed. There are, then, at least two kinds of meaning—propositional and implied—which the generative semantics approach might have the effect of collapsing into one.

We may take an example offered by a generative semanticist to illustrate that this collapse of propositional and implied meaning might have unfortunate consequences for literary analysis. Consider:

The police came into the room and everyone swallowed their cigarettes.

According to Robin Lakoff, the meaning of this sentence can only be fully understood by someone who is aware of the legal and social conditions surrounding the use of marijuana in our country.[29] This is clearly true; someone who is unaware of these conditions would look upon the conjunction of events in this sentence as temporally and causally absurd. But does it follow that the 'implied' meaning about marijuana and the 'explicit' meaning of the two conjoined sentences must be thought of as a single semantic result? The example proves that both kinds of meaning must be treated, but does it prove the generative semanticist's claim that they must be treated as one?

If we think of this sentence as, say, the first sentence in a short story, then there is good reason for treating its two meanings separately, as distinct, though related, phenomena. As Hemingway is once supposed to have said, it is often what you leave out of a story that makes it work, not what you put into it. One way in which this may be true is that if a writer leaves out something which might be predictably supplied by the reader, a kind of close co-operation between the reader and writer is established. Readers like to participate in a story; they do not like to be told everything; they enjoy having some things left out for them to infer through their own imaginative (but rule-bound) guesswork from the author's textual clues. Critical appreciation of the sort of things good writers characteristically leave out for the reader to construe, then, depends upon a methodological distinction between stated propositions and unstated implicatures. Propositional meaning can be formalized very well in a transformational model;[30] the overlaying contextual implications can be formalized with increasing success in a model of pragmatic meaning, often through the sort of rules of speaker/hearer co-operation that we find in grammars of conversational implicature.[31] But neither model replaces the other; nor can we collapse the two models into one and still guard safely the important distinction between the two kinds of meaning, a distinction by which the relation between the two meanings, as well as that between the reader and writer, becomes formally apparent.

Nowhere is this distinction more important than in the study of metaphor, which has been the object of a large share of the linguistic interest in literature. Michael Reddy, for example, fails to make the distinction in his attack on the provisions of a Chomskian grammar for identifying figurative propositions.[32] It has often been claimed, by those with a Chomskian orientation, that metaphor involves some kind of 'deviance' from literal discourse; the origin of this deviance these linguists identify as the violation of selectional restriction. For example, if one says

1 The rock speaks of hardness

he has spoken figuratively because he has violated the constraint on literal discourse which says, 'The verb *speak* may only be selected to occur, ordinarily, with a human agent.' Thus the transformationalist may show how the poet has manipulated an ordinary principle of language to achieve a special semantic effect. However, Reddy offers the following sentence as an example of metaphor which does not involve the above kind of selection deviance:

2 The rock is becoming brittle with age.

The 'metaphor' depends on pragmatic rather than linguistic criteria, he claims, as we may see by noting that the meaning would differ in the contexts of a geological expedition and a description of an old professor emeritus (p. 242).

But Robert Matthews points out that there is nothing IN Reddy's example that can be called metaphorical.[33] If sentence 2 is spoken while pointing at the old professor emeritus, it will indeed cause any reasonably intelligent and co-operative hearer to SUPPLY a metaphorical inference, like sentence 3 below, which does indeed involve a selectional violation:

3 The old professor emeritus is a rock.

The metaphorical *propositions* of sentences 1 and 3, then, are best studied through the lens of a model which can focus upon propositional content to identify the linguistic origins of the figurative meaning; transformational analysis offers a thoroughly acceptable choice for a student who wishes to study this phenomenon. On the other hand, the metaphorical *implications* overlaying a literal sentence like 2 in certain contexts are best studied through a model which can account for the sociological principles of co-operation between speaker and hearer in conjunction with textual and contextual cues; models of conversational implicature or speech act criteria present interesting and insightful choices to those who wish to study these phenomena. But these alternatives no more replace the transformational alternative than implicational meaning replaces propositional meaning in human language.

Several of the more insightful speech act approaches to literature, such as Hancher's in this anthology, themselves recognize the distinction between what a sentence SAYS and what a sentence may be used to DO.[34] Here, then, is an opportunity to explore the performative responses to and effects of an author's subtle clues as opposed to the logical truth structures of his explicit propositions. But appreciation of the subtlety is lost if the distinction between 'clues' and 'propositions' is dissolved in our overall theory, for no connection is conceivable, let alone analyzable, between two things which are not two but one thing.

Thus our theory ought to distinguish between what is articulated, what is induced from what is articulated, and what is inferred on other grounds, lest we commit the hubris of claiming to account for the entire compendium of human culture under the monolithic rubric of linguistics. The eclecticism which has allowed us to include many different models in this anthology, then, forbids us to accept the charges made by some of them that Chomsky's 'divide and conquer' distinction between competence and performance will produce a wholly inadequate theory. No single model in language theory need claim to do everything in order to do something worthwhile; furthermore, such methodological limitations and phenomenological distinctions as Chomsky made, even if somewhat ideal, often give rise to insights about the connections between contiguous phenomena which it would be impossible to understand under conditions of total methodological continuity. It was Chomsky's original demarcation of competence/performance criteria, in point of fact, which has now led to the interesting study of the relation between what he called 'linguistic' and 'extra-linguistic' meaning. Thus eclecticism in theoretical distinctions between alternative models is not ultimately disruptive to the unity of the theory as a whole; it is often under conditions of theoretical 'dissection,' as it were, that the otherwise inscrutable 'connective tissues' of the target phenomena become apparent.

Even if this multifarious situation in linguistic theory were not somewhat desirable for these reasons, it would remain a situation that is inherent in the nature of the case. The unifying intent, among most contemporary linguists, to describe the principles of human language intuition, automatically gives rise to a diversity of models. Simply put, there is so much to study in the complexity and magnitude of man's language that models which are to penetrate very far beneath the surface must be sharpened to a rather narrow focus. It has not proved to be the case that limiting oneself to the study of man's literary language in any way relaxes this necessity; in fact, it accentuates it. For literature, viewed as a distillation of man's perennial effort to shape his life, his culture, and all his world through language, forever presents the serious student with the feeling that the more he knows about it, the more he does not know about it. Since what he does not know is always outside the scope of the models of what he knows, he must forever be inventing new models or expanding the old ones to make them more powerful.

The practical danger in continually expanding a single model to make it more powerful is that this action also makes it more general. Of course, for theoretical purposes *per se*, the more general the model— that is, the more phenomena it can accurately explain with a single generalization—the more elegant it becomes. But a linguistic theory of literary language, if it is to have discretionary ability, must balance the need for elegance of abstraction against the need for incisiveness of detail; that is, it must equip itself to make powerful observations about the nature of literary language in general without losing its ability to pinpoint practical specifications about the nature of a literary text in particular. It is our belief that the need for generality can be met by linguistic theory as a whole, provided its practitioners will consent to individual models within the theory, models narrowly defined by specific objectives. To paraphrase something Kenneth Burke once said, if we fail to look specifically *for* something, we may find ourselves staring blankly *at* everything.

The process of defining objectives is often exactly the sort of pushing, pulling, going too far and then backing up that we see in the present state of linguistic scholarship. It is not a kind of debate which is unique to the field of language study, nor is it new within the field itself. Linguistics has always been both plagued and prodded by this difficulty in defining itself, because of the diversity of concerns to which the pervasiveness of human language drives it. But to anyone acquainted with the way human beings characteristically go about understanding themselves and their world, it is an exciting difficulty which ought to make one feel at home.

For it suggests that in modern linguistic theory we have exactly that sort of troubling multilateral perspective which is necessary in order to consider that old possibility that all the diverse fields of human knowledge must somewhere converge upon a point of truth. We can scarcely think of a more likely point of convergence than human language itself. And we would scarcely find a better place than literature in which to explore that old outrageous possibility, at least given the form in which modern linguistic theory has resurrected it again.

In conclusion, we believe that linguistic analysis of literature has revealed incisively some features of the language of literature: the very nature of literary language; the interrelationship of some of the syntactic, semantic, and figurative resources available; and pioneering explanations of not only readers' semantic interpretation of literary language, but also the affective impact of literary language upon them. The methods used, though not always eclectic, are initial attempts to explain more clearly than ever before readers' understanding of the tension between form and content in literature, purposeful semantic and syntactic deviation, the nature of ambiguity, and the diverse and multiple interpretations that readers may impose upon a word, phrase, or sentence—interpretations that may even differ from authorial intent but which may be legitimately held because of the rich multiguity in the objective structure of the text.

Linguistic theory has achieved these results through various models. At times, case grammar can explain the underlying semantic relations; in some instances, componential analysis is the most helpful way to elucidate the semantic interpretation of language by readers; pragmatics and speech act theory seem promising in accounting for interpretations that depend upon the social context or circumstance of an utterance or upon authorial intent or the persona of a work; and still other aspects—such as topicalization and narrative structure—may be understood by utilizing the classical concepts of deep structure, transformations, and surface structure as an analogy. The enlightened knowledge we now have gained about literary language must not stop because of the lack of a monolithic model, though there is reason to hope that a cohesive theory may evolve from the diversity of models. In any case, the merits of the results thus far point out that linguistic investigations of literature must continue.

NOTES

1 Donald Freeman, *Linguistics and Literary Style* (New York: Holt, Rinehart & Winston, 1970), p. 3.

2 For a good discussion of literary conventions not accessible through analysis of language, see William O. Hendricks, 'The Relation between Linguistics and Literary Studies,' *Poetics*, 11 (1974), pp. 5–22.

3 Jonathan Culler, *Structuralist Poetics* (Ithaca, N. Y.: Cornell University Press, 1975), pp. 113–14.

4 Stanley Fish, 'Literature in the Reader: Affective Stylistics,' *New Literature History*, 2 (1970), pp. 160–1.

5 See David Bleich, 'The Subjective Character of Critical Interpretation,' *College English* 36 (1975), 739–55.

6 Murray Schwartz, 'Where is Literature?', *College English*, 36 (1975), 756–65.

7 Helen Vendler, Review of *Essays on Style and Language*, ed. Roger Fowler, *Essays in Criticism*, 16 (1966), 457.

8 The distinction between 'ordinary' and 'literary' language has often been denied, for example, by Richard L. McLain, 'Literary Criticism Versus Generative Grammars,' *Style*, 10 (Summer, 1976), pp. 246–7. It is not necessary that, in defense of this modest distinction, we offer evidence of a total disjunction. Suffice it to say that the ability to utter and understand well-formed sentences is not tantamount to the ability to produce a successful literary work. The universal intuitions of sensitive readers of literature is that at least part of what makes a literary work successful is its masterful use of language. It follows, then, that the distinction between ordinary and literary language is one that has too broad an intuitive basis to be ignored either by linguists or critics. But as we argue below, the distinction is not in kind, but in use of the linguistic process. The literary artist has at his disposal no principle of language not accessible to the ordinary speaker; but the artist's selection and manipulation of these principles are effectively extraordinary.

9 See, for example, Noam Chomsky's *Language and Mind* (New York: Harcourt Brace Jovanovich, 1972).

10 See J. J. Katz, *Semantic Theory* (New York: Harper & Row, 1972).

11 This position is taken by Richard L. McLain, cited above in note 4.

12 Derek Bickerton, 'Prolegomena to a Linguistic Theory of Metaphor,' *Foundations of Language*, 5 (1969), p. 37.

13 Robert DeMaria, 'The Ideal Reader: A Criticial Fiction,' *PMLA*, 93 (May 1978), p. 463.

14 *Language Processing and the Reading of Literature* (Bloomington: Indiana University Press, 1978), p. XVI.

15 See Eugene R. Kintgen, 'Psycholinguistics and Literature,' *College English*, 39 (March 1978), 755–79.

16 Marcia Eaton, 'Good and Correct Interpretations of Literature,' *JAAC*, 29 (1970), pp. 227–33.

17 Northrop Frye, *Anatomy of Criticism* (Princeton University Press, 1957), pp. 117–118.

18 See, for example, Seymour Chatman, *Theory of Meter* (The Hague: Mouton, 1965), pp. 9–10; A. A. Hill, 'A Program for the Definition of Literature,' *University of Texas Studies in English*, 37 (1958), p. 46.

19 In S. Chatman and S. R. Levin (eds), *Essays on the Language of Literature* (Boston: Houghton Mifflin, 1967), p. 412.

20 Donald Freeman, Review of *Essays on Style and Language*, ed. R. Fowler, *Journal of Linguistics*, 4 (1968), pp. 109–10.

21 *Toward a Speech Act Theory of Literary Discourse* (Bloomington: Indiana University Press, 1977), p. 123.

22 See, for example, J. L. Austin, *How to Do Things with Words* (New York: Oxford University Press, 1962).

23 Jerrold J. Katz and Paul M. Postal, *An Integrated Theory of Linguistic Description* (Cambridge, Mass: MIT Press, 1964).

24 For this structure, we are using the model outlined in Mark Lester, *Introductory Transformational Grammar of English* (Atlanta: Holt Rinehart & Winston, 1971).

25 Pascal, *Pensee*; translated by W. F. Trotter (New York: Modern Library, 1941), p. 11.

26 Noam Chomsky, *Aspects of the Theory of Syntax* (Cambridge, Mass.: MIT Press, 1965).

27 Richard Ohmann, 'Generative Grammars and the Concept of Literary Style,' *Word*, 20 (1964).

28 Janet Dean Fodor, *Semantics: Theories of Meaning* (New York: Thomas Y. Crowell Co., 1977), p. 205.

29 As cited by Fodor, 1977, p. 205.

30 See Fowler's effort to redeem Ohmann's approach, R. Fowler, 'Style and the Concept of Deep Structure,' *Journal of Literary Semantics*, 1 (1972), pp. 5–24.

31 See P. Grice, 'Logic and Conversation,' in *Syntax and Semantics: Speech Acts*, ed. P. Cole and J. L. Morgan (New York: Academic Press, 1975), pp. 41–58.

32 'A Semantic Approach to Metaphor,' in Chicago Linguistic Society, Papers from the Regional Meeting #5, 1969, pp. 240–51.

33 Robert J. Matthews, 'Concerning a "Linguistic Theory" of Metaphor,' *Foundations of Language*, 7 (1971), p. 424.

34 Michael Hancher, 'Understanding Poetic Speech Acts,' *College English*, 36 (1975), p. 634.

PART II

Figurative language

The following chapters range in their approach from the examination of metaphor's philosophical foundations in language to a focus upon its 'literary' use in conversation. Bickerton's chapter (1) falls somewhere in between, for it demonstrates some of the ontological problems of using transformational grammar's hierarchies of semantic markers in the practical identification and interpretation of metaphor. Bickerton argues that the selectional restriction criteria for which these markers provide can do little more than identify metaphor as 'deviant' (since it allegedly violates these restrictions) and can do nothing to account for metaphoric production or to handle metaphor's subtle connotative effects. These matters he proposes to handle with the notion of 'attribute attachment,' which 'marks' a 'sign' (word) with a connotative meaning specifying how that word might be used metaphorically in appropriate speaker-hearer or writer-reader contexts. Reddy's parallel attack (chapter 2) on transformational selectional restriction as a tool for metaphor study is epistemological rather than ontological, although he, too, opts for speaker-hearer context sensitivity to metaphorical interpretation. Instead of viewing metaphor as a violation of *a priori* semantic categories (which gives rise to notions of 'deviance'), Reddy proposes to view it as an unconventional crossing of 'literal spheres of reference,' which are determined by actual usage conventions rather than linguistic intuitions. Matthews (chapter 3) attempts to rebut both Reddy and Bickerton in his defense of transformational grammar as a sufficient model for metaphor study. He argues that 'attribute attachment' cannot account for the production of *new* metaphor, since Bickerton's 'marked sign' presupposes some previous potentially metaphoric use of that sign. He also argues that Reddy's 'literal sphere of reference' and Chomsky's 'selectional restriction' amount to essentially the same thing, and that Reddy's contextually determined metaphors, which do not involve violations of selectional restriction, are not really metaphors; they are rather literal propositions which, in certain contexts trigger overlaying metaphorical implications that involve selectional violations when realized as propositions.

Reinhart (chapter 4) indicates that the debate over the above 'deviance' question in metaphor studies arises from the almost exclusive concentration of such studies upon 'focus interpretation' or the literal sense of a metaphor, which is often substituted for its figurative component or 'vehicle.' She points out that 'deviance' is indeed irrelevant to the literal focus, but she criticizes Bickerton and Reddy for ignoring the interests of vehicle interpretation which (presumably) must involve some notion of deviance. She finds the same problem in Van Dijk (chapter 5) who offers a formal pragmatic semantics for interpreting only the literal truth value of figurative speech acts whether these involve selectionally deviant (in his notation, 'sortally incorrect') propositions or not. However, Van Dijk calls for a model which can specify degrees of sortal incorrectness by reference to a topography showing the hierarchical relationships among sorts (or semantic categories) in logical space. Haley (chapter 6) answers this call with a map of lexical subcategories modeled after the Aristotelian/Ptolemaic universe so that the categories may be thought of as a hierarchical system of 'sorts,' or natural kinds displayed in a medium of psychological as well as logical space. Focusing upon Reinhart's 'vehicle interpretation,' he demonstrates how the crossing of lexical/sortal categories in metaphor effects poetic abstraction at the same time it effects a sense of parallel spatial sublimity. Lumsford (Chapter 7) further explains this method and illustrates it by application to the poetry of Byron and Shelley. He argues that the spatial model not only captures some of the obvious differences between the metaphors of these two poets, but that it also sheds new light on their more subtle differences.

In a more practical vein, Williams (chapter 8) offers historical evidence that synesthesia, one form of metaphor, operates and evolves according to predictable principles of semantic transference, indicating that diachronic data support the claims of synchronic theory to account for patterns of productivity in figurative language. Similarly, Ching (chapter 9) offers evidence that the erasure and replacement of semantic markers in oxymora illustrate the semantic transference from one word to another to explain both the deviant sense and the paraphrasable meaning of oxymora.

CHAPTER ONE

Prolegomena to a linguistic theory of metaphor

Derek Bickerton *

[Bickerton calls for a new linguistic theory of metaphor on the grounds that earlier theories, both linguistic and non-linguistic, have failed.

Pre-Chomskian theories of metaphor fail for two reasons:

1 The non-linguistic approaches do not account for the important process of metaphorical invention.

2 Most of the linguistic theories share the false assumption that mean- ing' exists only in the language, or only in the relation of speaker to hearer, or only in the relation of language to the natural universe.

Post-Chomskian theories of metaphor also fail for two reasons:

1 The existing generative-transformational approaches cannot distin- guish meaningful metaphors from mere anomalies, because they lump metaphors and anomalies together as 'deviant' without stipu- lating the restrictions that govern the appropriate metaphorical uses of a term.

2 The existing hierarchies of *a priori* semantic categories and sub- categories in generative-transformational grammar would have to be continually adjusted in absurd ways in order to accommodate the transfer of markers from one term to another in a true metaphor.

Bickerton argues that these shortcomings could be remedied by a linguistic theory of metaphor which acknowledges that meaning exists only in the relationship between speaker, language, and hearer. Such a theory would thus be mode-of-discourse sensitive and would stipulate the semantic pre-conditions for metaphorical usage on the basis of text type (poems, scientific journals, almanacs, etc.) and on the basis of speaker–hearer interaction. The mechanism for this stipulation would be the 'marked sign,' a word or term to which a specific, but essentially connotative, attribute of meaning has been attached. The attachment of this attribute to the term might then be construed to govern its metaphorical usage. A complete (but non-hierarchical) grid of known attribute attachments would thereby initiate a metaphor theory which would possess both creative and critical power to specify the potentially metaphorical meaning of any term.]

* First published in *Foundations of Language*, 5 (1969), 34–52.

I

Is a new theory of metaphor necessary? A decade ago, one might not have thought so. Metaphor has been studied, albeit non-systematically, since the time of Aristotle. But some recent developments, such as the growing interest of both linguists and philosophers in 'deviant utterances' and 'meaningless sentences', certain difficulties encountered in the field of structural semantics, and a direct concern with metaphor itself, evinced in the work of generative stylisticians such as Levin and Thorne, and in reviews of works on the subject in *Foundations of Language* by Hesse (1966) and Mooij (1967), combine to suggest that a new look at metaphor might be worthwhile. The needs of semantics in particular have been succinctly stated by Bolinger (1965, 567): 'A semantic theory must account for the PROCESS of metaphorical invention . . . It is characteristic of natural languages that no word is ever limited to its enumerable senses, but carries with it the qualification of "something else".'

II

Should a new theory of metaphor be a linguistic theory? Other approaches seem to have proved inadequate, in so far as no definition or theory yet proposed can be put to work to provide even an adequate taxonomy, let alone 'account for the process'. Aristotle at least tried to concentrate on formal aspects: 'Metaphor is the application of a strange term either transferred from the genus and applied to the species, or from the species and applied to the genus, or from one species to another, or by analogy' (*Poetics*, 1457B).[1] But Roman and Renaissance scholars, instead of trying to elucidate and develop this rather cryptic definition by clarifying 'strange', 'genus', 'species' and 'analogy', treated metaphor mainly as an ornament of rhetoric; a typical definition, echoing theirs, echoed in turn by countless school textbooks and primers of 'literary appreciation', is Blair's: '[Metaphor] is a figure founded entirely on the resemblance which one object bears to another. Hence it is much allied to Simile, or comparison; and is indeed no other than a comparison, expressed in abridged form' (1783, 295). Even as shrewd a critic as Richards felt able to remark that 'it would be easy to expound a grammatical theory of metaphor, hyperbole and figurative language, pointing out the suppressed "as if's", "is like's", and the rest of the locutions that may be introduced to turn poetry into logically respectable prose' (1929, 193). Easy or not, he was wise enough not to try.

More recent works are hardly more helpful. Wheelwright (1962), having divided metaphor into 'epiphor'—roughly, the traditional variety

—and 'diaphor'—the Symbolist juxtaposition of discrete images, which need not themselves be epiphors, to produce a whole distinct from its parts—admits that in 'the greatest cases of metaphor' the two are blended; cites as an example of such blending Donne's *A bracelet of bright hair about the bone* (which contains no metaphor at all in any previously accepted sense); and promptly redefines epiphor as 'the felt subterranean power to mean somthing more than the words actually say' and diaphor as 'evident from the utterly untranslatable character of each utterance' (ibid, 91). Turbayne (1962), while relatively free from the idiosyncratic jargon which Wheelwright permits himself— 'Metapoetics', 'steno-language', 'mythoid', 'the poeto-ontological question'—is equally prone to ground-shifting. Starting from a definition of metaphor as 'sort-crossing' (more or less equivalent to Ryle's 'category mistake') he confesses its use in illustration, and is finally obliged to concede that, for dealing with abstractions, metaphorical language is almost unavoidable. In this, as Miss Hesse points out, he approaches the view, shared apparently by some nineteenth-century philologists such as A. H. Sayce and Max Muller, that 'all language is metaphor'. But, while most words in a given language may have passed through a phase of metaphoric extension, it is relatively rarely that its speakers encounter anything they feel obliged to call metaphor.

Finally, in one of those perversely ingenious works whose errors reveal more than the truths of others,[2] Drange (1966) purports to examine 'meaningless sentences' but finds, uneasily and belatedly, that for much of the time he has really been talking about metaphor: 'Actually, a metaphorical sentence, taken literally, is invariably a type crossing. Hence, by my theory, it is unthinkable. It may be that this is precisely what is entertaining or challenging about metaphor. Since it cannot be taken literally, the reader or listener is forced into re-interpreting what is presented to him' (ibid., 215). Yet, he has already admitted that 'in many instances, what was once a metaphorical use has become almost literal (e.g. *she planted an idea in his mind*), (ibid., 174). This, together with the fact that his own definition of 'unthinkable propositions' is unthinkable,[3] demolishes his argument; for, if one metaphor can become 'literal', with no restrictions given, all can, and if a metaphor is only a special case of an unthinkable proposition, then the most unthinkable must be potentially thinkable, therefore fully acceptable by his own terms.

III

So far, then, non-linguistic approaches have done little more than obscure the issues, and it can be argued that they have failed precisely because they are non-linguistic. Moreover, most writers on metaphor share three implicit assumptions about language, all of which are probably false, viz.:

(i) *Words have fixed and definite meanings.* Drange, while regarding the sentence *smells are loud* as meaningless, accepts *a loud colour* for the strange reason that 'in the American College Dictionary, the seventh meaning given to *loud* is "excessively striking to the eye, or offensively showy, as colours, dress or the wearer, etc." ' (ibid., 14). Yet, while asserting elsewhere that 'unthinkability' (which he equates with 'meaninglessness') is time-independent, he fails to realise that *a loud colour* must once have seemed as 'meaningless' as *a loud smell—* and that, in the future, *a loud smell* might become, by a similar process, as 'meaningful' as *a loud colour.* One can only cite with approval Miss Hesse's comment on Turbayne: 'We must abandon the search for the "literal" or "proper" among the variety of meanings a word may have. Such a view of language is at present foreign to most structural linguists and linguistic philosophers, but it alone would be adequate to deal with . . . semantic problems in general' (1966, 284). It is still, apparently possible to accept 'L'arbitraire du signe', and reject what Firth was wont to call 'the cowness of cow', yet assume that, once *cow* has been firmly attached to cow, it is somehow out of its place in other company.

(ii) *The meaning of a sentence is the sum of the meanings of the words that compose it.* It is significant that when Richards wished to demonstrate the interaction of different levels of understanding in the interpretation of poetry, he should have chosen for his sample the line *Arcadia, Night, a Cloud, Pan, and the Moon—*five NPs paratactically linked, therefore as free from grammatical relationships (and thus from the semantic co-occurrence restrictions these entail) as any extended utterance could be; and should go on to discuss the parts played by 'the visual sensation of the printed words', 'tied images', 'free images', 'references', 'emotions', and 'attitudes'—anything and everything except syntax (1924, 116-33). In fact, syntactic structures strongly affect our interpretation, not only of poetry (as shown in Levin, 1962 and Bickerton, 1967) but of all modes of discourse. Moreover, co-occurrences of semantic category tokens may vary in interpretability according to the colligations in which they are found. Thus, a sentence such as *eternity is visible* might strike one as comparable with Drange's *the theory of relativity is blue*; yet *I saw eternity*, in Vaughan's poem 'The World' causes no such problems. (That it may in some way be validated by the co-text of the poem itself, or that 'we expect that sort of thing in poetry', is part, but only part, of the story.) Thus the inter-pretability of sememes within the frame Nom—Pres+be—Nom/Adj (in which most of Drange's examples of 'meaninglessness' are cast) may often be lower than that of the same sememes in different colligational frames.

(iii) *The interpretability of texts is mode-of-discourse free.* Everyone accepts that context can affect interpretation. Few realise that we need not go outside language to account for this. If it is accepted that every context of situation (or, to be more precise, situation plus role plus topic) produces its peculiar mode of discourse, and that these modes are formally distinguishable on at least one linguistic level, there is nothing to prevent us from referring interpretation directly to mode of discourse without bringing in extra-linguistic context at all. If we say that the language, or rather sublanguage[4], of scientific journals differs, and differs formally in a rule-predictable manner, from that of, say, hippies, we can say that *the theory of relativity is blue* is an unacceptable utterance in the first, but an acceptable (almost, in an account of an LSD trip, a predictable) one in the second. This merely means that our linguistic expectations adjust themselves to the mode of discourse we are receiving. If, in reading a poem, we encounter lexemes such as *moon, rose* or *autumn*, we are likely (indeed, without explicit indications to the contrary, highly likely) to give them values such as 'unattainable beauty', 'perfect beauty', and 'ripeness and/or decay', rather than 'satellite of earth', 'species of flower', and 'third season of the year'. But we would in no circumstances do this while reading an almanac or a horticultural catalogue.

These three assumptions may be regarded merely as different aspects of a more fundamental, but equally false, assumption: that meaning somehow exists in language, like water in a well, and is either there to be extracted from it, or sometimes, mysteriously, not. Yet when we say we have 'understood the meaning of an utterance', what in fact are we saying? That in the light of our linguistic competence, plus co-text and context (if any), we have given it an interpretation. In many cases, our interpretation will differ little, if at all, from those of others, which nourishes this illusion of 'meaning'; sometimes, however, it will not. Then our only appeal is to a consensus; grammars and dictionaries are merely this consensus at a further, more depersonalised remove. Moreover, should the consensus change, the right will be wrong, and vice versa. To a Colombian, *le provaca un tinto?* 'means' *quiere Vd un cafe?*, 'would you like a cup of coffee?', but to a Spaniard it 'means' *le hace pelear una copita?*, 'does a glass of wine make you fight?' Which is right? The question is ridiculous. But if meaning does not exist in language, neither can it exist merely in the speaker or hearer, otherwise we would be free to utter any combination of phones that pleased us, or to place on an utterance whatever interpretation we chose. Meaning exists, if anywhere, only in the relationship speaker-language-hearer, not in any one of the three, and least of all in any connection between language and the extra-linguistic universe.

IV

This connection is subtle enough to have misled some very acute linguists. Bazell, for instance, remarks: 'Both *green wine* and *yellow wine* are combinations seldom or never to be found. But the reason is different for the former, where it is a question of lacking material motive, and for the latter, where it is a matter of syntactic convention' (1953, 83). Now by 'material motive' Bazell presumably means that 'there is no green wine in nature', and by 'syntactic convention', that wine which is (at least to speakers of what Whorf called SAE) optically yellow is habitually modified, across several languages, by the adjective *white* and its equivalents. But even leaving aside the fact that interpretation of the spectrum is a linguistic variable, this will not do. What of Portuguese *vinho verde*, or, nearer home, *yellow rat* (which is not a rat either) or *green fingers*? Or take the following table:

iron-mine	*steel-mine
iron ore	*steel ore
ironworks	steelworks
iron magnate	steel magnate
iron production	steel production
iron girder	steel girder
iron determination	*steel determination
iron will	*steel will
iron discipline	*steel discipline

Bazell would presumably account for the non-occurrence of the first two items in the right-hand column, and the occurrence of the next four, by saying that while steel-mines and steel ore do not exist in nature, steelworks, steel magnates etc. do. But if he tried thus to account for the non-occurrence of the last three, he would be unable to account for the occurrence of the last three in the left-hand column. He would be obliged to treat these as metaphors, albeit somewhat moribund ones. But once he had done that, he would have to show why the last three in the right-hand column cannot similarly be treated.

In fact we are better off if we forget about 'nature' and 'material motive' altogether. The non-occurrence of *steel-mines* is only accidentally connected with the non-occurrence of steel-mines; *yellow rats* occurs, though there are no yellow rats. If there were something which described as a 'steel-mine', just as there are some persons who might be described as 'yellow rats', *steel-mine* would occur, even in the absence of steel-mines. The reason why no such thing exists is simply that, in English at least, no specific attribute has been attached to *steel*.

By 'specific attribute' is meant a particular quality, usually assumed to belong to the denotatum of a sign. Thus to *iron*, in English, is assigned the attribute 'hardness'. Natural as this may seem, it is in fact a fairly arbitrary process; hardness is only one of the attributes which iron might be supposed to possess (durability, weight, dark colour, etc.) and it possesses it to a lesser extent than many other substances, such as diamond, or, for that matter, steel itself. But to *diamond* has been attached the attribute 'value', perhaps also 'brightness'. And the arbitrariness of the process is further demonstrated by the fact that it is not interlingual: *hierro* has no metaphorical value in Spanish, but *acero* has; even in loan-translations, *iron curtain* and *iron lung* are rendered as *telon de acero* and *pulmon de acero* respectively. Spanish simply attributes 'hardness' to steel rather than iron, thus reversing the English relationship.

Lexemes which have such attributes assigned to them will henceforth be referred to as 'marked signs', and those with no attributes as 'unmarked signs'. It should be clear from the foregoing that nothing prevents a marked sign from being used in its unmarked, as well as its marked sense. In the latter, however, it will have a power of combining with, or substituting for, other signs, which its unmarked congeners will not possess.

The full significance of attribute-attachment will become apparent at a later stage of the argument. But before going further, it may be as well to reconsider the second of the two questions posed at the beginning of this paper; for, while grounds have been given for regarding non-linguistic treatments of metaphor as unsatisfactory, it remains to be proven that linguistic ones can do better.

V

To date, there has been no specifically linguistic treatment of metaphor, which, despite the recognised importance of its role in changes of meaning (cf. Stern, 1931, among others), has been regarded as somehow marginal in synchronic studies. In the work of generative grammarians, however, there would appear to exist materials for such a treatment. The introduction of semantic category markers into the lexicon by Chomsky (1965) and the theory of structural semantics elaborated by Katz and Fodor (1963) and Katz and Postal (1964) would appear to be directly relevant.

The current position as regards the first issue is stated by Lakoff (1968) as follows: all non-irreducible sentences may be derived from irreducible ones ('kernels'); all selection rules and co-occurrence restrictions (including semantic ones) apply at the latter level; and all such rules and restrictions remain constant through subsequent transformations (the corollary of which, that unacceptable kernels will continue to yield unacceptable sentences throughout subsequent transformations, is demonstrated in Bickerton, 1969). Thus it should be possible to disentangle the often highly involved chains of metaphor that one finds in poetry (and some other modes), separate out the kernels, and analyse each deviation from semantic norms in isolation. Thus—if we assume for the moment that we may legitimately treat metaphors as 'deviant'— we might divide them into classes, such as violations of major-category rules (*hearts that* SPANIEL'D *me at heels*), of subcategory rules (MISERY LOVES *company*) or of Katz-Fodor-Postal semantic projection rules (*the flinty and* STEEL COUCH *of war*). This would seem to offer to stylistics the tempting possibility of a readymade hierarchy of metaphor, wherein each level might be relatable to specific literary effects.

Unfortunately, while all metaphors may be regarded as rule-violations, not all rule-violations may be regarded as metaphors. Katz's **scientists truth the universe* is a major-category violation, but in no sense a metaphor. Similarly with subcategory violations; consider two sentences such as *poverty gripped the town* and **ability gripped the town.* Theoretically, the same subcategorial co-occurrence restrictions should apply to both: *poverty* and *ability* are both abstract nouns derived from adjectives which principally modify human nouns, *grip* is a verb that normally requires animate (*man, monkey*), animate attribute (*paws, fingers*), or inanimate artefact (*monkey-wrench, pliers*) subjects. But while the first sentence may be acceptable as metaphor, the second would almost certainly be regarded as 'meaningless'. As for violations of projection rules, these too are just as likely to produce 'nonsense' (**short hats, *green elbows*, etc.) as phrases which may be interpreted metaphorically. Thus there is no level of rule-violation at which metaphor and non-metaphor cannot coexist, and no means within the theory for distinguishing between them at any level.

Moreover, the Katz-Fodor-Postal formulation is itself deficient in at least two important respects. First, it fails Bolinger's 'modest requirement' that a semantic theory should 'relate the several senses of a word in terms of their probable derivation one from another' (1965, 566); there is no indication of how '(Male) (Young) fur seal when without a mate during the breeding time', '(Male) (Young) knight serving under the standard of another knight', and '(Human) who has the first or lowest academic degree' should have come to possess the same lexical exponent as '(Male) who has never married'—still less of why in the vast majority of cases we would give tokens of *bachelor* the latter sense. The last point must be left to a theory of sublanguages to explain, but the reason for the CHOICE of *bachelor* to carry the other three senses links up with the second deficiency.

Consider the two expressions *bachelor flat* and *bachelor girl*. The theory as it stands can account for the different deep structures involved, and show that the first (*the flat is for a bachelor*) entails no real mating of semantic incompatibles. But the second can only derive from *the girl is a bachelor*, a direct mating of incompatible elements ('N' a human-female—be—'N' a human-male) which should theoretically yield something with as low a probability of occurrence as Katz and Fodor's **spinster insecticide*. It would appear that the application of *bachelor* to females, like the previous one to seals, depends on some hitherto-unexplained power of lower-order 'distinguishers' (in this case, 'single', 'without a mate') to override higher-order 'semantic markers', such as Male or Human. But at least a high percentage of signs are thus capable of leaping categorial boundaries, and, however arbitrary the process may seem, speakers of a given language can regard particular results of it as falling 'inside' or 'outside' that language. Since the process must therefore form part of their linguistic competence, an adequate grammar is obliged to account for it.

For, faced, on the one hand, with utterances such as **she has stabbed my self-respect* or **quiet donkeying with my car*, and, on the other, by utterances such as *hearts that spaniel'd me at heels* or its humbler forerunner, *to dog someone's footsteps*, any native speaker of English should be able, not merely to distinguish between them, but to recognise the first pair as probably products of a non-native, the second as showing evidence of more than average skill in exploiting the resources of the language. To equate the two seems to me a denial of all that language is.

The question therefore arises, whether this inability of generative grammar to distinguish between metaphor and non-metaphor is a necessary or an accidental concomitant of the theory.

VI

Some of the leading generative theoreticians seem, from their original fields of study and/or current predilections, to be oriented more in the direction of logic than of practical linguistics. This may account for their '*p* or not *p*' approach to semantic problems, and for their rigid divisions between semantic categories, which even the admission of multiple category-membership cannot palliate (since even this does not permit of the continued free transfer of signs from one category to another). They thus render impossible the only question worth asking: what are the privileges and restrictions which govern such transfers?

There must be restrictions, otherwise there would be no theoretical limit to the free combination of signs, and a sign with unlimited privilege of occurrence, as McIntosh has pointed out (1966, 189, fn. 11), could have only grammatical meaning. There must be privileges, or languages would ossify; for every coinage or loanword there are countless transfers, and innumerable expressions such as *bachelor girl, loud colour, iron discipline*, etc. (which are not high flights of poetic metaphor, but the small change of everyday conversation) could never have come into use. What we lack is simply the key that will discover them.

VII

It was suggested, in Section IV, that certain attributes are attached to certain signs, making it possible for those signs to combine with, or stand in place of, other signs held to share the same attributes. Thus *soup* may be assigned the attribute 'density', so that it may then give the pilot's *soup* (for dense cloud conditions), the Londoner's *pea-souper* (for dense fog), *to be in the soup* (for 'to be in trouble'—*trouble* is dense rather than diffuse, cf. *forest of difficulties, slough of despond*, etc.) and so on.

One might be tempted, in tracing the origin of this process, to go back to the very beginnings of language, when, many writers on metaphor hold, the human race had only a limited stock of signs, consisting of 'the names of sensible objects', whose senses had to undergo metaphoric extension to be able to cover 'those mental objects, of which men had more obscure conceptions, and to which they found it more difficult to assign distinct names' (Blair, 1783, 280). Unfortunately though much has been written on the presumed origins of language (the various theories are ably summarised in Revesz, 1956), it is practically all speculation; and while it would not be unreasonable to conjecture that 'concrete' signs preceded 'abstract' ones, we have absolutely no evidence for this. We can, however, state what such a language or languages would have been required to do, for languages are still required to perform similar tasks in the face of far more complex circumstances.

It is likely, according to a noted anthropologist, 'that man began by applying himself to the most difficult task, that of systematising what is immediately presented to the senses . . .' (Levi-Strauss, 1965, 11); and that totemism and other beliefs and practices of primitive peoples are 'directly or indirectly linked to classificatory schemes which allow the natural and social universe to be grasped as an organized whole' (ibid., 135). Now the simplest form of classification is a binary one, and we may assume that at a relatively early stage of human development, there was set up a kind of conceptual grid based on binary oppositions—Concrete/Abstract, Animate/Inanimate, Static/Dynamic, Whole/Part, Dense/Diffuse, etc.

It is a characteristic of some of these oppositions that, since they form part of a process of progressive subdivision, they can be represented in a bidimensional tree model, as in Figure 1.1.

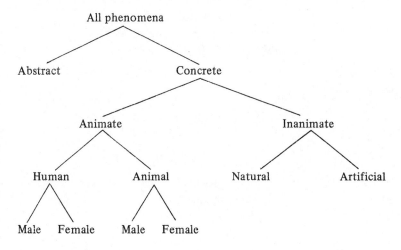

Figure 1.1

The similarity to generative tree-structures will be immediately apparent. It will also be clear that a number of further oppositions could be accommodated in such a system, at the cost of some redundancy, just as the Male/Female one is—thus Natural and Artificial could both be broken down into Liquid/Solid, and all categories into plus-Evaluative and minus-Evaluative (though here the picture would be complicated by the necessity of a third term, plus/minus-Evaluative, or 'morally neutral'). But as we incorporate further oppositions, some of which will divide, not one, but most, sometimes all, pre-existing categories, the complications of our picture will begin to multiply. Not only will the constant bifurcation appear increasingly superfluous, but (more important) the arbitrary nature of the ordering will become more and more apparent. For instance, if we were to follow *soup* along the branches of such a tree, we might extend our previous model as indicated in Figure 1.2.

Not only does this fail to exhaust all possible subdivisions (and it must be remembered that only a single branch has been followed through), but, in contrast with the earlier model, where the sequence was fairly unarguable, there can be no empirical grounds for preferring any system of ordering to any other. The order might just as well have been Liquid—Dense—Hot—Whole—Comestible—plus/minus-Evaluative, or one of other possibles. Yet it must here be emphasised that the oppositions under consideration (and many others) play as decisive a part in semantic relationships as do any of those treated in the Katz-Fodor-Postal formulation; this can readily be demonstrated by citing any of the countless unacceptable expressions which arise when they

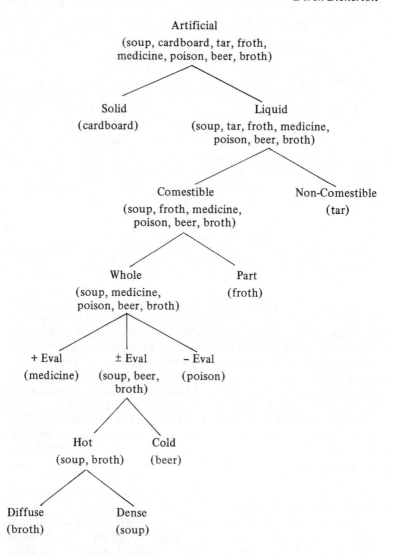

Figure 1.2

are breached, such as *scalding beer *the beer on the froth, *refreshing poison, *drink that cardboard*, etc.

Nor should we assume that such oppositions are necessarily subordinate to the earlier ones, e.g. animate/inanimate, etc. There may be times when we wish to group as a class (irrespective of their membership of other, incompatible categories) those signs characterised by

density—*fog, snow, soup, trees* (in a forest), *trouble*—or by coldness—
snow, beer, dogs' noses, (some) *hearts,* (some) *remarks*—or by any of
the terms in our other oppositions. There may be times when a 'lower'
opposition is more relevant than a 'higher' one. Indeed, the relationship between oppositions, and between the signs grouped under them,
may best be illustrated in the following way:

Let *A, B, C, D,* be categories in the two binary oppositions *A/B,*
C/D, and *a, b, c, d* be signs having membership of *A, B, C, D* respectively; and let *A/B, C/D,* intersect in such a manner that *a, b* fall on
contrary sides of the opposition *C/D,* and *c, d* on contrary sides of the
opposition *A/B.* Thus, with respect to *A/B, a, c* will fall within the same
category; but with respect to *C/D,* they will fall into different categories
We are then at liberty to draw one of the two following conclusions:

(i) That the intersection of *A/B, C/D* is mutually subdividing, so that
four discrete categories *AC, AD, BC, BD* are thereby set up.

(ii) That *a* and *c* are compatible by *C/D* and incompatible by *A/B,* i.e.
simultaneously compatible and incompatible.

Language, in fact, draws both. A large part of it (what is naively
termed the 'literal' part) runs according to the system of (i). But a
conceptual frame of mutually exclusive subcategories is far too rigid
to accommodate the Heraclitean flux which is our day-to-day experience; while we can hardly begin to think without setting up
categories, we need, for many practical purposes, to be able to make
connections between them, connections which a strict adherence to
(i) would make impossible. Thus the system of (ii) has to be invoked;
and, as we shall see, this system rules the attachment of attributes,
and the superstructure of 'true' metaphor which is erected on it.

That the foregoing illustration is no mere abstract schema, but is
closely related to the realities of language, may be shown in Figure 1.3.

We have merely substituted for *A/B, C/D* the oppositions Married/
Single, Male/Female, and for *a, b, c, d* the signs *husband, spinster,*
bachelor and *wife.* Our four mutually exclusive categories are then
Married-Male, Married-Female, Single-Male, and Single-Female. Thus
far, system (i); but *bachelor* is, as already noted, a marked sign, and
marked specifically for Single; thus, by virtue of system (ii), it is able
to across the boundary between *C* and *D,* and combine meaningfully
with a member of *D, girl.* Two points may be noted here. First, the
other three signs, being unmarked, cannot similarly combine, viz.
*spinster boy, *unmarried wife, *husband girl, etc. Second, while
bachelor girl might still prove an ephemeral creation, it might equally
be the thin end of a linguistic wedge whose ultimate result would be
the use of *bachelor* to denote young unmarried persons irrespective
of sex.

That a tree structure cannot represent both systems (and cannot
therefore serve as a model for the semantics of a language which contains

	Married	Single
	husband	bachelor

Male

Female

| | wife | spinster |

Figure 1.3

attribute-assignment and metaphor) may be shown by considering such an utterance as *take no notice of her—she's poison.* *Poison*'s derivation would show markers Concrete, Inanimate, Artificial, Fluid, Comestible, Whole, minus-Evaluative, Covert, and perhaps others. But for our sentence it is wholly irrelevant that *poison* has the first six—we are not suggesting the person referred to is a non-solid, can be consumed, etc.; only the last two matter. But, in a tree structure, any given node is regarded as dominated by the node immediately above it. Thus, if we wished to illustrate the above state of affairs, we would need a tree as in Figure 1.4, the absurdity (and ad-hocness) of which should be self-evident.

A more adequate model for a semantic system would be some kind of multidimensional grid, with no fixed rank-ordering of categories; this could only be represented in bidimensional terms by an analogue of a Jakobsen-Halle distinctive-feature grid (cf. Halle, 1964, 328)—though, needless to say, on a far larger scale.

It should by now be clear that the assigned attributes discussed in Section IV are, in most if not all cases, none other than the terms in the binary oppositions of the conceptual grid. Thus, while the choice of marked signs may be fairly arbitrary, the choice of attributes to attach to them is not; for the number of oppositions in a given language is almost certainly finite, probably quite limited (relative to the number of signs in its vocabulary), and possibly non-increasing. Signs marked with these attributes, or opposition-terms, can thus stand representative of the entire category to which they belong ('entire category' here being understood to mean the class of all signs which fall on the same side of the relevant opposition, not the smaller 'exclusive categories' set up by the intersection of two or more oppositions) and are then capable of combining with, or substituting for, other signs, marked or unmarked, which are members of the same entire category, even when the two belong to different exclusive categories. Needless to say, there is no biuniqueness condition in such a system;

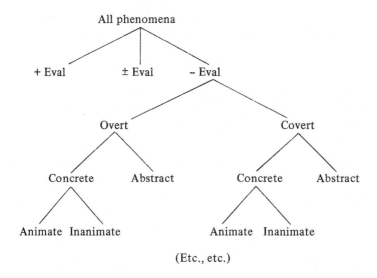

(Etc., etc.)

Figure 1.4

one entire category can be represented by several signs, just as (though perhaps more rarely) one sign can represent more than one entire category. In all cases, however, there appear to be restrictions on the use of such signs which are still very far from clear.[5]

It is by virtue of such a system that *iron* can combine with *will* or *discipline*, whereas *steel* cannot, or that *rat* or *monkey* can substitute for persons (of certain types) whereas *raccoon* or *lemur* cannot. In other words, it is thus that we compensate for the excessive rigidity of the exclusive-category frame, and are able to make those connections between apparently disparate fields which, for some of our purposes, seem to be as necessary as categorial distinctions. For it is surely significant that the incidence of marked signs will be found to be lowest, perhaps null, in specialised scientific writing, where concentration on a narrow sector of experience is mandatory; and highest in lyric poetry, where an attempt is made to syncretise, within a very limited space, as many different aspects of experience as the writer may think relevant to his theme.

VIII

It may be objected that little we have so far said relates to 'true' metaphors, in the sense of original and near-unique creations. These, however, may best be regarded as merely an extension of the system of attribute-assignment discussed above. A developed theory of metaphor, having first charted the latter, would then have to distinguish rigorously between four categories, which may be described informally as:

(i)   'literal' expressions (*iron bar, black cat*, etc.).
(ii) 'permanent' assignments (*iron discipline, yellow rat*, etc.).
(iii) 'temporary' assignments (*green thought, steel couch*, etc.).
(iv) 'meaningless' expressions (*steel-mine, procrastination drinks quadruplicity*, etc.).

Category (iii) is, of course, what most people mean by metaphor; and at an early stage the theory will have to deal with the suggestion that (iii) and (iv) are not really distinct categories, but that (iv) is simply potential (iii) awaiting validation by context of some kind. There, are, however, good reasons for believing that this is not the case, and, although the point is far too involved to be argued fully here, a reductio ad absurdum of the contrary position can be suggested. For, let us suppose that all members of an entire category could stand for that category, a privilege that would, of course, apply to each of the two or more members of any particular collocation. Now, since entire categories cross-cut, any member of one must also be a member of others, so that (unless the once-only assignment was somehow linkable with the existing system) there would be no way of knowing which entire category the sign(s) in question represented. We would thus be faced with a level of multiple ambiguity too high to permit of communication—a level which (as shown in Bickerton, 1967, 52–69) may already have been reached in certain poems.

The way in which the system of 'temporary' assignments (iii) develops from that of 'permanent' assignments can be suggested by a comparison between Marvell's near-unique *green thought* (*The Garden*, 1.48) and the commonplace *green fingers*. (In the present state of our knowledge, this treatment and all following ones must be regarded as tentative and informal to the highest degree.) *Green* may be taken as marked for Fertile and Young, and as having privilege of access to (among others) the exclusive category Human-Physical-Part, or rather to those members of it which fall on the same side of the relevant opposition(s). Thus *finger* or *thumb*, conceived of as agents of fertility (since we use them to plant, sow, water etc.) can combine with *green* to give *green fingers, green thumb*; whereas *ears* or *elbows*, neutral with respect to the opposition involved, would give only the anomalous *green ears, *green elbows*.

Within the system of (ii), however, *green*'s privileges would not extend to Abstract exclusive categories; they would do so only in the system of (iii), where they would still require adequate validation. ('Adequate', like so much else, must remain undefined for the present.) Thus *green ideas* and *green thought*, chosen by Chomsky and Ziff respectively (the latter apparently in ignorance of its history, cf. 1964, 395) as examples of 'semantic deviance', may be considered as having been validated, the second by Marvell's poem, the first posthumously, as it were, in a poem written (according to Voegelin, 1960, 59, fn. 3) by Dell Hymes. It may also be characteristic of some types of metaphor that, when an already marked sign such as *green* is used, an entailed attribute may substitute for its usual one; thus, with *green thought*, Natural rather than Fertile is assigned, as is indicated by the co-text: *Annihilating all that's* MADE *to a green thought in a green shade.* Similarly, in other expressions Immature (entailed by Young) may substitute for the latter, as in *greenhorn, green head on grey shoulders*, etc.

Metaphor may, of course, arise in several other ways, of which one may be illustrated by Shakespeare's *steel couch* (Othello, I.iii.231). Here, though neither sign is marked, *steel* belongs to the same semantic set (Names of metals) as the marked sign for Hard, while *couch* has a strong cognitive connection with the (Elizabethan) marked sign for Soft, *down*. The substitution for marked signs of their unmarked congeners probably also requires contextual validation, given in this instance by the occurrence of another 'hard' sign, *war*, in the same line, and two more 'soft' ones, *bed* and *down*, in the line following.

Thus in both cases the system of (ii) is only slightly extended, either by increasing the range of a marked sign, or substituting for the latter an unmarked one somehow related to it. It seems likely that other processes of metaphor-formation will likewise extend, rather than alter, the existing pattern of attribute-assignment.

So far we have considered only the synchronic component of a theory of metaphor. Such a theory, however, cannot be merely synchronic, otherwise it could neither account for the history of attribute-assignment (i.e. how countless expressions which must originally have seemed 'metaphorical' have now come to be accepted as virtually or completely 'literal') nor, what is perhaps more important, explain how countless other expressions, which may as yet not have occurred, may in the future pass through a similar process. For though in the present state of knowledge such a suggestion might seem wildly optimistic, the theory should have—if future processes prove to be modelled on past ones—at least some degree of predictive power.

Certain indications may be given as to how such processes work. For instance, attribute-assignment seems least likely to take place with signs which are hyponyms of others. The importance of hyponymy in semantics has been indicated by Lyons (1964); part of that importance lies in the fact that, while some signs marked minus-Evaluative and Dynamic (i.e. 'actively harmful') such as *hurt* and *wound* have privileges that extend even by system (ii) to Abstract categories—*to wound/hurt someone's pride/feelings/reputation* etc.—Hyponyms of these signs, such as *scratch, cut, slash* or *stab*, are not thus privileged (cf. **to* *scratch/stab/cut/slash someone's pride/feelings/reputation* etc.). That this rule is not universal can be shown by such exceptions as *a slashing attack* (as opposed to **a hurting attack*); but that it is fairly general can be demonstrated from other hyponymic sets, such as colour terms. Here, again, while main colour terms are usually marked—*red agitator, yellow rat, green fingers*, etc.—their hyponyms hardly ever are (cf. (*vermilion revolutionary*, **cerise mouse*, **ultramarine hands*, or any comparable expressions that may be produced).

Clearly this has something to do with the frequency of signs. Generic terms tend to occur more frequently than their hyponyms; and, broadly speaking, the rarer a sign's tokens are, the less likely it is to have attributes attached to it.

A further characteristic of the process is that it occurs more often between some categories than between others. The major ones involved seem to be Abstract and Animate (*time passes, prosperity grows, hopes wither*, etc.); Animal and Human (persons are *rats, lions, bears, monkeys* etc.); and Human and Artificial (*chairs* have *legs*; *needles, eyes*; and *clocks, faces* and *hands*, etc.).

Finally, it must be remembered that all privileges of marked signs are subject to purely syntactical restrictions similar to those which apply to unmarked signs. Take, for instance, *to face*; one can have *the car faced the bus, the bus faced the car, the car faced the house*, and *the house faced the sea*, but not **the house faced the car* or **the sea faced the house*; probably because *face* will only take Dynamic objects when the subject is also Dynamic, and will not take a Natural subject when the object is Artificial.

IX

It will be all too apparent that the foregoing paper has had perforce to ignore many aspects of metaphor, and skim all too lightly over others. This is partly because the field has been neglected by linguists for so long. I hope at least to have shown that any theory of natural languages which does not take metaphor into account will be inadequate to explain how such languages function; and to have provided at least the outline of a view of language within which an adequate linguistic theory of metaphor might be developed.

NOTES

1   Thus Hamilton Fyfe's translation (Loeb Classics ed., London, 1927). Turbayne quotes that of Ingram Bywater (Oxford, 1909), which begins 'Metaphor consists in giving *the thing a name* that *belongs to*

something else, (my italics). It is fascinating to note how Bywater, in trying to clarify the opacity of the definition, has succeeded, perhaps quite unconsciously, in smuggling into it several illegitimate suppositions about the nature of language, widely held, but with no shadow of foundation in the original text. Comparison with the latter will show the superior accuracy of Fyfe's translation.

2 It also takes little or no cognisance of much of the literature on the subject, e.g. Carnap, Ewing, Schaechter, Husserl, etc.

3 Which is, 'combinations of concepts which cannot be put together in thought' (142). Now, all concepts are abstract entities; only concrete entities can be 'literally' put together; therefore, 'to put together concepts' is a metaphor. But, all metaphors are unthinkable: therefore, the definition of 'unthinkable propositions' is itself unthinkable!

4 A theory of sublanguages may prove as essential a prerequisite for a theory of metaphor as a fully developed structural semantics. Such a theory is far too complex to discuss here (it will be the theme of a subsequent paper) but, briefly, it would treat 'a language' not as a homogeneous organism, but as a system of interrelated sublanguages, each with its specific social function. The means by which such a theory could be accommodated within a generative framework are set forth in De Camp (1968).

5 Some of these are syntactical (see the final paragraph in Section VIII). Others are far more obscure. Compare with *iron will*, etc., above, **iron hardship*, **iron devotion*, **iron danger*, etc. Or examine two bearers of minus-Evaluation, *black* and *ugly*. One can have *black day, black deed, black situation*, and *black sheep*; likewise one can have *ugly deed, ugly situation*, but *ugly day* is at least dubious, and **ugly sheep* either 'literal' or 'meaningless'. The answer to the latter may be that unmarked *ugly* can combine with (some) Animates, whereas in *black sheep*, usually treated as an idiom, both signs could be said to be marked. But the actual rules governing co-occurrence of signs are, of course, far more complex than the present rather cursory treatment might suggest.

REFERENCES

Bazell, C. E. (1953), *Linguistic Form* (Istanbul; Istanbul Press).

Bickerton, D. (1967), 'Meaning in Poetry', unpublished P.D.E.S.L. dissertation, University of Leeds.

Bickerton, D. (1969), 'The Linguistic Validity of Verb-Nominalising Transformations', *Lingua*, 22 (1967), pp. 47–62.

Blair, H. (1783), *Lectures on Rhetoric and Belles Lettres* (London: W. Strahan, T. Cadell).

Bolinger, D. (1965), 'The Atomization of Meaning', *Language* 41, No. 4, pp. 555–73.

Chomsky, N. (1965), *Aspects of the Theory of Syntax* (Cambridge, Mass.: MIT Press).

De Camp, D. (1968), 'Towards a Generative Analysis of a Post-Creole

Speech Continuum', paper read at the Conference on the Pidginiza-
tion and Creolization of Languages, U. W. I., Jamaica, 1968.

Drange, T. (1966), *Type Crossings* (Janua Linguarum, Series Minor,
44), (The Hague: Mouton).

Halle, M. (1964), 'On the Bases of Phonology', in *The Structure of
Language* (ed. by J. A. Fodor and J. J. Katz), (Englewood-Cliffs,
N. J.: Prentice-Hall) (henceforth SL), pp. 324–33.

Hesse, M. (1966), Review of Turbayne 1962, *Foundations of Language*
2, No. 3, pp. 282–4.

Katz, J. J. and Fodor, J. A. (1962), 'The Structure of a Semantic
Theory', in SL, pp. 479–518 (reprinted from *Language*, 39, pp.
170–210).

Katz, J. J. and Postal, P. (1964), *An Integrated Theory of Linguistic
Descriptions* (Cambridge, Mass.: MIT Press).

Lakoff, G. (1968), 'Instrumental Adverbs and the Concept of Deep
Structure', *Foundations of Language*, 4, No. 1, 4–29.

Lévi-Strauss, C. (1965), *The Savage Mind* (London: Weidenfeld &
Nicolson).

Levin, S. (1962) *Linguistic Structures in Poetry* (Janua Linguarum,
Series Minor, 23), (The Hague: Mouton).

Levin, S. (1964), 'Poetry and Grammaticalness', in *Proceedings of the
9th International Congress of Linguists* (1962) (The Hague: Mouton).

Lyons, J. (1964), *Structural Semantics: An Analysis of Part of the
Vocabulary of Plato* (Publications of the Philological Society, 20),
(Oxford: Blackwell).

McIntosh, A. (1966), 'Patterns and Ranges', in *Patterns of Language*
(ed. by A. McIntosh and M. A. K. Halliday), (London: Longman),
pp. 183–99 (reprinted from *Language 37*, No. 3, pp. 325–37).

Mooij, J. J. A. (1967), Review of Wheelwright 1962, *Foundations of
Language*, 3, No. 1, pp. 108–11.

Revesz, G. (1956), *The Origin and Prehistory of Language* (London,
Longman).

Richards, I. A. (1924), *Principles of Literary Criticism* (London:
Routledge & Kegan Paul).

Richards, I. A. (1929), *Practical Criticism* (London: Routledge &
Kegan Paul).

Stern, G. (1931), *Meaning and Change of Meaning* (Gothenburg:
Elanders boktryckeri aktiebolag).

Thorne, J. P. (1965), 'Stylistics and Generative Grammar', *Journal of
Linguistics 1*, No. 1, pp. 49–59.

Turbayne, C. M. (1962), *The Myth of Metaphor* (New Haven: Yale
Universty Press).

Voegelin, C. F. (1960), 'Casual and Non-Casual Utterances within
Unified Structure', in *Style in Language* (ed. by T. A. Sebeok),
(Cambridge, Mass.: MIT Press).

Wheelwright, P. (1962), *Metaphor and Reality* (Bloomington, Ind.:
Indiana University Press).

Ziff, P. (1964), 'On Understanding "Understanding Utterances" ',
in *SL*, pp. 390–9.

CHAPTER TWO

A semantic approach to metaphor

Michael J. Reddy *

[Like Bickerton, Reddy rejects the Chomskian notion that metaphor
may be defined and interpreted as a 'violation of selectional restriction',
or as a 'deviant' utterance, on the grounds that not all such violations
result in meaningful metaphors. (That is, sometimes these violations
result in mere anomalies.) But he offers two additional reasons for
rejecting Chomsky's selectional criteria for metaphor study:
1 Selectional restrictions and their connections to metaphor are
   unfairly presumed by transformational linguists to exist. According
   to Reddy, the facts of actual linguistic behavior do not uphold any
   presumption about the existence of such *a priori* intuitive categories,
   either in human language or in physical nature.
2 Selectional restrictions, even if presumed to exist, are not a necessary condition to metaphor. That is, both ordinary conversation and
   creative literature are filled with examples of statements which
   we are obliged to treat as metaphors (because of their context) even
   though they involve no selectional deviance or categorical violation
   in the Chomskian sense.
Thus Reddy opts for an essentially practical model of metaphor
which (like Bickerton's) would be sensitive to the pragmatic context
of text, speaker and hearer, rather than to the theoretical conditions
of an intuitive and sentence-bound syntax. Like Bickerton, Reddy also
rejects any notion of *a priori* semantic hierarchies for metaphor study
in favor of semantic considerations determined purely on the basis
of actual language use. However, unlike Bickerton, who employs
practical usage only for the purpose of marking individual words with
potentially metaphorical connotations, Reddy would employ practical
usage for the purpose of constructing 'literal spheres of reference,' which
are the 'normal limits of (conventional) referentiality' on individual
words. He would then define and study metaphor as an 'unconventional',
or novel use of a word, by reason of the fact that (in metaphorical usage)
no referent for a word can be found in its literal sphere of reference.]

*First published in *Papers from the Regional Meeting Annual*, 5 (1969), 240–51,
Chicago Linguistic Society.

1   To the extent that transformational grammarians have concerned themselves with the subject of metaphor, there has been a fairly general acceptance of an idea implicit in Chomsky's discussions of 'degrees of grammaticality.' (See especially Noam Chomsky, 'Degrees of Grammaticalness'.) This idea is that metaphorical language is 'semi-grammatical,' and is thus either caused by, or, at least, best approached in terms of the violation of some form of selection restrictions.

Perhaps 'acceptance' here indicates nothing more than an assumption. This was a plausible direction in which to proceed, as long as the purity of syntax was inviolate. And it had the further advantage of employing apparatus already necessary for syntactic analysis. But, whatever its status may have been, the survival of this view at the present time, when the majority of transformationalists have rejected not only selection restrictions, but the whole notion of an independent syntax, betrays a real lack of coherence in our growth as a science. We have attacked and destroyed the walls and the very foundations of a castle, and yet somehow left its battlements and fragile towers hovering undisturbed above the wreckage.

What is most disturbing about this situation, however, is the source of this collective inconsistency. There is, it seems, a kind of stigma about the subject of metaphor. It may be that it is too much akin to art or poetry. And under the remaining influence of nineteenth century Romanticism, the tendency is to think that art and especially poetry are somehow essentially nonanalyzable—some form of pure lyric gurglings. But neither is the structure of the Academy helpful in this respect: one is led to believe that man and departments of literature have 'rights,' as it were, on this subject. And imbedded, internalized norms dictate that one shall not do what is defined as 'another's thing.'

Or perhaps it is more simply a question of what language is most worth analyzing. In which case the conclusion must be that, apart from a few exceptions, we are most interested in the language found in reading primers and in language of such syntactic or logical complexity that it is rarely spoken. The language of children, because it is simple; the language of scientists because it is dear to our hearts.

In any case, the lag and the logical inconsistency in our understanding of metaphor persists because, for some reason, it is not considered important to bring it up-to-date. This has not been demonstrated, however, and thus the belief that what goes on in metaphor is peripheral to an understanding of language is simple presupposition. The question of its importance is an empirical one, not subject to academic boundaries.

In the present paper, I will take the position that metaphor is one of the more important and interesting of the phenomena involved in human communication. For in attempting to update the idea of metaphor somewhat, I have been confronted with a type of context sensitivity in the most mundane of utterances which present models simply do not allow for. All statements may be potential metaphors. And if this is the case, the phenomenon is probably far more important to linguists and departments of linguistics than it is to critics and departments of literature.

The object of this paper is thus threefold: to discuss, first of all, various reasons for not viewing metaphor as a deviation from some selectional norm; to explore, second, something of the real range of metaphorical language; and third, to propose and discuss some implications of an explanation of metaphor based on the concept of referentiality.

2 A major argument against approaching metaphor from the point of view of selectional deviance is, of course, simply that the existence of these restrictions, along with the form of analysis from which they sprang, have been called into question. At least one explicit argument (James D. McCawley, 'The Role of Semantics in a Grammar') has undermined the plausibility of such linguistic entities. And large numbers of proposals for the generation of sentences from underlying semantic rather than syntactic structures simply do not require this restriction on lexical items.

For the moment, however, let us ignore this fact, proceed as if there were no independent grounds for the rejection of these rules, and undertake a brief discussion of the consequences of analyzing metaphor in this fashion. In this case, there remain at least three very viable and, to my mind, compelling arguments against the position.

First, the assumption of, or the search for, some connection between selectional deviance and the phenomenon of metaphor is pre-judgment. As such, it immediately perturbs one's initial questions on the subject. Thus, in fact, although (2.1–4) represent the logical beginnings of a linguistic analysis of metaphor, (2.5) has been the starting point for those who accept this viewpoint.

What, exactly, is a metaphor?	(2.1)
What happens linguistically when people speak in this fashion?	(2.2)
What makes us take some utterances literally and others metaphorically?	(2.3)
Is there any relation between present models and what seems to be going on in metaphor?	(2.4)
What selection rules in the syntactic grammar were relaxed in generating this utterance, which I intuitively feel is metaphorical?	(2.5)

Second, consonant with a bad beginning, the way proceeds now into nothing less than a grammatical morass. Not all relaxations of selection restrictions result in metaphor. Many produce anomalies. Further elucidation, therefore, of the assumed or hoped-for connection between selectional deviance and metaphor requires investigation of this discrepancy. Which cannot be performed except on the basis of a fair number of real, adequately-formulated and tested sets of selection restrictions.

And if this is not already prohibitive and far from the point, then the syntactic form of most metaphors certainly renders it so. For most commonly occurring metaphors involve either propositional phrases, or modifiers derived from imbedded sentences of the form, 'X *is* Y.' Thus, at the very least, one must know what selection restrictions operate across 'is,' and have an understanding of how they behave in whatever underlies propositional phrases. To put it simply, this attempt to analyze metaphor plunges immediately into some of the least understood areas of the English language.

Finally, the strongest possible evidence that this entire point of view is indeed a prejudgment and not likely to yield an understanding of metaphor is the existence of a class of utterances with the following two characteristics: (1) they violate no conceivable sort of selection restrictions; and (2), they are precisely what we intuitively recognize as metaphors. Let us look at a few examples of this class.

Consider, to begin with, (2.6), a statement I made in the second paragraph of this chapter.

We have attacked and destroyed the walls and the very foundations
of a castle, and yet somehow left its battlements and fragile towers
hovering undisturbed above the wreckage.   (2.6)

This is a perfectly well-formed utterance about *castles, towers*, and *wreckage*. It violates no grammatical rules. In context, however, we processed it and understood it as a statement about such things as *pure syntax, the analysis of metaphor*, and an *odd situation in transformational grammar*. Another highly similar example is (2.8) in the context of (2.7).

He suspected that most of his listeners were sympathetic to the
position that selection restrictions were totally inadequate. (2.7)
But he attacked the sputtering tyrant once again, if only to place
his little penknife alongside the daggers of his companions.   (2.8)

(2.8) is exactly what is termed a 'metaphor,' but it has no trace of linguistic deviance.

Clearly, I have created these metaphors in each case by specifying a context before making a normal, non-deviant utterance. It is crucial to realize that non-verbal contexts, such as current events, or simply *the physical situation of the speaker and the listener*, can easily trigger the same kind of non-literal readings.

Thus, in the context of present-day university life in the United States, the second half of (2.9) will be processed as a metaphor.

> I stopped talking to the radicals because it is simply useless
> to chisel on granite walls.   (2.9)

Or consider the readings assigned to (2.10) in the context of (1) a group of people on a geology expedition, and (2) a group of students walking out of the office of some staunch old professor emeritus.

> The rock is becoming brittle with age.   (2.10)

In context (1), (2.10) will almost certainly function literally. In context (2), however, one can say with equal certainty that *part* of (2.10)—namely, 'rock,' and 'brittle'—will function metaphorically, while the rest remains perfectly literal.

There seems to be no need to belabor this point. Examples of this class of sentences can be constructed *ad infinitum*, and may be found without difficulty in everyday speech as well as literary works. A great deal more could be said about them. At most, they indicate, as I mentioned, that all statements may be potential metaphors.[1] At the very least, they are counterexamples to the notion that metaphor has a necessary connection with grammatical deviance.

3 The proposal I will offer as to the nature and perhaps cause of what occurs in metaphor is, I believe, a substantive one. But no proposal can reduce the innate complexity of this phenomenon. Nor can what I have to say, at this stage, be instantly and neatly formalized. I cannot—to make another metaphor—present you with a set of transistorized components that plug right into the back of your latest 70 watt grammar. I will now try to demonstrate the full range of the problem and attempt to ensure a clear understanding of the conceptual tools I hope to use in handling it.

4 To begin with, it is imperative that we confront the idea of selection restrictions once again. This time to question not simply their value for the analysis of metaphor, but their value and place in any analysis of the way humans communicate. For there is a sense in which this concept and the strict, generative mentality with which we began have exercised a real tyranny over our minds. Among other things, they have, I believe, blinded us to significant portions of the data we must explain. Some of this data is very important to the question of metaphor. I

have no choice, therefore, but to attack this dying Caesar once again.

The idea that human language, or any adequate model thereof, has a mechanism specifying some strings as *formally* correct and others as formally incorrect *on the basis of the way in which they connect concepts* mistakes the very nature of human knowledge and communication.

The grammatical device of selection restrictions rests on two very naive, epistemological fallacies which may be described in the following fashion. First, to embody in a grammar formally those restrictions which seem to operate in the normal, external physical world is to assume that all human utterances are directly and primarily concerned with describing this world. Second, to embody in a grammar those restrictions which seem to operate in the normal, external physical world is to assume that there is some normal, external physical world from which to extract them.

The fact of the matter is, however, that only a portion of human utterances are even intended to describe external events. And within this portion, such description takes place only secondarily, by means of the detailing of events internal to the speaker. And finally, because of the highly conglomerate and ever-changing nature of physical reality, there is no possibility of predicting those utterances which are intended to describe external events by any set of 'normal,' or 'distinctive' features.

To make these statements, which I regard almost as commonplaces of scientific epistemology, somewhat clearer, let me pose and give an answer to the 'fool's question.' What is a word? What is it that we communicate when we utter some 'lexical item'? What is, for example, a 'table'?

The only rational, non-metaphysical answer which may be given to this question is that the lexical item 'table' refers to an open class of actual, or recalled, or potential inputs to the speaker's sense modalities. *Events*, or *states*, if you will, *internal* to his complex system of devices for sampling what occurs around him.

By the term 'open class' of these events, I mean that membership in the set is specified only by rule, and therefore it cannot be enumerated. The rule, in the case of 'table,' as in that of most lexical classes, is that the events correspond to forms or gestalts of immense complexity. The rule for 'table,' for instance, involves allowances for everything from lighting conditions, distance, and angle of view, to decisions about purpose. Is it a 'table,' a 'footstool,' or a 'bench'?

A relatively firm implication of this answer is that the only bit of information communicated *primarily* and *directly* by the utterance of the word 'table' is *the speaker's decision to place some bundle of internal events in the class.*

In a very large number of cases, to which linguists have paid scant attention, this bundle of events is utterly internal to the speaker, and comprises part of what we call *dreams, desires, feelings, fears*, or strange, perhaps garbled *wishes*, or *memories*. It is therefore almost inconceivable that there could be some formal aspect of natural languages which would tend to make these utterances conform to relationships sometimes or even often observed in external events. And a more likely assumption is that the real formal mechanisms of language allow expression of internal and external events with equal ease.

And I repeat: only decisions about internal states are communicated immediately and directly by human utterances. And thus, even in statements intended by the speaker to be descriptive of the external, physical world, this description takes place only by virtue of the indirect, and highly complicated relationship between his gestalts and particular instances of physical events. This much is implied daily by our awareness that speakers may be mistaken, misinformed, or subject to an illusion or to mental aberrations.

To say this less precisely, but more simply, *speakers cannot and do not tell you about the world—they tell you about their experience of the world*. If linguistics is not to re-enact one of the most violent pseudo-arguments in the history of Western philosophy, we must understand very clearly that the external reality speakers *sometimes* talk about is neither the free and spontaneous creation of the human mind—as 'idealists' would have it—nor anything that exists apart from the human mind, and with which the human mind has some immediate, 'mystical' connection—as 'realists' will claim. Speakers do construct their worlds, but they construct them functionally, and according to rules.

But even this construct of the external world is not anything like the idea of selection restrictions assumes it to be. For we are continually supplementing our own rudimentary sensing devices with new and more powerful ways of gathering information about that which we call 'the external world.' Physical reality, we find, is infinitely on the move. And in the context of a real understanding of 'the external world,' concepts such as 'things,' as opposed to 'actions,' no longer apply. One is forced, following Whitehead's example, to speak only of 'events.'

Because human speakers have an intuitive knowledge or perhaps acceptance of this highly conglomerate nature of external reality, there exists an enormous variety of situations in which lexical classes such as 'air,' or 'table,' or 'house' will be validly and literally employed.

Consider, for the moment, that you are standing in a scientific laboratory. And that what you call 'air,' which is subject along with most of the rest of material reality to no less than three changes of state, is presently being made to change its states. In this context, you will probably utter sentences about 'air' 'blowing,' or 'splashing,' or 'breaking,' or 'splintering.' (4.1-2) are precisely the sort of thing you will say or hear.

Excuse me, but your air is dripping on the table.   (4.1)
How hard can you push on that air before it will break?   (4.2)

Or suppose you are looking at what you call a 'table' under a powerful microscope, or that you examine it with the probe of a Geiger counter. (4.3-5) are then valid, literal utterances.

Actually, as you will be able to see, the table swarms around more
violently every time I turn up the heat.   (4.3)
On the basis of these observations and some quick calculations,
I would say that the table is really about 68% empty space.   (4.4)
Perhaps you should not stand just there, John, the table seems
to be emitting gamma rays.   (4.5)

Perhaps you may retreat from all this to the normality of your home— but you may find it on fire and describe the experience with something like (4.6)

As I got out of the car, I saw my house crackling and roaring and
floating away into the atmosphere.   (4.6)

The concept of selection restrictions is, in a word, an epistemological blunder of the first rank. It is based on a false notion of what speakers have to communicate about. And it assumes a naive reality behind constructs such as 'things' that would have shocked even the Pre-Socratics.[2]

Heraclitus, you will remember, said: 'You cannot put your foot twice into the same "river".' We are in a position to know better. You cannot even put the same 'foot' twice into the same 'river.'

5 It is worth noting that none of the examples yet given in this paper have contained any irregularities in what one might call their formal semantic structure. The binding of the variables, the description of arguments, the distinct linkage of arguments with some but not other predicates, the compounding of propositions whereby some predicates with their arguments function as arguments for another predicate—all of this takes place in impeccable fashion. I must submit to you that these structures, these processes are the formal heartland of natural language. And that what we have called 'syntactic' structures should be considered in terms of their intricate relationships to these forms, and not as if they were anagrams generated in a semantic vacuum.

If there is any 'irregularity' about the phenomenon of metaphor, it is not, I think, anything which could be termed a deviance in *linguistic form*. What seems to be the defining characteristic of metaphor is rather something in the *referentiality* of the terms employed.

To explain this, let me say that I am using the concept of 'reference,' and will speak of 'referents,' in the way that logicians and natural language philosophers have used it. A 'referent' is *that which a word or group of words comes to refer to in the context of an utterance*. Thus, out of context, 'table' does not have a 'referent,' except in so far as it is the name of a lexical class. In (5.1), however, it has a precise, determinable referent.

Reddy's dining-room table is dirty. (5.1)

It is most important to realize that 'referentiality' is not synonym for 'meaning.' Although 'meaning' is often used in the sense of 'referentiality,' it has another very general sense which makes it imperative to keep these two terms separate. For one of the rules whereby human speakers decide on the membership of the complex lexical class 'the "meaning" of event X' allows the inclusion in the class of *anything which may be inferred from event X*. To someone in possession of given knowledge, anything may 'mean' anything. This usage is displayed in (5.2-3).

This skidmark means that my car was stolen. (5.2)
That paperclip on the floor means that the desk was rifled. (5.3)

Since this sense of the word applies to speech acts as well, the 'meaning' of an utterance or of a word in an utterance may be *whatever is implied by the fact of the utterance* or *by the choice of the word*. And this is clearly not the 'referent' of the word.

Let me now define the set of all possible referents which a word may have in human utterances as the 'sphere of reference' of this word. We have seen the word 'castle,' however, take in actual fact something best described as 'the theories of pure syntax' for its referent in the context of this paper. This would seem to suggest that the 'sphere of reference' for most words is actually the universal set, or everything. For if 'castle' may end up with something so remote and different as 'the theories of pure syntax' for its referent, what could one rule out?

It is possible, nevertheless, to speak of a subset of a word's sphere of reference which can be fairly well defined and is highly useful. This subset I will call the 'literal sphere of reference' and will define as the set of referents a word may, in context, *conventionally* or *literally* take on. The spontaneous and intuitive feeling that a word is operating metaphorically is, I believe, contingent upon the failure to find a referent for a given word *within* its 'literal sphere of reference.'

6 In order to make this concept somewhat clearer, and to show that, although they are complicated, literal spheres of reference can be delineated for various types of words, I include the following remarks on some general shapes this set can have.

At one end of the spectrum of types of literal spheres of reference are those connected with what one might call 'gross physical objects or activities.' I will continue to use 'table' as a paradigm case for words such as these. The literal sphere of reference of the word 'table' contains at least the four subparts given below.

First, all configurations of real sensory events from all or some of the speaker's sense modalities which conform to his gestalt 'table' are in the literal sphere of reference (LSR). I will make no attempt to define this gestalt. The only exceptions to this rule are where the gestalt has no configuration in the context of a given sense modality. Thus a 'table' may be something *seen* only, or *felt* only, but, normally not something *tasted* only, *smelled* only, or *heard* only.

Second, any of the above configurations, from all or only some of the sense modalities, as they are recalled, imagined, dreamed, combined, or otherwise shuffled about within the speaker's mind are also in the LSR. Notice that this includes constructions or combinations which may not occur at all external to the speaker's mind. In (6.1), the referent of the underlined portion may occur externally someday, but does not at the time of the speech act. In (6.2), however, the referent of the underlined portions will probably never occur external to the speaker's mind.

When I get rich, I will buy *my new Alfa Romeo.*   (6.1)
I dreamed about *this huge tree with eyes and ears* that kept
groaning.   (6.2)

Third, if the context is clear, any artificial or symbolic renderings of any of the above configurations belong also to the LSR. This, it seems, is a very important and beautiful generality. Crucial facets of the gestalt 'table' may be rendered in various ways in various artistic mediums. In a way that very much supports my arguments in Section Four, we also refer to these non-metaphorically as 'tables.' Consider the ambiguity of (6.3), which is completely dependent on the fact that 'table' may mean 'two-dimensional, colored rendering of some part of the gestalt "table".'

Picasso paints mostly tables and people.   (6.3)

Because of this capability, (6.5) is the normal way of saying what is much more precisely expressed as (6.4).

In the movie last night, the picture of Richard Burton was
represented as kissing the picture of Liz Taylor 5 times.   (6.4)
In the movie last night, Richard Burton kissed Liz Taylor
5 times.   (6.5)

Fourth, in specific situations such as the analysis of 'gross physical
objects or activities' into their component physical parts or events,
the LSR may contain any number of new or strange configurations,
because, in this context, learning may take place and the gestalt may
be subject to modification. Thus, examples (4.1-6) are, I believe,
literal utterances.

At the other end of the spectrum of literal spheres of reference are
those corresponding to what one might call 'relational' words. Consider
'pledge,' or 'claim.' The gestalt associated with each of these words
states simply that literal referents must *signify* a given relationship.
Since almost anything could do this, the LSR of these words is without
definite boundaries. Thus (6.6-7) are not metaphors.

Your only claim to the Erbacher estate was murdered last
night.   (6.6)
I took your pledge of eternal love and pawned it for
£30.00.   (6.7)

Another similar case is 'symbol.' (6.8) is not a metaphor, even though
the referent of 'symbols' is *the bull's ears.*

The bullfighter walked off with the bleeding symbols of
his victory.   (6.8)

In between these two extremes, there is an area which will require
some investigation. One of the ways that language seems to grow is
that metaphors become, after a time, literal usage. Thus there are a
great many words, such as 'latticework,' 'stolid,' or 'fruitful' which
do not, in my version of the language at least, seem to have sharp
divisions between concrete, root meanings and abstract extensions of
this meaning.

7 I will now offer the following hypothesis about the nature and
cause of metaphor.

What seems to be the defining characteristic of all instances of
metaphorical language is an abnormal or unconventional situation
with regard to the normal limits of referentiality on words. Metaphor
occurs, it seems, whenever words in an utterance do not have referents
within their conventionally defined, literal spheres of reference, as
described above. Please notice that this is an essentially negative

statement—I have not said that the words have, necessarily, referents outside of their literal spheres of reference. I have only stated that they do not have a referent *inside* this set.

The cause of this phenomenon is, I think, almost invariably the interaction between the context of an utterance and the literal spheres of reference of the terms involved. This, and this alone, is reason enough for linguists to be concerned with metaphor. Further study of this subject will reveal, I believe, a degree of context sensitivity as yet undreamed of in transformational models.

I will conclude with the following crude description of what seems to be a very general and crucial part of the processing of human utterances. As to how such things as metaphors might be *generated*, I have not the faintest idea at this point.

At some point in the processing of all utterances it seems, listeners and readers make decisions, very much on the basis of context, as to whether the words in the utterance have referents within their literal spheres of reference. Undoubtedly, this decision is contingent upon some search of the LSR in question. A positive result—that is, a more or less precise and determinate referent in the set, depending on the circumstances and on how precise and explicit the utterance is—allows processing to continue in whatever fashion it normally does.

A negative result however, causes two very different and interesting things to happen.

First, patterns of the gestalt or gestalts which defined the literal sphere of reference of the word in question are searched. Not with a view toward isolating some part of these patterns as the referent, but in an attempt to find analogies or similarities to events or configurations in the context of the utterance. A referent, or an area in which possible referents might lie, *may* then be determined on the basis of the context and the discovered similarities. It is possible, however, and in some cases even probable that different speakers will arrive at different referents, or that no one will arrive at any referent. For the utterance has stepped outside the conventional bounds of the language. And if it is no longer confined by them, then it is just as true that they are no longer guidelines to a unique reading.

But second, unique referents for those words which function metaphorically become less crucial to the understanding of the utterance. For the second sense of the word 'meaning,' which I described above, comes very much into play. The 'meaning' of the utterance is primarily *whatever is implied by the fact that something was expressed in this curious and unconventional fashion.* The symbolic connection of precise referents is less a bearer of information than the fact that the speaker chose such and such a word in such and such a context.

No one, I am sure, missed the information about my own attitude conveyed by the fact that I described selection restrictions as a 'dying

Caesar.' And although the referent of '70 watt,' in the phrase, 'your latest 70 watt grammar,' is not very clear, the implications of the phrase were obvious.

And finally, no one, I am sure, will miss the implications of the following metaphor—with which I shall end.

> We have our collective foot halfway through one of the major doorways to the human mind, and we must either go in completely —laboratory rats, Skinner, mystics, behaviorists, innatists, mentalists, religion, selection restrictions, and academic boundaries *notwithstanding*—or risk having that foot cut off. (7.1)

NOTES

1 This statement is probably too strong. A huge number of utterances are potential metaphors, however, and at least all those whose literal readings involve concrete objects or processes.

2 During the discussion period, it was claimed that selection restrictions had always been intended as descriptions of the internal or psychological states of the speaker. So that if the speaker thinks of 'air' as 'liquid,' the lexical item 'air' will be *+liquid*. This seems to be stretching the point somewhat. To my knowledge, selection restrictions have never been spoken of or written of in such fashion. Should they be, they must be considered an attempt to characterize what I have been calling the 'rule' or 'gestalt' which governs decisions about the employment of the lexical class in question. I frankly do not believe that any system of *features* will ever be adequate to do this task.

REFERENCES

Ayer, Alfred J. (1946), *Language, Truth, and Logic* (London: Victor Gollancz).

Chomsky, Noam (1964), 'Degrees of Grammaticalness', *The Structure of Language*, ed. Jerry A. Fodor and Jerrold J. Katz (Englewood Cliffs, New Jersey: Prentice-Hall).

Katz, Jerrold J. (1964), 'Semi-Sentences', *The Structure of Language*, ed. Jerry A Fodor and Jerrold J. Katz (Englewood Cliffs, New Jersey: Prentice-Hall).

Lenneberg, Eric H. (1967), *Biological Foundations of Language* (New York: John Wiley).

McCawley, James D. (1968), 'The Role of Semantics in a Grammar', *Universals in Linguistic Theory*, ed. Emmon Bach and Robert T. Harms (New York: Holt, Rinehart & Winston).

Whitehead, Alfred N. (1948), *Science and the Modern World* (New York: The New American Library).

CHAPTER THREE

Concerning a 'Linguistic Theory' of metaphor

Robert J. Matthews *

[In this defense of Chomskian grammar as a useful tool for metaphor study, Matthews offers a rebuttal to Bickerton (first article) and Reddy (second article).

He attempts to answer Bickerton in two ways:

1 Bickerton's notion of the 'marked sign' (a term whose potential metaphorical sense has been designated by the attachment of a specific attribute) deals only with metaphors that are already well known; it cannot serve to predict the potential uses of new, creative metaphors because the 'marking' of a term with a figurative sense could only occur through repeated metaphorical use of the term. Since new metaphors have not undergone such repeated use, the attachment of a specific attribute must be considered the result, not (as Bickerton says) the pre-condition, of metaphorical creation.

2 Bickerton's insistence on the distinction between metaphor and merely deviant utterances is not in keeping with his own call for a true linguistic theory of metaphor; this distinction depends, according to Matthews, on the intention of the speaker and hearer, which are matters of social performance rather than linguistic competence. A linguistic theory of metaphor, he maintains, ought to deal with competence in the Chomskian sense; the important competence distinction to be made in metaphor study is between deviant and non-deviant sentences.

According to Matthews, all selectionally deviant sentences are potentially metaphorical, and in fact are metaphorical in the proper linguistic and extralinguistic context.

Matthews also offers two rebuttals to Reddy:

1 Reddy's examples of 'metaphor' which involve no selectional deviance are not really metaphors at all; they are instead literal utterances which have underlying figurative implications. When these implications are themselves realized as sentences, they do indeed involve selectional deviance, contrary to Reddy's claim.

2 Reddy's 'literal spheres of reference' are essentially a notational

*First published in *Foundations of Language*, 7 (1971), 413–25.

variation on the lexical subcategories and selectional restrictions
posited by Chomsky.
In defense of these latter, Matthews argues that the lexical features on
which Chomsky's selectional criteria are based should not be mistaken
for *a priori* assumptions about psychological or physical reality. Because
these features should be viewed as delimiting only the discourse
environments in which words are commonly found in literal usage,
they make Reddy's literal spheres of reference a mere redundancy to
the Chomskian grammar.]

Recent discussions, apparently as a result of the continued interest
in 'deviant sentences' and 'meaningless utterances', have again called
our attention to the question of metaphor: a semantic theory, explains
for example the late Uriel Weinreich (1966, p. 471), is of 'marginal
interest if it is incapable of dealing with poetic uses of language, and
more generally with interpretable deviance'. More specifically, Bolinger
(1965, p. 567), requires that 'A semantic theory must account for
the **process** of metaphorical invention'. Bickerton (1969), convinced
that these exigencies demand a 'new look at metaphor' as well as a
'new theory', requires further that this new theory be linguistic because
thus far 'non-linguistic approaches have done little more than obscure
the issues, and it can be argued that they have failed precisely because
they are non-linguistic' (1969, p. 36).

While, of course, none would wish to deny the need to take a 'new
look' at metaphor, no one has yet bothered to explain exactly what
it is about metaphor that is to be 'accounted for': these discussions
of the role of metaphor in a theory of language seem to have by-passed
a careful formulation of the question in favor of theorizing. But the
continuing linguistic as well as philosophical interest in metaphor has
not been misguided: any attempt at a unified theory of language will
have to give an adequate account of this particular linguistic phenomenon. Such an account will be of central importance to the theory
not solely because of the high occurrence frequency of metaphor in
normal language use, but more importantly because of metaphor's
recognized affinity with the crucial notions of the grammaticality and
creativity (generative nature) of language. In consonance with the goal
of a unified theory of language, the subsumed theory of metaphor
would have to meet certain minimal requirements in order that we
could accept the theory as adequate. First, the theory of metaphor
would have to be such that it establish necessary and sufficient conditions for the distinguishing of metaphor from non-metaphor. This
first adequacy requirement is crucial to the theory of metaphor,
because unless a non-trivial characterization of this distinction can be
formulated the entire problem dissolves. Second, the theory of metaphor would have to be such that it accounts for how, in terms of

his linguistic competence, the speaker understands or interprets metaphors. It would be the assumption of any theory of metaphor which was subsumed under a more general theory of language that the native speaker of a language employs in his handling of metaphor the same linguistic 'tools' which he employs in his handling of non-metaphoric uses of language. We see that these two requirements for an adequate account of metaphor demand on the one hand an adequate distinction of metaphoric from non-metaphoric uses of language, and on the other hand an adequate account of the semantics of metaphor (how metaphor is interpreted) in terms of the semantic component of the more general theory of language.

While any adequate theory of metaphor would have to be articulated in conjunction with a more general theory of language, on the basis of the above two requirements it is not impossible for us to sketch an account of metaphor which will indicate what **considerations** will be important in such an adequate theory of metaphor, even in the absence of the more general semantic theory. In the present essay, I propose to present such an account of metaphor, approaching this goal first through criticism of the recent attempt by Bickerton (1969), to articulate a theory of metaphor. In this all-too-brief discussion and evaluation of Bickerton's contribution, it will be argued

1 that Bickerton fails to establish necessary and sufficient conditions for the distinguishing of metaphor from non-metaphor, and
2 that Bickerton's theory fails to confront the problem of how metaphors are interpreted or understood, once recognized.

In the second part of the paper, I wish to return to an account suggested by Chomsky (1965), but until now left undeveloped. The development of this suggestion, I wish to show, yields an adequate account of metaphor, meeting both of the aforementioned adequacy requirements.

In justifying his own attempt to present an adequate theory of metaphor, Bickerton observes that the various proposed theories have been less than satisfactory. He begins by outlining (1969, pp. 36-8), three false assumptions—

1 *'words have fixed and definite meanings'*
2 *'the meaning of a sentence is the sum of the meanings of the words that compose it'*, and
3 *'the interpretability of texts is mode-of-discourse free'*

—which he believes to underlie and consequently to have misled these earlier attempts. Developing no formal criteria for what he would consider to be an adequate theory of metaphor, these pitfalls of earlier attempts apparently serve as his sole formal guidance. Noting the affinity between the native speaker's competence for recognizing metaphors when they occur in discourse and this same speaker's competence for recognizing deviant sentences, Bickerton sees the distinguishing between 'potential' metaphor and simple deviance, in a context-independent manner, as the prime task or goal of a theory of metaphor. In explaining how it is that he will accept *bachelor girl* as metaphorical but not **spinster boy, hearts that spaniel'd me at heels* but not **she has stabbed my self-respect, green thumb* but not **green ears*, Bickerton resorts to the notion of a 'specific attribute': 'By "specific attribute" is meant a particular quality, usually assumed to belong to the denotatum of a sign. Thus to *iron*, in English, is assigned the attribute "hardness" ' (1969, p. 39). The assignment of a 'specific attribute' to a particular sign, he regards as arbitrary, but if the sign lacks such a 'specific attribute', the sign has no metaphorical use (at least with respect to the quality in question):

> Lexemes which have such attributes assigned to them will henceforth be referred to as 'marked signs', and those with no attributes as 'unmarked signs'. It should be clear from the foregoing that nothing prevents a marked sign from being used in its unmarked, as well as its marked sense. In the latter, however, it will have the power of combining with, or substituting for, other signs, which its unmarked congeners will not possess. (1969, p. 39)

On the basis of this notion of words (lexemes) as being 'marked' as potentially metaphorical, the distinction between potential metaphor and simple deviance supposedly becomes simple: you merely look to see if the deviant word is 'marked'. If the word is appropriately 'marked', then it may be metaphorical.

Bickerton describes his semantic model as a kind of 'multidimensional grid' with no fixed rank-ordering of categories, wherein, with respect to a particular binary opposition between categories (e.g., *married/single*), only one member of the category will be marked (e.g., *bachelor*, rather than *spinster*, within the category *single* with respect to the opposition *married/single*). Discussing these 'marked signs', Bickerton (1969, p. 47), explains:

> Thus, while the choice of marked signs may be fairly arbitrary, the choice of attributes to attach to them is not; for the number of oppositions in a given language is almost certainly finite, probably quite limited . . . and possibly non-increasing. Signs marked with these attributes, or opposition-terms, can thus stand representative of the entire category to which they belong. . . .

A fundamental difficulty with this account of how we recognize metaphors is clear: the proposed solution seems to beg the question. How do we determine which signs are 'marked' as potentially metaphorical if not through recourse to language use? No doubt the question as to whether or not a particular sign is in fact 'marked' will presuppose our being able to determine that it is potentially metaphorical, and not simply deviant, even before we have ascertained its 'marking'. But even supposing we do in some language-independent manner determine whether a sign is 'marked', how do we account for the bulk of examples of metaphor, namely those original and creative metaphors which do not (and could not) involve a 'marking' simply because they have not been previously constructed? There will most certainly be first occurrences of a given metaphor. Bickerton (1969, p. 48), bypasses this difficulty explaining that these 'true' metaphors 'may best be regarded as merely an extension of the system of attribute-assignment discussed above'. But it is precisely these 'true' metaphors with which we are concerned, and an argument by extension is not satisfactory.

But aside from the above difficulties, there are others which attach to this notion of 'marked signs': it is not clear whether this notion of 'marked signs' does in fact establish necessary and sufficient conditions for the distinguishing of potential metaphor from simple deviance as Bickerton seems to believe. While being 'marked' may be a sufficient condition for distinguishing a sign's use as potentially metaphorical, being 'marked' is definitely not a necessary condition for distinguishing a sign's use as potentially metaphorical. This is evident in Bickerton's own starred examples, for almost every utterance which he indicates as simply deviant (*), that is 'unmarked', in an appropriate context, might (can) be taken as metaphorical. For example, from Bickerton's *green ears* we can construct the metaphor *the sailor's profanity curled the seminarian's green ears.*

There is also a problem of uniqueness with respect to the 'marking' of signs which Bickerton fails to consider: for example, with *green ears* we can construct yet a second metaphor such as *the old lady listened with green ears to the young woman's tale, her envy growing by leaps and bounds.* It is apparent that the proposed 'marking' system is inadequate, but this inadequacy is radical: for every possible different context within which the sign can appear as metaphorical, an additional context-independent 'marking' will be required.

Given the proper context (linguistic and extralinguistic), almost any deviant sentence can be interpreted as metaphorical. As a consequence, the notion of 'marked signs' loses all efficacy: this notion does not therefore establish necessary conditions for distinguishing potential metaphor from simple deviance; and given the conceptual problems attaching to this notion, particularly in the case of 'true' metaphors, it is not clear that 'marking' establishes even sufficient conditions for distinguishing potential metaphor from simple deviance. Although Bickerton suggests that having distinguished potential metaphor one can then on the basis of the linguistic context satisfy our first adequacy requirement, he never in fact explains how this is possible.

There is no doubt that, as he claims, we can render any extra-linguistic context in terms of a linguistic context (mode-of-discourse), nor that whether a potential metaphor will be realized as a metaphor is a context-dependent phenomenon; nevertheless this notion of 'marking' fails to establish any necessary and sufficient conditions for the distinguishing of metaphor from non-metaphor. Hence, it is not clear what is gained by this notion (were it not beset with the aforementioned conceptual difficulties). What Bickerton has failed to show is that all deviant sentences are not in fact potential metaphors (i.e., 'marked signs').

But it is not clear in the first place why Bickerton believes that metaphor is to be explicated in terms of this competence distinction between potential metaphor and simple deviance. Brief reflection upon language performance, upon the occurrence of metaphor in discourse, should convince us that Bickerton's fundamental error in this notion of 'marked signs' was the presumption that the performance distinction between metaphor and non-metaphor was equivalent to the competence distinction between potential metaphor and simple deviance, rather than between deviant and non-deviant sentences. In normal discourse utterances are usually assumed to be meaningful, or in the case of deviant sentences, to be interpretable. In other words, in performance the question of whether or not a certain utterance is to be taken as metaphorical or as simply deviant does not arise except in certain un-usual contexts (e.g., linguistics discussions, discussions with new speakers of the language, etc.) where it is usually clear how the utterance is to be taken. And in cases where it is not clear whether the utterance is to be taken as meaningful, we are usually in a quandary as to whether or not the utterance is meant to be metaphorical or simply deviant. The dis-tinction between metaphor and simple deviance involves the intention on the part of the speaker or hearer to be metaphorical. The suggestion here is that the important competence distinction to be made is rather between deviant and non-deviant sentences.

What Bickerton (1969, pp. 41-2), takes to be an indictment against generative grammar—that generative grammarians have been satisfied to regard metaphor as an instance of interpretable deviance (this inter-pretability being highly context-dependent)—can now be seen as evidence of a more careful separation between performance and com-petence models, whereas Bickerton confuses the two, attempting to contrast the performance notion of metaphor with the competence notion of deviance. In short, Bickerton fails to recognize metaphor as a phenomenon of language use.

With respect to the second requirement on an adequate theory of metaphor—an account of how the metaphor is interpreted in terms of the speaker's single semantic competence—Bickerton is almost silent. It is not clear in his account how the understanding of metaphor is supposed to be related to the understanding of non-metaphoric sentences.

From the discussion of 'marked signs' though, it is apparent that Bickerton views the 'meaning' of the metaphor to be a direct consequence of the 'specific attribute' which is affixed to the sign by 'marking': thus to *iron* is fixed the 'specific attribute' of 'hardness'. The conclusion seems warranted that he considers the 'specific attribute' to be an adequate rendering of the 'metaphoric meaning' of the word: in other words, *iron will* is adequately paraphrased by *hard will*. Presumably, the metaphor *Richard is lionhearted* would be equivalently rendered by the non-metaphoric sentence *Richard is brave*, or perhaps *Richard is brave like a lion*. This substitution view, which regards metaphor as simply a stylistic ornamentation, has been sufficiently criticized elsewhere as to need no further comment here.[1] This Aristotelian view of metaphor arises in large part from the failure to realize that it is sentences, or more precisely deviant sentences which are intended as meaningful, and not 'metaphorical words' which are focal in the understanding of metaphors.

An account of metaphor as a deviant but interpreted linguistic structure involves the central notion of a **rule-violation** which formally specifies just what is meant when we designate a structure as 'deviant'.[2] Criteria for syntactic or semantic grammaticality are usually specified in terms of restrictions, both syntactic and semantic, on the kinds or classes of formatives which may occupy a particular position within a given structure. Given the verbal, the nouns which will serve as the grammatical subject and object(s) (if any) must meet certain selectional criteria, which in this paper I will call **selectional restrictions**,[3] if the sentence is to be non-deviant. Chomsky (1965, pp. 148-9) cites several examples in which there has been a failure to observe what he calls 'selectional rules':

1   (i)   *colourless green ideas sleep furiously*
     (ii) *golf plays John*
     (iii) *the boy may frighten sincerity*

or 'strict subcategorization rules':

2   (i)   *John found sad*
     (ii) *John elapsed that Bill will come*
     (iii) *John compelled*

The first set (1) differs from the second set (2) in that the deviance of the former may roughly be termed semantic as opposed to syntactic: the formatives in (1) have syntactically acceptable phrase structures, but the sentences are still in some manner deviant. In the sentence (1): (ii) for example, the verb *play* requires a subject with the lexical feature [+ animate] and an object with the feature [+ common]. The subject of (1):(ii) *golf* fails by being [− animate], and the object *John* fails by being [− common].

Selectional restrictions and their violations are in turn specified formally, as indicated by the above example, in terms of lexical features. A particular word or idiom referenced by a single lexical entry may be considered as a triplet of phonological, syntactic, and semantic features. (Words such as 'ball' (social affair) and 'ball' (spherical object) will by this definition receive separate entries in the lexicon, because it is only the phonological features which are shared.) The notion of lexical features, as I understand it, does not assume either the feature's psychological or physical reality. If, for example, a certain speaker regards wolves as immortal creatures, then, within that speaker's lexicon, the lexical entry *wolf* will have the lexical feature [+ immortal]. Neither should lexical features be understood as being semantically 'primitive': features of a lexical entry will themselves be lexical entries specified in turn by features, *ad infinitum*. In this respect lexical features should be viewed as delimiting the discourse environment within which the lexical entry is commonly found. Lexical features characterize the common uses of the lexical entry, and thus lexical features might best be viewed as elucidations of literal usage rather than as an analysis or definition of the lexical entry.

In discussing deviant sentences such as exemplified by (1), Chomsky (1965, p. 149), notes that

> It is necessary to impose an interpretation on them somehow—this being a task that varies in difficulty or challenge from case to case— whereas there is no question of imposing an interpretation in the case of . . . well-formed sentences . . . . Sentences that break selectional rules can often be interpreted metaphorically . . . or allusively in one way or another, if an appropriate context is supplied. That is, these sentences are apparently interpreted by direct analogy to well-formed sentences that observe the selectional rules in question.

In the short analyses which follow I will try to show that, as Chomsky suggests, the understanding of metaphor as a deviant, but interpreted sentence gives a full 'accounting' of metaphor, and more specifically I will attempt to demonstrate how, in terms of lexical features and the sentence's phrase structure, these deviant sentences 'are interpreted by direct analogy to well-formed sentences that observe the selectional rules in question'.

For a first example let us consider the following metaphor:

1 *the volcano burped*

This metaphor is structurally analogous to such literal counterparts as

2(a) *the man jumped*
2(b) *the volcano erupted*
2(c) *the man burped*

The metaphor (1) and the literal counterparts (2) have a phrase structure which is used semantically to make statements somewhat of the following nature: 'the noun of the sentence is asserted to be performing some action specified by the verbal'. The selectional restriction violation in (1) is seen to be one of a human attribute being predicated of an inanimate noun. Because of its common uses within non-metaphoric contexts (e.g., (2c)), the feature system of *burped*, besides such a feature as [+ human action], will include other features such as [+ emitted from mouth], [+ coming from within], [+ caused by gaseous pressure], [+ abrupt], etc., thus forcing a view of the volcano along lines specified by these features. Accepting the fact that a volcano is not a human being, the hearer of the metaphor may see the volcano's cone as lips, crater as mouth, vent as throat, etc., but this is not central to what it means to say that the volcano burped. Understanding the metaphor does not entail these associations.

It is often at this point that philosophers have raised the 'similarity' theory of metaphor which sees metaphor as based upon a similarity relation, noting that the metaphor trades upon similarities between the volcano and man (cone/lips, crater/mouth, vent/throat), but it should be seen that the explanation is not very enlightening as it explains our first metaphor *the volcano burped* in terms of other metaphors such as *the cone of the volcano is its lips*. More correctly, one might say that the metaphor 'creates' the similarities, in the sense that Black (1962) holds that metaphors 'organize' our view of the metaphor's subject (the subject of this metaphor being the volcano). The similarity theory does, however, contain an important insight: we are 'guided' in our interpretation of the metaphor both by the metaphor's phrase structure and by the meaning (non-metaphoric uses) of the constituent words of the metaphor, these constituent words being specified formally in terms of lexical features. The nature of this 'guidance' should become clearer in the following examples.

As a second example let us consider the following well-worn and much-discussed metaphor:

3   *the man is a wolf*

This metaphor, exemplary of a large class of metaphors, has a phrase structure wherein the copula relation is one of class membership: the man (a definite person) is asserted to be a member of the class denoted by 'wolf'.

As literal counterparts of (3) having the same phrase structure and also asserting a class membership, we might consider:

4(a)   *the man is a gentleman*
4(b)   *the man is a fool*
4(c)   *the man is a professor*

It is clear that there are no selectional restriction violations in these non-metaphoric sentences. For example,

4a'   *(the) man*   *is (a) gentleman*

+ animate	+ animate[4]
+ human	+ human
+ adult	+ adult
+ male	+ male
	+ well-bred
	+ courteous
	+ gracious
	+ considerate

Besides the shared features associated with *man* and *gentleman*, there are those unshared features associated with only the latter which delimit the class denoted by *gentleman*. With respect to these features *man* is neutral: for example, to be gracious or courteous is neither constitutive of nor disallowed in the *man*-system; attributing such features to *man* is allowed, however, by the selectional restrictions imposed.

In the associated metaphor, the feature systems of the constituents might be specified as follows:

3'   *(the) man*   *is (a) wolf*

+ definite	+ count
+ count	+ animate
+ animate	+ mammal
+ mammal	+ canine (− human)
+ human	+ quadrupedal
+ adult	+ tail
+ male	+ hairy
+ linguistic	+ nocturnal
+ bipedal	+ vicious
	+ predatory
	+ avoids man

Studying (3'), we note that selectional restrictions which *wolf* imposes upon the feature system of *man* have been violated: a member of the class having the feature [+ human] is being asserted to be a member of a class having the feature [+ canine (− human)]. Cognizant of this selectional restriction violation, we see that the *wolf*-system features which are not shared, including those which constitute the selectional restriction violation, are nevertheless asserted as delimiting a class to which the man denoted belongs.

The selectional restriction and its violation by the metaphor is crucial in differentiating (3) from (4a). It should be remarked that clustered around the [+ human]/[− human] selectional restriction violation there are associated violations, or more correctly, violations which specify in more detail just what is meant by the [+ human]/[− human] violation: for example, [+bipedal]/[+quadrupedal], [+ linguistic]/[− linguistic], [− tail]/[+ tail], etc. The *wolf*-features which are most important in 'organizing' our view of the *man*-system seem to be those which while retaining importance in the *wolf*-system are none-theless less directly implicated in the selectional restriction violation. With regard to our example, the features [+ hairy], [+ tail], [+ quadru-pedal], etc. which are most closely connected with the selectional restriction violation [+ human]/[− human] seem less important in understanding the metaphor than *wolf*-system features which are not closely involved in the violation, e.g., [+ vicious], [+ predatory], [+ nocturnal].

For a third example, let us consider the metaphor

5   *Macbeth murders sleep*

and the literal counterparts:

6(a)   *coffee disturbs sleep*
6(b)   *assassins murder people*
6(c)   *John washes floors*

From the examples we note that these sentences have associated with them the semantic expectation of someone or something acting upon, doing something to, or affecting something or someone else. In the metaphor (5), someone (Macbeth) does something (murders) to some-thing (sleep).

5′ *Macbeth . . .*	*murders . . .*	*sleep*
+ human	+ human agent	+ physical state
+ proper name	+ human victim	+ rest or quiescence
	+ act of killing	+ applies to animate
	+ malicious or	object
	premeditated	
	+ unlawful	

The selectional restrictions imposed by the verb upon the grammatical subject are satisfied: the agent is a human being. The selectional restric-tion imposed upon the grammatical object is, however, not satisfied: only a human being can be said to be murdered. The feature [+ human victim] of *murders* is violated as *sleep* is [− human].

In this particular metaphor it is very questionable in what sense our view is being 'organized' by the metaphor as Black (1962) suggests, except in the sense that the choice of **any** word rather than another to occupy a particular position in a sentence 'organizes' our view. By the same token, the similarity theory is also inapplicable: what is similar to what?[5] If one answers that *murders* is similar to words such as *disturbs*, this explanation of how metaphor is understood, too, says nothing significant about metaphor which is not equally applicable to **all** language: after all, *to rent* and *to lease*, and *to close the door* and *to shut the door* are somewhat similar also. The similarity and organization theories of metaphor exhibit a defect common to accounts of metaphor which concentrate upon the second adequacy requirement, while leaving the first in relative neglect: the assertions about this second requirement—how we understand metaphors, once recognized—are overly 'strong'. Supposedly giving an account of how we understand metaphor, these accounts in fact make a much broader statement about how we understand language in general, about how language predicates.[6]

As a final example I wish to consider the utterance (7) which Reddy (1969), has presented as representative of a large class of sentences which do not involve any sort of selectional restriction violation, but are nevertheless metaphors. Reddy's contention that there is such a class of metaphors must not be overlooked as it questions the assertion that deviance is a necessary condition for a sentence to be metaphorical.

7 *the rock is becoming brittle with age*

Reddy considers the readings of (7) in the context of (a) a geological expedition, and (b) a description of an old professor emeritus.

The question which Reddy does not consider is whether (7) should be termed a metaphor. Perhaps utterances of this type, although not metaphors themselves, are best viewed as having an underlying metaphor such as (8) which does involve a selectional restriction violation, as can be clearly seen in the attempt to explain (7) within the second context (b).

8 *the old professor emeritus is a rock*
9 *the rock is a soft shale*

The analysis of (7) in terms of the metaphor (8), as opposed to a reading such as (9), is precisely what differentiates the two contexts.

Reddy's rejection of the notion of selectional restrictions as central to an analysis of metaphor is more apparent than real: he accepts both the notion of metaphorical language as involving a non-literal usage of words ('the defining characteristic of all instances of metaphorical language is an abnormal or unconventional situation with regard to the limits of referentiality on words' (p. 248)) and the notion of metaphor as highly context-dependent. Instead of specifying the metaphoric *vs.* non-metaphoric distinction linguistically in terms of selectional restrictions, Reddy has rather specified this distinction in terms of psychological predicates.

Having completed the foregoing analyses, we are in a position to evaluate my own account of metaphor in terms of the two adequacy requirements. From the analyses we find that, as I suggested in the course of my criticism of Bickerton's account, the performance distinction between metaphor and non-metaphor is correctly characterized on the competence level in terms of a distinction between semantically deviant and non-deviant sentences. Selectional restrictions which exhibit the general non-metaphoric usage in terms of the lexical feature systems of the constituent words of a sentence are violated in the case of deviant sentences. The presence of a selectional restriction violation is thus a necessary and sufficient condition for the distinguishing of metaphor from non-metaphor, excepting of course those cases where the utterances are not intended to be meaningful.

With regard to the second adequacy requirement, we may conclude from the analyses that the metaphor is to be understood in the same manner as we understand the metaphor's literal counterparts, but the effect of the selectional restriction violation is to de-emphasize the features which figure in this selectional restriction violation as well as those other features most closely associated with it.

As opposed to Bickerton's theory, the foregoing not only renders a more adequate account of metaphor, but achieves this goal with a less weighty assumed conceptual foundation: no assumptions are made concerning the 'marking' of signs, 'multi-dimensional grids', etc. The semantic component of the more general theory of language of which a 'theory' of metaphor would be only a part is relatively unconstrained by the assumptions in the foregoing account.[7] Specifically, this account requires

1 the notion of syntactical and semantic deviance, and
2 the notion of lexical features (in the weak sense defined).

It should be pointed out that the first notion is likewise required by Bickerton's account, and that the second notion, I believe, is not incompatible with his conceptual model as this notion of lexical features does not assume the existence of semantic primitives or the existence of an hierarchal ordering of the features.

The failure to define what would be considered an adequate account of metaphor we see to be the major flaw in the accounts of metaphor discussed herein. These theories of metaphor have had the effect of over-emphasizing and transforming an important insight into a theory which is deficient by fact of its omissions and distortions. It will be sufficient perhaps if this account is equally illuminating, at least giving further emphasis to the importance of the competence-performance distinction in linguistic inquiry: while performance phenomena such as metaphor are most certainly within the realm of linguistic inquiry, it is particularly important in such analyses to conserve the distinction between language (competence) and the use of the language (performance).[8]

NOTES

1 See Black (1962), Beardsley (1958) and Khatchadourian (1968).
   An analysis and criticism of the more significant philosophical views
   of metaphor is also presented in my earlier paper (1970).
2 Within this paper it is assumed that in terms of a competence model,
   the notion of deviance is meaningful, having some intuitive basis
   for the speaker of a language.
3 I use the expression 'selectional restriction violation' in a wider sense
   than Chomsky's 'selection rule violation', including not only the
   deviant structures characterized by the latter but those characterized
   by strict subcategorization rule violations as well.
4 No attempt has been made to reduce the high redundancy of these
   lexical features because, as was pointed out earlier, no claim is being
   made that these features represent formally any more than elucidations of literal usage, and neither are these elucidations presumed
   to be exhaustive of a given speaker's usage of a particular word.
5 Proponents of a similarity theory have failed to notice that the terms
   of the supposed similarity relation differ depending upon the metaphor's phrase structure. For example, in (1) the supposed similarity
   relation would hold between *volcano* and *man* (the noun supposedly
   'replaced') but in metaphor (3) the similarity relation would have
   to hold between *man* and *wolf*.
6 The philosophical problem of metaphor seems to be closely analogous to that of 'seeing as': the various theories of metaphor show
   problems closely paralleling those arising in theories advanced as
   explanations of 'seeing as'. (See Wittgenstein's discussion of 'seeing
   as' in his *Philosophical Investigations*.)
7 Throughout this paper I have tried to stress the notion that an adequate account of metaphor is probably better viewed in terms of
   constraints upon the semantic component of a more general theory
   of language, rather than as a separate theory of metaphor.
8 I am indebted to Max Black for his helpful criticisms of an earlier
   version of this paper.

REFERENCES

Beardsley, Monroe (1958), *Aesthetics: Problems in the Philosophy
   of Criticism* (New York: Harcourt Brace).
Bickerton, Derek (1969), 'Prolegomena to a Linguistic Theory of Meta-
   phor', *Foundations of Language 4*, pp. 34–52.
Black, Max (1962), *'Metaphor', Models and Metaphors: Studies in
   Language and Philosophy* (Ithaca, N. Y.: Cornell University Press)
   pp. 25–47. (First appeared 1955, in *Proceedings of Aristotelian
   Society*, 273–94.)
Bolinger, David (1965), 'The Atomization of Meaning', *Language 41*,
   pp. 555–73.

Chomsky, Noam (1965), *Aspects of the Theory of Syntax* (Cambridge, Mass.: MIT Press).

Khatchadourian, Haig (1968), 'Metaphor', *British Journal of Aesthetics*, 8, No. 3 (July 1968), pp. 226–40.

Matthews, Robert J. (1970), 'On Metaphor' (unpublished thesis), Georgetown University.

Reddy, Michael J. (1969), 'A Semantic Approach to Metaphor', Papers from the Fifth Regional Meeting, Chicago Linguistics Society, 18–19 April 1969, Department of Linguistics, University of Chicago, pp. 240–51.

Weinreich, Uriel (1966), 'Explorations in Semantic Theory', *Current Trends in Linguistics No. 3* ed. T. Sebeok, (The Hague: Mouton) pp. 395–477.

CHAPTER FOUR

On understanding poetic metaphor

Tanya Reinhart *

[Reinhart indicates that the debate over 'deviance' in metaphor (as exemplified by the three preceding articles) is at a stand-off. No resolution to this debate is possible while linguists on both sides consider only 'focus interpretation' in metaphor, or the interpretation of the metaphor's 'literally' substitutable meaning. Those who reject the notion of 'deviance' are right as far as focus interpretation goes, because this process does not differ radically from the ordinary interpretation of a literal expression. (That is, both processes involve the selection of those semantic features which are compatible with the context and the erasure of those which are not; see Ching, Chapter 8.)

However, Reinhart points out that experienced readers of poetry are often more concerned with 'vehicle interpretation' in metaphor than they are with focus interpretation. Vehicle interpretation may be defined as the interpretation of that part of the metaphor's meaning which cannot be expressed literally. Whereas focus interpretation involves the selection of contextually appropriate literal concepts and the elimination of inappropriate ones, vehicle interpretation involves the imaginative synthesis of a whole new concept, one which is unique to the novel, creative vision implicit in the conceptual leap of the metaphorical expression *per se*. Though both processes are important, the 'double perception' entailed by vehicle interpretation presumably renders metaphor in this sense deviant from literal discourse.]

A recent debate in linguistic discussions of metaphor concerns the questions of whether there is such a thing as semantic deviance and whether metaphor can be treated as instance of such deviance. The notion of semantic deviance stems from early generative works such as Chomsky (1964; 1965), Katz (1964), and Ziff (1964). Within this framework meta-

* First published in *Poetics*, 5 (1976), 383–402.

An earlier version of this paper was presented at a meeting of the Greater Boston Stylistics Circle in May 1974. I would like to thank the members of the circle, particularly Paul Kiparsky, Mark Liberman, and Dick Oehrle, for their helpful comments. Still earlier, I profited from discussions with Wallace Chafe, John Searle, and especially, Benjamin Hrushovski.

phors are considered the result of violations of selectional restrictions. Jakobson has argued already in 1959 that this notion is extremely mis-leading, since there is no clear-cut distinction between literal and metaphorical expressions—both are even subject, in his opinion, to the same truth-conditional tests. Several more recent papers, such as Cohen and Margalith (1972), Reddy (1969), Bickerton (1969), Wissman Bruss (1975), and Gopnik and Gopnik (1973), follow this line, arguing in various ways against the concept of metaphor as deviance.[1]

To the extent that this deviance debate is of interest in the contem-porary linguistic scene, it is because it reflects (though not always expli-citly) a more crucial question: namely, is the process of understanding metaphor significantly different from the process of understanding literal expressions? The assumption which underlies the opponents of the notion of deviance is, basically, that it is not. The difference between understanding metaphorical and literal expressions is, on this assumption, at most a matter of degree. I will argue that no single yes/no answer is possible to this question, since, at least in the case of poetic or 'creative' metaphors, the process of understanding consists of two distinct proce-dures—one, to which I shall refer as *focus-interpretation*, is basically the same procedure as is applied to literal expressions, but the other, which will be labeled *vehicle-interpretation*, is unique to the understanding of poetic metaphor. As we will see in section 3, linguists, on both sides of the deviance debate, tend to consider focus interpretation only.

In arguing for hypotheses concerning the understanding of literary texts, the question of what counts as evidence is quite problematic. Des-pite the absence of extensive experiments concerning the way in which speakers understand poetic metaphors, however, evidence stronger than mere 'introspection' can be supplied by an examination of literary criti-cism. The critics' discussion of metaphors reflects, no doubt, the way in which they understand them. Hence, an analysis of their interpretative statements, as well as their theoretical assumptions, can serve as a source of information concerning the process of understanding metaphor. I will start, therefore, with a survey of the approaches to metaphor in literary criticism, in section 1. This survey will serve as initial evidence for the existence of the two procedures, which will be defined and further exemplified in section 2. The relation of these two procedures to the procedure involved in understanding literal expressions will be discussed in section 3, along with the linguistic approaches to metaphor.

1 The analysis of metaphor in literary criticism

Richards (1936), Black (1962) and Beardsley (1958) may serve as representative samplings of the theories of metaphor in modern literary criticism. Close examination of the assumptions underlying their articles will cover all the possibilities raised through various emphases and wording in the discussion of metaphor. The most convenient way of systematically presenting the data supplied by these three scholars is to examine how, according to the principles of their systems, they could have analyzed the same metaphor. Let us take the metaphor *riding the waves*, e.g.:

> I have seen the mermaids riding seawards on the waves
> (T. S. Eliot, *The Love Song of J. Alfred Prufrock*)

1.1. The definition of metaphor

To the question, why *riding the waves* is a metaphor, we would receive three different answers, based on the different definitions of metaphor: Richards would claim that it is a metaphor because it represents the interaction of 'two thoughts of different things' (1936: 93),(ostensibly, the one *riding a horse* and the other *floating on the wave*). Beardsley would say that it is a metaphor because the modifier, *riding* is incompatible with the noun, *waves*.[2] Black would try to grasp both ends—his definition of metaphor vacillates between a linguistic approach, similar to that of Beardsley, and Richards' 'epistemological' approach. His formal reply would be: this is a metaphor because *riding*, in the context of *waves*, is used in a non-literal sense. But comments scattered throughout the article reveal that non-literalness is not a sufficient condition for metaphor. A non-literal phrase is a metaphor only if it 'makes a connection between two systems of concepts' (Black 1962: 42). That is to say, the second part of his answer would be a variation on that of Richards.

1.2. The constituents of metaphor

The terms *tenor* and *vehicle* (to be referred to below as T and V), that Richards (1936) coined to denote 'the two thoughts' or 'the systems of concepts' that operate in every metaphor, have become accepted, in various names and guises, by most scholars of metaphor. Yet it remains very difficult to determine what exactly Richards, or any of the others, mean by these terms. One thing is clear: the T is something which is present in the given metaphorical phrases, while the V is something (word, referent, meaning?) which is not present, but which we construct when we interpret the metaphor. For *riding the waves* there are two possible analyses: either the T is *waves* and the V *horse* or the T is *floating on the waves* and the V is *riding a horse*.[3] It seems to me that from Richards's epistemological definition of metaphor, it is reasonable to conclude that he would choose the latter, since the T and V in this analysis are more likely to be described as the two complete 'thoughts' we have in mind. In Beardsley's system there is no place for the terms T and V. The two possible uses for these terms are determined by our understanding of what the metaphor is about. For Beardsley, the metaphor's constituents are determined solely by the grammatical structure of the metaphorical phrase. In the metaphor before us there are two constituents: noun—*waves*, and modifie.— *riding*, and we do not need any prior understanding in order to identify these constituents. On the face of it, Beardsley's proposal has great charm, for it provides us with a firm technical tool for analyzing the metaphor. But the real test of it would be in the next stage: can the assumption of these two constituents alone serve as a basis for a full interpretation of the metaphor (since this analysis does not enable us to introduce a constituent that will include the word *horse* or its features).

Black (1962), introduced into the discussion of the constituents of metaphor two pairs of terms: 'focus and frame' and 'principal and subsidiary subject'. An attempt to understand what these two sets of terms, particularly the second, should refer to would be fraught with difficulties. On the other hand, an explanation of the concepts underlying these terms is likely to be of crucial importance to the theory of metaphor. For in spite of the fact that it is not overt in his work, Black does, in effect, make the first distinction between two groups of constituents in metaphor, that may be developed into a decision between two distinct procedures of interpreting metaphor.

The way in which Black uses the terms 'focus' and 'frame' (F[E]) is clear: in our metaphor *riding* will be the focus, and *waves* the frame. But the definition of the terms is to a great extent deceptive. As was pointed out by Margalith (1970), Black vacillates between a semantic and a pragmatic definition of 'focus'. On the one hand, he speaks of focus as the non-literal, or metaphoric constituent in a metaphor; as distinct from the literal frame (Black 1962: 27); on the other hand, he says: 'Though we point to the whole sentence as an instance . . . of metaphor, our attention quickly narrows to a single word . . .' (1962: 27).

The contribution of the last statement to the identification of the focus is very dubious, since there is no guarantee that there is a focus of attention at all in a given metaphor. And what is more, if there is such a focus, there is no guarantee that it would always happen to be the semantic focus as well. The semantic definition, on the other hand, is misleading, since it assumes that the focus alone is the non-literal expressions, i.e. only it has undergone a metaphorical change (and see below).

A possible way to rescue Black's important distinction was suggested by Margalith (1970). Following Margalith, we can define the focus as the eliminable constituent of the metaphor:

Given a metaphoric (non-literal) expression $F_i[E_i]$, E_i is the focus, if it is possible to substitute E_j for E_i, so that $F_i[E_j]$ is a literal expression and $F_i[E_j]$ is 'similar in meaning' to $F_i[E_i]$.

For the sake of this discussion, we will define two expressions $F(a)$ and $G(b)$ as similar in meaning if the arguments (a) and (b) are referentially identical and the predicates F and G are intersecting in meaning. The definition of 'intersecting in meaning' will vary, of course, with semantic theories. However, it requires that there is at least one meaning constituent (or property, sub-predicate, restriction on application, etc.) which is shared by F and G.[4]

Given these definitions, in the metaphor (i) *riding on the waves*, the focus is *riding*. If we substitute, say, *floating* for *riding*, the result (ii) *floating on the waves* is a literal expression. The expression (ii) is, furthermore 'similar in meaning' to (i) since the arguments (*the waves*) are identical in (i) and (ii), and the predicates *riding on* and *floating on* share the property [advancing in space] (as well as several other properties that can be checked with Table 4.1 below). If, on the other hand, we substitute, say, *horses* for *waves*, we get the expression (iii) *riding the horses*, which is not 'similar in meaning' to (i), since the arguments in (i) and (iii) are not referentially identical. (If we substitute a synonym, or a referentially identical argument, for *the waves* the result (e.g. *riding on the surf*) fails the requirement that $F[E_j]$ should be a literal expression.)

The meaning of Black's (1962), second pair of terms—'principal subject' and 'subsidiary subject'—is even less clear. When he comes to detailed analysis, Black, like many scholars of metaphor, uses as examples only nominal metaphors (metaphors consisting of two nouns and a copula). This creates the impression that 'principal subject' and 'subsidiary subject' are additional and redundant terms for 'frame' and 'focus', respectively, since in *Man is a wolf, wolf* is both focus and subsidiary subject. The formal definitions that Black provides (in 1962, fn. 23) do not clarify matters much. The principle subject of F[E] is defined as: 'roughly, what F[E] is really about'. This is rough indeed, but nonetheless comprehensible.[5] The same cannot be said of the following definition: The subsidiary subject is: 'roughly what F[E] would be about if read literally'. This sentence as it stands makes no sense, since the point is precisely that there is no way of reading a metaphor literally, and 'read literally' F[E] is, thus, about nothing. The only way out is to define the subsidiary subject as the 'something' which the focus can modify literally. Or more exactly, given a metaphorical expression $F_i[E_i]$, the subsidiary subject will be defined as:

The frame, $F_j[\ ]$, in which the occurrence of E_i results in a literal expression $F_j[E_i]$ is not similar in meaning to $F_i[E_i]$.

According to these definitions, in the metaphor *riding the waves*, *the waves* is the principal subject (and see footnote 6), and the subsidiary subject is *horses*, since the occurrence of the focus *riding* in the frame [ ] *horses* would result in the literal expression *riding the horses* which, as we saw, is not similar in meaning to the metaphorical expression, according to the definition of similarity in meaning given above. Although Black does not offer any clear hint in this direction, it seems to me that he would agree to this analysis, since it provides the only possibility for translating the terms T and V, which Black is interested in preserving, to the terms of Black's own system.[6]

1.3. The interpretation of metaphor

The various proposals for analyzing the metaphor into its constituents suggested four words whose readings are likely to contribute to the process of interpreting *riding the waves*, namely: *waves, riding, horse* and *floating*.

Although the semantic theories of literary critics are very tenuous, it is possible to use them to draw up a list of approximate semantic features (or meaning constituents) for each word. This list does not necessarily correspond to the dictionary definition of each word: rather it conveys the 'system of commonplaces' associated with it by a given group of speakers (Black), as well as the 'connotations' (Beardsley) and the 'emotive weight' (Richards) of the word. This intuitive list would look something like Table 4.1.

On the basis of this list of features, the final interpretation of the metaphor will be made. In Black's words (1962: 45): 'The metaphor selects, emphasizes, suppresses, and organizes' the features of this list. It is necessary to decide which features are erased (e.g. blue, salty and eating fodder, are probably irrelevant), which features are transferred from the reading of one word to the other, and which new readings are created. This procedure of interpretation is conditioned by the decision that was made in the previous stage. The stage which determines the constituents of the metaphor is that which determined between which columns in Table 4.1 the process of transference of features will occur. Four possibilities were raised: Transference of features (or constituents of meaning) occurs:

1 between *riding* and *floating* (Black's focus).
2 between *waves* and *horse* (Black's principal and subsidiary subjects).
3 between *waves* and *riding* (Beardsley's noun and modifier).
4 between *floating on the waves* and *riding a horse* (Richards' T and V).

The choice of (1) assumes that the non-literal word in the metaphor is the focal word *riding*, and that, therefore, the only reading, which is

Table 4.1

waves − Animate	*horse* + Animate	*riding* [ ] + Animate	*floating* [ ] − Animate
advancing with rising and falling motions	advancing with rising and falling motions	advancing (in space)	advancing (in space)
immortal	mortal	on top of something (a horse)	partially on top of something (water)
blue			
salty	eats fodder		
absence of emotions	has certain feelings and intelligence	possibility of emotional response to the the object ridden	absence of emotional response
turbulent or calm	wild or obedient		
	noble animal	activity of noble people	
force	force	strength and domination	

by way of 'wanted', is the reading of this word, whereas no change will occur in the reading of the word *waves*. The theory of substitution that Black criticizes, would claim that the reading of the word *riding* in the context of this metaphor is precisely identical to the reading of the word *floating*. The theory of interaction, that he suggests as an alternative, would claim that it is created by a kind of interaction between the meaning constituents of *riding* and of *floating*. An interpretation which is based on this choice solely assumes, at any rate, that when we understand this metaphor, we in no way think of a horse.

The choice of (2) assumes that the metaphor involves a double perception of the concept of a wave and of a horse. Through this process, a change may occur in the meaning of the word *waves* in the metaphor, and it may acquire certain of the features of *horse*. A description of the metaphor as a metaphor of 'animation' rests on the choice of this possibility.

The choice of (3) does not differ much from that of (1). It too assumes that *riding* is the non-literal word. And an attempt to apply it (if it makes sense at all) has to arrive finally at a comparison between the meaning constituent of *riding* and meaning constituents similar to those which *floating* has in Table 4.1.

It seems to me that possibility (4) cannot impart additional informa-tion beyond that imparted by a combination of the conclusions of (1) and (2). It assumes that it is necessary to construct both the conept interacting with *waves* (2), and the reading of *riding* (1), and that the full meaning of the metaphor will be a combination of the information supplied by these two procedures. And this, in fact, is what a com-petent reader of poetic metaphor does when he interprets most (though not necessarily all) of the poetic metaphors.

The distinction between (1) and (2) as two discrete processes in-volved in the interpretation of metaphor is therefore the most significant conclusion to be drawn from the examination of the theory of meta-phor in literary criticism.[7] I will refer to the procedure underlying (1) as *focus-interpretation*. The procedure involved in (2), which in Black's terms requires the construal of the subsidiary subject, I will refer to as *vehicle-interpretation*, a term which is probably consistent with Black's intention, preserving Richards's original distinction.

2 The two procedures

2.1.

Let us examine now with more detail what is involved in the two pro-cesses. For convenience, the definitions of focus and vehicle are re-peated here:[8]

> Given a metaphorical expression $F_i[E_i]$,
> (i) E_i is the *focus* if it is possible to substitute E_j for E_i, so that $F_i[E_j]$ is a literal expression and $F_i[E_j]$ is similar in meaning to $F_i[E_i]$.
> (ii) The *vehicle* is the frame $F_j[\ ]$ in which the occurrence of E_i results in a literal expression, $F_j[E_i]$, where $F_j[E_i]$ is not similar in meaning to $F_i[E_i]$.

To illustrate again how these definitions apply to determine the focus and the vehicle of a given metaphor, consider the following famous metaphor:

> The yellow fog that rubs its back upon the window panes
> (T. S. Eliot, *The Love Song of J. Alfred Prufrock*)

In this metaphor, the focus is *rubs its back upon*, since we can substitute another expression for it, e.g. *touches, swirls against*, or *comes up against*, to yield a literal expression, such as *The yellow fog that touches the window panes*. This literal expression is roughly similar in meaning to the metaphorical expression according to the definition above, since its predicate intersects in meaning with the predicate of the metaphorical expression (although it is not, of course, identical in meaning to the metaphorical expression, and it cannot be considered in itself the full reading of the metaphor).

The vehicle in this metaphor is a cat (or some other animal which can be associated with the gesture of rubbing its back against things). This construal of the vehicle follows from the definition of vehicle suggested above, since if we put *rubs its back* in the frame *the cat* that [ ], the result is a literal expression: *The cat that rubs its back upon the window panes* which is not, however, similar in meaning to the original metaphor, being a statement about a cat rather than about the fog.

Identifying the focus and the vehicle provides the basis for the interpretation of a metaphor. The two procedures which follow are rather different in nature. Focus-interpretation assigns a reading to the focus expression which is a matter of selecting those properties associated with the focus expression which are relevant to the context. Thus among the properties of rubbing one's back, the properties of physical contact and of being in movement are consistent with the context of Eliot's metaphor, hence they can be selected. This procedure provides a rough understanding of what the metaphor is about, or what the actual situation which is being depicted is (the fog swirling against the window panes) and how it ties in with the wider context of the metaphor. However, if this level of understanding what the metaphor is about were to exhaust the full meaning of the metaphor, there wouldn't be much reason to use metaphor in the first place, since this part of the content of the metaphor can be expressed literally.[9] What is still to be accounted for is the 'image' aspect of the metaphor, which is captured by vehicle interpretation. Interpretive statements concerning a comparison or juxtaposition of two concepts in a metaphor, which are so frequent in literary criticism, reflect the operation of this procedure. The procedure of vehicle-interpretation does not have to assign a reading to the vehicle (since once the vehicle is construed, its reading is known). Rather, it has to do with establishing the relation between the two concepts involved—the fog and the cat, in the metaphor under consideration. Since in this metaphor both concepts are concrete, the image is rich in visual options—we can imagine a yellow cat and a yellow fog, both are in motion. There can be a similarity between the fuzziness of the cat's fur and the texture of the fog. The fog may be associated with a certain warmth, or even friendliness; there is something sensuous about this fog, which ties in with the atmosphere of the poem. Several other construals of the cat-fog relation are possible. The crucial point, however, is that although a partial

understanding of what the metaphor is about is possible on the basis of
the procedure of focus interpretation, a full understanding of the
metaphor performs also this double perception of a cat and the fog—
which is the procedure of vehicle interpretation.

Let us consider, now, the operation of the two procedures on a
more puzzling and harder to process metaphor, *blond absence*, coined
by cummings in:

> I mean that the blond absence of any program/except last and always
> and first to live/makes unimportant what I and you believe, . . .
>
> > *(Collected Poems*, no. 157)

The focus here is the adjective *blond* (its substitution will result in
a literal expression, similar in meaning to the metaphorical expression
e.g. *a positive absence*). Focus interpretation thus has to assign a reading
to this adjective. As is to be expected of cummings, the metaphor
is quite ambiguous. I have subjected it informally to several speakers
(who vary in the degree of their experience in poetry) and came
up with the following possible readings based on focus interpretation. For me and for several of my informants, this metaphor stands
roughly for:

(a) Positive, tempting, wonderful absence of any program (not having
     any program is a desirable situation)

Another informant thought that the metaphor means something like:

(b) Unspecified, unmarked absence (the absence is 'colorless'—it
     does not have any specific features)

A third informant came up with the rather original suggestion that the
metaphor means:

(c) A new absence of every program

Another possible interpretation, which I have not come across but
which I think could be ascribed to the metaphor in a proper context
is a 'metaphysical' one (religious, meditational, etc.):

(d) A pure spiritual non-carnal absence of any program (forming a
     program belongs to the material realm and as such it should be
     transcended)

The reason for the ambiguity of this metaphor is that the adjective
blond in Western cultures is a very 'rich' lexical item, i.e. it is associated
with many meaning constituents, some of which are inconsistent with
one another: (see Table 4.2). (The constituents above the dashed line
are of higher relevancy, and those below the dashed line are 'implied'
constituents, or connotations.)

Table 4.2

	blond	
	state	
	human patient	
	color	
yellowish		unmarked, colorless (unpigmented)
	color of hair	

_ _

	+evaluation (1. beautiful color of hair); (2. light vs. dark, as good vs. bad)	
innocent, pure (all angels and faeries are blond)		seductive, tempting (blond women are seductive)

young (for some people, blond
is associated with children)

In applying to this metaphor (in all the readings mentioned), the procedure of focus-interpretation ignores (or 'erases') the higher constituents [human patient], [color], and [color of hair], since these constituents are inconsistent with the context of *blond* in the given metaphor—the noun *absence*, being abstract, cannot have color properties or properties of humans. The various readings supplied to this metaphor are, then, the result of a selection of different items in the list of meaning constituents. The informant who chose (b) accounted for his choice by saying that *blond* means pigmentless and colorless, i.e. he picked out only this meaning constituent of *blond*. Interpretation (a) is based on the constituents [+ evaluation] and [tempting]. Reading (d) is due to the selection of the constituents [+ evaluation] and [innocent, pure]. The informant who suggested (c) is a very 'competent speaker of poetic language' and his account of his choice was that in Russian poetry *blond* tends to stand for the young hero.

A choice among the options in (a)-(d) provides the reader with a basic understanding of what is being asserted. What is still to be processed, however, is the image involved in the metaphor. The vehicle here (given the definitions above) is a person (since *a blond person* is a literal expression unrelated in meaning to *blond absence*). Speakers may vary with the degree of further specification that they assign to this person. All but one of the speakers I presented the metaphor to mentioned, in various ways, the fact that *absence of any program* is personified in this metaphor. Most of them observed further a comparison between the absence of any program and a woman. The specification of the vehicle correlates with properties which were selected in the stage of focus-interpretation: those who selected the reading in (a) saw a comparison to a blond and seductive woman: the informant who chose (c) drew a comparison to a young boy, while the informant who chose the reading in (b) is the one who overlooked completely the vehicle interpretation of the metaphor, and was surprised to hear that there is a comparison involved (though willing to accept it). This is consistent with the fact that this informant concentrated, in the stage of focus interpretation on a property of the *color* blond (unmarked, pigmentless), rather than on properties associated with humans who are blond.

What exactly is involved in the process of double perception of the two concepts is much harder to account for than the focus-interpretation (precisely since it is different from the more extensively studied process of interpretation of literal expressions). It should be observed as well that this process may differ significantly from metaphor to metaphor. Thus, we saw that in Eliot's metaphor the two concepts involved were concrete, and hence visual properties played an important role in the processing of the metaphor. In cummings's metaphor, on the other hand, there is no visual channel for the comparison, since it consists of an abstract concept. Although a personification of abstract concepts is common in allegory, cummings departs from allegory, choosing an abstract noun which denotes nothingness, hence no allegorical inter-pretation is really possible. The interaction which takes place is therefore conceptual (or abstract) rather than visual. Several interpretive state-ments can result from the processing of this interaction, e.g.

(a) Abstract entities have life, they are human agents in the world of cummings.

(b) Unlike Parmenides, cummings believes that the absence not only exists but is also potent.

(c) There isn't actually a borderline between existence and non-existence; absence can be just a mode of existence as attractive and vivid as that of a blond woman.

These statements do not, of course, exhaust the possibilities of dealing with the interaction presented by the metaphor. Those who have an image of a woman vividly associated with this metaphor may add that the metaphor implicitly states something about women, say, that they tend to live in the present and be more in touch with the primitive instincts of life. In any case, metaphors like *blond absence* indicate that the degree of specification assigned to the vehicle may vary. In metaphors which have been traditionally described as 'anima-tion', 'personification' or 'concretization' of abstract concepts, the vehicle can be construed merely as an unspecified person or object, and the metaphor can be assigned some vehicle-interpretation on the basis of this unspecified vehicle (as in statements a–c above). Further specifications of the vehicle (like *a blond woman* for *a person*) may vary more with speakers and are not necessarily possible for all metaphors.[10]

2.2.

A full understanding of a poetic metaphor is usually the result of the application of both focus and vehicle interpretation. (This is the case in all the metaphors discussed so far, for example.) However, the relative dominance of the two procedures of understanding a given metaphor may vary. On the one hand, different speakers may tend to emphasize one of the two procedures and overlook the other. Experienced readers of poetry often emphasize the procedure of vehicle interpretation, while inexperienced readers tend to overlook this aspect of the metaphor and attempt a 'literal substitution' or interpretation of the focus. This was the case with the informant who overlooked the personification in *blond absence* above. On the other hand, metaphors may differ inherently. In dead metaphors (like *iron will* and *roaring sea*) the vehicle has lost its vividness and, consequently, vehicle-interpretation does not apply. In some creative or innovative poetic metaphors, however, the focus interpretation may be less relevant, or even impossible. Thus, in cummings's *emancipated evening*, none, or close to none, of the meaning constituents associated with *emancipated* (the focus) can occur in the context of *evening*. Focus-interpretation is therefore virtually impossible though the metaphor can still be assigned a reading through vehicle-interpretation.

The best way to illustrate how the relative dominance of the application of the two procedures to a given metaphor may differ is to consider again actual interpretive statements offered for metaphors. We will consider the analysis by Leech (1969), of the metaphors below. At the same time, his analysis will serve as a further example of how the two processes discussed actually underlie the intuitive understanding of a metaphor.

[a] But ye lovers, that bathen in gladnesse
(Chaucer, *Troilus & Criseyde*, I)

[b] Sometime walking, not unseen/By hedge-row elms, on hillocks green/Right against *the eastern gate/Where the great sun begins his state*
(Milton, *L'Allegro*)

In our terms, in metaphor (a) the focus is the verb *bathen* and the vehicle is water. Focus-interpretation, thus, assigns a reading to *bathen* while vehicle-interpretation elaborates on the comparison between water and gladness. We will see that in this case, Leech's analysis reflects primarily the application of focus-interpretation and the contribution of vehicle-interpretation to his final understanding of the metaphor is only minor:

> The lovers' attitude to gladness is that they wholeheartedly commit themselves to it. Gladness becomes their element—they see nothing beyond it. Their delight is simple, uncomplicated, untarnished by worry, like that of a person enjoying the water—the natural gift of God.

> (Leech 1969: 155)

Leech's interpretation of the meaning of *bathen* in this context concentrates around two properties: totality and simplicity. The idea of totality is expressed in the first sentence of his analysis in which the key phrases *wholeheartedly, becomes their elements, see nothing beyond it* express the idea of a feeling which is total. This property of totality is derived from the connotation associated with *bathen* of being completely (or totally) immersed in water. The procedure of focus-interpretation ignores the physical aspects of this connotation and selects the connotation of totality as relevant to the context of the metaphor. We can recall at this point another famous metaphor which makes use of the connotation of totality associated with being immersed in water:

> Steep'd me in poverty to my very lips

> (Shakespeare, *Othello*)

The verbs *steep* and *bathen* share the connotation of being immersed in water, but *bathen* has furthermore the connotations of purity and of daily activity which *steep* lacks. These connotations are the source of the property of simplicity which is stressed in the second sentence of Leech's analysis ('Their delight is simple, uncomplicated . . .'), and no such property can be attributed to the focus of the metaphor from *Othello*.

The selection of the properties of totality and simplicity out of the meaning constituents of *bathen* reflects the application of focus-interpretation in Leech's understanding of the metaphor. The process of vehicle interpretation, namely, a direct comparison between water and gladness is hinted at in the concluding phrase of Leech's analysis— both water and gladness are 'the natural gift of God'—but it is not elaborated and it is clear that in Leech's understanding of this metaphor, the vehicle-interpretation plays only a minor role.

Although I agree with Leech's intuition concerning this metaphor—

and in my understanding too the interaction of *gladness* and *water* is not a dominant factor—it should be mentioned that different construals of this metaphor are possible. In Richards's (1939) analysis of the very similar metaphor from *Othello* which was cited above, the vehicle-interpretation is the major procedure which applies:

> For poverty, the tenor is a state of deprivation, of desiccation, but the vehicle—the sea or vat in which Othello is to be steeped gives us an instance of superfluity . . . .
>
> (Richards 1939: 105)

We see that in Richards's understanding of the metaphor, the vehicle—water—is vividly present, and he draws a direct contrastive comparison between poverty and water (the sea), which, furthermore, affects his (metaphorical) description of poverty as a state of desiccation.

Let us return now to Leech's analysis of the metaphor from Milton— *the eastern gate where the great sun begins his state*—and see that the relative dominance of the two procedures is reversed here. There are two focus expressions in this metaphor: *gate* and *begins his state* (as substitution for both of these terms will yield a literal sentence which bears some similarity to the meaning of the metaphor). The vehicle is a ruler or a king, whose occurrence in the context of the two foci will result in the literal sentence *the eastern gate, where the great king begins his state*. In Leech's statements concerning this metaphor, the result of vehicle-interpretation—namely, the comparison of the sun to a king, is emphasized:

> There is an obvious resemblance between the sun and a king: we look up to both; both are powerful, being capable of giving and taking away life; both are glorious and of dazzling brightness (the one literally, the other metaphorically). The eastern quarter of the sky is like a gate because it is the sun's 'entrance' to the sky.
>
> (Leech 1969: 155)

The interpretation of the focus expressions (namely, that *gate* stands for the eastern quarter of the sky and that *the sun begins his state* stands for the sun's rising) is only mentioned briefly in the last sentence of his statement.

3

Linguistic (or philosophical) analyses offered for metaphor have usually overlooked the procedure of vehicle interpretation. Without necessarily using the term 'focus', these analyses are based on the assumption that understanding a metaphor is basically a matter of what I have called here 'focus-interpretation'. It is interesting to note that this is equally true for approaches on both sides of the debate concerning the question whether metaphors are deviant expressions. Thus we can compare Ziff's (1964), and Bickerton's (1969), analyses of the metaphor *green thought* (originally coined by Marvell in 'The Garden'). Ziff considers the metaphor as an instance of a 'syntactically deviant utterance' (1964: 392). Bickerton, on the other hand, thinks that metaphors 'may best be regarded as merely an extension of the system of attribute-assignment' (1969: 48). In his interesting semantic framework, the term 'marked sign' stands for a sign associated with specific attribute; e.g. *iron* is marked for hardness, while *steel* is not. Therefore, we can find in daily speech the metaphor *iron will* but not *steel will*. In the case of creative metaphor further attributes may be assigned to the word. Despite this difference in their theoretical approach to metaphor, we can see that for both scholars the understanding of *green thought* is a matter of assigning a reading to the adjective *green*, which, given the definitions in section 2, is the focus of the metaphor. Here is what they say about this metaphor.

> Consider the utterance 'he expressed a green thought' .... the deviance of the sentence cannot be attributed to *thought*, it can only be attributed to *green*. Let E_i be the class of elements that can occur without syntactic deviance in the environment 'He expressed a ... thought'. Then we can relate the utterance to the regular grammar by invoking the rule $E_i \rightarrow green$.
>
> (Ziff 1964: 395)

> ... When an already marked sign such as *green* is used, an entailed attribute may substitute for its usual one; thus, with *green thought* 'natural' rather than 'fertile' is assigned, as indicated by the context —'annihilating all that's *made* to a green thought in a green shade.'
>
> (Bickerton 1969: 49)

Although Ziff and Bickerton are right, no doubt, in assuming that in order to understand what is meant by the metaphor *green thought* we have to understand what *green* stands for, from everything said in previous sections, it is clear that, in addition, the metaphor also involves (at least potentially) an image, or a double perception of two concepts. Outside the context of Marvell's work, this metaphor is ambiguous and several construals of the vehicle are possible. A construal of the vehicle as a plant will yield interpretive statements like the following:

A comparison is drawn between a thought and a plant. Through

this comparison, *thought* receives some of the properties of *plant*:
it has a certain kind of life; it grows and develops.

There is no mention in Ziff's and Bickerton's work of this option of
vehicle interpretation.

A 'sortal-semantics' alternative to the treatment of metaphor in
terms of selectional restrictions has been suggested in recent papers by
van Dijk (1975), and Guenthner (1975). Within this approach metaphors are treated as a subclass of sortally incorrect sentences. Very
roughly, a sentence is sortally incorrect if its 'predicate is applied to
an object of the wrong type, category, or sort' (van Dijk 1975: 177).
Those sortally incorrect sentences which can be assigned truth-value
in context are metaphors (although, as van Dijk points out, there are
other types of metaphor which are not sortally incorrect but rather
contextually false in their literal reading, e.g. *Peter preferred to pick
one of the local flowers*, where *flowers* refers to girls). Discussing
the interpretation of metaphors, van Dijk offers the following observations (where *Fa* is a metaphorical, or sortally incorrect, expression in
which F is the predicate):

> the conventionally determined logical region of the predicate F
> somehow CHANGES in an expression like *Fa*. This change, in
> most cases would be an EXTENSION in case F does not apply to
> a region of which a is a member. (1975: 189)

In other words, for van Dijk as well, the metaphorical process is the
change in the meaning of the focus, and metaphorical interpretation is,
thus, assigning a reading of the focus. This is carried out by a 'selection
procedure', which 'drops' certain of the predicate features. The details
of van Dijk's and Guenthner's proposals need not concern us here.
The relevant point, however, is that their approach provides a framework only for the treatment of focus-interpretation. However innovative this framework may be, it cannot (and does not intend to) provide
a full account of the process of understanding poetic metaphor.

This same neglect of vehicle-interpretation is found in all the other
linguistic or philosophical works mentioned in the introduction.[11] The
most insightful of these works are Margalith (1970), and Cohen and
Margalith (1972), which offer an inductive logic treatment of metaphor.
(Margalith (1970), also covers such problems as the notion of meaning
constituents and similarity in meaning, and the distinction between the
cognitive information conveyed by metaphors and their emotive or
aesthetic import.) The basic concept of what is involved in the understanding of metaphor is nevertheless the same:

The metaphorical meanings of a word or phrase in a natural language are all contained, as it were, within its literal meaning or meanings. They are reached by removing any restrictions in relation to certain variables from the appropriate section or sections of its semantical hypothesis. (Cohen and Margalith 1972: 735)

The treatment of metaphorical meaning in terms of 'removing restrictions' is probably more successful than the description in terms of dropping, or erasing, properties. However, its relevance, again, is only to the process of focus-interpretation. The same procedure cannot account for the construction of a whole new concept to be perceived simultaneously with the old concept, which I have referred to here as *vehicle-interpretation*.

There are two possible accounts of why linguistic analyses of metaphor have overlooked the procedure of vehicle-interpretation. The first is that most of these analyses tend to consider metaphors which occur in daily speech and often even dead metaphors, rather than poetic metaphors. It is true that in the metaphors of daily speech, the vividness of the image does not always play a crucial role. The other account is that the procedure of focus-interpretation can, perhaps, be considered more basic, or, in a certain sense, more crucial to the understanding of metaphor. As was said in section 2, interpretation of the focus enables the hearer to understand what is the basic (cognitive) content of the metaphor and what it is that the speaker talks about. Thus there is some sense of 'understanding metaphor' which does not involve the double perception carried by vehicle-interpretation. It is possible that this level of understanding metaphor (namely the one reached by focus-interpretations) is shared by all speakers of the language, while vehicle interpretation is a kind of privileged process introduced by poets and limited to creative usages of the language. The last hypothesis is, however, at best extremely speculative, in the absence of empirical studies of this issue.

We can now see that as far as the process of focus-interpretation is concerned, the opponents of the deviance approach are right and the claim that understanding metaphor does not differ radically from understanding literal expressions can be substantiated. We saw that this process involves the selection of those meaning constituents which are compatible with the context. The adjective *green*, for example, is associated with the meaning constituent, [color] and the positive connotations, like [freshness], [fertility], or with negative connotations like [unripe]. Given a metaphoric context like *green thought*, the property [color] is erased. With no further context, *green* is still ambiguous in this metaphor and either the positive or the negative connotations can be selected. The context can be more specific, forcing a further selection. Thus, given the sentence, *This conference is so dull that it's time that someone came up with a green thought*, the positive connotations of *green thought* will be selected, while the property [unripe] will be erased. On the other hand, in a context like *he's always publishing his green thoughts without even bothering to work out the details*, it is the positive connotations which are ignored.

Notice now that precisely the same procedure of selection of relevant properties takes place in the processing of literal expressions. Given a sentence like *What a beautiful green plant!* the property [color] is not erased, since it's compatible with the context. However, the property [unripe], [negative evaluation], and perhaps [fertile] are incompatible and hence erased. On the other hand, if *green* occurs in a sentence like *Don't eat this fruit: it's green*, the negative connotation [unripe] is selected. The difference between the processing of literal expressions and the focus-interpretation in metaphor is, therefore, at most a matter of degree, since in metaphor, the properties which are erased are usually of higher relevancy.

As we saw in the previous section, the procedure of vehicle-interpretation is clearly distinct—it does not involve a selection of meaning contituents but rather the construction of a whole new concept, which is to be processed along with the concepts given in the metaphor. The exact nature of the double perception involved in metaphor still awaits much study. In any case, this process is unique to the understanding of metaphor, or, perhaps, more generally, of figurative expressions (since some may argue that the same double perception takes place also in the case of simile, as in *her cheeks are like roses*). While it bears some similarity to the processing of visual images (like the montage in film, or a surrealist painting) there are no other linguistic constructions which require this kind of double perception.

Summary

This paper argues that understanding poetic metaphor involves two distinct procedures (discussed in detail): The first, *focus interpretation*, consists of identifying and interpreting the 'focus expression', resulting in some literal equivalent of the metaphorical expression. The second, *vehicle interpretation*, involves a process of 'double perception'. Previous linguistic analyses of metaphor have usually concentrated, within different frameworks, on the focus interpretation alone. It is argued that while this procedure does not differ significantly from ones applied in the linguistic processing of non-metaphorical expressions, the neglected procedure of Vehicle Interpretation is unique to the processing of metaphor.

NOTES

1 Independently of the question of metaphor, the notions of selectional restriction and semantic deviance were criticized in such
   generative semantics works as McCawley (1968: 1971), and Lakoff
   (1972), and defended in Moravesik (1970).
2 In fact, the terms which Beardsley uses are only 'subject' and
   'modifier' (while what the modifier does to the subject is named
   'attribution'). It looks like it didn't occur to Beardsley that a metaphorical engagement can happen between the verb and the object,
   as well as between other constituents of the sentence (e.g. the verb
   and the adverb in the famous 'sleep furiously'). But it would not
   be fair to take this fact seriously and to assume that his method
   cannot apply to our verb–object metaphor.
3 Also the decision to include the alternative possibilities in italics is
   not self-evident. It assumes that T and V are technical terms which
   determine the functions of *words* in a phrase. So that in principle,
   there are two further alternatives: the referents of the italicized
   phrases. The opinion that understanding metaphor requires considering (beliefs concerning the) properties of the objects or
   situations denoted by the words involved, rather than semantic
   properties of the words, is expressed in Fillmore (1975: IV–31,
   IV–32).
4 This definition of 'similarity in meaning' is quite arbitrary, and is
   unlikely to have much other use in any semantic theory. For
   example, by this definition, the sentences *Rosa sat down* and *Rosa
   stood up* would be defined as similar in meaning, since they have
   at least one intersecting property, say, [a change of body position].
   A more general definition of the focus can be stated in terms of
   truth conditions, roughly as the following:
       Given a metaphorical expression $F_i[E_i]$, E_i is the focus, if it is
   possible to substitute E_j for E_i so that $F_i[E_j]$ is a literal expression
   and $F_i[E_i]$ entails $F_i[E_j]$.
       (A parallel definition can be substituted also for the definition
   of the 'subsidiary subject', or 'vehicle', that will be offered directly.)
   In the metaphor (i) *the mermaids are riding on the waves,* a substitution of *floating* for *riding* results in (ii) *The mermaids are floating
   on the waves,* which must be true if (i) (interpreted in its context)
   is true, while a substitution of, say, *horses* for *waves* results in (iii)
   the mermaids are riding the horses, which can be false when (i)
   is true. Hence *riding,* but not *waves,* will be defined as focus.
       This general definition has, furthermore, the advantage of apply-
   ing equally well to all types of metaphors, including those in which
   the focus is a noun (e.g. a definite description). The definition of
   'similarity in meaning' can apply to these cases only if we treat
   definite descriptions as predicate-argument expressions (as, e.g. in
   van Dijk, 1975).
       For the sake of the present introductory discussion, however,
   the definition of 'similarity in meaning' has the advantage of not

making any mention of the interpretation given to the metaphorical expression as a whole, while the definition in terms of entailment depends conically upon the explication of the truth conditions of the metaphorical expressions, namely, upon the conditions for the interpretation of such expressions (since a metaphor can be assigned a truth value only under a proper interpretation).

5 In fact, the term 'principal subject' is indeed redundant since it will always be identical with the frame (or part of the frame). Taken literally its definition is extremely misleading since 'what the metaphor is really about' is a label for the meaning of a metaphor, and not for one of its constituents. And Richards has already warned us against confusing the tenor with the meaning of the metaphor. But what Black had in mind when he used this definition is probably something different. In subject-modifier metaphors like *man is a wolf* or *the sea roars*, the principal subjects *man* and *sea* can be described as 'what the metaphor is about' meaning simply that the metaphor says something about the sea, namely that it roars. In other words, the principal subject is what the focus modifies, or more generally (to cover also verb-object metaphors, like our₃), what the focus occurs with, namely the frame.

6 In copula-nominal metaphors (*man is a wolf*) the subsidiary subject would always be also the focus. The reason for that is that the subsidiary subject indicates the constructed noun (or object) which interacts with the one explicit in the metaphor. There is no need for such a construction in nominal metaphors, since both of the nouns (or objects) are explicit (man is compared to wolf). The suggested definition of the subsidiary subject will still hold for such metaphors with the additional convention that in these cases, the resulting literal sentence should be a tautology: *a wolf is a wolf*.

7 The difference between (1) and (2) is basically what Mooij (1975), describes in detail as the conflict between the monistic (1) and the dualistic (2) approaches to metaphor. Mooij tries, further, to provide arguments in favor of the dualistic approach, but concludes that it is possible that the problem does not allow a clear-cut solution. My claim here is that the solution is not a choice between the two approaches, but rather the realization that both represent procedures of understanding and that normally both apply to any given metaphor, although (as will be argued in section 2.2) their relative dominance may vary.

8 The discussion here will be limited to metaphors which involve a violation of selectional restrictions (or 'sortally incorrect' expressions). Another type of metaphors, known as 'replacement metaphors' (Brooke-Rose, 1958, Chap. 1), or 'symbols' (Hendricks, 1968), consists of expressions which have a literal reading (or are 'sortally correct'), but, in the context of their usage, their literal reading is not the one which is intended. Thus, the literal sentence *the royal court is going to the hunt* can be used metaphorically to describe lions stalking their prey. Or, in van Dijk's example

(1975), in the sentence *Peter prefers local flowers*, the noun phrase *local flowers* can stand for local girls. The definition of the vehicle suggested here does not, as it stands, apply to these cases. In such metaphors, the situation is the reverse of the one described above: the expressions *the royal court* and *local flowers* function as what I have referred to as the *vehicle*. Thus in these cases, the vehicle is given and the interpretation consists of constructing the *tenor* (roughly, the literal topic of the discourse). It turns out, then, that, as in the copula-nominal metaphors which were mentioned in footnote 6, in 'symbol' metaphors the focus and the vehicle are given by the same expression (though in copula-nominal metaphors the tenor is given as well). A more general definition of vehicle, which captures also these 'symbol' cases, is, perhaps, possible, but its elaboration goes beyond the points I want to make here.

9   This is basically the point behind Richards's (1936), warning against the identification of the tenor with the meaning of the metaphor and Black's (1962), arguments against the theory of substitution. Arguments against the hypothesis that the meaning of a metaphor is fully translatable into literal expressions are presented also in Barfield (1960).

10 The degree of specificity of the vehicle depends obviously also upon the information supplied by the focus. Thus, in the metaphor *oblivion spins its webs around us*, the focus *spins its webs* forces the specific vehicle—spider—and a mere description of the metaphor as 'animation' of oblivion misses the point. The same is true not only for metaphors involving abstract concepts. Both in *the sun laughs* (e.g. Donne: 'A Nocturnal upon s. Lucies Day') and in *the sun drinks tea with me* (adopted from Mayakovsky) the sun is personified. However, while in the first of the vehicles—a person—cannot be further specified, in the second, the focus may suggest a further specification of this person as an adult (possibly male), a friendly person, or a member of the same social class as the speaker, etc.

11 An outstanding exception to the linguistic tendency to ignore the vehicle-interpretation is Weinreich's work (1966, section 3.5). Although he does not draw a distinction between the two procedures discussed here, a close examination of his proposal will reveal that he basically has in mind the vehicle-interpretation only. Another exception is Leech's (1969) partly formal analysis of metaphor, which attempts, though not explicitly, to capture both procedures.

REFERENCES

Barfield, O. (1960), 'The meaning of "literal" ', in G. Watson, ed., *Literary English since Shakespeare* (London: Oxford University Press), pp. 22–34.
Beardsley, M. (1958), 'The logic of explication', in M. Beardsley, ed., *Aesthetics* (New York: Harcourt Brace Jovanovich), pp. 129–64.

Bickerton, I. (1969), 'Prolegomena to a Linguistic Theory of Metaphor', *Foundations of language 5*, p. 37.

Black, M. (1962), 'Metaphor', in M. Black, ed., *Models and metaphors* (Ithaca, N. Y.: Cornell University Press), pp. 25–47.

Brooke-Rose, C. (1958), *A grammar of metaphors* (London: Secker & Warburg).

Chomsky, N. (1964), 'Degrees of grammaticalness', in Fodor and Katz 1964, pp. 384–9.

Chomsky, N. (1965), *Aspects of the theory of syntax* (Cambridge, Mass.: MIT Press).

Cohen, J. and A. Margalith (1972), 'The role of inductive reasoning in the interpretation of metaphor', in D. Davidson and G. Harman, eds, *Semantics of natural language* (Dordrecht: D. Reidel), pp. 722–40.

Dijk, T. A. van (1975), 'Formal semantics of metaphorical discourse', *Poetics 14/15*, 173–98.

Fillmore, C. (1975), 'The future of semantics', *Berkeley studies in syntax and semantics* 1, IV, pp. 31–2.

Fodor, J. and J. Katz (1964), *The structure of language: readings in the philosophy of language* (Englewood Cliffs, N. Jersey: Prentice-Hall).

Gopnik, I. and M. Gopnik (1973), 'Semantic anomaly and poeticalness', *Journal of Literary Semantics 2*, pp. 57–63.

Guenthner, F. (1975), 'On the semantics of metaphor', *Poetics 14/15*, pp. 199–220.

Hendricks, W. O. (1968), 'Three models for the description of poetry', *Journal of Linguistics 1*.

Jakobson, R. (1959), 'Boas' view of grammatical meaning', *American Anthropological Association memoir no. 89*, pp. 140–5.

Katz, J. (1964), 'Semi-sentences', in Fodor and Katz, 1964, pp. 400–16.

Lakoff, G. (1972), 'Hedges: a study in meaning criteria and the logic of fuzzy concepts', (Papers from the Annual Regional Meeting of the Chicago Linguistic Society) 8.

Leech, G. (1969), *A linguistic guide to English poetry* (London: Methuen).

Margalith, A. (1970), 'The cognitive status of metaphors', unpublished dissertation (in Hebrew, to be published shortly in English).

McCawley, J. (1968), 'The role of semantics in a grammar', in E. Bach and R. Harms, eds, *Universals in linguistic theory* (Toronto, Montreal: Holt, Rinehart and Winston), pp. 124–69.

McCawley, J. (1971), 'Where do noun phrases come from?', in L. Jakovovits and D. Steinberg, eds, *Semantics: an interdisciplinary reader* (London: Cambridge University Press), pp. 217–31.

Mooij, J. J. A. (1975), 'Tenor, vehicle and reference', *Poetics 14/15*, pp. 257–72.

Moravesik, J. (1970), 'Subcategorization and abstract terms', *Foundations of Language*, pp. 473–87.

Reddy, M. J. (1969), 'A semantic approach to metaphor', CLS (Chicago Linguistic Society) 5, pp. 240–51.

Richards, I. A. (1939) ' "Metaphor" and "the command of metaphor" ', in I. A. Richards, ed., *The philosophy of rhetoric* (London: Oxford University Press), pp. 89–138.

Weinreich, U. (1966) 'Explorations in semantic theory', in T. Sebeok, ed., *Current trends in linguistics* (The Hague: Mouton), Vol. 3, pp. 395–477.

Wissman Bruss, E. (1975), 'Formal semantics and poetic meaning', *Poetics 14/15*, pp. 339–63.

Ziff, P. (1964), 'On understanding "understanding utterances" ', in Fodor and Katz 1964, pp. 390–9.

CHAPTER FIVE

Formal semantics of metaphorical discourse

Teun A. van Dijk *

[Acknowledging the limitations of a formal (logical) approach and remarking briefly on the value of a pragmatic approach (speech acts),
Van Dijk proceeds to offer a 'sortal semantic' approach to the study
of metaphorical discourse. A sortal category may be roughly thought
of as the underlying logical counterpart of the Chomskian selectional
type (co-occurrence class or lexical subcategory), for the explicit figurative proposition manifests its 'sortal incorrectness' linguistically as a
violation of selectional restriction. While Van Dijk allows that a given
sentence need not be sortally incorrect to be given a metaphorical
interpretation, he consigns sortally correct metaphors to a pragmatic
contextual component of the metaphor theory. His contribution to
this theory would be to suggest the outlines for a component in which
the truth conditions of metaphorical statements might be formalized in
logical terms; the sortal specification serves as his mechanism for this
because it 'assigns to each predicate of the language a region of logical
space,' or a sphere of possible (thinkable) objects to which that predicate may be applied.

He then calls for a topology of sortal categories in the form of
'concentric circles' surrounding each predicate of the language. These
concentric circles would reflect a hierarchy of abstract semantic features,
each succeeding circle defining an increasingly abstract region of logical
space for that predicate. The entire topology would then outline the
set of possible metaphorical extensions for each predicate (as well as
for all possible objects spanned by that predicate). It would also formalize the notion of 'semantic distances' which seem to increase between
the referents of a metaphor as the metaphor's degree of sortal incorrectness increases.]

* First published in *Poetics*, 4 (1975), 173–98.
    I am indebted to Dorothea Franck and Uwe Monnich for very useful pre-
liminary discussions about this paper. Suggestions by Hans Mooij and Francis
Ediline could, regrettably, not be integrated before the paper went to press.

1 Introduction

1.1 The aim of this paper is a discussion of some of the problems in the formal, i.e., logical, semantics of metaphorical language. A META-PHORICAL language is a language with metaphorical sentences or discourses, like natural language. A formal semantics specifies the conditions under which such metaphorical sentences may be said to have a truth value, viz. it defines the notion of an interpretation for a language including metaphorical sentences. The idea is not, as usual, to assign the value 'false' or a neutral value, e.g., 'non-sense', to all meta-phorical sentences, but to reconstruct formally the idea that metaphorical sentences may be true in a given context.

1.2 It goes without saying that only a fragment of a serious theory of metaphor can be covered by the formal semantics approach. I therefore must presuppose well-known the current linguistic and psychological work on the structure and the functions of metaphorical discourse and will focus my attention upon the properly logical and philosophical problems involved. Within these domains, again, I shall neglect both syntactic and pragmatic aspects of the problem. The idea of a semantics for metaphorical sentences will not be based on an independent syntax, so that the interpretations will be quasi-formal. As far as the pragmatic aspects are concerned: although it will briefly be argued that meta-phorical sentences can be interpreted only in context-determinate models, I shall have to leave out a detailed discussion of the pragmatic status of metaphorical aspects of conversation.

1.3 The semantics which will be introduced here must have a rather unusual feature in the theory of logic, viz. it must be SORTAL. That is, it only interprets those sentences which are sortally correct. In linguistic terms: it is a semantics accounting for selection restrictions. The problems involved here, both linguistic and logical, are considerable, and only part of them can be treated here; without many positive results, I am afraid.

The framework for the sortal semantics is basically the one con-structed by Van Fraassen and elaborated by Thomason. The novelty of our approach is the assumption that under specific conditions sentences which, 'superficially', are sortally incorrect may be assigned an interpretation. This idea brings us close to recent work in modal ('possible world') semantics for conditionals and counterfactuals, e.g., by Thomason, Lewis, Åqvist and others, in which the concept of 'similarity', e.g., between worlds, plays such a central role. Although research on these and related topics is merely in its first stage—where, indeed, 'theory' and 'metaphor' are still close—it may be hoped that such a formal, model-theoretic account provides a better basis for a theory of metaphor in natural language than the current linguistic attempts.

2 A remark on the pragmatics of metaphor

2.1 A sentence can be assigned a metaphorical interpretation only when a set of specific contextual conditions have been satisfied, especially with respect to the intentions of the speaker. As has been demonstrated by Dorothy Mack (Mack, 1975) the specific use of metaphors in conversation requires an examination of the speech act status of metaphorical utterances. Since the formal semantics will make abstraction from all relevant pragmatic features, making metaphorical utterances more or less 'appropriate', I make a remark on those pragmatic aspects before attacking the proper semantic problems (although it is difficult to fully separate semantics and pragmatics).

Within the general framework of the basic principles of rational conversational interaction as presented by Grice (1967), the utterance of a metaphorical sentence would, when taken 'literally', violate the basic cooperative principles of truth, relevance and manner. That is, a non-metaphorical interpretation would make the sentence false or non-sensical, irrelevant with respect to situation and discourse and— even when interpreted metaphorically—often a circumstantial 'way' of saying things or, more often, especially in literature, an obscure way of saying things.

However, as Grice has demonstrated, very often deviations from basic pragmatic principles have a reason, i.e., they remain within the scope of the Cooperation Principle for rational interaction. Metaphor is an example in case. The deviation, thus, is merely apparent, and the hearer knows that the speaker intends (to mean) something different than the 'literal' meaning of the sentence or at least implies additional meaning besides the literal meaning. The precise reconstruction of 'literal meaning' must await the following sections, and will here be taken in its usual sense, viz. as the 'normal', conventional meaning of an expression.

2.2 The appropriate use of metaphorical utterances in interaction is thus based on a general principle, e.g., something like:

(1) By uttering a sentence S in a context c_i, such that for all possible literal interpretations of S the utterance of S violates the principles of Truth and Relevance, the speaker implicates (that the hearer knows that the speaker intends) a meaning of a sentence S*, satisfying the mentioned principles and being semantically related with the meaning of S.

The pragmatic principle of metaphorical utterances might be formulated more precisely, but it will do for the moment, the more so while we cannot here go into the details of a pragmatic theory. Part of the principle, however, is semantic, and it must be made clear below under what conditions the literal meaning cannot 'receive' an interpretation. The purely pragmatic aspects involved are the following, among others:

(i)   The speaker knows that the hearer knows that S is false or non-sensical in c_i;

(ii) The speaker assumes that the hearer knows the semantic relation (operation) between S and S^* by virtue of his knowledge of the language and of a system of perception related to this language;

(iii) The speaker wants that the hearer interprets the uttered sentence S as if it were the sentence S^*;

(iv) The speaker, by uttering S and intending the meaning of S^*, wants the hearer to know that this indirect speech act has a specific reason (which may be non-conscious, like the wish to self-assessment by 'showing' linguistic virtuosity)—which in aesthetic contexts may be accomplishment of the specific speech act itself.

3   Sentence types

3.1 Taking both formal and natural languages as (infinite) sets of sentences, it is theoretically useful to distinguish between different types of sentences. Thus, in classical formal languages a clear distinction is made between those syntactically well-formed formulas which can be assigned a truth value, and those wff's which, for some reason or other, are not assigned a truth value. In natural language sentence-hood is determined by the grammar of that language, determining the possible phono-morphological, syntactic and semantic structures of each sentence belonging to the language. Sentencehood in natural language, however, is a rather fuzzy concept, and the grammar is merely an idealizing approximation to the notion 'sentence of a given language'. These methodological problems of linguistics will for the moment be put aside in favour of a more restricted analysis of some sentence types in formal languages.

3.2 The type of sentence which can be assigned a truth value is traditionally considered to be the declarative sentence in the present tense. Moreover, such classical valuations are bivalent, i.e., a sentence is either true or false, but not both.

It is well-known, however, that the set of MEANINGFUL or INTER-PRETABLE sentences of a language is much larger. First of all, tensed sentences are naturally true or false. Secondly, non-declaratives such as uttered in questions, commands, advices, requests, etc. may also receive some sort of interpretation: they may be said to be appropriate or non-appropriate in a given context, or—sticking to truth values—it may be argued that such sentences are MADE true or false in a given context. Finally, it has been attempted to introduce other, non-bivalent, truth values, e.g. 'indeterminate', 'zero', etc. for those cases where a (meaningful) sentence is neither true nor false.

One of the standard examples in the latter case is the non-satisfaction of the presuppositions of a sentence. Thus 'The a if F' is neither true nor false if a does not exist. Such and similar solutions are given in the valuation of some logical constants, especially material implication and negation.

From this brief discussion it appears that it is sensible to distinguish at least between the 'meaningfulness' of sentences on the one hand, and their 'valuation/interpretation' on the other hand. Probably the first property is a necessary condition for a sentence to have the second property, i.e., before we may know whether a sentence is (made) true or false we must know what it means. In other words, the extension of a sentence depends on its intension, viz. on the proposition it expresses.

3.3 Without pressing too much the extremely controversial distinctions mentioned above, we may distinguish a set of sentences which are MEANINGLESS for some reason. Meaninglessness may be determined at several levels in natural language: it may result from inadequate performance of phonemes and morphemes, the syntactic structure of the sentence may be ill-formed and finally, at the level of semantic representations, predicates may be used which do not 'apply' to the referring phrases (or at the object level: properties are assigned to individuals which these individuals cannot possibly have). In this case meaninglessness results from the SORTAL INCORRECTNESS of the sentence, i.e., a predicate is applied to an object of the wrong TYPE, CATEGORY or SORT. Since the terms 'type' and 'category' have numerous other meanings in logic and grammar the terms 'sort' and 'sortally (in-)correct' will be used here. Examples of sortally incorrect sentences are:

2   *The typewriter has a head-ache.*
3   *The square root of Susy is happiness.*
4   *May I please flow under your door?*

These sentences are sortally incorrect because in most normal contexts typewriters are not the 'sort' or 'kind' of thing which may have a headache, Susy (when understood to refer to a girl) cannot have a square root, nor can square roots be identical with, or have as a value, something of the sort of happiness. Finally, I (i.e., the speaker, hence a human) cannot have the property 'liquid', and hence I am not able to flow. In usual linguistic terms, we say in these cases that SELECTION RESTRICTIONS are violated.

A characteristic property of sortally incorrect sentences is that their logical negations are also sortally incorrect. This fact prevents us from simply treating sortally incorrect sentences as FALSE, although it might be argued that (external) logical negation should simply be read as 'It is not the case that . . .', which makes some of the sentences meaningful, but only at the meta-level where the meanings of expressions can be discussed.

As we shall see below, however, MEANINGFULNESS IS A RELATIVE AND GRADUAL CONCEPT. Sometimes, a sortally incorrect sentence expresses a proposition denoting an 'impossible fact', i.e., a state of affairs which cannot even be conceived mentally. This is certainly not the case in sentence (4), because I may well imagine a world where speakers-humans are non-compact (e.g. in Asimov's *The Gods Themselves*).

3.4 Finally, there is a type of sentence which is either plainly false or zero (e.g., for lack of presupposition satisfaction) or which is sortally incorrect, but which may nevertheless be assigned a normal (classical or non-classical) truth value, viz. truth in a given context. Those sentences are traditionally called METAPHORICAL. Some examples are:

5 *The car protested against such driving.*
6 *We have been beaten up by the pigs.*
7 *The sun laughed high in the sky.*
8 *this mind made war* [cummings].

Since these sentences are, when taken literally, sortally incorrect, their truth value is at least 'indeterminate'. However, we have the linguistic ability to interpret such sentences in a way such that they can be true or false. In the following sections it will be attempted to spell out the conditions under which sortally incorrect sentences may nevertheless be assigned a normal valuation. Notice, that a sentence need not be sortally incorrect in order to receive a metaphorical interpretation. Take e.g.:

9 *The king is back in office.*

where *king* may be metaphorical for an authoritative boss. But at the same time a literal interpretation of the sentence might, in a specific context (where kings normally work in their office), yield normal truth values.

4   Conditions on a theory of metaphor

4.1 A serious theory of metaphor must satisfy a number of methodological and empirical requirements. More specifically, a formal semantics for metaphorical sentences, part of such a more general theory, must account for a certain number of semantic facts. Some of these facts are the following:

(i)   some sortally incorrect sentences can, given the appropriate context, be interpreted metaphorically;

(ii) not all sortally incorrect sentences can be interpreted in the sense of (i);

(iii) for each metaphorically interpreted sentence there is at least one reading, the so-called 'literal' reading, such that the sentence is sortally incorrect under this reading or false/indeterminate in each possible world compatible with the context of utterance;

(iv) there are sentences which in a context c_i can be interpreted metaphorically, but not in a different context c_j;

(v)   a sortally correct sentence which is false or zero may, in an appropriate context, be interpreted metaphorically.

(vi) some metaphorical sentences have non-metaphorical counterparts having the 'same meaning', i.e., which are semantically equivalent [the translation principle for a class of metaphors] :

(vii) the metaphorical character of a sentence does not merely depend on its meaning or intension, but also on the extensions of its terms, i.e., it is determined by the (properties of the) individual referred to [the referentiality principle] .

Other facts and principles the theory should describe and explain will be mentioned below.

4.2 At the same time the theory should evaluate the traditional treatments of metaphorical sentences. Some major ideas from this tradition, which will not further be analysed here, are the following:

(i)   the substitution hypothesis: [the sun] *laughs* = [the sun] *shines brightly;*

(ii) the deletion hypothesis: *the sun* ⟨shines so brightly as if it⟩ *is laughing*;

(iii) the extension/reduction hypothesis: the predicate *laughing* does not only apply to humans but also to bright objects or to objects which make humans laugh.

Other versions and other proposals can be found in the literature. Our problem is: can such hypotheses be made explicit? In particular under what conditions may predicates be substituted, deleted, extended, or reduced? Below, it will become clear that the mentioned hypotheses all focus on a specific aspect of the interpretation of metaphorical sentences.

5   Sortal semantics

5.1 There are different ways to build up a semantics of natural language which is 'sortally sensitive'. I shall begin with a brief summary of the

attempt by Thomason, and shall subsequently discuss some of the particular and general problems involved in this approach or in any
attempt to provide a sortal semantics.

5.2 Thomason (1972), in his article 'A Semantic Theory of Sortal
Incorrectness', adopts several features from the semantic work of Van
Fraassen (1967, 1969, 1971). Valuations are given with respect to a
SORTAL SPECIFICATION. Only those sentences satisfying the sortal
specification can receive a bivalent interpretation. A sortal specification, then, is a function which assigns to each predicate of the language
a REGION of LOGICAL SPACE. A logical space is conceived as a conceptual network by Thomason, and Van Fraassen speaks of a set of
'points', 'possible individuals', or 'possible objects'. Such a possible
object, which in Thomason's terms may be viewed as an abstract 'role'
in semantic space, is constructed out of abstract properties, such that
predicates of the language can either apply or not apply to these
possible objects. Thus, the application of the predicate 'large' requires
the presence of a feature 'having dimensions', say. Individuals from a
domain D are said to be able to 'occupy' a point in logical space, i.e.,
they may become an instance of a possible object. The function determining this relation is the LOCATION FUNCTION: LOC, whereas a
REFERENCE FUNCTION: REF, selects the intended individual from
the domain for a given term of a sentence. Predicates are assigned a
subset $I(P)$ of the appropriate sort $E(P)$. A sentence is true if $ref(a)$, say
$d_i \in D$, is located at a point $loc(d_i)$ in the subregion $I(P)$.
    Let me give a concrete example to illustrate these ideas. Take the
simple sentence

10 *The boy is ill.*

The valuation of this sentence has basically two phases. It is first determined whether it is sortally correct and then it is determined what
(further) conditions make the sentence true or false. The sentence is
sortally correct because the possible object |boy| lies within the region
$E(ill)$, i.e., it is a member of the set of possible objects of which it may
be true or false to be ill. In other words: the predicate *ill* applies to
individuals to which also the predicate *boy* applies, probably because
of the fact that the possible object |boy| has the property ⟨organic⟩ or
⟨animate⟩ required for an object to be sane or ill. The rest of the valuation of (10) is normal. That is, the predicate *ill* or *being ill* is assigned
part of the region $E(ill)$. This part is the interpretation $I(ill)$ of the predicate. Next, the definite referring phrase *the boy* is assigned a particular
individual, say d_i—e.g. Peter—element of the domain of discourse.
This individual must be the only 'instance' of the possible object |boy|
i.e. $loc(d_i)$ must be an element of the |boy|-region of logical space.
The sentence is true iff $loc(d_i) \in I(will)$.

5.3 Such a sortal semantics requires a brief discussion about its philo-sophical foundations. It is clear from the literature on 'sorts' or 'types' that our understanding of the relations between (in-)significance in language and the structure of logical space is still very fragmentary (see e.g. Sommers, 1963; Drange, 1966). Thomason's notion of sort is close to the ideas put forward by Russell on the subject, where two objects are of the same type when the same (monadic) predicate is significantly (i.e., truly or falsely) predicable of both. Sommers himself proposes a more sophisticated approach combining ideas from Russell, Ryle, and Black. That is, he distinguishes between linguistically deter-mined types and ontological types, in the following way:

A-type: set of predicates of which every member spans every member of an a-type (and no member a non-a-type member);

a-type: set of objects spanned by a monadic predicate;

B-type: set of predicates significantly predicable of a thing;

β-type: set of things to which every member of a B-type applies.

In this terminology an A-type seems to correspond with what has been termed the 'content' of a term, or, in C. I. Lewis's terms the 'intension' of a predicate, also known as its 'connotation'. Hence it refers to those predicates which are included in a given predicate determining an a-type. Thus, the predicates *speak* and *think* belong to the A-type corresponding with the a-type spanned by the predicate *human* (see Van Fraassen, 1967).

The a-type would in that case correspond with the 'comprehension' (Lewis) of a predicate (called 'intension' by Carnap), where the set of objects is conceived of as a set of possible objects, in the sense of Van Fraassen and Thomason. In case the set of objects is meant of which the predicate is actually true—at a given moment—we would have to speak of the 'denotation' or 'extension' of a term or predicate.

Notice that the a-type is not very homogeneous. According to this definition all things which are 'thinkable' form a type, the things which are 'yellow' (or rather: which may be yellow), etc. Hence an a-type is a rather arbitrary finite subset of the power set of all possible objects.

A B-type is what we could also term a 'description' or 'characteriza-tion', or perhaps rather a 'possible description' of an object. However, a description is rather an (ordered) consistent subset of a B-type. At this point a distinction between generic and non-generic predicates should be made, and we enter the debate about essentialism: which properties are essential and which are non-essential of a given thing? The B-type could be split up accordingly. Thus, the predicate *boy* or *heavy* should somehow be distinguished from *falling* or *being painted yellow*.

The β-type, finally, is perhaps closest to our intuitive notion of a sort, type or kind. In case we are able to make a serious distinction between 'necessary' (analytic) and 'possible' (synthetic, contingent) predicates, the β-type would be specified in the same way, where the set of things to which a set of analytic predicates applies would be a 'natural kind' (for detailed discussion, see Kripke, 1972).

There are a large number of questions arising already from this brief discussion on the different possibilities to introduce sorts in the ontology for the semantics we need. What, for example, is the status of higher predicates? What constraints are needed to allow a sentence like *The boy runs quickly* and to mark off, somehow, a sentence like *The boy runs deeply*? Taking adverbs as higher predicates would suggest that we predicate something of a predicate, which would not very well fit into any of the kinds discussed above. Hence the need to allow processes and events to be serious individual objects, an assumption which would at the same time account for the admissibility of *a quick run* (or *the run was quick*) and the inadmissibility—in most contexts—of *a deep run* (or *the run was deep*).

Another difficulty is the status of predicates of higher degrees. In most of the discussion on sorts monadic predicates are used. Formally, the kind for a binary predicate like *love* would be a set of ordered pairs, viz. those of which the first member is human and the second any type of object. Nevertheless, in practice we would rather use the complex (abstracted) predicate 'being able to love something/somebody' as being applicable to humans, or in general to those objects 'having emotions'. Similarly for converses like 'visible', for those objects on which 'x is able to see [it]' is applicable.

5.4 What, then, are the consequences for a formal semantics taking sorts into account? Some predicates, like *happy* and *grunt* have precisely natural kinds as their range, viz. humans and pigs, say. Other predicates, like *big* and *yellow* do not seem to lie within 'natural' kind boundaries. The applicability of predicates, as Thomason suggests, is thus determined by the conceptual structure of the possible objects. It may be the case that some form of B-type, in Sommers's sense, determines these possible objects, viz. as a set of those possible individuals in logical space satisfying an n-tuple of predicates. Thus, the applicability of *big* would require a conceptual structure with a feature 'having dimensions', and 'yellow' would require 'coloured' or 'visible' as features. These 'features' themselves are identified by predicates, which in turn require a conceptual structure of certain possible objects in order to be applicable, say 'concrete' for both 'visible' and 'having dimensions'. Apparently, the set of conceptual features defining a possible object is (hierarchically) ordered.

The applicability of, say, *happy* on a possible object |boy| seems thus being determined by the existence of a possible object |happy boy|. Such an object is possible if there is a possible world in which there is an individual instantiating the possible object or individual concept. Similarly, *happy* is not applicable to |table|, because |happy table| is not a possible object, since a possible object with a feature |happy| must also have the higher ordered feature |having emotions|, requiring in turn |animate|, whereas |table| has at least a feature |non-animate|. The non-applicability of predicates, leading to the construction of impossible objects, is determined by a contradiction between two predicates for the basic conceptual features of an object.

Note that it is not easy to establish a clear distinction between linguistic (in-)significance and ontological possibility and absurdity (see Routley and Routley, 1969, 215 ff.). The second case pertains to objects (things, including events, etc.) which are possible or impossible, i.e. which may have an instantiation in some or in no possible world. The first case can be decided only on the basis of the 'meaning' or 'content' of the predicates used to refer to an object or to a property or relation. Thus the sentence *The yellow thing is square* is linguistically significant, but in case the definite description *the yellow thing* refers to a circle, the sentence denotes an impossible fact. In other terms, a fact-concept like |a yellow thing is square| which is 'intensionally' possible, may have fact-individuals as values which are impossible because the 'yellow'-concept may pick out things with properties which are inconsistent with those required for 'square' being applicable. In this example, thus, the sentence is sortally incorrect UNDER A GIVEN INTERPRETATION, which is determined by the context, viz. by the referents intended and their further properties. A sentence like *This circle is square*, however, is absurd under all interpretations, independently of context. Curiously, the last example, although expressing a plain contradiction, does not seem to be sortally incorrect, because the predicate *square* requires of a possible object to have (two) dimensions, which as such is not inconsistent with the predicate *circle*. Moreover, the sentence *A (the) circle is not square* is true, and would be indeterminate in case the non-negated version would be sortally incorrect.

5.5 It is clear that we cannot even attempt to solve here the numerous philosophical and logical problems involved. From the discussion above it seems that sortally incorrect sentences express a proposition which, under a given interpretation, 'denotes' a fact that is impossible in all physically possible worlds (situations, states of logical space) compatible with our actual world, i.e., those worlds having the same set of basic postulates (see Goble, 1973).

A serious insight into sortally incorrect sentences at the linguistic level and absurd or impossible facts at the ontological level requires previous understanding of the mechanisms of 'predication' and their corresponding operations in logical space. Should we maintain a fundamental distinction between 'substantive' concepts and 'attributive' concepts, the latter somehow presupposing the former? And does such a distinction correspond to a fundamental distinction between 'objects' and 'properties'? The objects of our world, values of (individual) concepts (see Scott, 1970), are topologically based selections of 'properties' of logical space. They are constant functions over changing time-space situations, continuous and structurally stable (for detail see Thom, 1972). The (non-analytic) assignment of properties, an operation expressed by predication on the linguistic level, produces non-stable objects like events/facts/states (Thom's CATASTROPHES), e.g., from |boy| a |happy boy|, where the 'boy'-properties remain constant but the set of properties 'applied' under the property 'happy' may change in different possible situations. Thus, the impossible concept |happy table| does not have a value in any physically possible world, compatible with our own, because the discriminating or constituting feature 'inanimate' of the table-concept conflicts with the 'animate' feature of the happy-concept. Taking 'happy' as a function, we would say that it is only defined for a domain of higher animates or humans, whereas it cannot assign an emotional state to tables since |table| itself has only values for a domain of inanimates.

5.6 Another feature of logical space to which more attention should be paid in order to be able to work out a complete theory of sortal semantics is the possibility of SIMILARITY and DIFFERENCE between its possible objects. Such an account is necessary for the description of DEGREES OF SORTAL (IN-)CORRECTNESS.

Consider the following sentences:

11 *The theory of relativity grunts.*
12 *The horse grunts.*

Intuitively, we somehow find (11) more 'strange' than (12). That is, we have less difficulty imagining horses that grunt than theories that grunt. A horse could have all its characteristic properties, and therefore being still (recognized as) a horse, but one, perhaps rather marginal biological feature, viz. the production of a different sound, could be different. In that case practically nothing of the 'horse'-properties would need to be different in order for a horse to be able to grunt. In other terms: a logical space where |grunting horse| is a possible object is less remote than a logical space where |flying horse| would be a possible object, because such an object would probably require such a horse to have wings. *A fortiori* so, in sentence (11), for grunting theories. A theory would be required to be a concrete object, perhaps even be animate, and at least have a sound-producing mechanism. In fact, we would hardly call such an object a theory, because it gives a fundamentally different 'coupe' from logical space.

A provisional statement about degrees of sortal incorrectness would perhaps run as follows:

13 A predicate *f*, applied to a term *a* in a sentence S_i, is LESS APPLIC-
ABLE than a predicate *g*, applied to the same term *a* in a sentence
S_j, if the set of predicates entailed by *f* which are also inapplicable
to *a* is larger than the set of inapplicable predicates entailed by *g*. A
sentence is sortally less correct if its predicates are less applicable.

Thus, in *The horse grunts* the predicate *grunt* does not entail a predicate which would be also inapplicable to *horse*, whereas in *The horse
is arguing* the predicate *argue* would entail at least the predicates *think*,
and *speak*, which are also inapplicable to *horse*. A semantic theory of
similarity relations in logical space would have to work out the topology
of possible objects. Intuitively, it is obvious that |horse| has a smaller
DISTANCE to the possible object |cow| than to |theory|. |Horse| is
connected with |cow| through all those properties designated by the
predicates entailed by *mammal*, and with |theory| perhaps only through
the most general feature |object|. In other terms: the intersection of the
conceptual structure of |horse| with that of |cow| is greater than that
with |theory|.

Similarly, we would have to account for the hierarchical structure of
the possible objects in logical space. The possible object |tree| somehow
'dominates' the possible object |oak| the set of oaks is included in the
set of trees, which seems to mean that |tree| is one of the features of
|oak|.

We will, however, leave these general discussions about the foundations of sortal semantics and now consider the specific problems in the
interpretation of metaphorical sentences.

6 Problems in the semantics of metaphorical sentences

6.1 The semantics of metaphorical sentences has a number of problems
well-known in the semantics of modal operators and of intensional
contexts in general: identity, substitution, opacity, etc.

First of all, Thomason's REFERENTIALITY PRINCIPLE in the
valuation of sortally sensitive sentences is problematic for metaphorical
sentences. That is, a sortally (in-)correct sentence must be so under
equivalent substitution. Yet, sentences which may be perfectly correct
under one description of an individual may be sortally incorrect under
another description, as we saw in some examples above, so that sortal
(in-)correctness must be determined at the object level in the interpretation. In metaphor, similarly, we start from a textually or contextually
determined discourse referent, remaining identical under any description, including its metaphorical description. The familiar scheme of
such sentences is then **Fa*, where *a* is a constant for the intended
referent and **F* is a METAPHORICAL PREDICATE, as in *He is a bear*

or *She is an encyclopedia*, significantly assertable of humans in certain contexts.

However, there are also cases in which the metaphorical predicate appears in the descriptive referring phrase as in sentence (9) and in sentences like

14 *Peter preferred to pick one of the local flowers*

where *flower* is intended to refer to a girl. Only under this referential condition sentence (14) is metaphorical. Under a literal interpretation it is not even sortally incorrect.

Such 'metaphorical referring phrases', however, must be treated as definite descriptions in general. As a general rule, definite noun phrases like *the Fx* may be derived only when the discourse referent has been introduced as the value of a term in an indefinite description in a previous sentence or in a pragmatically known proposition, including meaning postulates. Thus, the definite noun phrase *the local flowers* is 'grammatical' only when the interpretation specifies that the individuals referred to (viz. the local girls) have been mentioned before or are known to be intended by other contextual information. We will therefore assume that metaphorical referring phrases are derived from underlying structures in which the metaphorical term is introduced predicatively, e.g. as follows: 'the local girls are (like) flowers'. The same is true for such apparent indefinites like *Peter picked a local flower*, where the object noun phrase is equivalent with 'one of the local flowers'. Without previous identifying sentences a sentence like *Peter picked some flowers in the park* would, in a non-specific context, receive a normal, non-metaphorical interpretation.

Now, take the converse case, e.g. in the following sentence:

15 *The flowers in the park smiled at him.*

Such a sentence may be METAPHORICALLY AMBIGUOUS in the following way: either *flowers* is non-metaphorically referring to real flowers and *smile* is a metaphorical predicate for e.g. 'blossom' (in a certain way), or *flowers* is a metaphorical referring phrase, denoting girls, and *smile* is a normal predicate for girls. From this example it is clear again that a sentence is metaphorical only with respect to the model structures in which the previous sentences or pragmatic, contextual knowledge is interpreted.

The same holds for sentences which are not metaphorically ambiguous but which, in isolation, would not have been interpreted metaphorically:

16 *The lion roared.*

In this sentence *the lion* may be a metaphorical referring phrase to a strong man, say, where the predicate *roared* would, in order to 'stay in the image', be the adequate predicate for his cry. Such a sentence would be ambiguous in a narrative about a hunting party, but plainly metaphorical in a narrative about a battle in Flanders, say.

6.2 Another familiar problem arising in the interpretation of metaphor is whether identity is preserved under predicate substitution. In case of the local girls: as soon as it is implicitly or explicitly asserted that they 'are' flowers, we may freely use the referring phrase *flowers*. But the contextual identity *girls = flowers* will not hold in general, and the following sentences would be strange under a metaphorical interpretation:

17 *The government decided to give higher income to young flowers.*
18 *The flowers are requested to dress after the boys.*

The semantics of metaphor, thus, must guarantee that any form of identity or equivalence must be restricted to contexts with a specific structure.

In intensional contexts, e.g., in the scope of such verbs as *know, believe, dream, pretend*, etc., metaphors may be opaque:

19 *Peter thought (dreamt) that the flowers in the park smiled at him.*

Several possibilities are open here: (i) presupposed is that *girls = flowers*, such that Peter's dream objects are girls, (ii) Peter dreams/thinks that *girls = flowers*, (iii) Peter dreams about real flowers, and it is presupposed that *smile = blossom*, (iv) Peter dreams/thinks that *smile = blossom*, (v) Peter dreams about real flowers which are 'really' smiling, which would entail that they somehow have a face and mouth.

The opacity of some texts can of course be resolved in cases where the metaphor is not likely to be under the scope of the intensional verb:

20 *Ford pretended that he had been bugged by those dirty FBI pigs.*
21 *The young lady believes that her kid has been saved by the pigs.*

The general rule holding for such cases is that the speaker knows, believes, or assumes that the metaphorical identity or equivalence holds. That is, metaphorical equivalence statements, normally implicit in the discourse, are under the scope of pragmatic operators (speaker believes . . .). In other contexts it is obvious that the metaphor is under the scope of the intensional verb:

22 *The mayor, opening the new public park this morning, reminded the youth that trees and flowers are our friends.*

6.3 There is another case in which the (con)text influences the possibility of metaphorical interpretation. Thus, sentence (15) may very well receive a literal interpretation in a fable or fairy tale. Here animals or non-animate objects may systematically be assigned properties reserved to humans in our actual worlds. Hence, whether a sentence is metaphorical often depends on the sortal incorrectness of the sentence, but sortal incorrectness, as we saw, is determined with respect to interpretation in model structures with a set of possible worlds compatible with our own physical worlds. Thus, in her reply to Alice (Carroll, *Through the Looking Glass*, Chap. II), Tiger-lily may non-metaphorically utter: '. . . it's enough to make one wither to hear the way they go on.'

7   Metaphorical interpretation

7.1 With the problems mentioned above in mind, we now must specify the general conditions under which metaphorical sentences may receive an interpretation.

Recall that many metaphorical sentences are sortally incorrect whereas other metaphorical sentences would be contextually false under a literal interpretation. A sentence is sortally incorrect if the discourse referent occupying a given point (the possible object) in logical space is not a member of the interpretation domain of the sortal specification function for a given predicate. In other words: the individual would not satisfy the predicate under any interpretation. Example: *The theory grunts.*

The traditional idea associated with metaphorical sentences is that INSTEAD of the sortally correct sentence Ga, denoting a given fact, a sentence $*Fa$ is used, such that under a normal interpretation $*Fa$ is false or sortally incorrect. Since it may be maintained that Fa expresses a different proposition than $*Fa$, because $*Fa$ at least entails Ga and Fa does not, we shall distinguish syntactically between a given sentence Fa (receiving a literal interpretation) and its metaphorical counterpart $*Fa$. Whether the '$*$' symbol has a specific operator value, will be discussed below.

Furthermore, it is traditionally supposed that a sentence $*Fa$ may be used instead of Ga iff the predicates F and G have some sort of MEANING RELATION.

Following a brief suggestion made by Thomason, this would mean that the conventionally determined logical region of the predicate F somehow CHANGES in an expression like $*Fa$. This change, in most cases would be an EXTENSION in case F does not apply to a region of which a is a member. In our examples given earlier, this would mean that the predicate *flower* is extended such that its region not only comprises flowers but also girls (in a given context).

7.2 How can these ideas be made more explicit in the framework of a sortal semantics?

First of all, it must be established that at least two principles must be respected in any account:

(i) the structure of logical space (for a given language) does not change by the use of metaphorical sentences (as it is the case in the fairly-tale context);

(ii) the conventional meaning structures of the predicates of the language do not change by the metaphorical interpretation of a predicate.

The conclusion is that the 'metaphorical predicate' is (*ad hoc*) USED in a specific way, which indeed makes metaphorical interpretations pragmatical.

Nevertheless, although a given predicate may *ad hoc* be used in a specific way, there are general semantic principles determining under what conditions such *ad hoc* changes in the interpretation of predicates are possible.

Formally, the account would have roughly the following structure. Call the specific metaphorical meaning of a predicate F: F'. The interpretation V under a sortal specification E of the metaphorical predicate has a range $VE(F')$ large enough to have the referent a localized in it.

Such a formal account, however, would be simplistic and explain nothing, if other features are not built in. Since the range of F' is larger than that of F, the latter predicate must be less general. Hence some of the predicates (features) included in F must somehow be dropped in metaphorical contexts. In other words: F' must be constructed out of F by a SELECTION PROCEDURE. The intuitive idea of such a selection procedure is that those predicates entailed by F which are applicable only to a more limited region of logical space are dropped. On the other hand the remaining content of the resulting predicate must be specific enough to convey non-trivial information.

The selection procedure may make use of a specific SELECTION FUNCTION s with the set P of predicates of a language L_i as domain and co-domain. That is, s operates an ORDERING in P according to a SIMILARITY principle. In this way, each $f \in$ P is assigned a set M of predicates 'environing' f such that each element of M is more general than f. Hence it follows for any $g \in M$, and for any individual u that $f(u) \Vdash f(u)$.

The similarity function, however, must have a RELATIVE character. A predicate g may be more general than a predicate f with respect to a certain 'tag'. Thus, with respect to the tag [sex] the predicate *female* is more general than *girl*, whereas *youngster* is more general than *girl* with respect to the tag [age]. The function will therefore be indexed with the feature(s) with respect to which it operates on the predicates: $s_a(f) = g$. In generalizing we keep part of the included predicates constant, e.g. ⟨young⟩ when going from *girl* to *youngster*, whereas others are dropped, e.g. ⟨young⟩ when going from *girl* to *female*.

Since it is possible to drop several 'included predicates' we may introduce a linear set of subsets of M, viz. $M_1, M_2 \ldots M_n$. In our example we may thus go from *girl*, via *female* to *human*, dropping ⟨young⟩ and ⟨female⟩ respectively.

Each predicate is thus surrounded by sets of concentric circles, depending on the feature 'on which' we generalize. This topological structure of our concept language requires further analysis which cannot be given here.

7.3 We have already noticed that the extension of predicates by dropping part of their content is not arbitrary. The intuitive criterion is that the features which must remain are somehow TYPICAL. It is not typical of a pig that it has four legs, nor of a girl that she has hair. Hence the predicates *pig* and *girl* may not be used in an extended meaning in which the features ⟨having four legs⟩ and ⟨having hair⟩, respectively, are constant.

The consequence of this criterion is that the property underlying the extension may not be too general. We do not use a metaphorical predicate *table* to identify or qualify a flower because both are concrete objects. A typical property of a possible object (or more in general, at the linguistic level, a typical predicate/feature included in a predicate) need not be ontologically so. The choice of typical CRITERIA for the similarity function is pragmatically determined on the basis of cultural knowledge and beliefs. Thus, a pig need not be fat, physiologically speaking, but is typically fat with respect to other (semi-) domestic higher animals in the eyes of the members of a given culture. Thus we would need at least the following pragmatic postulate:

23 (For most *x*, and most *y*) [*(member of cultural group)* (*x*) & *(pig)*
(*y*) & B_x *(fat)(y)*]

where B_x is an indexed belief-operator.

So, the first condition is that it is generally believed that a given possible object has a property (or has this property in a remarkable degree) which other objects belonging to the same, more general kind, do not have (or do not have in this remarkable degree/way).

The second condition is that the usual 'name' for the possible object or attribute in question may be used for an individual of which it is predicated that it has this property.

Assuming that the predicate *flower* has the features ⟨beautiful, animate, fresh . . .⟩ typically, we may use this predicate in a context where this abstract feature structure is satisfied, e.g., where the possible object |girl| has an instance. Note that these specific features need not be defining the original concept, but may be contingent, contextually determined, features: the concept |girl| does not have |beautiful|, say as a 'necessary' property. In fact, this can be explained by the function of metaphors: we want to pick out and assign a specific contingent property of an individual, not the property the individual has anyway. The fact that flowers grow is therefore not a sufficient condition to use the predicate *flower* predicatively for humans, which also grow. In that case only the manner, e.g., the speed, of the growing may be selected for metaphorical predication if this is specifically different from the average type of growing.

7.4 The selection function does not necessarily have predicates as values which have a lexical expression in the language. These values may consist of an ordered n-tuple of features. Again this is precisely often one of the reasons for the use of metaphors. Since we have no predicate 'taking together' (con-ceiving) ⟨fat⟩, ⟨dirty⟩, ⟨animate⟩, ⟨stupid⟩ exclusively, we use a predicate, e.g., *pig*, signifying a possible object which has these properties inclusively. In case only one predicate has to be asserted this substitution is of course easier: *Peter is strong = Peter is a bear.*

7.5 The general truth condition for metaphorical sentences like **Fa* would thus become roughly the following:

24 $V(*Fa) = 1$ iff

(i) $V(Fa) = ?$
(ii) there is an F' such that $F' \in s_a(F)$
(iii) $V(F'a) = 1$
      (iff: $a \in IE(F')$)

In other terms the sentence is true just if the discourse referent, localized 'at' some possible object in logical space, is element of the region of the extended predicate F', viz. $E(F')$, including the intended interpretation of the predicate, viz. $IE(F')$. Hence the sentence is TRUE iff $loc(a) \in MIE(F)$, where MI is the metaphorical interpretation of the predicate F, which is identical with the 'normal' interpretation of the transformed predicate F', and where E is a sortal specification. The sentence **Fa* is FALSE iff condition (iii) does not hold, i.e., if a does not have the property F'. In other cases, e.g., if the similarity function has no values, the sentence is metaphorically speaking neither true nor false but 'indeterminate'. Keeping the first two conditions constant we guarantee that our metaphorical interpretations are bivalent. These truth conditions should be embedded in a more general set of pragmatic APPROPRIATENESS CONDITIONS. That is, although the conditions may hold, and thus a given predicate is metaphorically true of a given individual, it may be contextually inappropriate to use that meta-phorical predicate, as in sentence (17) for example.

7.6 From this still very imperfect formal account it emerges that in asserting **Fa* I basically assert *F'a*, where *F'a* is true iff *a* has the properties selected from *F* by the similarity function. This interpretation is context sensitive. Since a policeman will not IN GENERAL have the properties ⟨fat, dirty/mean, stupid⟩, *F'a* will not always be true and hence **Fa* may be false. The equivalence *policeman* = *pig* is therefore not analytic and substitution therefore not possible in all contexts. Nor may we use the predicate *policeman* to identify or characterize a pig, because a policeman does not have typical features which are contingently predicable of pigs. An unqualified substitution hypothesis is therefore inadequate.

8 Metaphors, comparisons, and counterfactuals

8.1 Selection functions have recently been used also in other formal semantic research. Especially in the semantics of certain connectives of the implicational type (material implication, entailment, counterfactual conditionals, causals, etc.) it has been fruitful to introduce selection functions operating on possible worlds. This work has been done by such scholars as Thomason, Stalnaker (see Stalnaker and Thomason, 1970), Åqvist (1973), and Lewis (1973).

In the interpretation of e.g. *if . . . then*—statements, we might formulate the truth condition such that truth is obtained if the consequent is true in all the possible worlds 'selected' by a function based on the truth of the antecedent. A proposition, which may be false in the actual world (of the speech context) may select those worlds in which it is true, ALL OTHER THINGS BEING EQUAL, for which it is further asserted that the consequent holds. Instead of selection functions other formal devices may be used, e.g., indexed alternativity relations between possible worlds ($w_o Rpw_i$) (see Lewis, 1973).

8.2 There are a certain number of formal properties of metaphors which recall these aspects of the interpretation of conditionals of different strength. As a first try we might construe the metaphorical sentence as an implicit conditional of which the antecedent must be true and select the possible situations in which the consequent, viz. the apparent metaphorical part may be true. When we take again the trivial example *Peter picked a local flower*, we would then rephrase it something like:

25 *If a girl would be a flower, Peter picked a flower.*

This is a rather strange indicative conditional, which is true in case *Peter picked a flower* is true in a possible situation which would be compatible with the actual (speech) situation, with the only difference that girls have 'flower'-properties in that situation. If the antecedent is false, the metaphor is neither true nor false, it would be metaphorically indeterminate, indeed, no metaphor at all. Weakened versions of (25) would be:

26 *If a girl could be called a flower* . . .

27 *If a girl* $\begin{matrix} \textit{would be} \\ \textit{is} \end{matrix}$ *like a flower* . . .

etc.

In all cases both antecedent and consequent are true/false in the actual world, which makes R at least REFLEXIVE. This is not strange, since the similarity relation is also reflexive: probably no world is as similar as w_i itself. Another reading of (25) would be:

28 *Provided girls are like flowers: Peter picked a flower.*

One of the advantages of such an approach would be the possibility to make explicit the METAPHORICAL POSTULATE required to interpret *Peter picked a local flower* or *The local flowers smiled at him*, where the definites had been explained earlier by the presence of a previous (textual or contextual, i.e. pragmatical) proposition. We could build out this hypothesis a step further by assuming that the implicit antecedent in fact should be a COMPARATIVE SENTENCE, e.g. like in:

29 *If girls are as beautiful (as . . . , as . . . .) as flowers, . . .*

where the *tertium comparationis*, which corresponds to the constant feature determining the selection function, is made explicit. In that case the antecedent would select exactly those situations in which girls are like flowers but relative to their property of beauty, say.

This treatment further would specify the exact relation between a COMPARISON and a metaphor. A metaphor is not a shorter version of the comparison from which the 'like' and the *tertium comparationis* are deleted (if this would yield a grammatical sentence at all), but a metaphor PRESUPPOSES a comparison. In that case, the comparison should be true for the metaphor to have a truth value, whereas the metaphor would be indeterminate if the comparison is false.

There are of course situations in which presuppositions of a given sentence are not satisfied by the context. The presupposed proposition in such cases may be said to be OBLIQUELY or INDIRECTLY ASSERTED together with the rest of the sentence. Similarly, in metaphorical sentences, the discourse referent may be introduced metaphorically such that it is characterized assertively by the specific predicates carrying the metaphorical transformation. The condition is, of course, that the discourse referent can be properly identified as the value of an individual concept by the following (con-)text.

8.3 In the account of the previous section the COUNTERFACTUAL character of metaphors did not yet come fully into picture, and therefore it is not fully satisfactory.

Let us take another example to illustrate this point. The metaphorical sentence *He is a bear* (as in the other examples it does not matter that the metaphor is rather trivial and even conventionalized) may be expanded as follows: *He is as strong as a bear.* The latter sentence is close in meaning to a sentence like:

30 *He is as strong as if he were a bear.*

Here the counterfactual is apparent in *as if* and in *were.* Now compare (30) with a normal counterfactual conditional like

31 *If he were a bear, he would be strong.*

In (31) the proposition *He is a bear* is false in the actual world, and no information is implied whether *He is strong* is true in w_o, although conversationally we normally infer that *He is strong* is (also) false in w_o. Sentence (31), when uttered, asserts however that *He is strong* is true in all those worlds where *He is a bear* is true. In fact his bear-hood entails his strength in those worlds. The alternative worlds in which *He is strong* is true are at least as similar as our own world with respect to the validity of the sentence *A bear is strong* in both.

In (30) the situation is inversed, so to speak. It is asserted (to be true) that he is strong and implied that he is not a bear. We therefore let *He is a bear* again be true in an alternative world; in all those worlds accessible from that alternative world, with the aid of *He is a bear*, it is true that *He is strong.* Now, the problem is that *He is a bear* is not true in w_o so that w_o does not seem accessible from w_i. One solution for this dilemma is to assume that, seen from the point of view of w_i, *He is a bear* is true in w_o, e.g., because *bear* is a predicate with a larger region in w_i. This, however, would require the construction, not only of alternative worlds, but also of ALTERNATIVE LANGUAGES, a task which might theoretically be interesting but of which the difficulties cannot be estimated at the moment. Intuitively, of course, the metaphorical use of predicates seems indeed an 'alternative' use of predicates, a use 'accessible' through the selection function, with the condition that part of the predicate-structure is kept constant. In order for the (partial) similarity to remain recognizable, we would need a SIMILARITY THRESHOLD, for which cognitive psychological research may provide empirical data.

Still, the explanation given is either too speculative at the moment or simply incorrect. Perhaps we should modify the account of the semantics of *as if* as follows: *p as if q* is true (in w_o) iff (i) *p* is true (in w_o) (ii) q is false in w_o (iii) q is true in most worlds in which *p* is true (in most worlds: $\sim(p \ \& \ \sim q)$). In fact, this is the semantic structure of an HYPOTHETICAL EXPLANATION. Take for example the following sentence:

32 *The streets are (so) wet, as if it has rained.*

The *as if* clause provides a possible explanation for the antecedent, because in most possible (physically) worlds it is the case that the streets are wet when it is raining. The converse of course does not hold: there may be other causes for the street to be wet, but the fact that in most situations the wetness of streets is caused by rain, is a sufficient reason to use an *as if* clause. Sentence (32), indeed, could even be used in cases where e.g., the firemen were the cause of the wet streets.

The very fact that other causes may be mentioned as explanation would be a satisfactory account of the possibility to give SEVERAL EQUIVALENT METAPHORS in order to assert the same fact. Indeed, in other cultures we might have *He is as strong as a horse/bison/ gorilla* .... If this approach is correct, a metaphorical sentence would be a shortened *as if* clause, of which the entailed consequent is deleted if it is a TYPICAL CONSEQUENCE. We will not here explore the further axiomatic properties of the *as if* connective/operator, although at first glance it would yield a satisfactory explanation of the modal character of metaphorical sentences like **Fa*.

REFERENCES

Åqvist, Lennart, (1973) 'Modal Logic with Substantive Conditionals and Dispositional Predicates', *Journal of Philosophical Logic* 2, 1–76.

Drange, Theodore (1966) *Type Crossings: Sentential Meaninglessness in the Border Area of Linguistics and Philosophy* (The Hague: Mouton).

Goble, L. F. (1973) 'A Simplified Semantics for Modal Logic', *Notre Dame Journal of Formal Logic* 14, 151–74.

Grice, H. P. (1967) 'Logic and Conversation', unpublished lectures (Berkeley, mimeo).

Kripke, Saul A. (1972) 'Naming and Necessity', in D. Davidson and G. Harman (eds) *Semantics of Natural Language* (Dordrecht: Reidel), 253–355.

Lewis, David, (1973) *Counterfactuals* (Oxford: Blackwell).

Mack, Dorothy (1975) 'Metaphoring as Speech Act:Some Happiness Conditions for Implicit Similes and Simple Metaphors', *Poetics* 4 221–56.

Routley, R., and V. Routley. (1969) 'Categories—Expressions or Things?', *Theoria* 35, pp. 215–38.

Scott, Dana (1970) 'Advice on Modal Logic', in: Karel Lambert (ed.),

Philosophical Problems in Logic (Dordrecht: Reidel), pp. 143–174.
Sommers, Fred (1963) 'Types and Ontology', *Philosophical Review*
    LXXII: 3, pp. 327–63.
Stalnaker, Robert C., and Richmond H. Thomason (1970) 'A Semantic
    Analysis of Conditional Logic', *Theoria* 36, pp. 23–42.
Thom, Rene (1972) *Stabilite structurelle et morphogenese* (Reading,
    Mass.: Benjamin).
Thomason, Richmond H. (1972) 'A Semantic Theory of Sortal In-
    correctness', *Journal of Philosophical Logic* 1, 209–58.
Van Fraassen, Bas C. (1967) 'Meaning Relations among Predicates',
    Nous 1, 161–79.
Van Fraassen, Bas C. (1969) 'Meaning Relations and Modalities', *Nous*
    3, 155–67.
Van Fraassen, Bas C. (1971) *Formal Semantics and Logic* (New York;
    Macmillan).

After this paper was written two books appeared which are highly
relevant to the topics treated in it: Leonard Goddard & Richard Routley,
The Logic of Significance and Context, Vol. I (New York: Wiley,
Halsted Press, 1973) and P. F. Strawson, *Subject and Predicate in
Logic and Grammar* (London: Methuen, 1974). Especially Goddard
and Routley's impressive book would have supplied a rigorous formal
basis for a sortal semantics.

Although much other work, especially linguistic and literary, has not
been mentioned in this paper because it has been mentioned by other
authors in this issue or because it is well-known to most readers of this
journal, I would like to mention another omission: in the discussion
on the conceptual structure of logical space I did not refer to the rich
recent research in cognitive psychology and artificial intelligence
(computer semantics), e.g. by Quillian, Schank, Anderson and Bower,
Kintsch, and others, where for example notions like 'semantic distance'
have been made explicit.

CHAPTER SIX

Concrete abstraction: the linguistic universe of metaphor

Michael C. Haley

[Pointing to the general provisions in language for the productivity and intelligibility of ordinary metaphor, Haley argues that generative grammar represents a powerful theoretical instrument for the study of poetic metaphor. In particular, such a grammar can isolate the underlying linguistic mechanism by which meaning is detached from literal, concrete reference and is then reconstituted as a novel, abstract configuration: Metaphor's violation of the constraints on literal discourse is what is responsible for the 'detachment,' and the semantic hierarchicalness of lexical subcategories is what is responsible for the 'reconstitution.'

He then proceeds to posit a broad topography of semantic categories as a hierarchy of predicative classes. The organizing medium of the hierarchy he calls 'psycho-lexical space,' a hybrid of 'perceptual space' and what van Dijk calls 'logical space.' Because perceptual space defines the field of literal concrete reference and because logical space defines the field of figurative semantic abstraction, Haley believes that his hierarchy can be used to map the systematic connection between concrete imagery and poetic abstraction. It is this connection, he maintains, which is responsible for the special performance conditions of figurative language in poetry as opposed to conversation—that is, poetic metaphor's condensation of linguistic history, its self-generating complexity, its subconscious contextual ease, and its world-transcending power.]

Long after the generative grammars have been replaced by other linguistic models, they will perhaps be remembered as the first systematic effort—at least in modern American linguistics—to account for the infinite creativity of human language. It seems natural, therefore, that generative grammar should lead linguists into the study of poetic metaphor, for this is possibly the most creative use to which human language can be put.

However, it seems equally natural, and on the same grounds, to raise objections to the study of poetic metaphor from the perspective of such a grammar. The most obvious objection is that the 'linguistic creativity' captured by generative grammar is only the sort of ordinary creativity we find common to men, not the sort of extraordinary creativity we find peculiar to poets. Chomsky (1957; 1965), for example, is interested in the universal linguistic competence that makes a potentially infinite number of sentences intelligible to the native speakers of a given language; that is, he is concerned with codifying the syntactic and semantic laws by which speakers and listeners generally agree that a sentence means what it says. But if we accept Robert Frost's (1966, p. 385) definition of poetry as 'the art of saying one thing and meaning another,' then we must face the fundamental question of whether or not a grammar constructed to illuminate the semantic laws of ordinary meaning can shed any light on the semantic laws of poetic meaning.

Even if we grant the specious assumption that a poetic metaphor does not, at any level, really 'mean what it says,' there is still good reason for answering the above question with a confident, 'Yes, the analysis of ordinary language is not only relevant but crucial to the study of poetic language.' This reason arises from the increasing evidence for the essential 'metaphoricity' or 'poeticalness' of ordinary language.

Consider the semantic evolution of the word *scruple* as a case in point. The original meaning of *scruple*'s ancestor was something like 'a small sharp stone, of the sort that gets in your shoe and worries you.' Over the centuries, the primary meaning of the word in American English has come to be 'a reluctance on the grounds of conscience.' Note that this evolution in meaning is no mere random change or drift; on the contrary, it strikes us as a rather teleological change, for it has a certain wit about it. The wit emerges when we realize that the 'small sharp stone' in the shoe is really a *metaphor* for 'moral reluctance'; and despite the fact that the colorfully quaint origin of *scruple* has dropped out of common knowledge, once we are reminded of it, we take conscious pleasure in finding the little worrisome pebble still there—for a 'scruple' is not an overwhelming moral principle that occupies a central position in our ethical system; it is simply a small point of conscience that we seldom think about until it turns up under foot to make us hesitate or to pang us if we tread upon it. Indeed, the metaphorizing of *scruple* is an instance of the sheer 'poetry' of ordinary language.

Scruple, along with the innumerable examples like it, is not offered here as evidence for the false notion that language, or even that metaphor, is all there is to poetry. Rather, it is only offered to suggest that the linguistic machinery underlying the productivity and intelligibility of poetic metaphor is implicit within the machinery of ordinary language. Thus grammars of ordinary discourse are not to be excluded from the study of poetical discourse on the grounds that poetic metaphor involves some peculiar kind of linguistic competence; for only the performance conditions of the two types of discourse may be shown to differ.

To be sure, these performance conditions which make the language of poetry distinctly different from that of ordinary discourse are vitally interesting. One difference seems to involve a contrast in the amount of time required for the metaphorical transference to be made complete, natural and convincing. That is, the poets among us are those who are able to achieve, in an instant of time, the sort of metaphorical conceptual leap which might take centuries for the ordinary process of semantic evolution to effect. *Scruple*, the reader will note, underwent no such conceptual leap; its evolution was very gradual, and it took centuries for those of us who are not poets to be convinced of it. Conversely, poetic metaphor leaps over those centuries, transcending time, accelerating the process by which word meaning—along with the world view delineated by word meaning—is convincingly made and remade. The 'ontogeny of meaning' we see in poetic metaphor recapitulates some vital stages in the 'phylogeny of language,' we might say.

This time differential gives rise to other interesting distinctions between poetic metaphor and the metaphorical provisions of ordinary language. But these distinctions, too, are matters of literary performance, not linguistic competence. For one thing, poetic metaphor seems to satisfy certain happiness or appropriateness conditions that ordinary metaphor often seems to violate. Subconscious contextual ease is one condition; that is, poets have a knack for making their metaphors fit the subliminal and mythological context of the lyrical situation. Complexity and novelty are other conditions, for poets create radically fresh, unpredictable tropes, each of which seems to produce a second, third, and fourth buried inside the first. Closely related to this self-generating complexity of poetic metaphor is its ability to create abstract correspondences between referents without the loss of their concrete senses. (Again, contrast *scruple*'s evolution, in which the abstraction of meaning is achieved almost totally at the expense of concretion.) It is this latter feature of poetic metaphor which, more than any other, seems to make it a creative, not merely an expressive, linguistic mechanism.

On the other hand, the language of non-poets ordinarily employs metaphor only to express meanings for which there happens to be no handy word, not to create novel configurations of meaning. For example, when a child identifies the oozing of sap from an injured plant as 'bleeding,' when a schizophrenic characterizes an anti-depressive medication as 'laughing,' when a New Guinea tribesman refers to cowardliness as the quality of having 'bones allsame water,' or when a nuclear physicist calls a magnetic subatomic particle a 'charm,' the power of metaphor is being invoked. But in each instance, it is the expressive power, not the creative power, of metaphor that we apprehend. To

get examples of truly creative metaphor, we shall have to turn to poems
like Shakespeare's 'That Time of Year,' where the metaphor of fall is
not simply a mechanism for naming the intangibles of old age, but a
mechanism by which we come to see both the seasons and the human
life cycle in an entirely new way and to discover the sense of order
that unites man and cosmos. Thus, whereas the rest of us use metaphor
merely to express how we view the shape of the world, poets use metaphor to rethink and to reshape the world view.

Furthermore, poets use metaphor to these creative purposes in
language schemes of such intuitive accessibility that the rest of us
can somehow participate in the imaginative constructions they place
upon the world. That is surely one of the most amazing things about
poetry: that I, who am no poet, can nevertheless see something of what
a poet sees through his poem. There could be no more relevant explanation of this than to note that I possess what the child, the schizophrenic,
the tribesman, and the physicist in the moment of discovery all must
share—the language of metaphor, that linguistic ability to conceive of
the 'unknown' as a novel reconstruction of the 'known.'

And it is because I possess this competence as an ordinary reader
that generative grammar is of unique value to the study of poetry.
For it can provide some primary insights to the general semantic
laws of metaphor, which are an important part of the ground rules
for the poet's rendezvous with the non-poet. Further, in isolating
these ground rules, generative grammar affords us an opportunity
to examine how poets manipulate or extend ordinary linguistic
competencies in order to effect the sort of extraordinary performance
conditions we have just been talking about: namely, the radical condensation of linguistic time, the subconscious contextual ease, the
self-generating complexity, and the 'world-reshaping' power associated
with the creative tension between concrete and abstract in poetic
metaphor.

In this paper, then, I would like to examine one part of the general
semantic system underlying metaphor and to demonstrate how this
system is rather specifically manipulated in poetry to produce the
special effects noted above.

First, let us look at the nature of the general semantic system of
metaphor. In particular, I am interested in the provisions of this system
by which the meaning of a word sign may be detached from its concrete referent and then reconstituted as an abstract configuration of
meaning. Without saying so, we have already seen this principle at work
with *scruple*, whose meaning 'grew' because it was 'detached' from its
'concrete referent' (the sharp little stone) and because it was then
'reconstituted' as an 'abstract configuration' (a point of conscience).
The provisions in human language by which this takes place broadly
distinguish the formation of human symbols from the animal use of

signs; but more narrowly, these provisions are precisely what make metaphor possible.

Let us use a very simple, ordinary sort of metaphor in order to examine this principle in more detail. I take the sentence

1 *every rock speaks volumes*

to be a figurative proposition, first of all, because it transcends some constraints on literal discourse, but secondly, because it does so without disrupting a possible interpretation. Specifically, it transcends these literal constraints in such a way as to provoke a figurative interpretation.

Now it is this 'transcendence' of the constraints on literal discourse which I take to be responsible for the initial 'detachment' of meaning from the 'concrete reference' of metaphor. Let us suppose that the concrete reference of *speaks* in sentence (1) is something of this sort:

to speak: to effect, or to behave as if to effect, *symbolic communication* peculiar to *human agency*, through the medium of *articulated vocal production*.

Note that this ordinary definition, viewed in the particular grammatical construction of (1), is *literally* incompatible with the concrete reference of *rock*, which is a 'non-human' agent. The sentence therefore 'violates,' or transcends, the constraint on literal discourse that requires human verbs to be used with human subjects. That is, the non-human features of *rock* clash with the human features of *speaks*, causing these features to be dislodged or 'detached' from their respective signs.

But this detachment, in turn, results in a 'reconstitution of meaning' as an 'abstract configuration,' for after the uniquely human features of *speaks* have been subtracted, what remains can indeed be predicated abstractly of a rock:

to speak: to effect, or to behave as if to effect, *symbolic communication*
$$\emptyset \quad \emptyset$$

In this way, the metaphor forces us to think of speech more abstractly than we normally do, as a 'passive' sort of communication by a symbol, requiring no voice, no agency, at least no human agency. Similarly, the metaphor requires us to think of *rock* more imaginatively than we normally do, for the detached human features of *speaks* have now been transferred to *rock*, creating a slight personification that sends us off in search of what rocks might be able to tell us. (Note that the verb *tell* has undergone a rather permanent 'abstraction' through the detachment of human agency.) This kind of detachment, as it is governed by syntactic relationships, can be formalized and made predictable under principles like the 'erasure and replacement of antonymous markers' discussed by Marvin Ching (1975); the subsequent transference of these markers has also been shown to be grammatically predictable by Owen Thomas (1969).

However, the provisions of the language for this process are not restricted merely to the syntactic operations of particular grammatical constructions; there are independently semantic provisions, as well, and it is one of these which the present paper focuses upon. Specifically, I am interested in the semantic *hierarchicalness* of human language which makes the process cognitively systematic.

Note that the abstraction of word meaning effected by metaphor is indeed highly systematic, regardless of the syntactic situation. Somehow speakers of English who read sentence (1) know, not only to subtract the feature 'human' from *speaks*, but to subtract the features of 'articulated vocal production' as well, and to leave the features of 'symbolic communication' intact. How do we know to detach and disregard some features of meaning from a word used metaphorically but at the same time to leave others of its features alone?

The answer is obvious if we examine the *levels of generality* that hold between the features of *speak* in our example. These levels might be represented by the following hierarchy:

COMMUNICATION

SYMBOLIC communication

HUMAN symbolic communication

VOCAL human symbolic communication

ARTICULATE vocal human symbolic communication

How do we know to subtract which features? If we recall that it is precisely the feature 'HUMAN' which is initially detached from *speaks* by its subject/verb juxtaposition with *rock*, then the answer is clear: The detachment of 'HUMAN' requires the detachment of 'ARTICULATE' and 'VOCAL' as well, since these features are subsumed under 'HUMAN' (in the hierarchy) and must logically stand or fall with it. But the elements of 'SYMBOLIC' and 'COMMUNICATION' are *not* affected by the detachment of 'HUMAN' since they are not subsumed under it and are therefore independent of it. The removal of the human link from this hierarchical chain thus removes everything that hangs upon that link and leaves only a remnant of the notion, 'speak':

COMMUNICATION
/
SYMBOLIC communication
/
∅

While this fragmented chain is only a remnant of meaning, it is a very powerful meaning, for it constitutes the exact abstract level at which the concrete absurdity of a talking rock becomes, not only intelligible, but believable.

By no means do all metaphors involve the simple subtraction or detachment of semantic features. Sometimes the process is a simple addition, or even a complex fission or fusion of features (Haley, 1975). But in all instances, the predictable alterations of meaning which we observe in figurative language would be unintelligible without some system of semantic generalization to unify the diverse particulars of metaphor's characteristically incompatible referents. A 'non-literal statement' is only an anomaly unless it refers us to some discoverable linguistic principle by which Aristotle's well-known dictum can be satisfied: 'A good metaphor implies the intuitive perception of the similarity in dissimilars.' It seems to me that the hierarchical nature of semantic features, as conceived by generative grammar in a system of lexical subcategorization, captures just such a discoverable principle. For the most dissimilar of all concrete referents are, at some higher level of semantic abstraction, found to be similar; a semantic hierarchy as a system of 'types' or 'sorts' embodies this condition accurately.

Of course, no single, universal 'lexical hierarchy' is known to exist, and all efforts to construct one have failed. Apparently, human beings have the unconscious ability to construct, dismantle, and reconstruct semantic hierarchies to fit the necessities of the task (Miller, 1956). But there is a startling unanimity among speakers of English regarding the relevant classes of semantic abstraction for particular lexical tasks (Anglin, 1970).

Furthermore, even the great variety of possible hierarchies, while *ad hoc* in nature, seems to consist of variations around a common theme. Certain lexical subcategories are ubiquitous in almost every connection —the human, animate, concrete, and abstract subcategories, for example—suggesting that the semantic hierarchies of English may differ in the fine details of their divisions more than they differ in the gross outlines of their classifications.

In the final part of this paper, then, I will present the gross outline for one hypothetical classificatory scheme which seems to exhibit a strong psycholinguistic reality for ordinary speakers of modern English in a variety of semantic tasks (Haley, 1975). Because the outline of this modern scheme nevertheless resembles the ontological hierarchy of a rather ancient extralinguistic world view, I believe it is especially relevant to the task of analyzing poetic metaphor which, as we have already seen, is distinguished by its power to transcend time and grapple with the shape of the world. And because the organizing medium of the hierarchy I will present is what I will call 'psycho-lexical space' (a close analogue to perceptual space), I believe that it is uniquely suited to give an account of the connection between the concrete reference of poetic imagery and the semantic abstraction of poetic metaphor. The broad, general scope of this scheme is intended to accommodate the vast ranges over which I believe poetic metaphor typically holds the concrete and the abstract in tension and in unity. As I have said, and as I will attempt to illustrate with a passage from Keats, it is this special connection between the concrete and the abstract in poetic metaphor which yields its radical condensation of linguistic history, its subconscious contextual ease, its self-generating complexity, and its 'world-reshaping' power.

I begin by positing the set of predicative categories with which my model hierarchy attempts to deal in Figure 6.1:

Noun Examples	Category	Predicate Examples
truth, beauty	BEING	to be, to seem
space, a point	POSITION	to be here, be there
light, force	MOTION	to move, to cross
hydrogen, anti-matter	INERTIA	to push, to pull
water, dust	GRAVITATION	to fall, to rise
rock, ball	SHAPE	to break, to strike
tree, flower	LIFE	to grow, to die
horse, fish	ANIMATION	to run, to swim
man, woman	INTELLECTION	to think, to speak

Figure 6.1

Because of its generality, there is no reason to believe that this list is exhaustive. But I offer two arguments for the intuitive importance of these categories for the study of poetic metaphor:

a   The list suggests a systematic hierarchy among the categories. Such a hierarchy is essential for any model which attempts to deal with poetic abstraction.

b   The categories also address themselves to some important perceptual types of concrete reference. Any truly adequate model of poetic abstraction must offer some account of the more salient sensory dimensions of poetic imagery.

By saying that this list of predicates implies a hierarchy, I mean that each category is conceived to be a subcategory of the class immediately above it in the list, as well as all categories above that class, of course. That is, INTELLECTION predicates are a subclass of ANIMATION predicates; ANIMATION, in turn, is a subclass of LIFE, etc. Such hierarchical relations among these lexical subcategories are well known in semantics.

However, if we move to the top categories on the chart, we begin to see some parallel hierarchical relations that have seldom been attended to in linguistics. Nouns matched as subjects for the MOTION predicates, for example, may also be predicated to have POSITION and BEING, but not vice versa. Not everything which can literally be predicated to have being can also literally be predicated to have position or motion. For example, I may be understood or disagreed with literally if I say, 'Truth exists,' but only figuratively if I say, 'Truth is here on top of the desk,' since abstractions like truth cannot occupy a literal position in space. To take another example, not everything which can be literally predicated to have MOTION can also be literally predicated to have INERTIA. I may be understood literally if I say, 'Light *moves* at 186,000 miles per second,' but only in a figurative sense if I say, 'Light *pushes* out the darkness,' because only things which are predicated to have mass in the ordinary sense of the word can push or pull (like pistons or elephants). Thus INERTIA predicates are a subclass of MOTION predicates, just as MOTION is a subclass of POSITION and POSITION a subclass of BEING. At the risk of resurrecting Aristotle yet a second time, I am attempting to suggest that these categories are systematically hierarchical.

But their features are not merely hierarchical. They also speak to a number of important perceptual or sensory concerns which define the ranges of concrete reference—shape, gravitational direction, mass, motion, position. The single most important way these categories address concrete sensory experience by reference is that they are organized in a medium of 'psycho-lexical space,' a close analogue to the perceptual dimension.

What is meant by this? It is a curious fact that most of the subjects who have served in psycholinguistic experiments with this model tend to think of abstract ideas as somehow 'spatially remote' from their own point of view, perhaps because of the abiding influence of Platonic thought in our culture. I must hope the reader will take my word for this upon a moment's introspection: Why, in the slang of our day, do we often call philosophers or dreamers 'spacy' 'way out' 'far out' or 'in orbit'? Why should we so often speak of abstruse theories as 'beyond' our understanding? Is it not because of the persistent metaphorical habit of Western thought, built right into our language, of representing the concrete and particular as 'down to earth' but the abstract and universal as 'lofty' or 'distant'?

The hierarchy I am positing accounts for this 'spatial' habit of mind. In his 'Formal Semantics of Metaphorical Discourse,' Teun A. van Dijk calls for a topography of semantic categories which 'assigns to each predicate of the language a region of logical space' (1975, p. 180). By 'logical space' he means the notion of 'semantic distance' which exists between the semantic categories by reason of their hierarchical structure' (p. 186). If we follow his advice and represent this hierarchy such that 'each predicate is surrounded by sets of concentric circles' (p. 191), we may see exactly how such a model can define the relations between categories as a function of logical space. This logical space then becomes the organizing medium for pure semantic abstraction. See Figure 6.2.

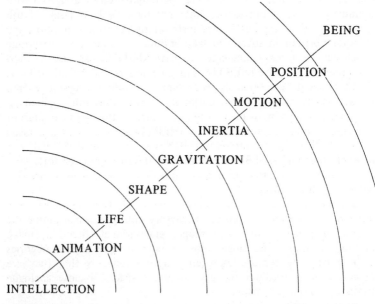

Figure 6.2

But it should also be clear how this model incorporates a kind of perceptual space, which serves as the reference field for concrete imagery. This is true because human experience (INTELLECTION) is here presented in a central position (from which, as it were, we 'view' the universe), whereas abstract experience (BEING) is presented in a perimetrical position, 'beyond' the universe and encompassing all. Between these two extremes we have a middle category labelled GRAVITATIONAL, since it divides the categories which are 'earth-bound' in our linguistic behavior from those which are not. On this account, the model bears an interesting resemblance to the old Ptolemaic astronomy, in which the earth, the realm of human life, was the center of a universe consisting of invisible spheres that were ruled by ascending degrees of divinity. If I am correct in saying that the higher levels of semantic abstraction in the language still occupy higher degrees of psycho-spatial expansiveness in our unconscious thought, perhaps I would be correct to suggest that the old geocentric theory, with its deep roots in the Western tradition, is not entirely outdated and quaint. After all, we all know that the earth orbits the sun, but we still *say* that it is the sun which comes up and goes down. It should not really surprise us to discover that our language still reflects that old egocentric point of view in ways which we have not previously suspected. Benjamin Lee Whorf has suggested that we unconsciously dissect the natural universe along lines laid down by our native languages (1956); I am suggesting that, in retrospect, we divide our most general categories for metaphor study along lines laid down by a world view dating back to the beginning of our literary tradition.

Let us turn to an illustration from that tradition, a selection from John Keats's *Endymion* (I, 453-6). Notice the complexity, the condensation, the world-transcending scope, and yet the ease and naturalness of the metaphor's displacement:

> O Magic sleep! O comfortable bird
> That broodest o'er the troubled sea of the mind
> Till it is hushed and smooth! O unconfined
> Restraint! imprisoned liberty!

I have chosen this passage because it exhibits both radical poetic abstraction and strong concrete imagery, but also because I believe the interplay between the abstraction and concretion is best understood in the context of a model like the one I am discussing.

Let us first take the metaphor apart. It is a rather complex one involving parallel 'comparisons' of sleep to a bird and the mind to a sea. Sleep broods over the mind in the same way a bird broods over the sea. But out of this dual analogy grows an even more complex one in which *sleep* is abstractly reconstituted as 'unconfined restraint.' Finally, Keats reverses the polarity of this paradox with the exceedingly abstract oxymoron of 'imprisoned liberty.' I have plotted this sequence of displacements in Figure 6.3.

Before I discuss what this displacement implies, the particular loca-

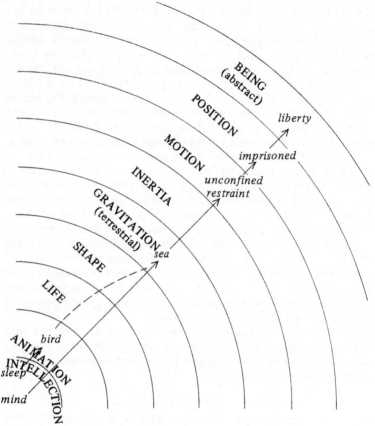

Figure 6.3

tions of the metaphor's words in Figure 6.3 requires explanation. First, it is important to remember that these categories represent *predicative* sorts: We locate nouns in a particular category on the basis of what may be literally predicated about them, and we classify all other parts of speech on the basis of the most distinctive literal feature of their predications. Thus, in Figure 6.3, *liberty* may only be classified with abstract BEING, since the only literal predication that may be made about it (if any at all) is that it exists; it cannot be literally predicated to exist in perceptual space (POSITION) or to possess the potential for MOTION or mass (INERTIA), etc. For this very reason, the expression *imprisoned liberty* is figurative, because the distinctive literal feature of the predicate *imprisoned* is precisely POSITION (assuming that *imprisoned* means 'to be limited to a certain space,' it cannot be predicated of an abstraction like *liberty*). This of course also explains why *imprisoned* is located in the sphere POSITION—it is literally a predicate of confinement in space.

But why, then, is *unconfined restraint* classified in the MOTION sphere instead of POSITION? For two reasons. First *unconfined*, especially in this connection, kinesthetically connotes motion. Second, the word *restraint* denotes force or energy, the distinctive feature of MOTION predicates. I am therefore classifying *restraint* as if it were a predicate on the grounds that it is derived nominal from the verb *restrain*. (Note that the same principle applies to the classification of *sleep*; viewed as a noun, it is abstract (BEING), not human (INTEL-LECTION), but semantically it is really only an ANIMATION verb— and in this context a human verb—used substantively as a noun; I have therefore classified *sleep* as if it were a verb of INTELLECTION.) While it may seem difficult to think of *restraint* as a type of MOTION, then, it is not difficult to think of it as a type of energy or to see that its underlying predicative structure designates a kind of motion (specifically, 'counter-motion'). It might be objected that *imprisoned* also designates 'counter-motion' in one sense; but I answer that *imprison-ment*, the analogous form to *restraint*, literally names a locational circumstance, not a kinetic activity as does *restraint*.

Happily, the placement of *sea* in Figure 6.3 is not so difficult to explain, for it is not so abstract. But it does illustrate another important principle of classification: The placement of a word in any given literal sphere of reference automatically *in*cludes that word within all higher, encompassing spheres, but *ex*cludes that word from all lower, more limited spheres, which are special subclasses. Any noun like *sea*, then, which we classify within the scope of predicates of (terrestrial) GRAVITATION, must not only be literally predicable of such verbs (e.g., *fall, rise, flow, drift*), but it must also be predicable of INERTIA verbs (like *push, pull, slam, crash*), because GRAVITATIONAL criteria are a subclass of INERTIAL criteria. On the other hand, *sea*—if properly located in the GRAVITATIONAL class—must NOT be literally predi-cable of SHAPE (like *shatter, crack, warp, explode*) or LIFE (*grow, die, flourish, wither*) or ANIMATION (*walk, run, sniff, snort*) or INTELLECTION (*read, speak, love, hate*), because these are all special, exclusive subclasses of GRAVITATIONAL (terrestrial) phenomena. In terms of what may and may not be literally predicated of *sea*, then, we see that its definition tells us it is correctly placed—for it is a member of that class of earth (GRAVITATION) substances (INERTIA) which can therefore move (MOTION), be located in perceptual space (POSITION) and thought to exist (BEING); but additionally, it is diffuse (no SHAPE), inorganic (no LIFE), unfeeling (no ANIMATION), and mindless (no INTELLECTION).

Of course, all of the things which cannot be literally predicated of *sea* by reason of its classification in the hierarchy rather nicely define the range of its figurative uses. For in Keats's metaphor, the sea is imaginatively endowed with all of these—shape, life, feeling, and mind. Let us return to the metaphor and notice how.

In Figure 6.3, note first that I have plotted the displacement of *sleep* to *bird*. This displacement initiates the 'tension' in the passage between concrete and abstract in two ways. First, it abstracts the concrete noun *bird* and concretizes the abstract noun *sleep*. But if we remember that *sleep* is really a verb used substantively as a noun, then we may see how *sleep* is actually made more abstract by its predication as a *bird*. The reason is that the context indicates the poet is concerned with his own experience of sleep (this is a very Keatsian type of sleep), with what human sleep is like. For this reason, *sleep* really seems to be working semantically as a predicate of INTELLECTION (in Keats, generally, sleep is a way of knowing). When *sleep* in this sense is predicated as *bird*, it is detached from its concrete or literal reference and reconstituted at a higher level in the hierarchy, because the subcategory to which *bird* belongs is at a higher level; that is, the displacement of *sleep* to *bird* moves it from its original, restricted sphere of INTELLECTION to a more generalized, all encompassing sphere of ANIMATION. Thus, at the same time Keats makes the abstract nominal of *sleep* more concrete through the predication *bird*, he makes it more abstract as well, for the semantic category of *bird* is more general and psycho-spatially remote than Keats's own peculiar, intellectual encounter with sleep.

Next, note that this bird is pictured brooding over a *sea* which, we are told, represents the human *mind*. This displacement reinforces the tension initiated by the first one: Lexically, *mind* is more abstract than *sea*, but contextually and semantically, the opposite is true. The mind in this passage is surely human mentality (INTELLECTION), so that when *mind* is predicated as *sea*, it is displaced to a more generalized category by reason of the broader scope of *sea*'s semantic class (terrestrial GRAVITATION) and by reason of the more 'vast' psycho-spatial sphere of this class. Thus the metaphor of *sea* and *bird* not only particularizes the intangibles of *mind* and *sleep*; it also serves to universalize them as well, by detaching them from the rigidly limited category of INTELLECTION and by moving them up the scale of BEING to the global sphere of terrestrial phenomena. Note that the movement toward this sphere produces a sense of both semantic and perceptual expansiveness; that is, the sensory experience of the mind during sleep is rather immediate, while that of a bird brooding over the sea is more remote, just as the semantic categories of *mind* and *sleep* are rather narrow, while those of *bird* and *sea* are more all-encompassing. When the narrow, immediate INTELLECTION (*mind, sleep*) is predicated as a broad, remote experience bounded only by earthly GRAVITATION (*bird, sea*), a kind of tension obtains and gives rise to the next part of the metaphorical sequence—*unconfined restraint*. In other words, the tension between concrete and abstract initiated by the first two tropes finds a rather natural culmination and expression in the kinetic paradox of *unconfined restraint.*

Further, it is the parallel semantic and perceptual (psycho-lexical) displacement of the metaphor's tenor up and out of its ordinary sphere of reference that makes the final oxymoron so climactic and 'world-reshaping.' That is, we build up to the ultimate abstract reconstitution of *sleep* as *imprisoned liberty* because the metaphor of *sleep→bird, mind→sea→unconfined restraint* leads us step-wise through the successively more abstract and expansive categories of INTELLECTION→ ANIMATION→GRAVITATION→MOTION→and (abstract) BEING.

But because we move *through* the mediating images of the bird and sea from the poet's mind toward pure abstraction, the abstraction is achieved without loss of concreteness. The universalized liberty in the final expression has been brought home by the particularity of a bird; the lack of confinement has arisen from the sea; and the quality of unlimited restraint has issued from the expanded prison of a poet's mind. To be in a prison that big, of course, is to be imprisoned by freedom. Keats has been turned loose, not so much by the freedom of sleep as by his own captivation with these perceptual images and by the figurative projection of his own mind into them. We may understand how this projection operates linguistically and capture something of that unleashed feeling for ourselves by reference to the chain of semantic categories to which those images belong; for these categories increase systematically—as the metaphor leads us through them—in their degree of semantic abstraction and in their parallel degree of spatial sublimity.

In a somewhat different way, Arthur Lovejoy spoke of the same phenomenon when he wrote in his classic work (1936, p. 139): 'The poet takes an imaginary voyage through space and at the same time conceives of this as an ascent of the Scale of Being.' My effort has been to show that a semantic scale, buried deeply in the nature of our language and ascending from INTELLECTION to pure BEING through the dimension of psycho-lexical space, still operates for us in metaphor. J. M. Murry once wrote (1968, p. 9), 'All metaphor . . . can be described as the analogy by which the human mind explores the universe of quality and charts the non-measurable world.' I suggest that metaphor can only chart the world through language, though it surely must require language in the hands of a poet to reshape the world. On all accounts, there would be no reshaping or charting of the world through poetic metaphor at all without the organizing power inherent in the hierarchical semantic structure of human language.

REFERENCES

Anglin, Jeremy (1970), *The Growth of Word Meaning* (Research Mono-
    graph No. 63) (Cambridge, Mass.: MIT Press).
Chomsky, Noam (1957), *Syntactic Structures* (The Hague: Mouton).
Chomsky, Noam (1965), *Aspects of the Theory of Syntax* (Cambridge,
    Mass.: MIT Press).
Dijk, Teun van (1975), 'Formal Semantics of Metaphorical Discourse',
    Poetics 4, pp. 173–98.
Frost, Robert (1966), 'Education by Poetry: A Meditative Monologue',
    in *The Play of Language*, ed. Dean, Gibson, Wilson (New York:
    Oxford University Press, 1971).
Haley, Michael (1975), 'Metaphor and the Linguistics of Space: A
    Psycholinguistic Model of Figurative Language', unpublished doc-
    toral dissertation, Florida State University.
Keats, John, *Endymion*, reprinted in *English Romantic Poetry and
    Prose*, ed. Russell Noyes (New York: Oxford University Press, 1956).
Lovejoy, Arthur (1936), *The Great Chain of Being* (Cambridge, Mass.:
    Harvard University Press).
Miller, G. A. (1956), 'The Magical Number Seven Plus or Minus Two:
    Some Limits on Our Capacity for Processing Information', *Psycho-
    logical Review 63*, pp. 81–96.
Murry, J. M. (1968), *Countries of the Mind* (Freeport, N. Y.: Books for
    Libraries Press).
Thomas, Owen (1969), *Metaphor and Related Subjects* (New York:
    Random House).
Whorf, Benjamin (1956), *Language, Thought, and Reality* (Cambridge,
    Mass.: MIT Press).

CHAPTER SEVEN

Byron's spatial metaphor:
a psycholinguistic approach

Ronald F. Lunsford

[Lunsford uses a psycholinguistic method, developed by Michael C. Haley in 'Concrete Abstraction: The Linguistic Universe of Metaphor,' to examine the imagery in Byron's *Childe Harold's Pilgrimage*, Canto III, and Shelley's 'Ode to the West Wind.' Mr Haley's method builds on the transformational approach to metaphor which views it as the product of co-occurrence violations, adding to the transformational method features which indicate the psychological space of a word's referent in relation to the individual using that word. This analysis— together with I. A. Richards's terms, 'tenor' and 'vehicle'—allows one to see the spatial distance in metaphor. For example, Mr Haley's method would show the referent of the vehicle 'lion' in sentence 1 to be psychologically closer to the tenor 'John' than the vehicle 'rock' in sentence 2.

1 John is a lion.
2 John is a rock.

In using this method, Lunsford finds that Byron and Shelley make use of similar types of metaphor: The imagery in both of the analyzed poems moves non-Human things toward the Human and humans toward the non-Human. But he also finds significant differences. Byron's metaphor continually projects the poet as far away from the Human as possible while Shelley's metaphor has the effect of displacing the poet from the Human to 'things' that are relatively close to the Human.

Lunsford then brings this analysis to bear on the question of whether Byron was imitating Shelley. He finds that whatever Byron's original intentions in writing *Childe Harold*, Canto III, his language itself militates against any charge of plagiarism.]

Literary critics from Aristotle on, recognizing that metaphor is one of the essential ingredients of poetry, have sought methods to investigate its crucial role. But until recently, these investigations have not proceeded on the assumption that metaphor is a linguistic process which can be investigated by linguistic methods. Only in recent years has linguistic theory (i.e. transformational theory) provided the tools which make it possible to investigate the linguistic foundations of metaphor.

A most important tool, I. A. Richards's concept of 'tenor' and 'vehicle,'[1] is not the product of transformational theory, but the transformational theory combines nicely with Richards's terminologies to explain the effect of metaphor. As Owen Thomas demonstrates in his *Metaphor And Related Subjects*,[2] the 'turn in meaning' in metaphor is the result of selection restriction violations between the tenor and the vehicle of a metaphor. In Thomas's example

His grandfather is a child when it comes to money.

(p. 21)

there is a violation in linguistic features between the two words 'child' and 'grandfather.' His feature analysis of 'child' follows:

'child'

$$
\begin{bmatrix}
+ \text{ noun} \\
+ \text{ common} \\
+ \text{ countable} \\
+ \text{ animal} \\
+ \text{ human}
\end{bmatrix}
$$

$$
+ \begin{Bmatrix} \text{infant} \\ \text{unborn offspring} \end{Bmatrix}
$$

$$
+ \begin{Bmatrix} \text{boy} \\ \text{girl} \end{Bmatrix}
$$

$$
+ \quad \text{time before puberty}
$$

$$
+ \begin{Bmatrix} \text{son} \\ \text{daughter} \end{Bmatrix}
$$

$$
+ \quad \text{descendant}
$$

(p. 21)

Of course the word 'grandfather' shares some of the features with 'child'—for example, + noun, + human—but since there is at least one feature that the two words cannot share, there is a selectional violation, a 'turn in meaning' of a word—in this case 'child'—and hence, the creation of a metaphor.

Such an analysis is an important first step in accounting for the meaning of metaphor; but it is just a first step, for, as literary critics are well aware, a complete treatment of metaphor must include the patterns developed by multiple metaphors. The layman recognizes these patterns intuitively. If one speaks of grandfather as a 'child' in regards to his money and goes on to call him a 'pack rat,' a pattern develops that will allow an interpretation: roughly, grandfather is very childish with his money, hoarding it all to himself, with little regard to others. However, if the first metaphor is followed by another such as—Grandfather is a 'lamb'—there is an entirely different interpretation: grandfather is very child-like, free with his money, with little regard to himself.

The selection restriction analysis of metaphor reveals graphically the patterns that literary critics have been intuiting. For example, it represents the literary critic's discovery that a certain work's images pattern around disease by marking the vehicles of the metaphors, + disease. If the only use of this linguistic analysis were to represent formally what the literary critic had already discovered intuitively, however, the analysis would be of little value. But, it can do much more: it can facilitate real discoveries about the nature of reality and language by providing insight into how language is a reflection of an individual's reality.

This point is sufficiently important to warrant further explanation, and some examples. If the features for the word 'child' given in the transformational analysis—as represented by Thomas's features—were the only information linguistic analysis could provide, one could argue that it contributed little. When the individual thinks of the word 'child,' he may not be conscious of the feature, + descendant, but when this feature is brought to his attention, he immediately recognizes it as a property of the word's meaning. Thus, the analysis has not told him anything he did not already know. But psycholinguistic experiments, first performed by the author and Michael C. Haley,[3] indicate that in addition to all the features listed in the transformational analysis, there are other psychological features, features that do reveal information that is new in the sense that it is so much a part of the culture of the individual as to be unnoticeable.

One such experiment involved giving subjects a number of triads (groups of three words) such as 'child,' 'flower,' and 'rock' and asking them to group together the two words that were most alike. The subjects grouped 'flower' and 'rock' together, and, in a space provided for comments, many responded that flower and rock were 'out there.' There is nothing in the transformational feature analysis that would predict this grouping; in fact, it might be interpreted to predict that 'child' and 'flower' would be grouped together because both are + living while 'rock' is – living.

This psycholinguistic research suggests, then, that individuals categorize the words in their lexicons by a system of criteria much more complex than the transformational feature analysis would indicate. It also suggests that much of what individuals know about the words in their language is entirely below the level of consciousness. (When subjects were shown that they were categorizing words according to physical proximity to them, they were surprised.) Finally, it suggests that while many patterns of metaphor are susceptible to intuitive criticism, that many are not, and that a psycholinguistic examination of the properties of words may provide new insights into metaphor.

This study is an attempt to sketch what one such model, a model developed by Michael C. Haley and outlined in the previous chapter 'Concrete abstraction: the linguistic universe of metaphor' can offer to the study of Romantic imagery, specifically the imagery in Byron's *Childe Harold's Pilgrimage*, Canto III, and Shelley's 'Ode to the West Wind.' Before examining the poetry, we will need to sketch Mr Haley's psycholinguistic framework.

Mr Haley proposes a linguistic model which can account for the connection between psychological space and a speaker's knowledge about how a word may be used. He postulates that individuals categorize words in their lexicons according to a physical (or in the case of an abstract term, the lack of a physical) relationship between the individual and the referent of that word, that despite the apparent demise of the Ptolemaic world view, man still thinks of himself as the center of the universe and categorizes the elements in his universe accordingly.

Mr Haley represents this categorization by means of a selectional restriction feature analysis. In addition to all the other information an individual uses in processing a word is information which places that word's physical relation to the individual. Unlike semantic markers which are bi-valued (+ or –) this information consists of many—at this point Mr Haley posits nine—categories into which an individual can place a word; or, in other words, an individual can assign one of nine category features to a word. (See Table 7.1 for a list of these categories.)

This categorization determines co-occurrence possibilities—thus it is necessary to categorize predicates as well as nouns. A noun and a predicate may co-occur, in a literal statement, if they belong to the same category. However, a noun and a predicate which can co-occur in a literal statement do not necessarily belong to the same category because the categories are hierarchically arranged. As is demonstrated graphically by the concentric circles in Figure 7.1, a category includes

Table 7.1

Category	Noun		Predicate	
	type	*example*	*type*	*example*
BEING	Abstractions	truth	Being	exist
COSMIC	Spatialities	space	Position	be here
ENERGETIC	Energies	light	Motion	cross
SUBSTANTIAL	Substances	hydrogen	Inertia	push
TERRESTRIAL	Earth-bound substances	water	Gravity[4]	fall
OBJECTIVE	Objects	glass	Shape	break
LIVING	Flora	plant	Life	grow
ANIMATE	Fauna	horse	Animation	run
HUMAN	Humans	man	Intellection	think

all categories less specific than it; for example, HUMAN implies ANIMATE, LIVING, etc., but BEING implies nothing else.

The co-occurrence possibilities of nouns and predicates are illustrated in the following sentences.

		Noun Category	Predicate Category	Literal Reading
1(a)	Truth exists.	BEING	BEING	Yes
(b)	The truth broke in on him.	BEING	SHAPE	No
2(a)	The man exists.	HUMAN	BEING	Yes
(b)	The man was broken.	HUMAN	SHAPE	Yes
(c)	The man thought about it.	HUMAN	INTELLECTION	Yes

These sentences illustrate the fact that only BEING predicates may be paired, non-metaphorically, with 'truth,' a BEING noun. Sentence 1b is metaphoric. On the other hand, any predicate may be paired, non-metaphorically, with man (HUMAN). The operative word here is *may*; for if the reader objects that 2b *may* be metaphorical, he should take note that it *may* be literal as in the case of a piece of heavy machinery running over the man. Under no circumstance *may* 1b be interpreted literally.

A noun is labelled according to the most specific category of predicates that it can literally pair with. In calling a category 'specific,' one denotes that it contains items which the individual possesses specific information about; and, of course, the individual knows more about those things which are close to the realm of the human. For example, the individual can know only that the referents of BEING nouns 'exist.' The individual knows not only that 'space' (COSMIC) exists, but also that it is 'out there;' and he knows that 'lightning' (ENERGETIC) exists, that it has a space and that it 'moves.'

These categories provide a new vantage point for examining the perennial question of how sincere and original Byron's *Childe Harold*, Canto III is. While he acknowledges that Wordsworth's poetry influenced him (indirectly, through Shelley), Byron denies Wordsworth's charge of plagiarism.[5] If Byron is not plagiarizing, does Canto III recount a real transcendent experience like those recounted by Wordsworth's *Prelude* and Shelley's 'Ode to the West Wind'? A comparison of Byron's metaphor in Canto III with Shelley's metaphor in 'Ode to

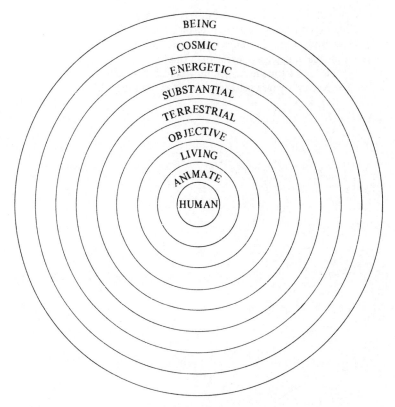

Figure 7.1

the West Wind' reveals differences which suggest that Byron is not merely mimicking Shelley.

In *Childe Harold*, Canto III, Byron undertakes what would seem to be the same quest that Shelley undertakes in 'Ode to the West Wind': the attempt to effect a union of the poet and Nature. And the patterns of the metaphors in the poems are similar. Both poets use their metaphorical language to humanize Nature (i.e., draw elements of Nature in toward the HUMAN) and to de-humanize the poet (i.e., thrust the poet out into Nature).

An example of the first pattern of movement occurs in stanza XIII of Canto III.

> Where rose the mountains, there to him were friends;
> Where roll'd the ocean, thereon was his home;
> Where a blue sky, and glowing clime, extends,

He had the passion and the power to roam;
The desert, forest, cavern, breaker's foam,
Were unto him companionship; they spake
A mutual language, clearer than the tome
Of his land's tongue, which he would oft forsake
For Nature's pages glass'd by sunbeams on the lake.

XIII

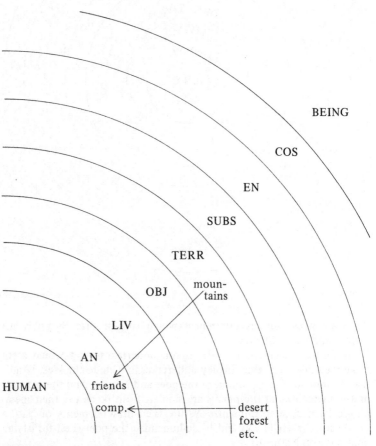

Figure 7.2

Figure 7.2, a 'metaphor map' based on Figure 7.1, charts the movement of these metaphors. Line one of this stanza contains a simple metaphor, 'the mountains were friends.' Thomas's analysis would account for this metaphor by assigning to 'mountains' the feature

- living and to 'friends,' the feature + living. Mr Haley's psycholinguistic model accounts for the metaphor in a similar manner by assigning TERRESTRIAL to the word 'mountain' and ANIMATE to the word 'friends'; in doing so, however, it pictures the movement effected by the metaphor in a way that Thomas's analysis does not. The pairing of 'mountain' with 'friends' has the effect of bringing close to the HUMAN (i.e. to an adjacent category) an element of Nature, 'mountain,' that is quite removed from the HUMAN (four categories, as shown in Figure 7.2).

Another example of the movement from non-Human to Human occurs in lines five and six, the metaphorical statement being 'the desert, forest, cavern, breaker's foam,/Were companionship . . .' Again, the subject nouns belong to the category TERRESTRIAL and the predicate 'be companionship to' is ANIMATE.[6] In calling the 'desert,' 'forest,' etc. 'companionship,' Byron is once again drawing the non-Human in toward the category HUMAN.

The second type of movement, the projecting of the self into the non-Human, is illustrated in the following lines:

> I live not in myself, but I become
> Portion of that around me; and to me
> High mountains are a feeling, but the hum
> Of Human cities torture: I can see
> Nothing to loathe in nature, save to be
> A link reluctant in a fleshly chain,
> Class'd among creatures, when the soul can flee,
> And with the sky, the peak, the heaving plain
> Of ocean, or the stars, mingle, and not in vain.
>
> LXXII

Near the end of this stanza, the poet wishes his soul, an attribute of Humans[7] and thus HUMAN, to be projected out into the 'sky,' the 'peak,' and to 'mingle' with the 'ocean' and 'stars.' The movement is from HUMAN to TERRESTRIAL ('sky,' 'peak,' 'ocean') to SUBSTANTIAL ('stars'). (See note 4 for a discussion of the categorization of 'stars.')

The same two patterns of metaphor movement are present in Shelley's 'Ode to the West Wind.' Shelley's poet draws Nature in toward the HUMAN in the first line of the poem: 'O Wild West Wind, thou breath of Autumn's being.' Since breathing is a distinctive characteristic of the category ANIMATE, the wind (TERRESTRIAL) is brought to the ANIMATE. Then, in stanza IV Shelley projects the poet into the non-Human, specifically, the OBJECTIVE ('leaf') and the TERRESTRIAL ('cloud,' 'wave').

> If I were a dead leaf thou mightest bear;
> If I were a swift cloud to fly with thee;
> A wave to pant beneath thy power . . .
>
> IV ll. 43-5

This brief comparison reveals similarities between the metaphor in the two poems, similarities that the intuitive critic can recognize without the aid of any formal linguistic method. However, the method developed in this essay reveals significant differences which are not so apparent as the similarities.

Byron's metaphor in Canto III is an attempt to attain a transcendent experience by getting as far away from the HUMAN as possible. Rousseau is Byron's model for this experience:

> His love was passion's essence—as a tree
> On fire by lightning; with ethereal flame
> Kindled he was, and blasted; for to be
> Thus, and enamour'd, were in him the same.
> But his was not the love of living dame,
> Nor of the dead who rise upon our dreams,
> But of ideal beauty, which became
> In him existence, and o'erflowing teems
> Along his burning page, distemper'd though it seems.
>
> LXXVIII

Rousseau moves from the HUMAN to the LIVING ('tree') to the ENERGETIC ('fire,' 'lightning') and, finally, disappears into BEING: 'his love was ideal Beauty.'

Shelley's ode contains a different pattern of metaphor movement. The poet is first projected into the LIVING ('leaf'), and then into the TERRESTRIAL ('wave'); but Shelley stops short of the trip to the stars[8] and pulls the poet back toward the human:

> Make me thy lyre, even as the forest is:
> What if my leaves are falling like its own!
> The tumult of thy mighty harmonies
> Will take from both a deep, autumnal tone,
> Sweet though in sadness. Be thou, Spirit fierce,
> My Spirit! Be thou me, impetuous one!
>
> V ll. 57-62

These lines contain the climax of the poem, for which Shelley uses imagery that displaces man only three categories from the HUMAN, in comparing the poet (HUMAN) to a 'lyre' (OBJECTIVE) and 'leaves' (LIVING and OBJECTIVE; both because these leaves are dead).

The imagery in Shelley's climactic scene clearly contrasts with the overall imagery in Byron's poem. To establish this fact, let us examine the climactic passage in Canto III, Childe Harold's transcendent experience.

> All Heaven and Earth are still—though not in sleep,
> But breathless, as we grow when feeling most;
> And silent, as we stand in thoughts too deep:—
> All Heaven and Earth are still: From the high host
> Of stars, to the lulled lake and mountain-coast,
> All is concentered in a life intense,
> Where not a beam, nor air, nor leaf is lost,
> But hath a part of Being, and a sense
> Of that which is of all Creator and Defence.

LXXXIX

Here Harold experiences the unity of all the elements in Nature, but he is completely lost in the experience. It is almost as if he has given up any position or space to dissolve into BEING and thus be able to move freely among the elements of Nature—'beam' (ENERGETIC), 'stars' (SUBSTANTIAL), 'lulled lake and mountain-coast' (TERRESTRIAL), 'leaf' (LIVING).

What does this contrast suggest about the two poets? One would not want to go so far as to say this imagery is exemplary of all the metaphor of Byron and Shelley, that Byron always projects man out into BEING and that Shelley never does.[9] But one can say that Shelley is quite fond of the lyre metaphor, with its picture of the poet co-operating with Nature in the making of harmonious music[10] and that Byron, in this most transcendent of his poems, does not use this metaphor, or any metaphor which pictures man in some 'thing.' As Byron says in stanza LXXV, Harold 'contemns/All objects,' preferring to soar above them, to move toward BEING. In order to achieve this transcendent experience, Byron must imagine man out of any spatial existence, thus, in effect, removing man from the experience.

Shelley's frequent use of metaphors which allow the reader to identify the poet lends support to Irene Chayes's comment on 'Ode to the West Wind.'[11]

> This is by no means an identification by the speaker with the wind in which he loses his individual identity; he does not say 'Let me be thee,' as he would necessarily be saying if the 'individual' here were indeed being 'merged' with the general.

Chayes is claiming that Shelley believes the individual can merge with Nature without losing himself entirely. Chayes's criticism is supported by the following passage from Shelley's *Defense of Poetry*:[12]

Man is an instrument over which a series of external and internal
impressions are driven, like the alternations of an ever-changing wind
over an Aolian lyre, which move it by their motion to ever-changing
melody. But there is a principle within the human being, and perhaps within all sentient beings, which acts otherwise than in the
lyre, and produces not melody, alone, but harmony, by an internal
adjustment of the sounds or motions thus excited to the impressions
which excite them.

Here Shelley is talking specifically about the writing of poetry, but
the comments would seem to apply as well to the experience poetry
speaks of. For Shelley, there is that in man that makes him essential
to the experience, as well as to the recounting of the experience in
poetry.

What does this contrast suggest about the originality of *Childe
Harold*, Canto III? In his fine book *Byron and the Dynamics of
Metaphor*,[13] W. P. Elledge claims that in Canto III Byron is attempting
to conjure up for himself the experience which Shelley has undergone,
by writing poetry stylistically similar to Shelley's. He maintains that

Interpretation of those rare 'mystical' moments in his [Byron's]
verse must then be regulated by a recognition of Byron's real experience among the Alps . . . In the poetry he wrote about responses
to Nature which he wanted to feel, exaggerating the love for natural
phenomena in order to convince himself that such affection was
possible. (p. 44)

Elledge points to the similarities between Byron and Shelley's poetry
in supporting his contention. However, the differences in their poetry,
as shown in this study, suggest that if Byron began in an attempt to
imitate Shelley, he did not follow through in that attempt. He could
have slavishly copied Shelley's poetry (including his images); but, he
did not. At some point, Byron's language took over making the poem,
and the experience recounted, his.

One final question: what does such a psycholinguistic analysis as this
offer the literary critic? It offers him the possibility of allowing the language of a poem to 'show' meaning that might otherwise be missed.
For years critics have felt that Byron's other poetry, such as that in
Manfred, militated against interpreting the experience in *Childe Harold*,
Canto III, as Shelleyan, or Wordsworthian; yet they were aware of
similarities between the experience Byron recounts and those recounted
by Shelley and Wordsworth, and many were forced to charge Byron
with imitation or vacillation. This analysis of Byron's language reveals
a significant difference between Shelley and Byron, a difference which

shows the Byron of Canto III to have some of the same misgivings about man that the poet in *Manfred* possesses.

The critic is often troubled by the paraphrasing involved in explicating a poem. He is somewhat like the translator who attempts to convey information from one language to another, knowing that something is bound to be lost and wishing that his audience could receive the message in the language it was written in. This linguistic approach to poetry allows the poet to tell the reader what he means in the language that he writes in: his metaphor.

NOTES

1 I. A. Richards, *The Philosophy of Rhetoric* (New York: Oxford University Press, 1936), pp. 89–112.

2 Owen Thomas, *Metaphor and Related Subjects* (New York: Random House, 1969).

3 Subsequent to these initial experiments, Mr Haley wrote a doctoral dissertation in which he conducted numerous experiments and made applications to literature. 'Metaphor and the Linguistics of Space: A Psycholinguistic Model of Figurative Language,' unpublished Ph. D. dissertation, The Florida State University, 1975.

4 'Gravity' here refers to the Earth's gravity. Obviously, things outside the Earth's gravity possess a gravity of their own, but this fact is not registered in the mental construct of the 'Earthling.' Another point that should be mentioned here is that because of the hierarchical nature of these categories, an entity must both have 'shape' and be within the Earth's gravity to be in the OBJECTIVE category. Thus, 'star,' which refers to an entity that has shape (perhaps a better example would be 'planet' since it is not gaseous, but Byron does not refer to 'planets'), is SUBSTANTIAL because it is not within the Earth's gravity. 'The star is falling' is metaphorical until the star actually enters into the Earth's gravity.

5 Moore records Wordsworth's charge. Lord John Russell, ed., *Memoirs, Journal, and Correspondence of Thomas Moore*, 8 vols. (London: Longman, Green, 1853–56), III, p. 161.

6 Here I take some liberties with the concept of predicate. However, the structure could have been explained as two nouns joined by a *be* verb, in which case it would still be metaphorical. 'Companionship' would be categorized as ANIMATE on the strength of Mr Haley's direction that his categories contain not only words that refer to a certain class of phenomena but also words that refer to attributes and distinctive characteristics of members of the class. In saying that 'companionship' is ANIMATE, one is saying that nothing less specific than ANIMATE can have, or be, 'companionship.'

7 Some may wish to attribute souls to animals and thus classify this noun ANIMATE. Doing so will not hurt our argument.

8 The star is Byron's consummate image for this transcendent experience. Note stanza LXXXVIII

   Ye Stars! which are the poetry of Heaven!
   If in your bright leaves we would read the fate
   Of men and empires,—'tis to be forgiven,
   That in our aspirations to be great,
   Our destinies o'erleap their mortal state,
   And claim a kindred with you; for ye are
   A Beauty and a Mystery, and create
   In us such love and reverence from afar,
   That Fortune,—Fame,—Power,—Life, have named themselves a Star.

9 In fact, in *Adonais* Shelley writes poetry that sounds very much like
   the poetry Byron is writing in Canto III.

                          XLII
          He is made one with Nature: there is heard
          His voice in all her music, from the moan
          Of thunder, to the song of night's sweet bird;
          He is a presence to be felt and known
          In darkness and in light, from herb and stone,
          Spreading itself where'er that Power may move
          Which has withdrawn his being to its own;
          Which wields the world with never wearied love,
          Sustains it from beneath, and kindles it above.

                          XLIII
          He is a portion of the loveliness
          Which once he made more lovely: he doth bear
          His part, while the one Spirit's plastic stress
          Sweeps through the dull dense world, compelling there,
          All new successions to the forms they wear;
          Torturing th'unwilling dross that checks its flight
          To its own likeness, as each mass may bear;
          And bursting in its beauty and its might
          From trees and beasts and men into the Heaven's light.

   However, there are some differences. It is still possible to identify
   the poet, Keats, in this experience. His 'voice' is in the music and
   'He' is a presence to be 'felt and known.' In stanza LXXXIX of Canto
   III, Byron's poet is nowhere to be found.
10 Shelley uses the lyre metaphor in 'Alastor,' 'Hymn to Intellectual
   Beauty,' and in his *Defense of Poetry*. For a perceptive discussion
   on the Romantics' use of this metaphor, see M. H. Abrams's 'The
   Correspondent Breeze: A Romantic Metaphor'; in M. H. Abrams,
   ed. *English Romantic Poets* (New York: Oxford University Press,
   1960), pp. 37–54.
11 'Rhetoric as Drama: An Approach to the Romantic Ode,' *PMLA*,
   79 (March 1964), p. 72.

12 Donald H. Reiman and Sharon B. Powers, eds, *Shelley's Poetry and Prose* (New York: W. W. Norton and Co., 1977), p. 480.
13 W. P. Elledge, *Byron and the Dynamics of Metaphor* (Nashville: Vanderbilt University Press, 1968).

CHAPTER EIGHT

Semantic Laws

Joseph Williams *

[Williams considers some general laws, or trends, by which word meanings develop and change through metaphorical extension. However, he notes that most of these 'laws' are based upon statistical probability alone and do not have predictive power. The problem of discovering predictive laws of semantic change reduces to the problem of discovering internal, universal, and cognitive trends that parallel one another across many languages, as opposed to external, temporal, and cultural trends that are peculiar to a given language. He cites the semantic development of color categories and the metaphorical transfer of sensory words from one empirical category to another as possible examples of the universal type of trend. That is, if it is true that the historical development of color terms and the transfer of sensory terms from one category to another follow rather stable patterns of evolution across many languages, then it might be said that these processes reflect universal cognitive principles that, stated as scientific laws, would have predictive power. Williams notes that those few metaphorical transfers which break the laws in question tend to die out of the language, thus corroborating those laws even in the violation of them. But Williams's observations seem to go beyond the question of how to make a prediction about the directions of semantic change; they also suggest that the processes of metaphorical invention and extension may be studied further as reflections of some universals in human psychology, instead of simply as the accidents of word usage that pertain to individual linguistic cultures.]

Historical semanticists have searched for laws, or rules of semantic change, much as historical linguists studying sound patterns and grammatical structures have. In the nineteenth century, a group of Germanic philologists were able to formulate laws of phonological change in the Germanic languages that were of very great explanatory power . . . Inspired by their success, semanticists set about looking for equally powerful laws of semantic change.

*First published in *Origins of the English Language* (New York: Macmillan, 1975), pp. 207-11.

Unfortunately, they have met with very limited success. There are a few tendencies that we can discover in the previous data:

1 Words for abstractions will generally develop out of words for physical experience: *comprehend, grasp, explain*, and so on.
2 Words originally indicating neutral condition tend to polarize: *doom, fame, predicament, luck, merit.*
3 Words originally indicating strong emotional response tend to weaken as they are used to exaggerate: *awful, terrific, tremendous.*
4 Insulting words tend to come from names of animals or lower classes: *rat, dog, villain, cad.*
5 Metaphors will be drawn from those aspects of experience most relevant to us: *eye of a needle, finger of land*; or most intense in our experience: *turn on, spaced out, freaked out*, for example.

But these only approximate statistical tendencies. They are not laws fulfilling the usual requirements of a law: that it not only explain relevant past events, but predict future events as well. The odds are that a word for an abstract cognitive or emotional process will develop out of an earlier concrete reference, but we cannot take any given word with concrete reference: *rock* or *push* and predict that it will evolve into a word referring to abstract experience. And the reverse has happened with originally abstract words like *dull, blunt, keen*, and *soft*. All originally referred to nonphysical referents.

A change that has been given the name of 'law' and often cited as one of the best examples of a law is that suggested by Gustaf Stern: Adverbs meaning *rapidly* before 1300 developed into adverbs meaning *immediately*. Adverbs meaning *quickly* after 1300 did not. This, of course, is peculiar to English and limited to a particular point in time. At best, it is a restricted generalization about the past, not a law that encompasses the future.[1]

We must, however, distinguish two kinds of predictions:

(1) In some cases, we have to base a prediction on relevant external forces. A culture will invariably assign meanings it **must** develop to the words it uses most frequently or can create most easily. Thus a generalization about, say, euphemism, is entirely culture-dependent in regard to the tabooed and non-tabooed areas in which euphemisms will be used.
(2) On the other hand, there may be universals of change which, because they are so regular and so general, reflect internal influences either peculiar to the particular language or to human language and cognition in general. It has been claimed, for example, that all human languages obey a very general law for the development of color terms.[2] The development has seven states and each stage must be passed through in sequential order. The order can be represented in terms like this:

$$\begin{bmatrix} \text{white} \\ \text{black} \end{bmatrix} > \text{red} \overset{\nearrow}{\searrow} \begin{bmatrix} \text{green} \\ \text{yellow} \end{bmatrix} \begin{bmatrix} \text{yellow} \\ \text{green} \end{bmatrix} \overset{\searrow}{\nearrow} \text{blue} > \text{brown} > \begin{bmatrix} \text{purple} \\ \text{pink} \\ \text{orange} \\ \text{grey} \end{bmatrix}$$

I   II   III   IV   V   VI   VII

That is, all languages have nonmetaphorical words for black and white. Such words may exhaust the spectrum. If there are only three terms, the third one will be a word for something approximating red. Stages III and IV may occur in either order: green and yellow will be the next words to develop, but they may develop in either order. Once those five words have developed, then blue and brown will follow, themselves to be followed by the next four in no particular order.

As the authors of this research have suggested, there are eleven universal potential color categories, and those colors develop in a fixed order. If they are correct, this is surely an example of cognitive-linguistic interaction and a very powerful semantic 'law' dependent not on any particular cultural organization but rather only a particular level of cultural complexity.

There may be another law of semantic change in English where mental processes interact with a cultural milieu to create new meanings for old forms. Words for sensory experience fall into five basic categories.

Tactile: *mild, soft, smooth, even, hard, rough, harsh, coarse, dull, dry, keen, sharp, hot, cold, warm, cool, heavy, light, dry, bland, hard.*

Gustatory/Olfactory : *piquant, pungent, tart, bitter, cloying, acrid, acid, sweet, sour, vapid, tangy.*

Visual (dimension): *high, low, thick, thin, deep, shallow, wide, broad, narrow, full, big, little, flat, steep, small, level.*

Visual (color): *clear, light, bright, brilliant, fair, dark, dim, faint, pale.*

Aural: *quiet, loud, shrill, strident.*

We can expand these basic categories by transferring words from one category to another: *hot music, loud colors, sharp tastes, sour smells,* and so on. But not all metaphors are equally comfortable: *loud heights, wide smells, bright edges, low tastes* (i.e., parallel to low sounds on a sensory dimension not the sense of vulgar tastes). At first glance, we might assume that we randomly select our metaphors, since many of these are perfectly clear even though we never or rarely use them. A loud height is certainly higher than a quiet one.

But the historical development of these metaphors in English reveals a pattern that approaches the regularity of a law that might be represented like this:

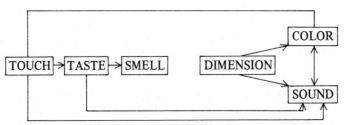

That is, in English (and possibly many other languages), words referring primarily to tactile sensations will, if they transfer at all, transfer to taste (*sharp tastes*), color (*harsh colors*), and sound (*soft, sounds*). Taste words will transfer to smell (*sour smell*) or to sound (*sweet sounds*). There are no primary, non-metaphorical smell words in English (or in many other languages, interestingly enough). Dimension words may transfer to color (*deep red*) or to sound (*high sound*). Color and sound words trade metaphors (*dark sounds, quiet colors*).

There is a second regularity: Each successive transfer follows the same sequence. That is, once *dull* transferred from tactile to vision, it transferred on to sound, but not back to taste/smell or dimension. Each successive transfer of a word is determined by the most 'advanced' meaning of the metaphor.

And there is a third regularity: If a sense transfer violates either of the first two regularities, that sense development tends to disappear. For example *soft taste*, a sense not usual in standard English, was active for a time after *soft sounds* had developed, a violation of the 'most advanced sense' constraint. That taste meaning subsequently disappeared. *Shrill* developed touch and taste senses, contrary to the main principle. Neither sense has maintained itself in the language.

There are a very few exceptions to this generalization: *Mellow* developed senses out of the predicted order; *faint* developed a smell/ taste sense after earlier transferring from the meaning 'feigned' or 'simulated' to color. *Sharp* transferred to angles, perhaps on the model of Latin *acute*. *Flat* and *thin* transferred to taste. But when all the transfers are taken into consideration, these exceptions constitute less than one per cent of the total data.

This kind of research into the semantic development of an entire field of words as opposed to tracing the history of a single word is little explored at the moment, largely because the data is so difficult to assemble. We require what we do not yet have for any language: An historically organized *Roget's Thesaurus*, a resource that would list every word that has ever referred to any sense listed under the category of that sense along with the earliest and latest citations of that word with that sense. Without such a resource historical semanticists are forced to read dictionaries entry by entry, searching for senses and words that at one time may have referred to a particular referent but no longer do. How, for example, would we discover all the words that at any time have ever referred to say, taste? These have: *asper, coarse, cold, poignant, rough, smart, soft, warm, acrid, austere, dulcet, eager, acute, high, small, loud,* and *shrill.*

Problem 1: Here are some sense words with their etymological sources. Does this information confirm or contradict the generalization about sense transfer? *sweet* (Pleasing to any sense), *bitter* (from biting), *acid* (from *ac-* = sharp), *acrid* (from *ac-* = sharp), *tart* (sharp pain), *cloy* (prick with a nail), *piquant* (piercing or stinging), *pungent* (to prick), *shrill* (rasping or grating, earlier to scrape or abrade), *quiet* (calm, peaceful), *dulcet* (sweet to taste or smell), *blunt* (unclear of sight), *keen* (intelligent), *soft* (producing agreeable sensations), *coarse* (ordinary), *dull* (unintelligent), *harsh* (rough and hard to touch, then to taste). How do these fit in: *eager, poignant, austere, brisk*?

Problem 2: Many of these words also apply to abstract situations and to personality: *a dark moment, a rough time, a warm personality, a dry humor,* and so on. Are there any generalizations to be made regarding the sequence of development of these transfers? You will have to consult the *OED* for dates.

NOTES

1 Stern, Gustaf, *Meaning and Change of Meaning with Special Reference to the English Language.* Göteborg, Sweden, 1931.
2 Berlin, Brent and Paul Kay, *Basic Color Terms, their Universality and Evolution.* Los Angeles and Berkeley, 1969.

CHAPTER NINE

A literary and linguistic analysis of compact verbal paradox

Marvin K.L. Ching *

[Ching argues that literary but non-linguistic treatments of oxymora are often inadequate in that they call attention only to the paradoxical, contradictory character of these expressions and fail to show how a 'sensible meaning' can be derived from them. Limiting himself to oxymora of the adjective-noun construction and employing a theoretical extension of Katz's notion of semantic markers (constituents of word meaning), Ching offers an explanation of what actually occurs when informants on his questionnaire interpret the 'sense' beyond an oxymoron's nonsense.

While the paradoxical 'nonsense' of an oxymoron is definable in terms of Katz's principles governing antonymy, the interpretation of an oxymoron's intuitive sense requires some principles governing 'the erasure and replacement' of such antonymous markers. That is, Ching's informants seem to interpret an oxymoron by cancelling out the contradictory features of meaning in one word ('erasure') and by putting in their place the opposing features of the other word ('replacement'). Ching offers two general rules which seem to govern this erasure and replacement of semantic markers in oxymora:

1 The semantic markers of a word with only a few markers will erase and replace the antonymous markers of a word with many markers. That is, if a word has only a few markers, then these markers seem to be less expendable, less susceptible to erasure. Therefore, they tend to dominate the opposing markers of the other word which, because it has more markers, can afford to give some of them up.
2 If both words in the oxymoron have about the same number of semantic markers, those of the modifier tend to erase and replace the opposing markers of the head noun.

Thus sometimes the markers of the head noun erase and replace those of the modifier, and sometimes the reverse is true, depending on the relative quantity of markers belonging to the modifier and head. These principles not only explain how readers can agree on the interpretations

*First published in *College Composition and Communication*, 26 (1975), 384-8.

for some oxymora, but they also explain how readers may legitimately disagree upon the interpretations of others. More importantly, these principles show how oxymora, depending upon their syntactic and semantic structure, can produce differing emphases—for informants appear to give greater interpretative focus to that word in the paradox whose markers (for one of the two reasons given) dominate those of the other.]

Soundless wailing. Timid rage. Prudent carelessness. Careless prudence. Wild justice. Does a compact verbal paradox of the adjective-noun construction mean more than a mixture of contradictory ideas? Literary handbooks classify compressed paradoxes, like those cited above, under the word *oxymoron.* Literary authorities usually describe the oxymoron as a compact paradox, a joining together of contradictory words which produces an epigrammatic effect. But literary dictionaries go no further. They do not tell us whether the contradictory ideas ever combine to form a sensible meaning or whether the ideas presented by the conflicting words forever remain a contradiction. As a form of paradox, however, an oxymoron often does convey a meaning other than the ostensibly contradictory one. After all, a paradox is only a 'seeming' or 'apparent' contradiction, not a real one.

Through the use of Jerrold Katz's theory of semantic markers, as found in his book *Semantic Theory*, 1972, I shall show how readers on a questionnaire I administered interpret some kinds of oxymora. I shall not give all of the possible interpretations readers assign to these oxymora. Because of restrictions of space, I shall show how readers commonly interpret these oxymora through a phenomenon which I shall call *erasure and replacement.*

But first, a brief word on what semantic markers are. Semantic markers may be conceived of as the constituent concepts of a word. For example, the word *chair* may be conceived of as being composed of the following concepts or semantic markers: (+ object), (+ physical), (+ non-living), (+ artifact), (+ furniture), (+ portable), (+ something with legs), (+ something with a back), (+ something with a seat), and (+ a seat for one). Words are contradictory to each other—that is, they are antonyms of each other—if they hold at least one semantic marker in common and if they share at least a pair of semantic markers which are antonyms of each other. Moreover, the antonyms must be grouped according to a common principle. These generalizations may be illustrated by the words *bride* and *groom.* These words are antonyms of each other because both words have the semantic marker (+ human) and both words share a pair of semantic markers which are antonyms of each other: that is, (+ male) in *groom* and (- male) in *bride.* They are also antonyms because the pair of antonymous semantic markers are antonymous on the common principle of sex.

Semantic markers thus give us the sense of contradiction in an oxymoron. For example, *soundless wailing* may be interpreted to be contradictory because both words hold in common the semantic marker (+ audio); both words share antonymous markers, (– sound) for *soundless* and (+ sound) for *wailing*; and the antonyms have the common principle of auditory sensation.

Semantic markers may also help us to see what occurs when the semantic markers of the adjective and the noun in an oxymoron are combined to form a semantic reading. The interaction of these markers may aid us in seeing what occurs when readers interpret oxymora. The semantic markers may help us to explain readers' intuitions in their interpretations of oxymora.

On the questionnaire which I administered, readers were given the oxymoron *soundless wailing* in this context:

> Where is there an end of it, the soundless wailing,
> The silent withering of autumn flowers
> Dropping their petals and remaining motionless;
> Where is there an end to the drifting wreckage,
> The prayer of the bone on the beach?

Readers commonly interpreted this phrase from T. S. Eliot's *Four Quartets*[1] as 'unspoken sorrow or sadness,' 'silent despair,' or 'an expression of grief without sound.' These answers may be explained by an interaction of semantic markers, which I have chosen to call *erasure and replacement*.

Suppose the markers for *wailing* are

(+ produce sound)

(+ vocal)

(+ reason: emotion)
$\begin{Bmatrix} (+ \text{ sorrow}) \\ (+ \text{ pain}) \end{Bmatrix}$

(The braces in this analysis indicate that one or all of the markers enclosed may be chosen.) It seems that the semantic marker (– sound) of the modifier *soundless* in the phrase *soundless wailing* erases and replaces the markers (+ sound) and (+ vocal) of the head. The semantic marker (– sound) erases and replaces all the markers of wailing that relate to the concept of sound—(+ produce sound) and (+ vocal) so that only the reason or the cause of the utterance is left: the emotion of sorrow or feeling of pain. The result is as follows:

(– sound)   (+ reason: emotion)
                                                                       (+ sorrow)
                                                                       (+ pain)

Thus, readers tended to give answers like 'unspoken sorrow or sadness,' 'silent despair,' or 'an expression of grief without sound' when they interpreted the oxymoron. Notice that it is the semantic marker of the modifier which erases and replaces its antonym in the head.

However, take the oxymoron *thunderous silence* (from Edward Corbett's *Classical Rhetoric for the Modern Student*, 1971). Probably most of us would think a *thunderous silence* to be an ominous or threatening silence. Here there is a reversal as to which word in the modifier-head construction is acted upon and which word does the erasing and replacing. The direction of *erasure and replacement* in *thunderous silence* is from the head to the modifier rather than from the modifier to the head. From readers' responses to various oxymora, I have discovered that it is the word with the fewer semantic markers that does the erasing and replacing. Therefore, in both *soundless wailing* and *thunderous silence* the marker (– sound) erases and replaces the marker (+ sound).

When both words in an oxymoron tend to have about the same number of semantic markers, it seems that it is the markers in the modifier that erase and replace those in the head.

I quoted on the questionnaire the oxymora *prudent carelessness* and *careless prudence* from Gerald Kennedy's *The Lion and the Lamb: Paradoxes of the Christian Faith*, 1950. I asked my readers this question:'Do these phrases differ in meaning or do they mean the same: *prudent carelessness* and *careless prudence*? Explain.' Before examining readers' responses, however, let me analyze these words. Both *prudence* and *carelessness* may share semantic markers having to do with the possession or the lack of these ideas:

wisdom
conscious awareness
planning
watchful concern

The word *prudence* must always contain the semantic marker (+ wise). However, though *prudence* often conveys the concepts of planning or forethought, awareness, and attentive concern, the word may have a reading showing a negation of these markers. That is, *prudence* may be wisdom, but wisdom without conscious awareness, planning, or watchful concern. The word *prudence* must always have (+ wise) as a marker, but the other markers are + or –, depending upon how the word is used:

+ wisdom
± conscious awareness

± planning
± watchful concern

In contrast, *carelessness* does not require showing the possession of any of these concepts. Instead, different readings of the word must show the lack of at least one of these concepts. For example, the familiar reading of the word *carelessness* has the marker (- wise): *carelessness* often means a lack of discernment of good judgment. But *carelessness*, in other readings, does not mean a lack of wisdom. Instead, *carelessness* may mean a lack of planning or conscious awareness or attentive concern. In other words, the word *carelessness*, depending on its use, may be shown as follows:

± wisdom
± conscious awareness (one must be a minus)
± planning
± watchful concern

For comparison, the two words may be shown side by side:

prudence	*carelessness*
+ wisdom	± wisdom
± conscious awareness	± conscious awareness
± planning	± planning
± watchful concern	± watchful concern

This analysis helps to explain why readers tend to think of *prudent carelessness* as favorable in meaning and why they differ on interpretations of *careless prudence*. The reason most readers think that *prudent carelessness* shows a desirable situation or characteristic is that the modifier has a semantic marker like (+ wise) that erases and replaces its antonym (- wise) in the head word. The reason that readers often consider *careless prudence* unfavorable or pejorative in meaning is that the modifier has a semantic marker like (- wise) that erases and replaces its antonym (+ wise) in the head word. On the other hand, in readings of *careless prudence* that are favorable, the modifier has a semantic marker like (+ wise) and thus does not contradict the marker (+ wise) of the head word. Instead, one of the other markers of the modifier is antonymous with a marker in the head word and erases and replaces its antonym in the head word. For example, the semantic marker (- planning) of the modifier erases and replaces its antonym (+ planning) in the head word. Therefore, a *careless prudence* may be a wisdom that has risen without planning; it may be a wisdom that has a spontaneous origin.

I shall now cite some responses of readers to the pair of oxymora *prudent carelessness* and *careless prudence*. The first set of interpretations indicates directly or indirectly (that is, by inference) that the marker of the modifier, whether (- wise) or (+ wise), is the one which does the erasing and the replacing of its antonym in the head. This direction of erasure and replacement causes readers to feel *prudent*

carelessness to be favorable in meaning and *careless prudence* to be unfavorable or pejorative:

> *prudent carelessness*: as in 'Rosemary Woods exercised prudent
> carelessness in erasing the tapes.' (not necessarily pejorative)
> [parenthetical material written by the reader.]
> *careless prudence*: 'You exercised a rather careless prudence in
> ignoring your boss's tax evasions.' (pejorative)
> [parenthetical material written by the reader.]
> They differ. *Prudent carelessness* is a virtue and *careless prudence*
> is a vice. The adjective in both cases determines the normative value.
> *prudent carelessness*: means that the carelessness is really planned
> or wisely thought out. One judges when it would be wise for him
> to appear careless.
> *careless prudence*: suggests that one is careless in making decisions
> requiring care and wisdom.

Other interpretations of the pair of oxymora emphasize the degree
of calculation, premeditated evaluation, fore-planning, or conscious
control. The constituent concepts having to do with the presence or
absence of planning, awareness, or attentive concern in the modifier
erase and replace their antonyms in the head word. Therefore, when
prudent is the modifier, the amalgamated meaning of *prudent* and
carelessness indicates the ideas of planning or awareness or attentive
concern; when *careless* is the modifier, the amalgamated meaning of
careless and *prudence* indicates the ideas of lack of planning, awareness, or attentive concern. When *prudent* is the modifier, the oxymoron
always conveys the idea of wisdom in the amalgamated reading of the
modifier and the head word. If *carelessness* as the head word has a
semantic marker (- wise), the semantic marker (+ wise) of the modifier
erases and replaces its antonym in the head word. On the other hand,
if the modifier is *careless*, the semantic marker of the modifier may
be (+ wise) or (- wise). If the marker is (+ wise), the semantic interpretation of the oxymoron *careless prudence* is favorable; if the marker
is (- wise), the meaning of the oxymoron is pejorative because the
marker erases and replaces the antonym (+ wise) of the head word.

> These generalizations explain the following set of readers' responses:
> *prudent carelessness*: means a deliberate carelessness undertaken
> in the belief that it will be beneficial or at least if it is not deliberate
> the results are nevertheless desirable or wise.
> *careless prudence*: means a wisdom that is not always practical
> or that is not careful to take into account all the relevant issues.
> [The expressions] Differ. *Prudent carelessness* means that in some
> instance it was wise to appear careless. Since the carelessness was
> premeditated, it is ironic, not true carelessness at all. *Careless*

prudence means an inadvertent prudence. The results were prudent although the action was not given forethought.

The first phrase [*prudent carelessness*] indicates a careless behavior that is deliberate and intentional. Such a person is very aware of what he is doing. The second phrase [*careless prudence*] indicates a prudent behavior without concern or care for the consequences of such behavior. Example: a person who is very prudent about his actions, but does not care if such actions hurt others.

One individual's interpretation of *careless prudence* in an oral interview also shows the modifier erasing and replacing its antonym or antonyms in the head word: 'a wisdom that is not uptight; a wisdom that is freely given.' The concept in the modifier of lack of planning, attentive concern, or awareness conveys the notion of spontaneity and the free bestowal of prudence.

Because the direction of *erasure and replacement* is from the modifier to the head word (it is the modifier that does the erasing and the replacing), readers feel an emphasis of meaning placed upon the modifier. The head word is interpreted or filtered through the modifier when both the modifier and head word have about the same number of semantic markers.

What may we learn from readers' interpretations of *soundless wailing* and *prudent carelessness* and *careless prudence*? First, we may say that the oxymoron is not as nonsensical as its etymological origin suggests. It is not merely 'sharply' or 'pointedly foolish.' Besides the obviously contradictory interpretation, the oxymoron does yield a semantic reading. One linguistic process which occurs in the amalgamation of the adjective and the noun is a combining rule which I have called *erasure and replacement*. It seems that the direction of movement in *erasure and replacement* is determined by the number of semantic markers in one constituent as compared to the number of semantic markers in the other constituent. If one constituent has fewer markers than the other, then it is the marker or markers in this constituent that erase and replace their antonyms in the head word. On the other hand, if both adjective and noun seem to have the same number of semantic markers, the direction of *erasure and replacement* is from the modifier to the head word. *Erasure and replacement* is one combining rule which helps us to explain readers' intuitive interpretations of oxymora. It is different from the regular combining rule for modifier-head constructions in denotative language, which Katz calls a Boolean union, a union which is of an additive type.

NOTES

1   T. S. Eliot, 'The Dry Salvages,' in *Four Quartets* (New York: Harcourt, Brace, 1943), p. 22.

PART III

Stylistics

We have grouped the following articles according to our understanding of their differing perspectives and emphases with regard to style:

1 those that emphasize 'content' as a constant and 'form' as a variable, which alters only the effect and not the essence of 'content,' have been placed in the section entitled 'Style as Choice';

2 those that emphasize the contributions of 'form' *to* 'content,' or which believe that 'form' changes or even creates 'content' (so that there can be no clear distinction between the two), have been placed in the section entitled 'Style as Meaning';

3 those that emphasize the special meaning or effect of style arising as a new synthesis from the dialectic of a 'form/content' interaction have been placed in the section entitled 'Style as Tension between Meaning and Form.'

The expressive machinery of a dialectic seems appropriate, for this third category does appear to be a relatively new upshoot from the classic debate between the alternate schools represented in (1) and (2). The very existence of this third category illustrates the principle of eclecticism which we believe is already at work to make linguistic criticism of literature increasingly feasible and worthwhile. It may be noted that those in the 'Style as Choice' school tend to be transformationalists; those in the 'Style as Meaning' school tend to be generative or pragmatic semanticists; those in the 'Style as Tension' school may perhaps combine the best of both. In all instances, the scholars from all three sections seem to be selecting models of description which are appropriate to their texts and objectives. From Pavel's transformational theory of macro-text structure in Russian folk narratives to Ching's case-grammar analysis of oxymora, the subtleties and complexities of the inscrutable form/content connection in literature are revealed through the investigation of that same connection in language.

Style as choice

CHAPTER TEN

Some remarks on narrative grammars

Thomas G. Pavel *

[Using a Chomskian transformational model, Pavel sketches a grammar
for the narrative. After briefly treating earlier linguistic-based studies
of narrative structure, Pavel discusses the advantages of a transformational model, showing how Chomsky's distinction between competence
and performance is useful in dealing with structures larger than the
sentence (his example is the folk-tale). Once he has established that a
transformational grammar may be applied to structures larger than the
sentence, he must decide what the basic unit (or initial symbol in the
phrase structure component) will be. Pavel notes that T. A. van Dijk
has proposed the text as the basic unit; however Pavel argues that the
narrative sequence should be seen as the basic unit, basing his argument
on the fact that when the text is composed of more than one narrative
it is impossible to generate a text by means of the phrase structure
component. According to Pavel, the transformational component,
operates on the output of the phrase structure component to produce
the text. Even though Pavel makes use of semiotic approaches, his
model is essentially Chomskian in separating syntax from semantics,
thus allowing for a 'style as choice' approach.]

1 Theory and corpus

In recent years the study of narrative structures has been pursuing two
basic goals: the extension of the domain of objects with which the
theory deals, and the refinement of the theory itself. When Propp
(1928a) estalished the bases of NARRATOLOGY (a term introduced
only later by Todorov, 1969) he used Russian fairytales as his point of
departure; the new science effectively encompassed, yet narrowly
defined, the characteristics and limits of this homogenous corpus.
Propp's successors extended the application of his method to similar

*First published in *Poetics*, 8 (1973), 5-30.
I am grateful to A. J. Greimas, M. L. Rivero, T. A. van Dijk, and D. Walker for
comments on an earlier version of this paper. The paper was translated into
English by Raymond St Laurent.

objects. Dundes (1964), for example, analyses a corpus which has the same nature as the one studied by Propp: it consists entirely of folk tales. The importance of Dundes' innovations resides primarily on the theoretical level. Dundes was one of the first to point out the similarities between the problems of narratives and those of descriptive linguistics, and to systematically introduce linguistic concepts into the field of narrative analysis. These concepts are taken mainly from Kenneth Pike's tagmemic theory, an offshoot of post-Bloomfieldian linguistics.[1] But the significant extension of the domain of narratology must be credited to the effects of the Paris School of Semiotics, whose major representatives often analysed texts much more complex than folk-tales: the novels of Bernanos (Greimas, 1966), the *Decameron* (Todorov, 1969), Antoine de La Sale's novel *Petit Jehan de Saintré* (Kristeva, 1970), biblical narratives (Chabrol and Morin, 1971), and mystery novels (Eco, 1966). As to the theoretical innovations introduced by this School, these are in the main due precisely to the necessity of explaining phenomena which characterize WRITTEN literature (as opposed to folklore). Bremond (1966, 1968) introduces the notions of 'narrative possibility' and 'choice'. Kristeva (1970) develops the notion of 'subject'—in the phenomenological sense of the term. Todorov (1966, 1968) deals with rules which account for the psychology of the characters—rules which would be impossible to formulate, or even postulate, in the narrower methodological framework used by Propp wherein each character is automatically assigned to one (or more) functions. Barthes (1966) constructs a complex network of notions aimed at distinguishing phenomena which are specifically literary—to note, in an analysis of folk-tales, the role of CATALYSTS, of INDICES, and of INFORMANTS would be much more restricted. This approach, once assumed, allows the theory a greater scope in establishing its own constraints: it may proceed by deliberately widening the corpus under analysis, as does Chatman (1969) who devises a method for the description of psychological literature, or, it may set as its goal the construction of more extensive and more powerful models on the theoretical level, as exemplified by Greimas (1970).

2   Narratology and linguistics

As with all new disciplines, the theory of narrative structures borrowed some of its concepts from more firmly-established neighbours: literature, anthropology and linguistics. We know that many of these concepts were taken from linguistics. The epistemological reasons for linguistics' particular influence on the related human sciences, especially within the last two decades, remains to be explained. In fact it seems that linguists themselves were not always pleased about the extended use of their

methods. Dundes (1964) relates the history of the American distributionalists' dissatisfaction with the efforts made to apply their notions
to anthropology. This same suspicion about the application of linguistic
concepts to extra-linguistic domains is found in Europe, but there
this attitude remains, in general, peripheral. As is brought to our
attention by Greimas,

> ni Saussure, ni Hjemslev, ni Jakobson, ni l'ensemble de la tradition
> saussurienne dans ce qu'elle a de plus remarquable, ne se sont jamais
> enfermes dans le domaine linguistique *stricto sensu* . . . . Dès ces
> premières formulations [Hjelmslev's glossematics] la théorie linguis-
> tique ne peut manquer d'affirmer sa vocation à l'universalité
> (1970: 20).

This dedication to universality was to evolve into the constitution of a
'non-linguistic' linguistics (the term is Martinet's), into a semiology (or
semiotics), whose goal is to develop and construct a general theory of
language as a symbolic system. Reciprocally, any science to which
linguistic methods are successfully applied becomes an object of semio-
logy/semiotics.[2] It seems historically evident that the annexation of
narrative structure by semiology/semiotics was preceded—and made
possible—by the infiltration of linguistics into anthropology, inaugurated
by Claude Lévi-Strauss (1955, 1958). Significantly, the first studies
wherein structuralist concepts were applied to narrative structures
were written by anthropologists (Claude Lévi-Strauss, 1955; Köngäs-
Maranda, 1962; Dundes, 1964). It is still too early (and too close at
hand) to undertake a review of linguistic influences on narratology;
however, let us examine some of the concepts borrowed from the
major trends in twentieth-century linguistics.

In Köngäs-Maranda's early studies the influence of linguistics was
filtered by the structural anthropology of Lévi-Strauss. It is important
to note at this point that the notion of transformation which Köngäs-
Maranda used—after Lévi-Strauss—and which is also found in Greimas
(1970), is quite different from the Chomskian notion of transformation. We shall return to this point later. Greimas's structural semantics,
and its applications to narratology, is a continuation and development
of the Hjelmslevian glossematics, yet it accepts many of the discoveries
of Lévi-Strauss' anthropology. As mentioned above, Alan Dundes
introduced post-Bloomfieldian principles into narratology. Todorov's
Grammaire du Décaméron apparently connects various European
structuralist theories to this study. Julia Kristeva's contribution is the
integration of certain concepts of Saumjan's generative model. Zellig
Harris's discourse analysis has also a prominent influence on European
research of text-structures—Isenberg (1971) and Harweg (1968) are
two examples among many. Finally, with Greimas (1970), van Dijk

(1970, 1971, 1972), Vuillot (1971), Chatman (1971), and in part
Kristeva (1970) and Todorov (1970), narratology also begins to adopt
a transformational generative (TG) outlook—and more recently and
emphatically, a definite TG perspective.

3 Ideality of grammar

One of the first problems which presents itself when TG theory is
applied to narrative structure is that of the nature of the relationships
between narrative COMPETENCE and textual PERFORMANCE.
According to Chomsky (1964), the central fact which any linguistic
theory must account for is the following: 'A mature speaker can
produce a new sentence of his language on the appropriate occasion,
and other speakers can understand it immediately, though it is equally
new to them' (1964: 50). This means that using a limited amount
of linguistic data acquired early in his life, every human being develops
his innate faculty of language by 'constructing' for himself a competence which enables him to produce any new utterance in his (native)
language. This competence, which, in Chomsky's interpretation, is
closely parallel to the Saussurian notion of *langue*, 'can be represented,
to an as yet undetermined extent, as a system of rules that we can
call the grammar of his language' (Chomsky, 1964: 51).[3] The representation of competence takes the form of a finite set of rules (instructions)—
of different types—which lead to the generation or the identification of
a theoretically infinite set of correct sentences in the language in question while also assigning a structural description to each sentence.
Performance, on the other hand, defined as effective use of language
in concrete situations, depends not only on competence but also on a
whole series of other factors. To grasp the relationship existing between
the grammar and 'real' sentences, we must keep in mind that if on the
level of competence we speak of CORRECT, or GRAMMATICAL,
sentences, on the level of performance we find the notion of ACCEP-
TABILITY (Chomsky, 1965: 2052). The acceptability of a sentence
depends not only on its grammaticality; it is also subject to specific
constraints e.g. the limited capacity of linguistic memory. We cannot,
for example, exceed certain limits of length when using embedded
structures. The grammar then, operates as an IDEALIZATION in
relation to the actual facts on the performance level. The competence
represented by a grammar is that of an IDEAL speaker, one who knows
the language 'perfectly' and who is not subject to the limits imposed by
memory, interference, etc. This ideal speaker would, furthermore, be
immortal, for his competence allows him to utter an infinite number of
sentences of infinite length. Obviously, death eventually intervenes;
but even if the speaker does not succeed in uttering ALL the sentences—

of FINITE length—which his competence allows, he is nonetheless capable of uttering ANY of these permissible sentences. If it is true that he is forced—in some way—to CHOOSE among sentences, this choice— at least theoretically, and only for the set of sentences of finite length— is still a FREE choice. This operative idealization of grammar is in no way exaggerated, for every sentence produced by the grammar is REALLY possible. Would not the same situation validly exist when dealing not with sentences only, but with narrative structures and texts?

For T. A. van Dijk, a text and/or narrative structure theory[4] which follows a TG model must be '*productive*, c'est-à-dire engendrer (formellement) un ensemble infini de textes a partir d'un ensemble fini de règles et d'éléments lexicaux. La théorie visée ici rendra compte d'une competence textuelle . . .' (van Dijk, 1972: 182). The 'productivity' of a grammar is purely formal, which means that it is no more a model of text PRODUCTION than of text RECEPTION. Although the neutrality that grammar has in relationship to the speaker-listener dichotomy has been often underlined in transformational studies, given how easy it is to slide from the mathematical and linguistic meanings of such terms as 'generative', 'generate', 'produce' to their commonly accepted meanings in daily language, it cannot be overemphasized that a grammar which 'produces' or 'generates' a set of objects (sentences, texts, etc.) does in fact no more than ENUMERATE these objects and assign to them a structural description.[5] It is of course possible to conceive of some models of linguistic production or linguistic reception which incorporate the results of generative grammar but a grammar itself is not seen as functionally related to the speaker-listener dichotomy. The relations between grammar and reception may play an important role in narratology in regard to certain stylistic effects, such as false interpretation when reading mystery novels, and in general all decoding–control devices (Riffaterre, 1971), but these cannot be explained unless the grammar being used is previously assumed to be independent of production/reception.

If we conceive of the grammar which generates (i.e., enumerates and structurally describes) a set of narratives as a mechanism consisting of an inventory of symbols and of a set of rules (of different types), and if this mechanism is sufficiently precise, we can safely assume it will generate a very large number of texts. If, furthermore, this mechanism contains recursive rules, the number of generatable texts is infinitely large. The problem thereby posed is the nature of the correlation which exists between this infinity of objects and the intuition of the speaker/listener. In other words, before undertaking the application of a formal system to narratology, we must be sure that the formal notions introduced do NOT conflict with the existing ontological or aesthetic intuitions of the speaker/listener in a culturally-defined context. The main contribution of a formal system, as Chomsky himself often points out, lies NOT ONLY in its formal validity—and thus in its coherence and unity—but also in its capacity to account for observable truth on the common-sense or intuitive level. To use two terms from Hjelmslev (1943), it is not so much a matter of its being ARBITRARY as of its being ADEQUATE.

It seems that if we limit our interests to certain categories of narratives, chances are strongly in favour of some sort of correspondence between the notion of an infinity of generatable texts and elementary intuition. In the area of folk-tales, for example, we find between the possible generative grammar of a certain genre of tales and the tales themselves, the same type of relationships which exist between the grammar of a language and the possible sentences of that language as generated by that grammar. Folk-tales do not compose a static, closed corpus: each RACONTEUR may change the story at will and can invent new stories which his audience unmistakably recognizes as being folk-tales. The grammar is potentially capable of generating an infinity of tales. This infinity will never be realized completely, but nothing prevents the appearance of any of the potentially generatable stories of that grammar. In the same manner that an ideal speaker of a generative-based grammar can produce all the correct sentences of a given language (and that these sentences are all recognized by the ideal listener), the ideal raconteur is capable of telling any 'well-formed' tale, which accordingly, is recognized by his audience. This analogy can be stretched a little farther, just as linguistics has the right and the need to distinguish between competence and performance, so too has narratology of folk-tales. Narrative grammar in this case represents the ideal narrative competence, while the study of performance deals with certain supplementary constraints which, applied to 'well-formed' stories on the competence level, render them 'acceptable'. As in TG grammar, these constraints are most apparent when dealing with recursive rules. It has been illustrated that a narrative grammar of the *Thousand and One Nights* must make use of such rules in order to explain the embedding of stories within other stories (Todorov, 1970; Gerson, 1972). As we know, recursive rules may be applied an infinite number of times, resulting in sentences—or in our case, stories—which are infinitely long. It is obvious to any reader of the *Thousand and One Nights* that continuous embedding of stories within stories has no theoretical limit, that the number of 'nests' in a 'nested' story cannot be determined *a priori*. It is equally obvious, on the other hand, that this embedding mechanism is drastically limited on the level of performance by extra-grammatical restraints such as, for example, the limited capacity of memory. Other similarities between TG grammars and the narrative grammar of folk-tales are equally—and as easily—acceptable on the intuitive level. We are here referring to such notions as grammaticality, semi-sentences (Katz, 1964), idiomatic expressions, etc., for which there undoubtedly exist corresponding notions in the narratology of folk-tales. Not only is there nothing in the linguistic definition of the sentence which opposes the theoretical existence of an infinity of sentences, some of which are infinitely long, but furthermore, a correct definition of the sentence MUST account for this possibility. Similarly in the cultural definition of the folk-tale, there is nothing which prevents the theoretical existence of an infinite number of possible stories, some of which are of infinite length. Much to the contrary, it is 'of the essence' of folk-tales, that each story represents the unique realization of ONE possibility from among an infinite number of possibilities.[6] We can already realize that, historically and culturally, folk-tales' 'creativity' is related to their oral character. The grammar which has folk-tales as output, does not therefore generate TEXTS, if by text we refer to such works as *The Fairie Queene*, or *Tristram Shandy*.

We must now distinguish two different meanings of the term TEXT. On the one hand, TEXT may be defined as 'any sequence of sentences having a certain coherence', and in this weak sense of the term each folk-tale is a text. On the other hand text may be defined more rigorously as 'any unchangeable sequence of sentences which has a strong cohesion and the unchangeable character of which is related to a value system of some sort'. In its weak sense, the text does not enter into the sphere of interest of narratology; but we shall discuss this aspect shortly. In its stronger meaning, the 'text' is very similar to the notion which Zumthor (1963) called MONUMENT (as opposed to document); that is, a specific use of language resulting from 'the radical tendency to surpass the contingent' which corresponds to the need of representing (and to constituting) a network of values. If in the weak sense of the term text, there is nothing to prevent the grammar from producing an infinite number of texts, in the stronger sense of the word this potential infinity is excluded. The text in its stronger sense, is, by definition, unique.

In what sense then can we speak of the infinity of generatable objects of a narrative grammar? Suppose we had succeeded in establishing a grammar capable of generating, without errors, Racine's *Andromaque, Bérénice, Bajazet,* and *Phèdre.* Suppose also that this grammar, beyond generating Racine's texts, also assigns to each of these tragedies a correct structural description. Without going into detail at this point as to the form which such a grammar should have, it seems evident that if this grammar resembles in any way a narrative grammar of folk-tales, it would generate NOT ONLY the required tragedies but also an indefinitely large number of other tragedies of the same type. But this would contradict the cultural definition of tragedy, a definition centering on the uniqueness of the literary object. The notions of 'competence' as well as the 'ideal' character of a grammar would thereby become void. The conclusion which seems to impose itself is, then, that a TG grammar would generate (in this type of situation) a vast number of objects which do not correspond to any reality, and that the very principle behind this production would not correspond to any cultural intuition.

Without formally testing the uniqueness of literary works, especially in certain types of cultures, note that this uniqueness is partially compensated by certain common characteristics which create groups of works—otherwise individually unique—appearing as a 'family of objects' to both the authors and readers/listeners of these works. Even in cultures where a literary work is considered to be a highly original and unique product, it is easily perceived that every work belongs to one LITERARY GENRE or another. There are instances where we even notice that this membership to a genre is guaranteed by a system of rules which the author himself must respect. In literary debates, the nature of literary creativity is often discussed in relation to the systems of existing rules: partisans of the 'traditional' approach see literary creativity as the production of new 'objects' within the existent rules—a sort of 'rule-ordered creativity'—whereas those who advocate a 'modernistic' approach hold that creativity also produces new rules—more or less a 'rule-changing creativity'. On another level it is often the case that an author's particular 'trademark' is easily recognizable, not only in matters of textual stylistics, but also in his organization of narrative material according to the recurrence of certain processes which seem to be the result of the application of some unique rule(s). Certain of Racine's characters for example, especially those who are subjected to violent—and for different reasons, forbidden passion, follow in the course of their amorous misadventures a pre-ordered sequence:

1 They are struck by 'love at first sight'
2 they recognize the interdiction related to their passion, and attempt to overcome this passion, sometimes believing they have succeeded
3 finally realizing the futility of their opposition, they acquiesce to the situation.

This sequence which is found in *Andromaque* (Oreste), *Bérénice* (Antiochus), *Mithridate* (Xiphares), and *Phèdre* (Phèdre and to some extent Hippolyte) has always seemed to be typically 'Racinian', often in opposition to the attitude which Corneille imposes on his heroes in similar situations.[7]

The existence of such literary phenomena as the pastiche and parody reinforce our conviction that certain literary regularities are observable and usable for the production of literary objects resembling the 'unique' literary objects.

If such is the case, these regularities should be considered as a sort of 'competence' representable by means of a generative grammar. This grammar would not have as its aim the generation of a unique work or even the set of unique works but rather to account for the fundamental regularities as perceived on different levels. If this hypothesis is correct, it should be able to represent, by means of a grammar, the observable regularities in an author's work and the regularities in a literary genre or type—perhaps especially within a certain period or within a particular literary moment. If these attempts succeed, we may eventually discover very general phenomena—LITERARY UNIVERSALS, as it were —and there would be no reason preventing the eventual formulation of a 'general and reasoned' narrative grammar.

4 Narrative structure and text

In order to better delimit the characteristics of such a grammar, it seems that a brief discussion of some notions already examined by narratologists would be useful. It should be pointed out that although these comments are influenced by transformational linguistics to a large degree, many aspects are nonetheless traceable to Greimas's semiotics. While the latter often appears to hold an analytical viewpoint, some of its concepts will be used within a generative framework. As we shall see, this reversal, far from lessening the interest of these concepts of Greimas's, adds a wider value to their validity.

One of the most interesting contributions made by Chomsky (1957) to linguistic theory was the formalization of the immediate constituent (IC) method of syntactic analysis. Immediate constituent analysis, practised intuitively for centuries, and given a coherent theoretical status by American distributionalists, emphasizes the importance of hierarchical syntactic dependencies within a sentence. Note that these dependencies have always been granted a syntactic relevance and that the best criterion for their discovery has often been intuitive.[8] In a certain sense we could say that the native speaker/listener has a natural 'feeling' for the unity of the sentence,

1 *My friend came yesterday.*

He divides this sentence naturally into *my friend* and *came yesterday*. He feels that *my friend* is further divisible into *my* and *friend*; etc., etc.. In a Chomskian representation of this phenomenon, the dependency hierarchy can be generated by a grammar consisting of a set of symbols (including an initial 'root' symbol) and a certain number of rewrite rules. In Chomsky (1957) the initial symbol, S, corresponded to the intuition—common to all languages—of the basic unit called SENTENCE. The first rewrite rule, $S \rightarrow NP + VP$, corresponded to the division of a sentence into a nominal phrase followed by a verb phrase. A nominal phrase was further rewritten as Determiner + Noun. To these rewrite rules correspond ordered graphs, in the form of labelled trees which are graphic representations of the dependency hierarchies. The initial symbol corresponds to the root of the tree, and each symbol corresponds to a labelled node. If a sequence of symbols is dominated (in a tree) by a single node X, then this sequence is a constituent of the type X. For example in a simplified tree-representation (Fig. 10.1, *my friend* 'constitutes an' NP; and NP + VP 'are a' Sentence.[9]

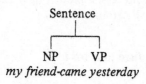

Figure 10.1

In presenting a narrative grammar in a form parallel to that of a TG grammar, one of the first problems encountered is the choice of an initial symbol. While tradition facilitates this choice for linguistics, in narratology this is not the case. The grammar presented by T. A. van Dijk (1970, 1971) proposes the text as the starting point:

La derivazione (la generazione, la produzione formale—che non s'identifica con la scrittura 'performanziale') di ogni testo inizia percio nel seguente modo (banale):

1 $T --- F_1, F_2, \ldots F$
   $F --- \ldots$
   $\ldots$
   etc.

e via di seguito, in mode recorrente, per tutte le frasi del testo.

But the author is aware of the difficulties raised by such a rule:

Tuttavia sarebbe abbastanza semplicistico limitarsi a questa ritra-scrizione lineare. L'idea intuitiva (apercettiva) della *strutturazione di un testo* potrebbe essere presa come un'indispensabile ipotesi susseguente, poiché un qualsiasi insieme stocastico di frasi non constituisce necessariamente un testo.

In order to account for the text's STRUCTURE, van Dijk introduces a complex structural variable S which functions on several levels: phonological, syntactic, and semantic. On the semantic level this variable S_{sem}

> consista di un data numero di semi e di classemi, che devono ricorrere nel'intero testo. Un dato sema 'tematico' e strutturatore sottosta, per esempio, a certi connettori (pro)nomi: Io o Egli. Un dato sema, a base classematica 'dinamismo', si riscntra, per sempio, nelle 'funzioni' di Propp. . . (van Dijk, 1970: 149-50).

As has already been noted, the term TEXT has two meanings. In the weak sense, a text is a set of sentences having a certain coherence. The means by which this coherence is realized have been an object of study since Harris (1952a and b) right up to Bellert (1970), in a linguistic framework interested largely in transphrastic phenomena. Without going into the details of these studies, it seems that they are all specifically oriented toward the study of the interrelations between the different SENTENCES of a text, relations which are usually best explained as dependencies between classes of elements found within the sentences. This concept 'from sentence to text' which can be paralleled to Harris's concept of syntax as a 'from morpheme to utterance' analysis, is found in the early era of interpretive semantics. A text cannot, however, be 'just another type of sentence' for it is itself composed of a number of interrelated sentences. In this 'from sentence to text' view, the interpretation of a text would comprise (a) the interpretation of each sentence, (b) the co-relating of these interpretations by some device which accounts for the concatenation relating these sentences. But if we accept this view, the interpretation of a text becomes almost a type of finite-state machine wherein the interpretation of each sentence allows us to pass from one state to another.

Chomsky (1963), has shown that certain languages CANNOT be generated by a finite-state machine. These languages share one common characteristic: in order to describe them, a simple linear description of their sentences is insufficient, for discontinuous elements and dependencies must also be accounted for. For example, a language (XX) having an alphabet a and b and whose sentences are *aa, bb, abab, baba, aaaa, bbbb, aabaab*, and in general all sentences composed of a sequence X of elements a and b followed by this same sequence X cannot be generated by a Markovian model.

It is evident that in many narrative texts (if not in all) this type of structure is to be found. To take a very simple example; let us briefly examine the following excerpt from a Sherlock Holmes story:

> Both of us were surprised, I think, to perceive that our caller was a young lady. . . . Gently Sherlock Holmes took the travelling-case

from her hand, and pushed an armchair towards the fire . . . "I thank
you Mr. Holmes," replied the young lady . . ."They say, sir, that
you can read into the human heart." . . . "They overestimate my
powers," he answered, smiling. "Beyond the obvious facts that you
are a lady's companion, that you seldom travel yet have recently
returned from a journey to Switzerland, and that your errand here
concerns a man who has engaged your affections, I can deduce
nothing."

The young lady gave a violent start, and I myself was taken aback.

"Holmes," cried I, "this is too much. How could you possibly
know this?"

"How, indeed?" echoed the young lady.

"I see it, I observe it. The travelling-case, though far from new, is
neither worn nor battered by travel. Yet I need not insult your intelligence by calling attention to the paper label of the Hotel Splendide
at Grindelwald in Switzerland, which has been affixed with gum to
the side of the case."

"But the other point?" I insisted.

"The lady's attire, though in impeccable taste, is neither new nor
costly. Yet she has stayed at the best hotel in Grindelwald, and she
arrives in a carriage of the well-to-do. Since her initials, 'C. F.', do not
match the 'M' on the carriage panel, we may assume her to occupy
a position of equality in some well-to-do family. Her youth precludes
the position of governess, and we are left with a lady's companion.
As for the man who has engaged her affections, her blushes and
lowered eyelids proclaim as much. Absurd, is it not?" (Doyle and
Carr, 1971: 6-7).

Let us assign a letter to each of Holmes' deductions and to its 'logical'
source, as follows:

(a) The young lady does not travel often; her case is neither new nor
     used.
(b) She has come from Switzerland; the hotel's label is affixed to her
     case.
(c) She is a lady's companion in a wealthy family; there is a contra-
     diction between her modest attire and the luxury of the hotel
     (where she stayed) and the carriage (whose emblem does not
     match her initials).
(d) She is concerned with the well-being of a loved one; her blushes
     and lowered gaze when he is mentioned.

If we ignore, for the time being, the difference in the order of the
deductions and their explanations, the essential core of this narrative
fragment may be represented as a sequence *abcdabcd*. Other deductions-
explanations sequences, to be easily found in mystery novels, may be
represented as sequences like *aacc, abcabc, aa* etc. These sequences

belong, therefore, to a language not generatable by a finite-state grammar.[10] In order to account for the narrative structure of a text, it is not sufficient to consider it merely as a concatenation of sentences: we need a more powerful grammar which will also explain the structural relations between various parts of the text.

We have just demonstrated that the conception which seemingly explains the global meaning of a text by the concatenation of the meanings of its individual sentences is inadequate for a theory of narrative structures. We now propose to show that the notion of text is not the hierarchically primary notion, and consequently, in a narrative grammar which has a TG format, the use of 'text' as initial symbol in the base component is neither advantageous nor sufficiently productive. In order to show this more succinctly, we need only examine the relationship between narrative structure and text.

There is at least one phenomenon at the textual level which shows that the text is a reality derived from its relation to an abstract structure which is hierarchically primary. In particular we are referring to what Todorov (1966) calls ALTERATION: two independent—or nearly independent plots are developed simultaneously (and alternatively) within one text. In *Phèdre,* for example, the spectator witnesses the development of two different narrative sequences (albeit related by a common character): the love of Hippolyte for Aricie, and the Phèdre-Hippolyte conflict. There is an almost total lack of connectedness between the scenes dealing with the story of Hippolyte and Aricie, and those dealing with Phèdre's situation. An extreme example of a text wherein two totally independent narratives alternate is Faulkner's novel *Wild Palms.* In order to account for this type of text, a mechanism is needed which first GENERATES the narrative structures, then by a series of operations similar to transformations, mixes the narrative sequences to give them their final format. Accepting the distinction made by Greimas and Rastier (1968) between superficial SURFACE STRUCTURES ('une grammaire sémiotique qui ordonne en formes discursives les contenus susceptibles de manifestations. Les produits de cette grammaire sont indépendants de l'expression qui les manifeste') and MANIFESTATION STRUCTURES (which 'produisent et organisent les signiants'), we would have to conclude that the text is related to the manifestational aspect[11] and therefore belongs to a later stage of the narrative-generating process. Another argument in favor of this interpretation of 'text' is the frequently-found phenomenon of assembling different texts into a set because of their narrative structure-type: the set of *Electra*-type tragedies, the set of different textual arrangements and adaptations of one play, etc. The same narrative structure is manifested by completely different texts. We know, for example, that Racine wrote his tragedies first in prose before converting them into verse.[12] It would be extremely uneconomical to generate the prose text and the verse text of the same tragedy separately. On the other hand, if we generate only the narrative structure and then introduce the differences at the textual level, this would be much more satisfying intuitively as well as 'fitting in' better with the reality of the situation. In van Dijk, 1971 and 1972, we find a certain number of arguments similar to those presented above: according to van Dijk we must distinguish between the DEEP STRUCTURE and the SURFACE STRUCTURE of a text. These two terms are easily relatable—and even coincide with—what we have been calling narrative structure and text.

5   Remarks on the base component

The preceding analysis has been suggested both by Chatman (1971) and by van Dijk (1971, 1972) who propose transformational formalization of narrative grammar. The initial symbol used by Chatman (1971), who follows Todorov (1969), is S (narrative sentence). This notion, amply detailed in Todorov (1969), corresponds to that of SENTENCE in linguistics. Just as a linguistic sentence is divided into NP + VP, the narrative sentence is divisible into AGENT and PREDICATE. The notion of narrative sentence (or 'proposition') is useful when dealing with the analysis of a narrative into smaller meaningful segments. As both Todorov (1969) and Chatman (1971) clearly show, a narrative proposition is a 'local' reality. Narrative propositions combine to form narrative sequences which, in turn, may combine to form larger units. What is of main interest to us is the possibility of generating structures which are more general than narrative propositions. The latter would be introduced as concrete realizations of more abstract symbols and in so doing approach more closely the original concept of narrative structure held by Propp:

> Le contenu tout entier d'un conte peut être énoncé en des courtes phrases ressemblant à celles-ci: les parents partent dans la forêt, ils interdisent aux enfants d'aller dehors, le dragon enlève la jeune fille, etc. Tous les *prédicats* reflètent la structure du conte, tous les *sujets*, les *compléments* et les autre parties du discours definissent le sujet (Propp, 1928a: 141).

This brief quote clearly shows that for Propp the narrative structure is more abstract than the narrative propositions and this structure organizes them into a coherent whole. At the same time we can incorporate Greimas's view which states: 'La récit, pour avoir un sens doit être un tour de signification, il se présente, de ce fait, comme une *structure sémantique simple*. La narration, considérée comme un tout, nécessite donc une structure hiérarchique du contenu' (1970: 187).

The initial symbol, then, must be NARRATIVE STRUCTURE. The first rewrite rule (the first step in 'generating' a tree) must correspond to some major cut or division within the narrative and should be intuitively recognizable. We shall attempt to show that the role of narrative categories can be fulfilled by certain of Propp's functions, or by similar functions, and that these are subject to the effects of the phenomenon called EXPANSION. Propp's classification of the functions found in the Russian fairy-tales (numbering thirty-one) are as follows:

1	absence	11	departure	22	rescue
2	interdiction	12	the first function of the donor	23	unrecognized arrival
3	violation	13	the hero's reaction	24	see 8a
4	reconnaissance	14	the provision	25	the difficult task
5	delivery	15	spatial translocation	26	task accomplished
6	fraud	16	struggle	27	recognition
7	complicity	17	marking	28	exposure
8	villainy	18	victory	29	transfiguration
8a	lack	19	lack liquidated	30	punishment
9	mediation	20	return	31	wedding
10	beginning counter action	21	pursuit		

Propp suggested the possibility of reducing this inventory by pairing the functions according to their interdependence. Thus INTERDIC-TION is implied by a VIOLATION. In Greimas (1966: 164), the following functions are combined: 2 & 3, 4 & 5, 6 & 7, 9 & 10, 12 & 13, 16 & 18, 21 & 22, 25 & 26, 28 & 29 and 30 & 31; but even this reduction leaves a system which is far too complex. Greimas asks, then 'si le couplage de fonctions ne peut recevoir une justification méthodologique qui le rendrait opérationnel...' (Greimas 1966: 195). If we consider, for example, the functional pair INTERDICTION–VIOLATION 'en dehors de tout contexte syntagmatique, il apparaît comme un catégorie sémique, dont les termes sont à la fois conjoints et disjoints, par consequent formulable par *s* vs. non *s s* = sème' (Greimas, 1966: 195). These two functions together are the realization of a 'breach of contract' by opposition to the pair MEDIATION-HERO'S COUNTER ACTION which realize an 'establishment of contract'.

The dependencies which Greimas describes with the aid of semic categories can be represented in tree form. It is clear that the symbols INTERDICTION and VIOLATION can be joined to a common node which would be labelled, ultimately, BREACH OF CONTRACT. Likewise, the symbols 'mediation' and 'hero's counter action' (if these symbols in fact belong to the grammar) would be dominated by a node labelled ESTABLISHMENT OF CONTRACT. From here it is only a short step to conjoining both of these nodes to a single higher node.

On the other hand, as has often been noted, Propp's functions are not all of equal importance: RECONNAISSANCE and DELIVERY for example can be related to DECEIT but the latter does not depend on the existence of a 'reconnaissance' nor on the attainment of some information. Conversely, these two functions could not exist without the FRAUD to which they contribute. We must therefore recognize that in this case—and in many others—there exists a type of syntactic dependency which is fairly common. The sequence 'reconnaissance-delivery-fraud' represents, in distributionalist terminology, an 'expansion' of the 'fraud' just as the sequence *these hopeful people* is equivalent to an expansion of the noun (Harris, 1951: 274). If all the while we realize that the pair 'reconnaissance/delivery' is joined only to 'fraud' and not to the pair 'fraud/complicity' we may represent the sequence (a linear sequence, according to Propp):

1   reconnaissance + delivery + fraud + complicity,

is underlaid by a tree showing these hierarchical dependencies. The whole of the sequence would be represented (and dominated) by an initial node, tentatively labelled SEQUENCE.

2
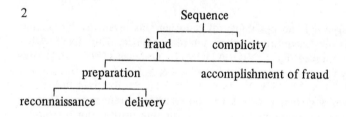

The following rewrite rules correspond to this tree representation:

3   Sequence → Fraud + complicity
4   Fraud → (Preparation) Accomplishment of fraud
5   Preparation → Reconnaissance + delivery

As can be seen, these three rules can generate another sequence representable as

6
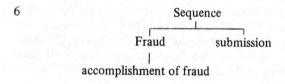

We do not know if a narrative grammar of Russian fairytales should include THESE particular rules, but it is reasonable to conclude, at least that (2)–(5) are valid representations of the relations between the functions of sequence (1).

This type of rule also allows us to include a phenomenon which, due to the nature of the corpus studied by Propp, was not recognized until much later. At issue here is that which Bremond (1964, 1966), calls the NARRATIVE POSSIBILITIES. In his two studies Claude Bremond shows that the linearity and solidarity which, according to Propp (1928a), unite the functions do not correspond to narrative reality. The narrative processes can manifest themselves as a succession of possibilities and can be divided into three stages: one function initiates or triggers the process; a second function actually realizes, or accomplishes, the process; the third function terminates, or delimits the whole of the process. These functions may be called: (1) Initial, (2) Procedural, (3) Terminal. The initial function is followed by the procedural function which may/may not be fulfilled. If completed, the procedural function is followed by the terminal function which, in turn, may represent either a 'follow-through' or a 'checkmate' of the process. In the case of DECEIT, the following schema is one representation:

7   Initial   Procedural   Terminal

$$\text{Fraud to be accomplished} \begin{cases} \text{accomplished} \\ \text{not accomplished} \end{cases} \begin{cases} \text{succeeds} \\ \text{fails} \end{cases}$$

In order to introduce the narrative possibilities more easily into our grammar, suppose that in sequence (1) the realization of 'submission' does NOT depend on the success of the 'fraud', and that the fraud is triggered by the sequence 'reconnaissance–delivery'. Our primary interest here is to be able to introduce the representation of (7) into the grammar.

The fact that there is a process to be fulfilled (a deceit to be achieved) is indicated simply by the choice of the symbol 'Fraud' when rewriting the symbol which precedes—and dominates—it. In our example, this choice is rendered mandatory by rule (3). To indicate the possible choice between accomplishment/non-accomplishment of the deceit it is sufficient to modify rule (4) such that the symbol 'Fraud accomplished' cannot be chosen:

$$4 \quad \text{Fraud} \rightarrow \begin{cases} \text{Preparation} \\ \text{(Preparation) Accomplishment of Fraud} \end{cases}$$

Finally, to indicate that the deceit accomplished may be successful or may fail, a supplementary rule must be introduced:

8 Accomplishment of Fraud → $\left\{ \begin{array}{l} \text{Fraud succeeds} \\ \text{Fraud fails} \end{array} \right\}$

In applying rules (3), (4') and (8) we get the tree representations (9)–(11)

9

```
                    Sequence
                       |
            ┌──────────┴──────────┐
          Fraud              Complicity
            |
        Preparation
```

10

```
                    Sequence
                       |
            ┌──────────┴──────────┐
          Fraud              Complicity
            |
        ┌───┴──────────────┐
    Preparation          Accomp.
                         of Fraud
                            |
                      Fraud succeeds
```

11

```
                    Sequence
                       |
            ┌──────────┴──────────┐
          Fraud              Complicity
            |
        ┌───┴──────────────┐
    Preparation          Accomp.
                         of Fraud
                            |
                       Fraud fails
```

There are two other representations corresponding to (10) and (11) which do not have the symbol 'Preparation', which in rule (4') cannot be chosen if 'Accomp. of Fraud' is chosen. Notice that if in a grammar we wished to show that complicity was a consequence of the function 'Fraud succeeds' and ONLY of this function, we would have to reject (3) and modify (8) to read:

8' Accomp. of Fraud → $\left\{ \begin{array}{l} \text{Fraud succeeds + Submission} \\ \text{Fraud fails} \end{array} \right\}$

Finally, before going on to look at transformations, let us justify our choice of the initial rule. In linguistics, rewriting sentence as NP + VP seems natural. Yet as Robins (1967) and Lyons (1968) note, the discovery of the parts of speech resulted from long and laborious study spanning several centuries. In narratology, as we have previously seen, this study is just beginning. Consequently, all propositions such as that which follows, and which aspire to universal applicability, are subject to disproof. We shall adopt the following as our first rewrite rule:

12 Narrative Structure → Inversed Content + Posited Content

The two symbols on the right correspond to two notions used by Greimas (1966).

> Une sous-classe de récits dramatisés (mythes, contes, pièces de théâtre, etc.) est définie par une propriété structurale commune: la dimension temporelle sur laquelle ils se trouvent situés, est dichotomisée en un avant et une après. A cet *avant* vs. *après* discursif correspond un 'renversement de la situation' qui, sur le plan de la structure implicite, n'est rien d'autre qu'une inversion des signes du contenu. Une correlation existe ainsi sur les deux plans:

$$\frac{\text{avant}}{\text{apres}} \simeq \frac{\text{contenu inversé}^{13}}{\text{contenu posé}}$$

6 Transformations

The narrative structure of a given tale can be represented, as suggested by Propp (1928a), by the sequence of PREDICATES (functions) which compose the tale. The base component of the grammar, which represents narrative competence, generates hierarchical structures in the form of labelled trees whose symbols are often identical to Propp's functions. This base grammar cannot generate the correct terminal strings of the narrative predicates. To show that a series of transformational rules applicable to the output of the base component is needed, let it suffice to mention a few typical cases which are similar to linguistic phenomena requiring the use of transformations. Chomsky (1963) and Postal (1964) showed that a language (XX) whose sentences are composed of two identical sequences, for example *aa, bb, abab*, etc., cannot be context-free and therefore cannot be generated by a syntagmatic grammar. In order to generate this language using a context-free base-grammar component, transformation rules must be introduced. As we have seen, certain narrative effects—such as the relationship between the deductions and the 'indicators' the detective uses in mystery novels—must be described as sentences of an (XX)-type language, which therefore brings us to the conclusion that the use of transformations in a narrative grammar is necessary. Another type of situation which is most economically resolved through the use of transformations is that of 'discontinuous constituents'. The three stages through which Racine's star-crossed lovers must pass in their forbidden passion (which fulfills the role of 'violation' in relation to a previously-set 'interdiction') are, as we have seen:

1 love at first sight,
2 resisting the passion,
3 resistance failed; succumbing to the passions.

To simplify the base component of our grammar and to clarify the relation between love's first blow and its second ('De mes feux mal eteints je reconnus la trace', *Andromaque*, v. 86) we can postulate the following rules:

13 Violation → Passion + Resistance
14 Passion → 1st desire + Invincible passion.

A transformation should then rearrange the symbols of the terminal string and should be something like:

15 T passion overcomes resistance
    1st desire + invincible passion + resistance →
    1st desire + resistance + invincible passion

Another function of transformation rules would be to allow for the construction of generalized grammars. For example: in the narrative grammar of Russian fairytales the pair 'interdiction/violation', is only indirectly linked to 'defiance', and belongs to the preparatory aspect of the tale, or CORRELATIVE CONTENT (Greimas, 1970). Usually the character who accomplishes this defiance is not the same as the one who carries out the 'violation'. In Racine's tragedies, as a counter-example, the 'interdiction/violation' on the one hand and the 'defiance' on the other (if we can consider the 'recognition' of the passion as being roughly equivalent to a defiance which causes a lack of equilibrium in the Racinian universe) are conjoined to the same node: INVERSED CONTENT. A more general grammar would first of all produce the more abstract of the two narrative situations, and would then introduce the other by means of an adequate transformation. A set of transformations of this type would serve to characterize a literary genre, or an author's particular narrative style.

The transformations mentioned so far are indispensable for the generation of acceptable terminal strings. These strings of narrative predicates are far removed from actual texts. To obtain, not the text, but at least the narrative texture—that is, the organization of the narrative material of the work—we must introduce a system of textualization rules whose input is the output of the preceding transformation rules. It is at this stage that we must account for such phenomena as narrative alternation and flash-back techniques wherein the textual sequence does not coincide with the sequence of narrative predicates. In order to tackle the thorny problem of textualization we must first resolve the problem of the status of the terminal symbols. Are these MINIMAL units as Propp supposed, or are they bundles of narrative propositions? If the latter proves valid, a narrative grammar of the type proposed herein can make effective use of the important conclusions drawn by Greimas (1970), and Todorov (1969, 1970), regarding the typology of narrative propositions.

In conclusion, let us point out that the term 'transformation' is used here with precisely the same meaning as found in the writings of American transformationalists. As we know narratology originated through the efforts of anthropology and was for a long time solely its device. We have also seen the extent of Lévi-Strauss's influence on the development of narrative structures. Thus it comes as no surprise that the term 'transformation' has a particular, and specifically different, meaning in some previous studies in narratology than it does in the Chomskian transformational tradition in linguistics. In the latter, transformations constitute a set of rules, one of the main characteristics of which is that more than one symbol may be posited to the left of the double arrow ($\Rightarrow$ 'rewrite as'). In the Chomskian sense, transformations apply to underlying tree-structures which are already derived from a base component, and map (i.e. transform) these initial trees into other, structurally different, trees. A Chomskian transformation is *par excellence* syntactic and since Chomsky (1965) it has been accepted that transformations 'do not change meaning.'[14]

In order to grasp the significance of Lévi-Strauss's conception of transformation, as found in the work of Greimas, Köngäs-Maranda, or Kristeva let us briefly re-examine the formula proposed by Lévi-Strauss for myth:

$$|f_x(a) : f_y(b) : : f_x(b) : f_a - 1 (y)|$$

As explained by E. Köngäs and Pierre Maranda in Köngäs-Maranda, 1971: 26-27:

if a given actor (a) is specified by a negative function F_x (and thus becomes a villain) and another one (b) by a positive function F_y (and thus becomes a hero), (b) is capable of assuming in turn also the negative function, which process leads to a 'victory' so much more complete that it proceeds from the 'ruin' of the term (a) and thus definitely establishes the positive value (y) of the final outcome.

Lévi-Strauss's outcome indicates a mediation process by which a certain state of affairs is transformed into the inverse situation. It seems that this semantic relationship between two contents linked by a mediation is the widest acceptable application of the term transformation in semiotics. Greimas (1966) uses this term unambiguously when speaking of TEST, a function which he calls PERFORMANCE (1970) and which constitutes the kernel of the MEDIATION: 'le role de l'épreuve se précise: elle prend en charge une structure de contenu donnée . . . et la transforme, par une opération mythique . . . en une structure de contenue différente de la première' (1970: 221). The use of the term 'transformation' by Elli Köngäs-Maranda in Chapter 4 of Köngäs-Maranda (1971), may be assigned this same interpretation.

In the grammar we have been proposing, the 'mythic' transformation of contents corresponds to the semantic interpretation of first re-write rule:

12   Narrative Structure → Inversed Content + Posited Content

Note also that in Propp (1928a), and in Maranda (1971: Chapter 3), the term 'transformation' has yet a third meaning. This time, a transformation accounts for the relationship between a folk-tale and a myth, a myth and another myth, etc. In this sense, the application of a transformation is somewhat analogous to transformation as proposed by Harris (1957). In Harris's theory no distinction is made between deep and surface structures, and the transformations, far from being applied to abstract underlying structures as is the case with Chomsky, transform real sentences into other real sentences. Harris's transformations are strictly syntactic while those proposed by Maranda function with semantic elements. The theoretical similarities between the two however, are striking.

NOTES

1 For a summary of Dundes, 1964, see Bremond, 1968.
2 Greimas (1970) distinguishes these two terms. According to him 'on pourrait reserver le nom *sémiotiques* aux seules sciences de l'expression, en utilisant le terme, reste disponible, *sémiologie* pour les disciplines du contenu' (1970: 33).
3 It is of some relevance here to note Chomsky's epistemological caution. In this formulation the rules only REPRESENT competence. Later, certain proponents of generative grammar expressed more radical opinions. Without discussing the psycholinguistic experiments which attempted to measure the temporal length of transformational derivations occurring in the human brain, let us cite a characteristic passage from one of Chomsky's later students on this issue: 'It has been suggested by critics of generative grammar (e.g. Hockett, 1968) that it has become caught in the fatal trap of taking its theoretical entities such as rules, ordering, underlying base forms, etc; for real entities, whereas they actually, according to Hockett, are only tools to be used for analysing the real entities such as phonemes and morphemes. Historically, linguistics supports exactly the opposite conclusion in an especially direct way. We have seen that sound change and analogy is change in the grammatical system of a language, including precisely the rules and their order. If these real events then, are changed in the rules and their order, then the rules and their order must be real entities too' (Kiparsky, 1970: 314).

4 We are using and/or in a loose sense; later we shall see that in this context a choice must be made between and/or, and that this choice has some theoretical consequences.

5 It would be even more erroneous to believe that competence follows the rules as ordered in the grammar in a 'chronological' way, or that it relates a phonetic representation to a meaning rather than relating a meaning to a phonetic representation. On this question of 'directionality of mapping' and its role in recent polemics between various representatives of interpretive *vs.* generative semantics, see Lakoff (1971), who in note 2 refers the reader to Chomsky (1971).

6 All this is valid, of course, if considering the 'ideal' raconteur, as described in classical theory of folklore.

7 For a recent account of critical works on Racine, see Roubine, 1971.

8 It should be recalled that in Bloomfield (1933), meaning is considered to be the best means of determining immediate constituents.

9 For more recent developments concerning base rules (of the constituent type) see Chomsky (1965) and McCawley (1968). The adherents of the various 'generative semantics' approaches view these base rules in a totally different light, theoretically, than does Chomsky. A mathematical treatment of some aspects of TG grammar is found in Brainerd, 1971; Chap. 5.

10 Dundes (1964), who retains some of Propp's functions and groups them into pairs, and Greimas (1970), who divides narrative structure into 'Inversed Content' and 'Posited Content' show that this type of language is highly characteristic of narrative structures.

11 Throughout this discussion TEXT has been used in its weaker sense. It is evident that in its stronger sense, there is even less validity to the use of text as a starting point for a generative grammar.

12 The prose sketches of Racine's completed tragedies are not extant. They were probably destroyed once each play was finished in verse. The only existing prose fragment, the beginning of *Iphigénie en Tauride*—incomplete—has no corresponding version in verse. Even though we cannot speak of TEXT in the stronger sense of MONUMENTARY TEXTS—in regard to these lost prose tragedies—they suffice to show our meaning of text in the weaker sense.

13 The notions originate in the works of Claude Lévi-Strauss.

14 For a recent discussion of this condition, see Barbara Hall Partee, 1971.

REFERENCES

Barthes, Roland (1966), 'Introduction à l'analyse structurale des récits', *Communications 8*, pp. 1–28.

Bellert, Irena (1970), 'On a Condition of the Coherence of Texts', *Semiotica 2*, pp. 335–63.

Bloomfield, Leonard (1933), *Language* (New York: Holt, Rinehart & Winston).

Brainerd, Barron (1971), *Introduction to the Mathematics of Language Study* (New York: American Elsevier).

Bremond, Claude (1964), 'Le message narratif', *Communications 4*, pp. 4–32.

Bremond, Claude (1966), 'La logique des possibles narratifs', *Communications 8*, pp. 60–76.

Bremond, Claude (1968), 'Posterite américaine de Propp', *Communications 11*, pp. 148–64.

Chabrol, C. and Morin, L. (eds) (1971), 'Sémiotique narrative: Récits bibliques', *Langages 22* (numero special).

Chatman, Seymour (1969), 'New Ways of Analyzing Narrative Structures', *Language and Style 2*, pp. 3–36.

Chatman, Seymour (1971), 'Compte-rendu de Todorov, 1969', *Language Science 17*, 52–4.

Chomsky, Noam (1957), *Syntactic Structures* (The Hague: Mouton).

Chomsky, Noam (1963), 'Formal Properties of Grammars', in Luce, Bush, and Galanter, pp. 323–418.

Chomsky, Noam (1964), 'Current Issues in Linguistic Theory', in Fodor and Katz, 1964, pp. 40–118.

Chomsky, Noam (1965), *Aspects of the Theory of Syntax* (Cambridge, Mass.: MIT Press).

Chomsky, Noam (1971), 'Deep Structure, Surface Structure and Semantic Interpretation', in Steinberg and Jakobovits, *Semantics* (London: Cambridge University Press, 1971), pp. 183–217.

van Dijk, Teun A. (1970), 'La metateoria del raconto', *Strumenti critici* 12, pp. 141–64.

van Dijk, Teun A. (1971), 'Some Problems of Generative Poetics', *Poetics 2*, pp. 5–35.

van Dijk, Teun A. (1971), 'Aspects d'une théorie générative du texte poetique', in Greimas *et al.*, *Essais de semiotique poetique* (Paris: Larousse, 1972), pp. 180–206.

Doyle, A. Conan and J. Dickson Carr (1971), *The Exploits of Sherlock Holmes*, (New York: Random House).

Dundes, Alan (1964), *The Morphology of North American Indian Folktales* (Helsinki: Academia Scientiarum Fenica).

Eco, Umberto (1966), 'James Bond: Une combinatoire narrative', *Communications 8*, pp. 77–93.

Fillmore, Charles J. and D. T. Langendoen (eds) (1971), *Studies in Linguistic Semantics* (New York: Holt, Rinehart & Winston).

Fodor, Jerry A. and Jerrold J. Katz (eds) (1964), *The Structure of Language* (Englewood Cliffs, N. J.: Prentice-Hall).

Gerson, Sylvia (1972), 'Profondeur motifémique et prolifération narrative' (ms.).

Greimas, Algirdas, J. (1966), *Sémantique structurale* (Paris: Larousse).

Greimas, Algirdas, J. (1970), *Du sens* (Paris: Seuil).

Greimas, A. J. *et al.* (1972), *Essais de semiotique poetique* (Paris: Larousse).

Greimas, A. J. and Francois Rastier (1968), 'Les jeux des contraintes semiotiques', in Greimas, *Du sens* (Paris: Seuil, 1970).

Hall Partee, Barbara (1971), 'On the Requirement that Transformations Preserve Meaning', in Fillmore and Langendoen, *Studies in Linguistic Semantics* (New York: Holt, Rinehart & Winston, 1971), pp. 1–29.

Harris, Zellig S. (1951), *Methods in Structural Linguistics* (Chicago: University of Chicago Press).

Harris, Zellig S. (1952a), 'Discourse Analysis', *Language 28*, pp 1–30.

Harris, Zellig S. (1952b), 'Discourse Analysis: A Sample Text', *Language 28*, pp. 274–94.

Harris, Zellig S. (1957), 'Co-occurrence and Transformation in Linguistic Structure', *Language 33*, pp. 293–340.

Harweg, R. (1968), *Pronomina und Textkonstitution* (Munchen: Fink).

Hjelmslev, Louis (1969), *Prolegomena to a Theory of Language* (Madison: University of Wisconsin Press).

Ihwe, Jens (ed.) (1971), *Literaturwissenschaft und Linguistik, 1: Grundlagen und Voraussetzungen* (Frankfurt am Main: Athenäum).

Isenberg, Horst (1971), 'Uberlegungen zur Textheorie', in Ihwe, *Literaturwissenschaft und Linguistik, 1* (Frankfurt am Main: Athenaum, 1971).

Katz, Jerrold, J. (1964), 'Semi-sentences', in Fodor and Katz, *The Structure of Language* (Englewood Cliffs, N.J.: Prentice-Hall, 1964), pp. 400–16.

Katz, Jerrold J. and Jerry A. Fodor (1964), 'The Structure of a Semantic Theory', in Fodor and Katz, *The Structure of Language* (Englewood Cliffs, N. J.: Prentice-Hall, 1964), pp. 519–43.

Kiparsky, Paul (1970), 'Historical Linguistics', in Lyons, 1970, pp. 302–15.

Köngäs-Maranda, Elli and Pierre Maranda (1962), 'Structural Models in Folklore', *Midwest Folklore 12*, pp. 133–92.

Köngäs-Maranda, Elli and Pierre Maranda (1971), *Structural Models in Folklore and Transformational Essays* (The Hague: Mouton).

Kristeva, Julia (1970), *Le texte du roman* (The Hague: Mouton).

Lakoff, George (1971), 'On Generative Semantics', in Steinberg and Jakobovits, *Semantics* (London: Cambridge University Press, 1971), pp. 232–96.

Lévi-Strauss, Claude (1955), 'The Structural Study of Myth', *Journal of American Folklore 68*, pp. 428–44.

Lévi-Strauss, Claude (1958), *Anthropologie structurale* (Paris: Plon).

Luce, R. D., R. Bush and E. Galanter (1963), *Handbook of Mathematical Psychology, II* (New York: Wiley).

Lyons, John (1968), *Introduction to Theoretical Linguistics* (London: Cambridge University Press).

Lyons, John (ed.) (1970), *New Horizons in Linguistics* (London: Penguin).

McCawley, James (1968), 'Concerning the Base Component of a Transformational Grammar', *Foundations of Language 4*, pp. 243–69.

Postal, Paul M. (1964), 'Limitations of Phrase Structure Grammars', in Fodor and Katz, *The Structure of Language* (Englewood Cliffs, N. J.: Prentice-Hall, 1964).

Propp, Vladimir (1928a), *Morphologie du conte*, trans. by M. Derrida *et al*. (Paris: Seuil, 1970).

Propp, Vladimir (1928b), 'Les transformations du conte merveilleux', in Propp, (1928a), pp. 171–200.

Riffaterre, Michael (1971), *Essais de stylistique structurale* (Paris: Flammarion).

Robins, R. H. (1967), *A Short History of Linguistics* (London: Longman).

Roubine, Jean-Jacques (1971), Lectures de Racine (Paris: A. Colin).

Steinberg, Danny D. and Leon A. Jakobivits (eds) (1971), *Semantics* (London: Cambridge University Press).

Todorov, Tzvetan (1966), 'Les catégories du récit littéraire', *Communications 8*, pp. 125–51.

Todorov, Tzvetan (1968), *Littérature et signification* (Paris: Larousse).

Todorov, Tzvetan (1969), *Grammaire du Décaméron* (The Hague: Mouton).

Todorov, Tzvetan (1970), 'Les transformations narratives', *Poétique 3*, pp. 322–32.

Vuillot, G. (1971), 'Exercices sur de courts textes', in Chabrol and Morion, *Sémiotique narrative Langages 22* (1971).

Zumthor, Paul (1963), *Langue et techniques poétiques à l'époque romane* (Paris: Klinchsieck).

CHAPTER ELEVEN

Inversions and deletions in English poetry

George L. Dillon

[Dillon's article compares the deletions and inversions in English poetry from Spenser to the Victorians with the deletion and inversion transformations which operate in modern English prose. He concludes that the rules by which these poetic inversions and deletions are generated are similar to certain optional transformations which function in ordinary English; thus, for Dillon, style is choice—and attempts to categorize the differences between the two sets of rules, showing the poetic rules to be extensions of and deviations from these ordinary English transformations. He gives poetic examples of rule extensions and deviations, working his way toward the statement that 'one should assume the minimum of difference between poetic syntax and that of ordinary language . . .' He then outlines the ways in which poets use these deletions and inversions:

1 to order information to focus on a constituent (presentational)
2 to represent complex psychological experience (imitative)
3 to achieve rhyme and metrical effects (prosodic).

Dillon treats the first two briefly and goes into some detail in discussing the third.

He no longer uses this approach in analyzing style. He has changed to a psycholinguistic model, which is reflected in *Language Processing and the Reading of Literature: Toward a Model of Comprehension* (Indiana University Press, 1978).]

It is well known that English poets from Spenser to the Victorians employed certain inversions and deletions in their poetry which were described in Classical and Renaissance rhetorics as 'schemes of words.'[1] A sample of unusual orders is given in Chatman's *Introduction to the Language of Poetry*.[2] While some of these re-orderings and deletions are indeed characteristic of poets from Spenser to Tennyson, they are also fairly common in modern, non-poetic English. To understand what is unusual about the syntax of these poets, it is necessary to describe the re-orderings and deletions precisely and to compare them to des-

*First published in *Language and Style* (1975), 220–36.

criptions of optional transformations of Modern English such as those given by Ross, Emonds, Postal, Hankamer, Grosu, and other grammarians.[3] Despite certain obscurities about Modern English and the notion of 'common optional transformation,' such a comparison is possible and, I hope to show, quite interesting.[4] There is a further advantage to giving these inversions and deletions precise formulation, namely that the derived structure of the line will show extra junctures and ϕ symbols which should correlate with altered prosodic properties and thus in many cases explain why the inversion was made. The first part of this article will describe the poetic transformations and the second will survey some of the poetic purposes served by them.

The actual inversions and deletions can be described by rules which resemble common optional transformations, but differ from them in certain ways. There are rules which

(i) operate as in non-poetic Modern English but
    (a) affect a broader range of elements (e.g. deletions under identity)
    (b) are ordered or written slightly differently (Topicalization, PP-Fronting)
    (c) are triggered by a broader range of environments (S/V Inversion)
(ii) differ from any rule of Modern English (Verb-Final) (the ones to be discussed also differ from rules of ENE)
(iii) affect structures which are normally Islands (i.e. immune to chopping)

These items characterize unusualness of syntax: in fact, most of them could be viewed as relaxations of constraints on transformations in Modern English (i.e. 'licenses'). We can describe in what ways and to what degrees a poet's language is unusual in terms of them. To be precise, however, they characterize formal unusualness, or unusualness of syntactic rules—there are some very complicated sentences in Milton, for example, that are not formally unusual, so that there is no direct correlation between unusualness as here defined and difficulty of reading. The rules do, however, characterize a kind of extra syntactic competence required of the reader. I will exemplify rules of each type in the following sections.

1.1. Deletion of Subjects and Direct Objects (D. O.): Conjunction Reduction and Gapping in Modern English delete certain elements in conjoined structures under identity. The Node-Raising option of Conjunction Reduction deletes the first of two identical D. O's when it is the last element in the Verb Phrase:

    John killed, and Mary cleaned, the game.

Conjunction Reduction also deletes the Subj. of the second conjunct when it is identical to the Subj. of the first:

John killed and cleaned the game.

Gapping deletes the second V or ADJ predicate:

John killed a bear and Mary, a lynx.

In my speech, Verb Phrase-deletion usually leaves an Auxiliary verb or *do* when deleting a second VP, but some writers describe it as leaving no trace, or allowing the trace to be deleted:

John killed a bear, and Mary (did so) too/as well/also.

All of these optional deletions occur in the poetry and are not unusual.

There are, however, a number of unusual deletions as well, where the deleted element would normally be pronominal in Modern English. D. O's are deleted to the right:

1 When rocks impregnable are not so stout,
Nor gates of steel so strong, but Time decays?
(Shakespeare, *Sonnets*, 65)[5]

2 For this Infernal Pit shall never hold
Celestial Spirits in Bondage, nor th'Abyss
Long under darkness cover.
(Milton, *Paradise Lost*, I.657-9)

3 Our purer essence then will overcome
Their noxious vapor, or enur'd not feel
(*Paradise Lost*, II. 215-16)

4 Chaste Matrons praise her, and grave Bishops bless;
(Pope, 'Epi. Sat.' I.146)

5 for she can so inform
The mind that is within us, so impress
With quietness and beauty, and so feed
With lofty thoughts, that . . .
(Wordsworth, 'Tintern Abbey' 125-8)

6 For I will fly to thee
Not charioted by Bacchus and his pards,
But on the viewless wings of Poesy,
Though the dull brain perplexes and retards;
(Keats, *Ode to a Nightingale* 31-4)

7 That ever with a frolic welcome took
The thunder and the sunshine, and opposed
Free hearts, free foreheads—
(Tennyson, 'Ulysses' 47-9; here deleted element is a PP: *to them*)

According to Hankamer's account of Conjunction Deletion, however, the constraint against 'gapping' D. O's is a language-specific output condition for English.[6] In these lines it is apparently lifted. There are also cases of deletion of the second Subj. when not identical to the first Subj. but rather to the D. O. or other NP in the first sentence:

8   Nor do we find him forward to be sounded
             But with a crafty madness keeps aloof
                            (Shakespeare, *Hamlet*, III.i.8)

9   For Cloten,
             There wants no diligence in seeking him,
             And will no doubt be found.
                            (*Cymbeline*, IV.iii.19-21)

10   This is that banish'd haughty Montague . . .
             And here is come
                            (*Romeo and Juliet*, V.iii.49-52)

11   He . . . did set uppon us flying both for feare
                            (Spenser, *Faerie Queene*, VI.i.16)

12   the gods, that gave good eare
             To her bold words, and marked well her grace,
             Being of stature tall as any there . . .
                            (*Faerie Queene*, VII.vi.28)

13   Into the Heart of *Eve* his words made way,
             Though at the voice much marveling
                            (Milton, *Paradise Lost*, IX.551-52)

14   wond'ring at my flight and change
             To this high exaltation; suddenly
             My Guide was gone, and I, methought, sunk down.
                            (*Paradise Lost*, V.89-91)

This freedom of deletion of Subjs. under identity is not confined to poetry, however, but is characteristic both of conversation and prose. Thus while these deletions are among the relatively unusual options the poets allow themselves, they are not unique to the poetic language.

1.2. Fronting transformations: Most of the rules of Modern English that 'front' constituents are used by these poets: Topicalization,[7] Left-Dislocation,[8] PP-Fronting, Adjective Phrase-Preposing. I have found virtually no cases where the NP fronted by Topicalization moves

beyond its original clause, and so adopt the following formulation of
Topicalization which might better be called NP-Fronting:

$$[_s\text{X--NP--Y}]_s$$
$$1 \quad 2 \quad 3 \Rightarrow$$
$$2 \,\#1 \quad \phi \quad 3$$

I will assume that PP-Fronting, though formally very similar to NP-
Fronting, is a distinct rule. Both are frequently applied to the same sentence, usually leaving the verb in clause-final position. Interestingly, the
usual order of application seems to be NP-, then *PP*-Fronting, so that
the D. O. immediately precedes the Subj., as in the following lines:

15   And over all a blacke stole shee did throw
                              (Spenser, *Faerie Queene*, I.i.4)

16   Against the Poets *their own Arms* they turn'd
                              (Pope, 'Essay on Criticism', 106)

17   In golden Chains the willing World she draws
                              (Pope, 'Epilogue to the Satires': Dialogue I, 147)

18   High on *Parnassus'* Top her Sons she show'd
                              (Pope, 'Essay on Criticism', 94)

19   But since like slaves his bed they did ascent
                              (Dryden, *Absalom and Achitophel* 16)

20   By falsities and lies the greatest part
            Of Mankind they corrupted
                              (Milton, *Paradise Lost*, I.367-68)

Roughly the same thing happens in the following lines, where the
D. O. (or head of the D. O., or at least the first element to the right of
the V) immediately precedes the Subj.:

21   Of these the vigilance
            I dread
                                        (*Paradise Lost*, IX.157-58)

22   Life piled on life
            Were all too little, and of one to me
            Little remains
                                        (Tennyson, 'Ulysses,' 24-6)

23   But of this frame the bearings, and the ties,
            The strong connexions, nice dependencies,
            Gradations just, has thy pervading soul,
            Look'd thro'?
                                    (Pope, 'Essay on Man,' I.29-32)

Notice that while (15)-(20) all violate the Kuno and Robinson 'Double-Dislocation Constraint,' they do so in the less radical 'non-crossing' way.[9] Crossing would give the order O PP S V.

1.3. Subject/V Inversion: Emonds (pp. 11-24) gives a considerable list of initial elements which optionally or obligatorily trigger S/V Inversion. Among these are

Directional Adverbs, PPs: Away ran John. Into the house ran the cat.
NEG-Advs: Seldom, never, rarely have so many owed so much to
   so few.
Compared Adjs.: Most important has been the secretary's testimony.
Locative PP: On every wall hangs a portrait of Lenin.

All of these optionally trigger S/V Inversion in the poetry, but so do a wide range of other preposed elements, usually optionally:

(a) Preposed ADJ and participles (inversion usually only with *be*, not *seem* or *appear*):

24   Vain is her wish
                                    (Wordsworth, *Prelude*, I.130)

25   tender is the night
                                    (Keats, 'Ode to a Nightingale,' 35)

26   Coldly thy rosy shadows bathe me, cold
            Are all thy lights, and cold my withered feet
            Upon thy glimmering threshold.
                                    (Tennyson, 'Tithonus,' 66-8)

27   pleasing was his shape
            And lovely
                                    (Milton, *Paradise Lost*, IX.503-4)

28   Cut is the branch that might have grown full straight,
            And burned is Apollo's laurel bough
                                    (Marlowe, *Dr Faustus*, xix.20)

(b)   Time adverbials:

29   After many a summer dies the swan
                                    (Tennyson, 'Tithonus,' 4)

30   some hour before you took me from the breach of the sea
was my sister drowned
> (Shakespeare, *Twelfth Night*, II.i.19)

31   Soon had his crew
Op'n'd into the Hill a spacious wound
> (Milton, *Paradise Lost*, I.689-90)

32   now shalt thou be moved
> (Shakespeare, *Henry IV, Part I*, II.iv.366)

33   Then wilt thou not be loath
To leave this Paradise, but shalt possess
A paradise within thee, happier far.
> (*Paradise Lost*, XII.586-88)

34   Then felt I like some watcher of the skies
> (Keats, 'On first looking into Chapman's Homer,' 10)

35   Once again
Do I behold these steep and lofty cliffs
> (Wordsworth, 'Tintern Abbey,' 4-5)

(c) *so, therefore:*

36   So have I a noble father lost
> (Shakespeare, *Hamlet* IV, vii.25)

37   So shall the World go on,
To good malignant, to bad men benign,
Under her own weight groaning
> (Milton, *Paradise Lost*, XII.537-9)

38   Therefore am I still
A lover of the meadows and the woods
> (Wordsworth, 'Tintern Abbey,' 102-3)

(d)   Direct Objects[10]

39   Full many a glorious morning have I seen
> (Shakespeare, *Sonnets*, 33)

40   But horse and foot knew Diamond to wield:
With curtax used Diamond to smite,
And Triamond to handle spear and shield,

But spear and curtax both usd Priamond in field.
(Spenser, *Faerie Queene*, IV.ii.42)

41   But answer made it none
(Shakespeare, *Hamlet*, I.ii.215)

42   That rudeness that hath appeared in me have I learned from
my entertainment.
(Shakespeare, *Twelfth Night*, I.v.203-04)

There well may be differences in the set of elements triggering S/V
Inversion for each poet, but in general it seems that S/V Inversion can
be triggered by a considerably wider range of elements than in Modern
English. Note that in (29), (34), (40), and (41) the entire verb inverts
with the Subj.
2.   Rules of type (ii): Verb-Final and Prep./NP-Inversion
2.1 Verb-final: All of the poets employ an optional rule which inverts
a verb and its complement. I will call this rule Verb-Final, though it
must be written to apply either to AUX + (ADV) + V or just to V,
and to all of the complement to the Verb, or just the D.O. Further,
the 'V' may be participial, or, more rarely, ADJ:

43   And salt too little which may season give
To her foul-tainted flesh
(Shakespeare, *Much Ado about Nothing*, IV.i.140-1)

44   Yet he her followd still with corage keene
(Spenser, *Faerie Queene*, III.iv.51)

45   The feends do quake, when any him to them does name
(*Faerie Queene*, III.iii.12)

46   she had this knight from far compeld.
(*Faerie Queene*, I.i.5)

47   Great wits are sure to madness near ally'd
And thin partitions do their bounds divide
(Dryden, *Absalom and Achitophel*, 11)

48   With secret joy indulgent David viewed
His youthful image in his son renewed
(*Absalom and Achitophel*, 33)

49   Where'er she turns, she finds
Impediments from day to day renewed
(Wordsworth, *Prelude* I.130-1)

50   And little town, thy streets for evermore
                Will silent be
                            (Keats, 'Ode to a Grecian Urn', 38-9)

51   For close designs and crooked counsels fit
                            (Dryden, *Absalom and Achitophel*, 55-6)

52   That she hath thee is of my wailing chief
                            (Shakespeare, *Sonnets*, 42)

53   what to your sense is due
                            (Pope, Essay on Criticism, 564)

54   For heav'nly minds from such distempers foul
                Are ever clear.
                            (Milton, *Paradise Lost* IV.118-19)

55   these steep woods and lofty cliffs,
                And this green pastoral landscape, were to me
                More dear, both for themselves and for thy sake.
                            (Wordsworth, 'Tintern Abbey ,'157-9)

An approximate statement of Verb-Final then is:

$$\underbrace{X\text{-}AUX\text{-}(ADV)\text{-}}\ \left\{ \begin{matrix} V \\ ADJ \end{matrix} \right\}\ \text{-}Y$$

1	2	3	4	$\Rightarrow$
1	$2/\phi$	ϕ	$4 + \phi/2 + 3$	

When the Subj. is missing (due to Imperative or Conjunction Reduction), the result of Verb-Final is formally identical to Topicalization—both are used in the following passages:

56   One common note on either lyre did strike,
                And knaves and fools we both abhorrd alike.
                To the same goal did both our studies drive
                The last set out the soonest did arrive.
                            (Dryden, 'To the Memory of Mr. Oldham,' 4-7)

57   The day with cloudes was suddeine overcast,
        And angry Jove an hideous storme of raine
        Did poure into his Lemans lap so fast,
        That every wight to shrowd it did constrain,
        And this fair couple eke to shroud themselves were fain.
                            (*Faerie Queene*, I.i.6)

The SOV order resulting from Verb-Final seems to be distinctively poetical in Milton: Ronald Emma found many instances of it in his samples of Milton's poetry, but none in the prose (*Milton's Syntax*, p. 145).

One apparent constraint on Verb-Final is that it does not apply if a PP has been fronted. That is, the order PP S O V does not occur. The sense of this would seem to be that the worst kind of 'Double Dislocation' is one where two constituents are dislocated in opposite directions. The rationale may be that the position of the verb is normally crucial for determining grammatical relations, and if that is altered no other dislocations are possible. However, this does not discriminate between Verb-Final and Subj./V Inversion, and O V S does occur (39–42), though fairly rarely. More research is needed on Subj./V Inversion before we can grasp the relevant differences between the two movements.

2.2. Prep./NP Inversion: Henry Peacham in 1577 noted an 'abuse' by poets which involves the inversion of the Prep. and NP of a PP: *'all Italy about I went* which is contrary to the plain order that placeth that saying thus *I went about all Italy. Now hope and fear between I stand* for *I stand between hope and fear*' (*The Garden of Eloquence*, f.iiii verso). This inversion is common in Spenser (e.g. *Faerie Queene* L.i.4, 11) and not uncommon in Shakespeare and other Elizabethan writers.[11] This inversion rule is of type (ii). Interestingly, it is not used to any noticeable degree by poets later than Shakespeare: Ronald Emma found only one occurrence of it in all of the passages from Milton's writings he examined (*Milton's Syntax*, p. 128); there is another one, however, in *Paradise Lost* IX.543.

3. Rules of type ii: Island-Chopping

A syntactic grouping is said to be an Island if it is immune to the removal (chopping) of its elements by such transformations as Topicalization or PP-Fronting. The classic example of an Island is a Co-ordinate NP. When, for example, the second of two coordinate D. O.'s is topicalized, the result is bad:

* Mary John kissed Sue and.

This is worse than chopping of the first conjunct:

? Sue John kissed, and Mary.

This seems to be because the latter can be viewed as derived by Conjunction Deletion:

John kissed Sue and J~~ohn kissed Mary~~

followed by Topicalization of the first D. O., which is not yet in a co-ordinate structure. This application of Topicalization is perhaps unusual in that it does not apply to the topmost S. One reads this sentence with an intonation break at the comma, suggesting that what follows is a kind of afterthought—that is, it is not dominated by a higher S. I will assume that sentences with Topicalization of the *first* of co-ordinated D. O.'s are a little odd, but not radically so. Milton employs Topicalization in this way:

58   his gestures fierce
                 He mark'd and mad demeanor
                        (Milton, *Paradise Lost*, IV.128-9)

59   Sea he had searcht and Land
                              (*Paradise Lost*, IX.76)

There are also instances of it in Pope (see (75), below). In (60) we seem to have PP-Fronting of *for contemplation* as well as Verb-Final. Here a co-ordinate NP does seem to have been split:

60   For contemplation hee and valor form'd
           For softness shee and sweet attractive Grace
                      (*Paradise Lost*, IV.298-9)

In (61) Verb-Final seems to have inverted the participial adjective with the (Prep.) and first NP of a co-ordinate structure:

61   he seem'd
          For dignity compos'd and high exploit
                      (*Paradise Lost*, II.110-11)

It is not clear to me whether moving something into a co-ordinate NP is as radical as moving one conjunct out, or even if this is a meaningful question. Example (62) seems derived by PP-preposing of *to him* next to the verb (a usual transformation of English), followed by Verb-Final again moving the V into a co-ordinate NP

62   For wee to him indeed all praises owe
            And daily thanks
                      (*Paradise Lost*, IV.444-5)

The following lines contain a truly unusual splitting of co-ordinate NPs which are complements to the noun *noise*:

63   where the noise
          Of riot ascends above thir loftiest Tow'rs,
          And injury and outrage
                      (*Paradise Lost*, I.499-501).

The derivation of these lines is certainly not obvious and is so unusual that one is inclined to read *injury* and *outrage* as co-ordinate with *noise* despite the semantic hash this makes of the lines. The difficulty here, as in (60), is the non-repetition of the Preps. If they were present, the lines would be less problematic. Perhaps a 'licentious' extra rule of 're-peated Prep. deletion' is involved, though this is scarcely a strong basis for postulating such a rule.

So much is still controversial about the transformations of conjunction reduction, deletion, and gapping, that it is premature to conclude that certain lines violate the Co-ordinate Structure Constraint or require a special 'poetical' kind of operation to derive them. It is not at all clear, for example, that the lines from Milton cited by Grinder and Elgin as illustrating a typical violation of the CSC do in fact involve a violation:

> is not the Earth
> With various living creatures, and the Air
> Replenisht
>
> (*Paradise Lost*, VII.329–31)[12]

These seem derivable via VP-deletion (ignoring the Q and NEG)

the Earth be replenisht with v.l.c. and the ~~Air be replenisht with v.l.c.~~

followed by Verb-Final. The methodological moral here is that one should assume the minimum of difference between poetic syntax and that of ordinary language, placing the burden of proof on those who claim that lines are highly unusual. A second moral is that one must consider the grammar of the poet as a whole.

With regard to other co-ordinate nodes, predicate Adjectives and participial phrases seem to prepose with only slight awkwardness in Modern English:

Disgusted John was and weary of life.

Again, only the first conjunct can prepose, and the situation is similar to that with *Sue John kissed, and Mary*. There are many examples of this in the poetry:

64   pleasing was his shape,
            And lovely

(Milton, *Paradise Lost*, IX.503–4)

65   Sober he seemde, and very sagely sad

(Spenser, *Faerie Queene*, I.i.29)

66   Most blameless is he, centred in the sphere
            Of common duties, decent not to fail
            In offices of tenderness
                                    (Tennyson, 'Ulysses,' 39–41)

Again, however, Milton will split co-ordinate ADJ's and participles
when they are nominal modifiers. This is said to be distinctive of
Milton's style.[13]

67   with wand'ring steps and slow
                                    (*Paradise Lost*, XII.648)

68   th'upright heart and pure
                                    (*Paradise Lost*, I.18)

The following may be regarded as imitations, though they lack the co-
ordinating conjunction:

69   Days of sweet leisure, taxed with patient thought
            Abstruse, nor wanting punctual service high
                                    (Wordsworth, *Prelude*, I.43–44)

70   unbroken cheerfulness serene
                                    (*Prelude*, I.114)

71   but thy strong Hours indignant
                                    (Tennyson, 'Tithonus,' 18)

There is a kind of dislocation peculiar, as far as I know, to Milton,
which at first sight seems to violate another Island constraint known
variously as the Left Branch Constraint or the Frozen Nucleus Constraint.[14] The construction involves a relative clause whose head noun
is the determiner in a higher NP:

72   and deify his power
            Who from the terror of this Arm so late
            Doubted his Empire
                                    (*Paradise Lost*, I.112–14)

73   As being the contrary to his high will
            Whom we resist.
                                    (*Paradise Lost*, I.161–2)

74   Thir children's cries unheard, that pass'd through fire
            To his grim Idol.
                                    (*Paradise Lost*, I.395–6)

These certainly present perceptual problems to the reader, forcing him to look for the head noun modified by the relative clause in a place he would not usually find it (roughly the same problem occurs in (13) and (14)). It appears, however, that these are derivable by Extraposition-from-NP and are not violations of the formal constraints mentioned above. The same is true of (78) below. A true violation would be of the form of

His high will whom we resist opposes our exploits.

This discussion of Island violations has been highly inconclusive, but it does suggest that one must be very careful before claiming that these poets flaunted the constraints with abandon, particularly in view of our ignorance about Island constraints generally.

A few preliminary conclusions can now be drawn. The first is that it is impossible to draw a sharp line between poetic inversion and dele-tion and ordinary optional transformations. This is particularly clear in the case of the deletions considered and Subj./V inversion. The second is that it is undesirable to do so, for otherwise we would miss the degree of similarity involved. The only extra rules we have added are Verb-Final and P/NP inversion. It is important that these can be described as transformational rules, because it means that only syntac-tic constituents are affected; this is a considerable constraint on random reordering, and is a kind of structural option that can be learned by the reader—indeed, must be and is learned by every reader of Spenser, Milton, and Pope. In the following section I will show that formulating these inversions and deletions as transformations has the additional happy consequence of predicting the prosodic properties of the lines. This, of course, must be the case if these inversions and deletions are transformations.

The functions of, and hence possible motive for, inversions and deletions can be roughly grouped into three classes: presentational, imitative, and prosodic. By presentation I mean the ordering of the information in the sentence to focus on a constituent by fronting it, or to front old information ('theme'), or to establish a parallelism with the patterning of information of previous lines, or to delay a piece of information for climactic effect. I will not illustrate most of these, since they often require several lines of context to clarify and are well-known in the criticism of individual authors. One example of 'climax' will illustrate what I mean by that term:

And now his heart
Distends with pride, and hard'ning in his strength
Glories.

(*Paradise Lost*, I.571-73)

By imitative, I have in mind passages in Milton, Pope, and Wordsworth which represent complex psychological experiences such as confusion, growing apprehension, deceptive or misinterpreted experience. Stanley Fish's *Surprised by Sin* (Berkeley and Los Angeles: University of California Press, 1967), for example, discusses many passages in *Paradise Lost* where the reader is forced by the syntax to repeat in himself the experience being described. In Wordsworth's *Prelude* there is a similar use of inversion to represent the mind groping toward illumination. Countless passages could be cited. Pope also uses inversions and deletions in this way. Consider, for example, the following passage on women's pursuit of fleeting pleasures, where the lines imitate the fitful yearnings for the ungraspable:

75   Pleasures the sex, as children Birds, pursue,
         Still out of reach, yet never out of view,
         Sure, if they catch, to spoil the Toy at most,
         To covet flying, and regret when lost:
         At last, to follies Youth could scarce defend,
         'Tis half their Age's prudence to pretend;
                           (Pope, *Moral Essays* II, 231–36)

Again, everyone has, no doubt, his favorite passages which illustrate this function of inverted and deleted syntax, and this class needs no further description.

The least-studied motives for inversion have to do with prosodic effects, and I will conclude by discussing these in more detail. Several functions come under this heading:

  (i) movements to get a rhyme-word
  (ii) movements to render a line metrical, or less metrically complex
  (iii) movements to manipulate a caesura or other pauses in the line.

i. In what seems to be his earliest piece of criticism, Dryden makes fun of those who apply Verb-Final in blank verse to achieve elevation in style, and while conceding its usefulness for rhyming, says 'I should judge him to have little command of English whom the necessity of a rhyme should force often upon this rock.'[15] Getting a rhyme word is not the only usefulness of Verb-Final, however. Since bisyllabic verbs in English, unlike nouns, are generally stressed on the final syllable, a bisyllabic verb will give a stress in the final syllable of the line, giving the 'strong' ending much sought by the writers of the heroic couplet (as well as Milton, by the way). It is certainly no accident that the majority of examples of Verb-Final and also fronting operations that leave the verb in line-final position do create either a rhyme word or a stress in final position. There are cases, however, when other motives seem to be at work.

ii. There are, for example, lines that would be sadly unmetrical had the

inversions not been applied. Compare, for example, other versions of
(20) with the lines as written:

20   By falsities and lies the greatest part
              Of mankind they corrupted
              They corrupted the greatest part of mankind
              By falsities and lies
              By falsities and lies they corrupted the
              Greatest part of mankind

Another example is the Verb-Final in example (50).
iii. The rule of Topicalization written above introduced a clause-boundary
(#) between the fronted material and the rest of the original sentence.
This is phonologically realized as a sharp fall-rise intonation break
which can function as a line-final pause or medial caesura. If we compare the first line of 13 with the un-preposed form,

13   Into the Heart of Eve his words made way
              His words made way into the Heart of Eve

we see that while both are metrically simple and end with a stressed
syllable, there is a more marked caesura following *Eve* in the line as
written. One possible motive for fronting operations, then, is to introduce a clause-boundary into the middle of a line which would otherwise
lack it. A more complicated difference in line-dynamics occurs in
example (19) when the line as written is changed to one involving Verb-
Final:

19   But since like slaves # his bed # they did ascend
              But since they did ϕ his bed like slaves ascend

The rewritten line does have a caesura which I perceive as falling at the
original site of the moved verb, but the line as written has two pauses
associated with the two clause-boundaries introduced by the double
application of the fronting operations. There are other rather clear
examples of caesuras introduced by Verb-Final:

54   For heav'nly minds ϕ from such distempers foul
              Are ever clear
              For heav'nly minds are ever clear from such
              Distempers foul.
49   Impediments ϕ from day to day renewed.
              Impediments renewed from day to day.

This suggests that the null-symbol introduced by Verb-Final is not in fact deleted in surface structure but remains and receives phonological realization, though the precise phonetic facts are obscure to me. The point is that the movement leaves a 'hole' which can function as the nucleus of a caesura. Note that in (15)-(19), (56), and (57), if Verb-Final had been applied instead of the fronting transformations, 'holes' would have been left after the first, second, or third syllables—e.g.

56   That every wight to shroud it did constrain
        That it did ϕ every wight to shroud constrain

If this hypothesis about null-symbols is correct, then all deletions should leave 'holes.' This is difficult to check in the case of Gapping or Conjunction Reduction because rewriting with the deleted elements present adds syllables to the line. Perhaps the following rewriting of Pope's famous couplet is a reasonable test case:

76   *Authors* are partial to their *Wit*, 'tis true,
        But are not *Criticks* to their *Judgment* too?
                    ('Essay on Criticism,' 17-18)
        Aren't Critics partial to their judgments too?

The rewritten line lacks the pronounced caesura of Pope's second line. In general, a poet seems to have a choice between keeping a prono-minalized element, which gives him an unstressed syllable, or deleting it, which gives him a 'hole.' I think such deletions even introduce secondary pauses in lines where a clause-boundary provides the primary caesura—this contributes a certain tension to the line, like the winding up of a spring that wants release in the following line or lines. An example of this occurs in Pope's professedly juvenile piece 'On Solitude' (I will mark clause-boundaries and holes):

77 Whose herds ϕ with milk, # Whose fields ϕ with bread, #
    Whose flocks supply him with attire, #
    Whose trees in summer yield him shade, #
            In the winter ϕ fire.

Holes and boundaries contribute to the nervous energy of (75)

75 Pleasures # the sex ϕ, as children ϕ Birds, pursue, with bread #
    ϕ Still out of reach, # ϕ yet never out of view, #
    Sure, # if they catch ϕ, # to spoil the Toy at most, #
    To covet ϕ flying, # and regret ϕ when ϕ lost: #
    At last, # to follies ϕ Youth could scarce defend, #
    'Tis half their Age's prudence to pretend ϕ #

Where both holes and boundaries occur at the same spot, extremely
sharp caesuras are present. The last line moves very quickly as it dissi-
pates the stored energy of the previous lines. Although my terms are
becoming quite impressionistic, I think there is much to pursue here
toward describing how lines move dynamically. One last example,
where the acceleration of the later lines is clearly imitative:

78   Him # the Almighty Power
              Hurl'd φ headlong # flaming # from th'Ethereal Sky
              With hideous ruin and combustion down
              To bottomless perdition, # there to dwell φ
              In Adamantine Chains and penal Fire, #
              Who durst defy th'Omnipotent to Arms.
                                               (*Paradise Lost*, I.44–9)

Notice finally that all of the functions of inversions and deletions
occur at once: Verb-Final may get a poet a rhyme word stressed on the
final syllable, but it also leaves a 'hole'; the fronting transformations
may be used to focus on an item, but they will also insert clause-
boundaries. Talent, with respect to versification, might be regarded as
the ability to 'over-determine' an inversion or deletion, not to use it
solely for rhyme, but at the same time to make use of its other consequences happily.

I think the most surprising conclusion to be drawn from this survey is
that the lines examined do not greatly differ formally from the output
of various optional rules of Modern English. Only the extra rule of
Verb-Final had to be postulated, and it would seem to be an outgrowth
of the normal order in dependent clauses in OE. The rule describes a
syntactic option (or group of options) taken by poets for centuries.
The main difference in freedom of deletion, deletion to the right of
D. O's, is, if we adopt Hankamer's analysis, the lifting of an English-
specific output condition and not the reflection of any fundamentally
different deletion process. Finally, a number of lines which appear to
violate Island constraints turned out not to do so. This conclusion
is surprising for at least two reasons: first, as modern readers, we expect
poets to transcend the bounds of syntax; second, it is hard to believe
that such perceptually difficult passages as (74) and (75) are not highly
deviant syntactically. But I believe I have adequately demonstrated
that the source of complexity, or perplexity, in Spenser, Milton, and
Pope is quite different from that in, say, e. e. cummings or Dylan
Thomas. There is, I believe, a rather sharp discontinuity between the
'language' of the former and latter poets which recent work in stylistics
tends to obscure.

My crucial assumption has been that these inversions and deletions are to be regarded as syntactic rather than post-syntactic or a-syntactic. That is, the inverted or truncated line is still to be viewed as a surface structure. An alternative view would be that these processes are essentially post-phonological, simply reorderings and deletions of strings. This is the way Grinder and Elgin view their rules of 'literary language' (*Guide*, p. 177). For the class of reorderings and deletions described here, however, it seems very clear that the assumption that the derived structures are still structures which determine phonological realization is a fruitful one, for it has proved possible to show how these processes alter the sound of the line. I feel very strongly, moreover, that this is the way most of these poets expected and desired to be read. Suppose we encounter the sequence NP NP V—the modernist might want to consider the shimmering possible relations among these constituents, but I believe the poets considered here would expect us to analyze this as either O # S V or S O V, whichever is correct in context, and to read the line that way. We cannot appreciate the intricacy, and the power, of this language unless we, as readers, do the kind of syntactic work outlined in this paper.

NOTES

1 Veré Rubel, *Poetic Diction in the English Renaissance* (1941; rpt. New York: Kraus Reprint Co., 1966); George Williamson, 'The Rhetorical Pattern of Neo-Classical Wit,' *Modern Philology* 33 (1936), 55–81; Sister Miriam Joseph, *Shakespeare's Use of the Arts of Language* (New York: Columbia University Press, 1947); William K. Wimsatt, 'Rhetoric and Poems,' *English Institute Essays*, 1948; Alexander Ward Allison, *Toward an Augustan Poetic* (Lexington: University of Kentucky Press, 1962); William Boman Piper, *The Heroic Couplet* (Cleveland: Case Western Reserve University Press, 1969).
2 Seymour Chatman, *An Introduction to the Language of Poetry* (Boston: Houghton Mifflin, 1968).
3 John Robert Ross, *Constraints on Variables in Syntax*, Diss. MIT 1967 (available from the Indiana University Linguistics Club); Joseph Emonds, *Root and Structure Preserving Transformations*, Diss. MIT 1970 (available from the Indiana University Linguistics Club); Paul Postal, *Crossover Phenomena* (New York: Holt, Rinehart & Winston, 1971); Jorge Hankamer, *Constraints on Deletion in Syntax*, Diss. Yale 1971; Alexander Grosu, *The Strategic Content of Island Constraints*, Ohio State Working Papers in Linguistics, No. 13 (Columbus: Ohio State Department of Linguistics, 1972).
4 One obscurity here is—do we mean by 'common optional transformation' one that does not produce stylistic elevation (e.g. Particle Movement, Indirect Object Movement)? If there is a stylistic component in a grammar, as suggested in Chomsky (*Aspects of the Theory of Syntax* [Cambridge, Mass.: MIT Press, 1965], pp. 126–7,

221-2), where does it begin? Or, do we follow Jacobs and Rosen-
baum (*Transformations, Style, and Meaning* [Waltham, Mass.:
Xerox, 1971]) and say that *all* optional transformations are stylistic?
5 Citations of Spenser from *The Complete Poetical Works*. ed. R. E.
  Neil Dodge (Boston: Houghton, Mifflin, 1936); of Shakespeare
  from *The Complete Works*, ed. Alfred Harbage (Baltimore:
  Penguin Books, 1969); of Milton from *Complete Poems and
  Major Prose*, ed. Merritt Y. Hughes (New York: Odyssey Press,
  1957); of Dryden from *The Best of Dryden*, ed. Louis Bredvold
  (New York: Ronald Press, 1933); of Pope, from *Poems*, ed. John
  Butt (New Haven: Yale University Press, 1963); of the Romantics
  from *English Romantic Poetry*, ed. Harold Bloom (Garden City:
  Doubleday, 1963); and of Tennyson, from *The Complete Poetical
  Works*, ed. W. J. Rolfe (Boston: Houghton Mifflin, 1898).
6 *Constraints on Deletion*, pp. 242–52.
7 The nativeness of Topicalization has been missed by most scholars.
  Angel Day in 1592 and John Smith in 1657 cited examples of it as
  instances of 'anastrophe' (Day) and 'hyperbaton' (Smith):

  'Faults no man liveth without' where order requireth 'No man
  liveth without faults' (cited in Joseph, *Shakespeare's Use*, p. 294)

  Ephesians 2.1: 'And you hath he quickened, who were dead in
  trespasses and sins' (John Smith, *The Mysterie of Rhetorique Unvail'd*
  [London, 1657] p. 200). Smith is citing the Authorized Version.

  Ronald Emma found seventeen instances of it in his sample of 451
  lines of Milton's poetry. On the other hand, those who knew of its
  use in earlier English have thought it characteristic of 'the greater
  freedom of ENE word order' (Emma, *Milton's Syntax* [The Hague:
  Mouton, 1964], p. 140). However, I recently came across the
  following passage in the *New York Times*. Speaking of Solzhenitsyn,
  Hedrick Smith says, 'Marxism he has thrown off without choosing a
  new political doctrine. Neither capitalist nor Communist economics
  does he regard as a source of good. Politicians he has scored in *Gulag
  Archipelago* as mere "boils on the neck of society preventing it from
  freely moving its head and arms" ' (*New York Times*, 17 Feb. 1974,
  Sec. 4, p. 1, col. 8).
8 I have several examples of Left-Dislocation from Shakespeare (*Rape
  of Lucrece*, 1. 1208; *Lear* IV.vi.77; *Ric. III*. V.iii.268–69) and from
  Wordsworth ('On Man, On Nature, and on Human Life,' 34 ff.,
  50 ff.), but Milton seems to have preferred Topicalization. John
  Smith's second example of hyperbaton from the Authorized Version
  involves it: 'Ephesians 5.3, But fornication and all uncleannesse, or
  covetousnesse, let it not be once named amongst you, as becometh
  Saints' (Smith, *Mysterie*, p. 200).
9 Susumo Kuno and Jane Robinson, 'Multiple Wh Questions,' *Linguistic Inquiry* 3 (1972), p. 477.
10 This order is fairly rare in Milton (and, I think, later poets): Emma
   found only two occurrences in the 431 clauses of his sample.

11 See E. A. Abbott, *A Shakesperian Grammar* (1870, rpt. Dover Books, 1966) par. 203; also Wilhelm Franz, *Die Sprache Shakespeares in Vers und Prosa*, 4th ed. (Halle/Saale: Niemeyer, 1939) par. 426.

12 Cited in *A Guide to Transformational Grammars* (New York: Holt, Rinehart, 1973), p. 185.

13 F. T. Prince, *The Italian Element in Milton's Verse* (Oxford University Press 1954), p. 113.

14 *Strategic Content*, pp. 128, 202-5.

15 *Of Dramatic Poesy and Other Critical Essays*, ed. George Watson (London).

Style as meaning

CHAPTER TWELVE

Stylistic analysis and literary interpretation

H.G. Widdowson *

[Widdowson begins his article in agreeing with the literary critics' charge that much linguistic criticism of literature has been inimical to aesthetic appreciation. He cites as a reason for this fault the linguists' tendencies to value descriptive linguistic analyses more highly than intuitive approaches and to concentrate on the means (the language of literature) to the exclusion of the product. Widdowson calls for a wedding of linguistic and literary methods, a wedding which will 'set linguistic evidence in correspondence with intuitive judgment . . .' In order to demonstrate his proposed method, Widdowson uses linguistic methods to analyze Frost's poem 'Stopping by Woods on a Snowy Evening,' in the belief that 'If a linguistic analysis really can contribute anything to an understanding of a poem over and above that promoted by the literary approach, then there ought to be something more to be said about the poem than has been said already.' He begins in showing how a study of the poem's syntax can provide insights into the poem's meaning: the fact that the syntax is arranged to focus on a possessive word 'whose' is correlated with the theme of possession which runs throughout the poem. He uses a semantic feature analysis to show that the poet's lexical choices also function to create the theme of possession. By means of these analyses, Widdowson shows language, the means by which literature (the product) is achieved, to be essential to and indivisible from that product.]

Stylistics, understood as the linguistic description of literary texts, is regarded with suspicion by many literary scholars. This suspicion seems to arise from a feeling that the linguist's orientation to the study of language has not shown itself to be relevant to an understanding of the way literary texts make their total impact, and is of its nature inimical to aesthetic appreciation. I think this suspicion is to a large

*First published in *The Use of English*, Vol. 24, no. 1 (1972), pp. 28–33, now published by Hart-Davis Educational, Granada Publishing. The substance of this paper was incorporated in one of the chapters of Widdowson: *Stylistics in the Teaching of Literature* (London: Longman, 1975).

extent justified. There has been a tendency for linguists who have concerned themselves with literary texts to suggest that an analysis in terms of the theoretical units of descriptive linguistics yields information of an intrinsically more essential kind than that which results from the impressionistic approach of the literary scholar. But of course the units which the linguist deals with are those of the abstract system of the language, and to analyse texts in terms of such units is to treat such texts primarily as exemplification of the system. Such an analysis will yield information of interest to the linguist, but this information will not necessarily of itself reveal the nature of literary texts as communication, and it cannot be regarded as in any sense more basic than the literary scholar's intuitive grasp of the communicative import of the literary use of language. In order to understand what it is that a writer is trying to express, we must know what means he is using in relation to the linguistic resources he has at his disposal. Hence it is difficult to see how the linguist can fail to make some contribution. But understanding the means is clearly not enough. We must also know what ends are achieved in terms of the communicative effect of the language used. It is this which the literary scholar is trained to perceive.

One might perhaps say that the linguist's orientation leads him to focus on the means, and his most common mistake is to assume that these are of over-riding importance, so that once they have been described, an understanding of the ends will automatically follow. The literary scholar's orientation, on the other hand, leads him to focus on the ends, and his most common mistake is to assume that these can be understood without any very precise reference to the means. The view has sometimes been put forward that stylistics might be regarded as a method for accumulating linguistic evidence which the literary scholar can draw upon to support his intuitive judgments. It seems to me that it is a mistake to separate means and ends in this way. If stylistics is to make any real contribution to criticism, it must be considered as the study of literature as a mode of communication, and in such a study, means and ends must be given equal weight and shown to be interdependent. Only in this way, it seems to me, can we ensure that a linguistic description of literary texts is not merely an arid analytic exercise and a literary description not merely a piece of subjective self-indulgence.

What I want to do in this short paper is to present an exercise in stylistics considered as a characterisation of literature as communication. I propose, therefore, to take up a position intermediary between the linguist and the literary scholar and, as far as my competence permits, I will set linguistic evidence in correspondence with intuitive judgment, giving neither any particular priority. This means that I shall proceed shuttlecock-wise, moving from intuitive impression to linguistic observation and vice-versa, adducing evidence to support aesthetic judgments and allowing the evidence to develop further hypotheses as to its significance.

I have chosen as text for analysis the well-known poem by Robert Frost: 'Stopping by Woods on a Snowy Evening'. One of my reasons for choosing it is that it is well-known: it appears frequently in popular anthologies and is often included in literature syllabuses for secondary schools both in this country and overseas. It therefore represents a challenge, since one might suppose that everything that could be said about it has already been said. If a linguistic analysis really can contribute anything to an understanding of a poem over and above that promoted by the literary approach, then there ought to be something more to be said about the poem than has been said already. A second reason for choosing this poem is that it is free of linguistic oddity. Because the linguist's prime interest in literature is in the manner in which it exemplifies the language system, a good deal of stylistic analysis has focused on poetry which violates linguistic rules. Thus, poets like Dylan Thomas and e. e. cummings have received attention out of all proportion to their literary worth because their work has interesting implications for linguistic description. Such a concentration of effort on work which many literary scholars would regard as having only limited literary merit lends support, of course, to the suspicion I mentioned earlier that the linguist's orientation to language study is irrelevant to literary appreciation. Since my point is that such an orientation can be made to be relevant, Frost's poem is a good one to choose.

Stopping by woods on a snowy evening

> Whose woods these are I think I know.
> His house is in the village though;
> He will not see me stopping here
> To watch his woods fill up with snow.
>
> My little horse must think it queer
> To stop without a farmhouse near
> Between the woods and frozen lake
> The darkest evening of the year.
>
> He gives his harness bells a shake
> To ask if there is some mistake.
> The only other sound's the sweep
> Of easy wind and downy flake.
>
> The woods are lovely, dark and deep,
> But I have promises to keep,
> And miles to go before I sleep,
> And miles to go before I sleep.

Perhaps the first thing that one notices, if one is looking at the language of the poem without troubling about what it is attempting to convey, is the preponderance of pronominal forms in the first verse. *I* occurs twice in the first line, and *his* occurs twice as well: once in line 2 and once in line 4. In addition, we have *he* and *me* occurring in line 3. There may, of course, be nothing in the least significant about these elementary observations, but we may take them as a beginning and see where they lead us.

Let us now speculate that the 3rd person is associated with the notion of possession, basing our speculation on the slender evidence of the double occurrence of *his*. With this in mind, the next thing we might notice is that the idea of possession is given prominence at the very beginning of the poem, in that the phrase *Whose woods* is placed in thematic position. That is to say it has been moved from its normal place in the word-order of the sentence and put in initial position where it acquires the status of the theme of the sentence. This observation might lead us to surmise that the theme of the poem as a whole has something to do with possession as well as something to do with woods.

We may now turn to consider the two occurrences of *his*. Its first occurrence is in the phrase *his house*, and its second in the phrase *his woods*. We notice that in each of their two appearances in the first verse, the woods are represented as being possessed. Furthermore, since *house* and *woods* are both associated with *his* in the parallel phrases in which they occur, we might look into the possibility of their being represented as having some kind of semantic equivalence. Since *his* only occurs in the two phrases *his house* and *his woods*, there does seem to be an implication that houses and woods are conceived of as being the same kind of thing, and that the woods are possessed in the same way as the house is possessed.

Let us explore this possibility further. The lexical item *house* may be distinguished from the lexical item *wood* in that its semantic specification in the lexicon of the language would include the feature/+ artefact/, whereas the specification for *wood* would not. The two items are not therefore semantically equivalent in the language code. If they are to be taken as semantically equivalent in the context of this poem, either *house* must lose its feature/+ artefact/ or *wood* must acquire it. At this point, we might turn our attention to the rather striking verb *fill up* in line 4.

Fill up would be specified in the lexicon as being associated with artefacts rather than with natural objects. That is to say, we would normally think of glasses, bottles, petrol tanks as filling up, rather than woods. The oddity of the phrase: *To watch his woods fill up with snow* arises because *wood* does not have the features/+ artefact/ and /+ receptable/ as items like *bottle* and *petrol tank* do. It acquires these featues in this context. Thus, of the two possibilities mentioned above, the evidence would seem to suggest that the woods are being represented as artefacts, and possessed in the same way as houses are possessed.

Possession bestows right of ownership. We are perhaps now in a position to suggest why it is that the first thing which is expressed in the poem is a sense of trespass. The first verse expresses the poet's feeling that he has no right to stop because somebody else has already acquired total rights over the woods by virtue of possession. They have thereby become part of the human world of rights and obligations which the poet as a member of society is bound by, so that even to stop and look at the woods is to infringe some social law of private ownership.

We may now turn to the second and third verses. Here, we notice, the woods are no longer represented as pieces of real estate: *his woods* become *the woods* and artefacts and items of rightful property become aspects of nature. But the theme of possession as being associated with human values and institutions is continued. The possessive, this time related to the first person, recurs in *my little horse*. The horse is shown to be very much a part of the world of human values. Not only is he possessed but he also possesses: *his harness bells*. Furthermore, whereas the item *horse* has in the lexicon the feature/- human/, in the context of the poem it acquires the feature of humanness. The horse is represented as reacting like a human being: he does not understand why he should be made to stop where there is no human habitation, and where, therefore, there can be no justification for stopping in terms of any normal social requirement.

The sound of the harness bells, which might be said to suggest the world of human affairs, is contrasted with the sound of the wind in verse 3. Whereas the sound of the bells is caused by a sense of human values, that of the wind represents a freedom from the constraints which such values impose: the wind is 'easy' in the sense that term has in the expression 'free and easy'. Furthermore, the fact that the two phrases *easy wind* and *downy flake* occur in combination and are structurally and rhythmically alike suggests that the adjectives are intended to be understood as referring to the same kind of quality. That is to say, the implication seems to be that it is of the nature of wind to be easy in the same way as it is of the nature of snowflakes to be downy: these are intrinsic properties in each case. We might say, then, that in the second and third verses, the woods, the wind and the falling snow are seen as symbolising a natural freedom from constraint, a world apart from that which is circumscribed by a human system of rights and obligations.

At the beginning of the last verse, the word *woods* appears again as the theme of the sentence in which it occurs. This time, however, it is both theme and subject in a simple attributive sentence. The effect of this is to provide the woods with an independent reality, having values which are not attached to them by virtue of being possessed, but which are intrinsic properties: just as the wind is naturally easy, so the woods are naturally lovely, dark, and deep. These qualities are contrasted with human values as the theme of possession is restated. Whereas, however, possession in the first verse is associated with rights, in the last verse it is associated with obligations. The use of the verb *have* is interesting here. As a lexical verb, *have* carries the meaning of possession, but as modal auxiliary (in expressions like *I have to go* for example) it carries the meaning of obligation. In the expression *I have promises to keep*, these two senses of *have* are compounded. This might be shown as follows:

I have promises
I have to keep promises   *I have promises to keep*

One might say that what is being suggested here is that the first person in the poem has promises in the same sense as the third person has woods, but the possession of promises does not bestow rights, it imposes obligations.

Finally, we might notice that the connection between the first and second lines is elliptical and is open to two interpretations. The lines, are, I think, generally understood to mean something like the following:

The woods are lovely, dark and deep but (I cannot stay to enjoy them any longer because) I have promises to keep.

If, however, one takes it that the woods, together with the wind and the snow, represent a kind of elemental freedom from the kind of constraint which controls human lives, then one might think of these lines as having something like the following meaning:

The woods are lovely, dark and deep, (and represent as such a reality of elemental freedom) but (my reality must be that of social constraints and this is represented by the fact that) I have promises to keep.

Only in sleep is there freedom from responsibility.

What I have attempted to do in this analysis is to show how linguistic clues can lead to interpretation. I do not claim any special objective status for the interpretation which I have suggested, but only that it gives a definite shape to my own intuitive sense of what the poem is about. However, it is worth pointing out perhaps that the theme which this interpretation brings out: that of the reality of social constraints, of rights and obligations, in opposition to that of natural freedom, is one which often occurs in Frost's poetry (most strikingly, perhaps, in 'Mending Wall').

In conclusion, it seems reasonable to suggest that the stylistic approach which I have adopted here might provide a means whereby people like schoolchildren and students, whose intuitions are not trained to perceive significance or who find it difficult to give articulate expression to what they do perceive, can get at the meaning of poetic communication. Furthermore, such an approach necessarily involves making students aware of the way the language operates in its normal communicative use. It is perhaps not too fanciful to suggest that it might provide a means whereby the study of language and literature can be meaningfully related to their mutual benefit.

CHAPTER THIRTEEN

Syntactic deviation and cohesion

Irene R. Fairley *

[Fairley analyzes five cummings poems in an attempt to show that cummings uses syntactic deviation as a structuring device. At the same time she shows how this syntactic deviation functions as meaning in cummings's poetry. She treats three short poems—'a like a,' 'Tumbling-hair,' and 'Me up at does'—showing how cummings uses deviant syntax to create the structure of a whole poem. For example, in 'Me up at does,' he uses deviant syntax to place the topic of the poem, the poisoned mouse, in a central position, syntactically and typographically. Fairley's discussion of 'All in green went my love riding' and 'when god lets my body be' demonstrates cummings's use of syntactic deviation to effect coherence in longer poems. In 'All in green went my love riding,' Fairley finds deviant patterns repeated in such a way as to link various stanzas with one another: the similarities in deviance cause the reader to parallel the stanzas and, in doing so, discover unifying threads in the poem. Syntactic deviance functions in a similar fashion in 'when god lets my body be.' Fairley shows how the syntactic deviance creates the poem's structure, which is the basic metaphor, and thus an integral part of the meaning of the poem.]

In 1963, in a class on English Structure at M. I. T., Professor Noam Chomsky introduced examples of word order violations from a poem written by e. e. cummings, entitled 'Me up at does'—it had appeared in *The New Yorker* that week. Professor Chomsky called our attention to the poem as containing sequences that are not permissible in standard English. His examples led me to study cummings's syntactic deviations; they are of interest to linguists curious about rule violations. cummings's counter-grammatical devices have drawn considerable attention because of the boldness of the deviations.

There is another just as interesting, but, I believe, overlooked facet of cummings's irregular syntax—the function of syntactic deviation as a device of structural cohesion. cummings's cohesive deviation

* First published in *Language and Style*, 6 (1975), pp. 216–229. The author has incorporated a revised version into her book *e. e. cummings and ungrammar* (Searington, N.Y.: Watermill, 1975).

is an aspect of his style to be recognized as equally important and innovative as his idiosyncratic use of specific syntactic deviations.[1]

There are, to be sure, instances of cummings's using syntactic deviation conventionally as a device of foregrounding, so that the deviations do not pattern or appreciably alter the statement of a poem. In such instances deviation provides relief and contrast within a context of otherwise parallel and regular constructions.

In the single occurrence (inter-sententially), deviation creates tension and may reduce the redundancy of a statement, but when repeated intrasententially it can reinforce understanding. cummings often sustains deviation to provide through its repetition a level of patterning within a poem. Instances, or tokens of a particular type of deviation, thus form a set of equitable items. For example, functional shifts pervade the sonnet 'true lovers in each happening of their hearts,' preparing the reader for the final instance: 'their eyes would never miss a yes.' Deviant compounds such as 'dream-send,' 'moan-loll,' 'moon-cease,' correspond in the poem 'riverly as a flower.' Violations of cooccurrence restrictions pattern in the poem beginning 'the hours rise up putting off stars and it is.' In cummings's poems, repetition of a type of deviation becomes another source of motif.

More subtle and innovative, though, is cummings's use of syntactic deviation to relate levels within the organization of the poem. 'a like a,' a brief poem, illustrates this principle.

> a like a
> grey
> rock wanderin
>
> g
> through
> pasture
> wom
>
> an creature whom
> than
> earth hers
>
> elf
> could
> silent more no
> be

Although syntactically the poem is a fragment, an expanded noun phrase lacking a main verb or predicate, the nominalization is functional, since the poem conveys an Imagist description rather than an action or prediction. Theme and form are joined in cummings's selected deviations.

A common method of dealing with fragments is to assume that a complete sentence is recoverable, and to seek the nearest equivalent grammatical statement. Constituents in this poem suggest to me three underlying sentences and a derivation that is in harmony with the expression of the poem.[2] Setting aside inversions, the sequence could be derived as follows: from two simple sentences, 'a woman creature is like a grey rock,' 'she (or it) is wandering through pasture,' which can be combined by relative clause embedding to form a matrix sentence, and one complex sentence, 'earth herself could not be more silent than her,' which in turn can be embedded into the matrix. The entire sentence can be subsequently nominalized and the main verb *be* deleted, to provide the sequence of the poem. Relative clauses identify and describe and are therefore a suitable vehicle, given cummings's statement, while reduction and nominalization allow for compression. Because *be* has a high probability frequency and is readily reinserted, its omission is minimally disruptive. Deletion of *be* when it functions as a 'neutral' copulative is a device used to increase the imagistic effect of descriptions, and has been favored by twentieth-century poets.[3]

The major ambiguity (attributable to relative clause reduction) furthers an identification of woman and rock. Is the woman creature or the grey rock wandering through pasture? It is difficult to determine. Since the participle is placed between the two noun phrases, like a squinting modifier, it may apply to either. 'Wander' calls for an animate subject, but the placement of the participle makes 'rock' also a possible head noun. Both selections involve deviance, one conflicting features, the other impermissible word order. The ambiguity suggests indistinctness perhaps due to distance. 'Silence' indicates distance as well, and only slight movement. cummings's typographical concentration defines a limited movement, and even the semantic value of the participle 'wandering' is countered by association with a 'grey rock.' The total effect is of stasis.

cummings skilfully selects and manipulates verbs so as to minimize the expression of action. The main verb *be* has been deleted, and functioning within the subordinate clause, 'be' is dislocated so that it closes the poem. That single final token stresses the descriptive mode, recalling all the deleted (or suppressed) instances of *be* (in accordance with the suggested derivation) while avoiding surface repetition.

Several levels in the poem are integrated by the impermissible shift of the 'like' modifier to a position before the noun; a visual and syntactic axis is established. 'Woman creature' is postponed and centered, her position—possibly a location in the field—is supported typographically and lexically by an equal distribution of words and lines, and at the phonological level: 'wom/an creature whom.'[4] Syntactically, the shift permits 'woman creature' to be both preceded and followed by descriptive comparative clauses, giving an impression of balance to an entirely left-branching sequence. Centering of the noun phrase contributes to the overall impression of quiescence and equilibrium.

All of the ungrammatical features of 'a like a,' the deletions and dislocations, function to relate syntactic, semantic, and visual levels into a consistent whole. They are not incidental, but are crucial to the structure of the poem and to its rendering of the image of woman in field preserved at an instant in time.

> Tumbling-hair
>   picker of buttercups
>   violets
>   dandelions
>   And the big bullying daisies
>   through the field wonderful
>   with eyes a little sorry
>   Another comes
>   also picking flowers

A similar cohesion can be found in 'Tumbling-hair.' The poem is organized as a pair of contrastive images, or characterizations, hinged by the phrase 'through the field wonderful,' which can be syntactically attributed to either unit and divides them about equally in terms of word count and visual grouping. The first unit, a fragment, depicts spontaneity, exuberance; the second sentence, grammatically regular, a person sad or conventional, perhaps engrossed in thought. The contrast is expressed through a network of synonymous and antonymous typographical, semantic, and syntactic elements.[5]

With hair tumbling, the first person gathers flowers, identified by concrete nouns as violets, daisies and dandelions, scattered typographically as in a field. 'Wonderful' ambiguously describes both the person's involvement in the activity and the field.[6] The syntax is incomplete, abbreviated, but not confusing. What has been deleted can be easily reconstructed in context on the basis of remaining constituents. Also, possible replacements occur in the paired grammatical sentence. A missing verb of motion pointed to by the typography, the activity designated by 'picker,' and the predicate complement 'through the field,' is reinforced by 'comes' in the second description. From the phrase 'with eyes a little sorry' we might borrow 'with' for the opening: 'with Tumbling-hair.'[7] These insertions would further the already partial parallelism, indicated by 'another,' and 'also picking flowers.'

The parallelism is, of course, deliberately incomplete. 'Wonderful' provides a hinge with ironic overtones, for, typographically represented, the movement of 'Another' is confined, in keeping with the activity abstractly and flatly designated as 'picking flowers,' and corresponding to the syntax that is conventional, unimaginative. The 'Tumbling-hair picker' is characterized by a syntax that is free, unconventional in its deviation. Syntactical form thus characterizes the two persons.

At least three levels correlate to form the composition. Visually, the typography suggests first broad and spontaneous, secondly circumscribed movement. Lexically, we find a contrast between colorfully concrete and flatly abstract descriptions. And syntactically, the composition alternates from imaginative and deviant to conventional expression.

'Me up at does' is still another poem in which syntactic deviation is cohesive. The burden of relating structure and statement rests more obviously upon the syntactic component in this poem.

> Me up at does
>
> out of the floor
> quietly Stare
>
> a poisoned mouse
>
> still who alive
>
> is asking What
> have i done that
>
> You wouldn't have

The speaker is startled, his confusion communicated by jumbled speech. It is, curiously, what we might expect of a poisoned mouse, but the imagined speech of the mouse is in standard order, straightforward and concise. The irony of the situation, the emotional reversal, is conveyed by impermissible word order. Inversion of the prepositional object ('Me up at') and the adverbial inversion ('still who alive') are errors that belie agitation. The auxiliary 'does' is also dislocated, so that it functions ambiguously, expressing at once emphasis, 'a poisoned mouse *does* quietly stare,' and disbelief, 'does a poisoned mouse quietly stare?'

In 'Me up at' and 'still who alive' cummings preserves the constituent unit while disturbing the internal sequence. More disruptive dislocations of the entire indirect object ('Me up at'), place adverbial ('out of the floor'), and finite verb ('does') within the sentence, serve to postpone the matrix subject, 'a poisoned mouse.' The noun phrase is emphatically centered (visually as well) so that modification precedes and follows, a pattern cummings favors. Because it is delayed, 'a poisoned mouse' surprises the reader, as well as the speaker in the poem.

As in the two previous poems, organization and meaning depend upon syntactic deviation to the extent that correction of the deviant sequences would irreparably alter formal relations, causing a collapse of both unity and rhythm. In each of the poems cummings has included deviation as an element of poetic structure.

cummings did not limit a supportive role for deviant syntax to his brief poems. In longer poems he combines repetition of deviation with a cohesive function in patterning that secures the unity of the poem. 'All in green went my love riding' has a complex sequence of stanzas, with alternately repeated patterns incorporating constituent dislocations. The syntactic level of the poem is a pervasive parallelism based on syntactic deviation.[8]

> All in green went my love riding
> on a great horse of gold
> into the silver dawn.
>
> four lean hounds crouched low and smiling
> the merry deer ran before.
>
> Fleeter be they than dappled dreams
> the swift sweet deer
> the red rare deer.
>
> Four red roebuck at a white water
> the cruel bugle sang before.
>
> Horn at hip went my love riding
> riding the echo down
> into the silver dawn.
>
> four lean hounds crouched low and smiling
> the level meadows ran before
>
> Softer be they than slippered sleep
> the lean lithe deer
> the fleet flown deer.
>
> Four fleet does at a gold valley
> the famished arrow sang before.
>
> Bow at belt went my love riding
> riding the mountain down
> into the silver dawn.
>
> four lean hounds crouched low and smiling
> the sheer peaks ran before.
>
> Paler be they than daunting death
> the sleek slim deer
> the tall tense deer.
>
> Four tall stags at a green mountain
> the lucky hunter sang before.

> All in green went my love riding
> on a great horse of gold
> into the silver dawn.
>
> four lean hounds crouched low and smiling
> my heart fell dead before.

Four distinct stanza patterns are formed by the surface interlacing of semantic and syntactic features. Stanza 1 clearly groups with 5, 9 and 13, stanzas 1 and 13 being identical. Stanza 5 varies the pattern by changing lexically and syntactically two modifying phrases while preserving the larger syntactic pattern (adverbial phrase, finite verb, subject noun phrase, gerund, two adverbial complements). Stanza 9 echoes the modifications of 5, with additional lexical variation.

An even stronger congruence exists among the set of stanzas 3, 7 and 11, which, excepting substitutions for some lexical items, does not vary in grammatical structure (adjectival predicate, finite verb, subject pronoun, predicate complement, two appositive noun phrases).

The second stanza links with 6, 10, and 14, the major variation being lexical, a change in subject noun phrase in each repetition of the pattern (predicate noun phrase as object, subject noun phrase, finite verb, preposition). The noticeable variant is the final substitution: 'my heart fell dead before,' in which noun phrase and verb are marked semantically as well as syntactically.

The fourth set, stanzas 4, 8, and 12, contains more variation, but limited entirely to lexical items within the subject and object noun phrases. The grammatical structure remains stable (predicate noun phrase as object, subject noun phrase, finite verb, preposition). The lexical substitutions in all four sets are synonymic and metonymic, supporting while varying the network of correspondences like the incremental repetition of ballads.

This quaternary stanzaic system based on syntactic and semantic correspondence represents only part of the structure of the poem. Another axis of organization follows a binary principle, complementing the semantic opposition of the lovers' struggle as hunger ('my love') and prey (the speaker's heart). Each lover has a dual identity, one as four hounds, the other as four deer. There are two systems of correspondence—one quarternary and one binary, observed as well in the distribution of grammatical features.

Stanzas pair, advancing the descriptive level, then the narrative. But they also alternate regarding focus. Triplets (stanzas 1, 3, 5, 7, 9, 11, 13) describe first the pursuer, then the pursued. Likewise, couplets (stanzas 2, 4, 6, 8, 10, 12, 14), designating relative positions during the hunt, alternately focus on hounds and deer. The topic of a triplet is introduced in the first line and functions as sentence subject. The topic of the couplet, also introduced in the first line, reflects the focus of the previous triplet, but functions as an object thus introducing another feature of grammatical alternation. The grammatical subject of the couplet, on the second line, serves as a transition to the next triplet.

Glancing at stanza 3, we can see how this alternation works. The subject 'they,' referring back to the 'merry deer' of the previous couplet, is echoed in the appositive noun phrases that conclude the triplet, and then referred to again in the topic of the following couplet: 'Four red roebuck.' But the syntactic subject of the couplet does not occur until the second line: 'the cruel bugle,' and it, in turn, is echoed in the subject of the following triplet: 'Horn at hip went my love.'

It is also interesting to note how cummings augments a sense of action by reversing constituents in couplets. He misleads us into thinking that the first NP VP is the main NP VP. We are likely to read the first line as a sentence with a finite verb, until we come to 'and smiling,' which forces us to re-evaluate, reading the entire first line as a noun phrase with a reduced relative clause modifier, and as object of the preposition 'before.' Dislocation, then, results in a dual reading of the lines, as a series of actions and a statement of spatial relationships. But because the device is repeated and stylized, only the first instance is disruptive.

Even syntactic deviation is made to conform with the extravagantly regular patterning that characterizes this poem. A very general correspondence of deviation holds among odd stanzas and among even stanzas. Triplets are characterized by verb/subject inversion, a predicate complement in initial position, and paired phrasal modifiers in terminal position. In couplets constituents are reversed, with the object of the preposition in initial position. Postponement of the subject noun phrase is common to all stanzas, triplets, and couplets, but triplets have additionally inversion of the subject and verb. In respect to deviation the duple rhythm of the poem could be presented as two counts alternating with one. Couplets show inversion ($\gamma.\beta \rightarrow \beta.\gamma$), triplets both inversion and discontinuity.[9] Syntactic deviation is integral to the pervasive parallelism and to the binary organization of the poem. Repetition and intricate linking of features, including features of deviation, contribute importantly to the textual coherence of the poem.

Consider still another, and final, poem. Formal structure (English sonnet) and syntactic divisions are less obvious, and deviation, as dislocation, is incorporated more subtly. Unifying devices and interrelationships are much less conspicuous in 'when god lets my body be.'[10]

when god lets my body be

From each brave eye shall sprout a tree
fruit that dangles therefrom

the purpled world will dance upon
Between my lips which did sing

a rose shall beget the spring
that maidens whom passion wastes

will lay between their little breasts
My strong fingers beneath the snow

Into strenuous birds shall go
my love walking in the grass

their wings will touch with her face
and all the while shall my heart be

With the bulge and nuzzle of the sea

While there is lexical repetition, it is not prominent. The auxiliaries 'shall' and 'will' alternate, and prepositions repeat but in differing sentence positions. Quatrains are semantically parallel, having synonymous images, each quatrain presenting an image of death and regeneration, each including a 'shall' sentence that predicts regeneration from the dead body and a 'will' sentence that describes response from the living. A couplet concludes the poem, climaxing the series of images in the identification of 'heart' and 'sea.'

The closing reveals in 'the bulge and nuzzle of the sea' the underlying rhythm of the poem and the key to its composition. Lines pair contrary to rhyme, sentence, and quatrain units, but in doing so emphasize syntactic dislocations within each sentence. This oppositional pairing approximates the motion of the sea, to and fro and overlapping. Undulating movement is represented graphically, lines corresponding to crests, the spaces between them to troughs, the poem, then beginning and ending with the peak of a crest. Determining wave units from crest to crest, as it is customarily measured and illustrated in geology texts, accounts for the rhyme scheme across paired lines. In cummings's poem the initial and final crests figuratively join—simultaneous with the completion and renewal of the cycle of life and death.

He must have had in mind the oscillating movement that defines waves—particles of water move circularly returning to a point close to origin. Syntactically, the poem can be considered a single sentence with an introductory dependent clause: 'when god lets my body be'. Since a final period is lacking, the sentence is potentially circular. The closing line returns us to the opening, rhyme concurring in the completed wave. The elimination of punctuation is as appropriate as the selected deviation, which is dislocation. cummings's sea image effectively ends the poem as it aligns the semantic with other structural levels. All levels of the poem converge in an elaborate metaphor.

The strongest syntactic congruence is found, not at the surface level, but at the level of syntactic deviation (somewhat below the surface of the wave). Corresponding dislocations link the first and second quatrains—the first sentence of each pairing by two features, topicalization (shift to an initial position, before subject and verb, of an adverb or an item that has the sense of predicate object or complement) and verb/subject inversion; the second sentence by topicalization. (It is an alternation similar to that of 'All in green went my love riding.') In the third quatrain internal parallelism holds, with complement/verb inversion common to both sentences (see Fig. 13.1). The pattern of topicalization and verb/subject inversion reiterates in the couplet.

lines

1	when god lets my body be
2	From each brave eye shall sprout a tree
	3 2 1

5	Between my lips which did sing
6	a rose shall beget the spring
	3 2 1

	3
3	fruit that dangles therefrom
4	the purpled world will dance upon
	1 2

	3 1
7	that maidens whom passion wastes
8	will lay between their little breasts
	2

	1
9	My strong fingers beneath the snow
10	Into strenuous birds shall go
	3 2

	1
11	my love walking in the grass
12	their wings will touch with her face
	3 2

Figure 13.1

The rhythmic effect of these dislocations can be ascertained by reading the deviant sequences in normal order. Topicalization, especially, complements the central metaphor in creating an impression of overlapping, and all the dislocations are emphasized by cummings's seemingly

perverse distribution of couplets. But the semantically shifting relationships between subjects and objects and the introduction of new pairs
with each image assures a progressive thrust.

Given the matrix of dislocations, the third quatrain is certainly
marked—forgrounded—as only those two sentences begin conventionally
with subject noun phrases: 'My strong fingers' and 'my love.' It is
amusing—and characteristic of cummings—to have redefined the relationship of deviation to regularity in the context of the poem. The
change to verb phrase inversion maintains a form of correspondence
(within the quatrain) but varies the overall rhythm of the poem. In
this respect and in the apportionment of correspondence generally
(phonologically, lexically and grammatically) 'when god lets my body
be' is less symmetrical than 'All in green went my love riding,' which
may be too lyrical for contemporary taste.

1 When God lets my body be from each brave eye shall sprout a tree;
   Fruit that dangles therefrom the purpled world shall dance upon.
   Between my lips that did sing a flower shall beget spring;

2 When God lets my body be,   7

   From each brave eye shall sprout a tree,   8

   Fruit that dangles therefrom   6
                  will
   The purple world shall dance upon.   8
                  did
   Between my lips that no more sing   7

   A flower shall beget (the) spring,   7

   That maidens whom passion wastes   7

   Will
   Shall lay between their little breasts.   8

   My strong fingers beneath the snow   7

        strenuous
   Into slender birds shall go,   8

   My love walking in the grass   7

                    will touch on her face.
   Their wings shall seek e'er they pass.   7

And all the while shall my heart be   8

With the bulge and nuzzle of the sea.   9

3   When god lets my body be from each brave eye shall
                        sprout a tree;
         Fruit that dangles therefrom the purpled world will
                        dance upon.
         Between my lips which did sing a rose shall beget
                        the spring,
         That maidens whom passion wastes will lay between
                        their little breasts.
         My strong fingers beneath the snow into strenuous
                        birds shall go.
         My love moving in the grass their wings will brush
                        on her face.
         And all the while shall my heart be with the bulge
                        and nuzzle of the sea.

A comparison of earlier versions of the sonnet reveals some of cummings's deliberate refinements.[11] Three of the drafts (for which no order is specified in manuscript) show a relatively conventional and static distribution, although the syntactic dislocations are already present and dominate structurally. In a fourth version we perceive cummings working toward the subtle scheme of the poem, bringing the ryhme scheme, line divisions, and typographical distribution of lines into a complex relationship with syntactic units. In the fourth version, I believe, the metaphor of the poem is established.

4   When God lets my body be

                 from each brave eye shall sprout a tree,
                 fruit that dangles therefrom

                 the purpled world will dance upon.

                 Between my lips which did sing
                 a rose shall beget the spring,

                 that maidens whom passion wastes

                 will lay between their little breasts.
                 My strong fingers beneath the snow

                 into strenuous birds shall go

                 my love walking in the grass
                 their wings will touch with her face.

And all the while shall my heart be

With the bulge and nuzzle of the sea.

'All in green went my love riding' and 'when god lets my body be' prove an innovative bonding of syntactic deviation and parallelism, the last a recognized major element of verse. In all of the poems considered—varying in theme and verse form—syntactic deviation functions as a source of correspondence, of integration and structural cohesion. In short, cummings indicates that deviation may be structurally supportive, may function much like lexical, grammatical, and phonological features, to unify a poem.

The range of devices from overt repetitions to subtle and intricate patterns is interesting as a factor of cummings's individual style, and I hope that this analysis reveals his selections of deviation as being carefully calculated rather than anarchic or frivolous, as some critics supposed. cummings may use deviations more frequently than most poets and may have a wider range of options, but he also appears to use them in unique contexts. In those contexts, and given their cohesive functions, cummings's deviations may indeed be original uses of irregular syntax. But while original, they are not without ties to literary tradition. cummings's deviations are manipulations of possibilities inherent in English syntax, and I would expect a diachronic study to show that his innovations follow guidelines long in existence in English poetry.[12]

NOTES

1 Earlier versions of this paper were presented at the New England Linguistic Society Meeting, October 1971, McGill University, and at the Linguistics and Literature Section of the April, 1972, meeting of the Northeast Modern Language Association at Skidmore College.
  The analyses that follow are directed to cummings's special use of irregular syntax; they are not intended as complete studies of individual poems. The poems by cummings are from *Poems 1923–1954* (New York, 1954), with the exception of 'Me up at does,' which is included in *73 Poems* (New York, 1963).
2 The derivation is not intended to represent cummings's creative process. Unfortunately, manuscripts are not available for this poem.
3 The verb *be* is optionally deleted in certain standard English constructions; poets have always extended the options. For a discussion of fragmentary style see William E. Baker, *Syntax in English Poetry, 1870–1930* (Berkeley, 1967).
4 In his commentary on the free verse stanza of the poem, Norman Friedman, *e e cummings, The Art of His Poetry* (Baltimore, 1960)

p. 99, notes the series of puns, remarking on 'wom/an creature' and 'hers/elf.' He identifies the poem as a description of a New Hampshire country wife.

5 During the discussion at NEMLA Richard Kennedy, of Temple University, suggested that the poem with its original title, 'Epitaph,' as it appeared in *Eight Harvard Poets* (Cambridge, 1917), referred to the rape of the mythical Persephone. Following that interpretation, the contrast can be seen as one figure spontaneously gathering flowers, while another, Hades, closes in with more direct movement, picking flowers to cover his purpose. cummings dropped the title, including the poem under TULIPS, as V in the group of 'Chansons Innocentes' in *Tulips and Chimneys* (New York, 1923), and subsequently as III of that same group in *Poems 1923–1954*. Title removed, a more broad interpretation is possible.

6 'through the field is wonderful' is multiply ambiguous in regard to both the function of the entire adverbial phrase and of the single modifier 'wonderful.' This kind of productive ambiguity that allows for complementary interpretations is characteristic of cummings's poems.

7 Disregarding the parallelism there would be other options. For example, adding the definite article would result in a type of impermissible adjectival modification that cummings frequently employs: 'the Tumbling-hair picker.'

8 Two interpretations of this poem have appeared. Barry Sanders in *The Explicator*, 25 (November 1966), 23, describes the speaker as an unrequited lover whose heart is captured by the classical goddess, the huntress Diana, and mentions a cyclical, seasonal structure. Will C. Jumper in *The Explicator*, 26 (September, 1967) 6, has taken issue with Sanders's interpretation, insisting that the gender of the speaker is female, that the speaker recounts in courtly fashion the tale of her lover's fatal hunt. He argues that 'the structure of the poem is not "cyclic" but is merely a sophisticated improvisation on the ballad pattern with repetition and repetition with variation throughout.' Personally, I agree with Sanders and hold to a male speaker and a figurative hunt (green is the color traditionally associated with feminine riding habit), but the identification of gender is not crucial to my analysis. It is necessary, however, to recognize the play of a sexual or binary opposition. Also, both observations regarding the structure of the poem would seem to have some validity, and are, I believe, supported by the following discussion of two related stanzaic systems and the structural complexity of the poem.

To the reader who wishes to pursue the structure of 'All in green went my love riding,' I recommend also an essay by Philip J. West, 'Medieval Style and the Concerns of Modern Criticism,' in *College English*, 34 (March, 1973), which presents an analysis of the poem from oral-formulaic premises.

9 These terms are used after the manner of Dolores M. Burton in her essay on Shakespeare's syntax, 'Toward a Theory of Deviant Word Order,' *Proceedings–1968 ACM National Conference*, 801–5. Two

of the dislocations observed in this poem—complements to initial position and verb/subject inversion—recur frequently in cummings's poems. These and other dislocations are treated at length in my dissertation, 'Syntactic Deviance in the Poetry of E. E. Cummings: A Stylistic Investigation,' Harvard University, 1971. In concluding Chapter V, I outline three rearrangement rules, conceived as late stylistic adjustments in a generative grammar of English, that derive cummings's major constituent dislocations. The rules are presented in rough form and at best represent the kind of formalization which may eventually be possible in stylistics. They resemble options in English, both diachronic and synchronic; not surprising, since cummings is innovating within the context of English syntax. Rule (1), topicalization, moves items (noun phrase, adverb, predicate phrase) in main and subordinate clauses. Rule (2), V/S inversion, shifts the finite verb. A third rule, O/V inversion, reorders within the verb phrase. To return to the analysis of 'All in green went my love riding,' it is of interest that the dislocations when accounted in terms of these rules, as reiterative and alternating rule application (rules 1 + 2 in triplets, rule 1 in couplets), confirm the binary principle of organization.

10 Robert E. Wegner, in *The Poetry and Prose of E. E. Cummings* (New York, 1965), p. 57, mentions this poem as one of a group reflecting cummings's belief in reintegration. Wegner states that in cummings's view 'dying is an extension of life, for the individual who responds with love to the phenomena of his existence.'

11 cummings's manuscripts and poems are included by permission of the Harvard College Library and the estate of Marion Morehouse Cummings.

12 Many of cummings's inversions echo devices of Milton, Shakespeare, Keats, and Hopkins, and the pattern 'adverb-verb-subject' is one that even Hemingway uses (as in the narration of 'Big Two-Hearted River'). There are clearly predilections in English which are reflected in conventional devices and in their various extensions. The problem of defining style, or of identifying idiosyncratic devices, involves comparisons at many levels, but those comparisons still elude us. Morton W. Bloomfield, 'Generative Grammar and the Theory of Literature,' *Proceedings of the Tenth International Congress of Linguists* (Bucharest, 1970), argues in support of a complex comparative matrix, essential to both a theory of literature and of style. Other references I have found helpful to my approach are Bloomfield's 'The Syncategorematic in Poetry: From Semantics to Syntactics,' in *To Honor Roman Jakobson, Essays On The Occasion Of His Seventieth Birthday* (The Hague, 1967); Roman Jakobson, 'Grammatical Parallelism and its Russian Facet,' *Language,* 42 (1966), pp. 399–429; George M. Landon, 'The Grammatical Description of Poetic Word-Order in English Verse,' *Language and Style*, 1 (1968), 194–200; and Samuel R. Levin, 'The Analysis of Compression in Poetry,' *Foundations of Language*, 7 (1971), pp. 38–55.

CHAPTER FOURTEEN

Wallace Stevens: Form and meaning in four poems

Samuel Jay Keyser *

[If form and content are intertwined, the study of form should provide valuable insights into meaning. Keyser tests this assumption by carefully analyzing the form of four Wallace Stevens poems. He uses a Case Grammar approach in analyzing 'Death of a Soldier' and finds a connection between the poem's agentless verbs and its theme of the inevitability of death. In 'Poetry is a Destructive Force,' the syntactic and phonological chiasmi mirror the semantic reversals in the poem. Similarly, the syntax and phonology adumbrate the content of 'Anecdote of the Jar.' The syntax functions to stress rhyme words crucial to meaning. Rhymes and alliteration draw attention to the effects the jar has on the wilderness around it. Finally, Keyser analyzes the syntax of 'The Snow Man,' showing that the syntactic confusion is integral to the poem's meaning. As one reads the poem, getting more and more linguistic information, he must continually re-evaluate the syntactic structures; Stevens's message is that in order to get a clear perception of reality, one must continually change his perspective.]

Introduction

It is a commonplace of literary criticism to observe that form and content in a poem are closely related. It is less common, however, to encounter explicit analyses of particular poems which support this commonplace. The analyses which follow will attempt to do this. Four poems by Wallace Stevens will be analyzed from a formal standpoint. Then an attempt will be made to show how the formal analysis is closely related to what the poem is about.[1]

The Death of a Soldier

Let us look at a poem which appeared in the 1923 collection called *Harmonium*. The poem is one which Yvor Winters (1937, 70) includes

*First published in *College English*, 6 (1976), pp. 578-98. Copyright © 1976 by the National Council of Teachers of English. Reprinted by permission of the publisher and the author.

in a list of poems which according to him rank Stevens as being '. . . probably the greatest poet of his generation.' The text of the poem follows:

The Death of a Soldier

> Life contracts and death is expected,
> As in a season of autumn.
> The soldier falls.
>
> He does not become a three-days personage,
> Imposing his separation,
> Calling for pomp.
>
> Death is absolute and without memorial,
> As in a season of autumn,
> When the wind stops.
>
> When the wind stops and, over the heavens,
> the clouds go, nevertheless,
> In their direction.

The verbs in the poem can be divided into two distinct types, finite verbs and nonfinite verbs. Finite verbs are those which take endings that agree with their subjects in number. For example, in *He works*, the end *-s* is determined by the third person singular subject, *he*. Nonfinite verbs show no such agreement. We list these verbs with their corresponding subjects, expressed or otherwise, in (1) and (2) below:

1 *finite verbs*	2 *nonfinite verbs*
Life contracts	(who) imposing his separation
death is expected (by someone)	(who) calling for pomp
soldier falls	
he does not become a three-days personage	
Death is absolute and without memorial	
the wind stops	
the clouds go	

A notion which plays a role in the semantic and syntactic structure of many languages, including English, is agency. The agent of a verb is normally but not necessarily the animate instigator of whatever action the verb describes. For example,

3 (a)   John opened the door with a key.

(b)   The door opened.
(c)   The door was opened by John.
(d)   The door was opened.

In (3a) *John* is interpreted as the instigator of the action of door-opening in marked contrast to (3b) where the subject *the door* is clearly the recipient of the action of the verb *open*. In such sentences we normally understand that *John* is capable of exercising voluntary control over the action of the verb. It is for this reason that agents are left to be animate.[2] If we look at these two sentences, however, we see that not every subject of a verb can be interpreted as the agent. Moreover, the agent of an action may appear in a position other than subject position. This is illustrated in (3c) where the passive construction has the agent as object of the preposition *by* and the recipient of the action as subject of the sentence. From (3d) we see that it is possible to suppress an agent altogether.

Armed with the notion of agent we return to the verbs in ((1)-(2)) and recategorize them in terms of whether or not an agent is present. These judgments are by means automatic and require some critical appraisal, but the recategorization that appears in ((4)-(5)) will hopefully do:

4 *finite verbs*

A VERBS WITH AGENT	B VERBS WITHOUT AGENT
	life contracts
	death is expected
(none)	soldier falls
	he does not become
	Death is absolute
	wind stops
	clouds go

5 *nonfinite verbs*

A VERBS WITH AGENT	B VERBS WITHOUT AGENT
(who) imposing his separation	(none)
(who) calling for pomp	

The obvious feature of this categorization is a systematic asymmetry. All the finite verbs in the poem have subjects which are not understood as agents, while all the nonfinite verbs have subjects which are. Before we consider the significance of this asymmetry, let us focus attention on the reasons for the categorization in (4) and (5). Beginning with (4) we note that these verbs can be further subdivided into verbs which can never take an agent because of their inherent meaning and verbs which can but do not in this poem.

6 *finite verbs*

A Can never take an agent	B Can take an agent but do not in this poem
is	contract
become	is expected
fall	stop
	go

Recall that agency requires an action verb. Since *is* does not describe an action, its subject cannot be an agent. Similarly, *become* describes a state. One becomes something but *become* itself is not an action. Its subject too can never be understood as an agent. The verb *fall* in the line *the soldier falls* describes an action that has happened to the subject but not an action which the subject can bring about through his own instigation. *Fall* is like *die* or *live* in this respect and its subject can not be its agent.

The verbs in (6B) can take agents in other contexts in English, though it is clear from inspection of the contexts in the poem that the subjects are not agents. Compare

7 (a) life contracts
   (b) the wind stops
   (c) the clouds go

with

8 (a) God contracts life.
   (b) God stopped the wind.
   (c) God goes everywhere.

In the examples in (7a.-c.) the verbs, like *fall* above, describe actions which have happened to the subject but not actions which the subject has instigated. These contrast with (8a.-c.) where the subject is simultaneously the instigator. In the poem *contract, stop* and *go* have happened to *life, wind* and *clouds* but there is no indication of any agency for these events.

A word needs to be said about *is expected*. In the line *death is expected, death* is the goal of *is expected*, not the agent. It is in other words, the grammatical subject of the sentence but the semantic object. The semantic subject of the verb has been suppressed from the line, and left vague. Therefore *is expected* is categorized as not taking an agent.[3]

We turn now to the nonfinite verbs in (5). These are *imposing* and *calling for* and they occur in sentences related syntactically to sentences like:

9 The three-days personage imposes his separation.

and

10 The three-days personage calls for pomp.

In (9) the role of the subject, i.e. *three-days personage* as agent of *imposes*, is clear and requires no comment. The second of these has *three-days personage* as subject of the verb *call for*. Now *call for* has two meanings which are possible here. The first is the meaning 'order, demand' and in this meaning *three-days personage* is also an agent, paralleling (9). The second meaning is 'require, need' and in this reading *three-days personaage* cannot be an agent. The parallel with *impose* suggests the agentive reading and we assume that *impose* and *call for* are agentive verbs.

Having made the judgments outlined above, we return to the asymmetry observed earlier; namely, that finite verbs in 'Death of a Soldier' occur with grammatical subjects which are not agents while the nonfinite verbs do take agentive subjects. There is, however, a peculiarity of the nonfinite verbs. These verbs appear in syntactic constructions in which the agents have been deleted; that is, they do not occur on the actual surface of the poem. This enables us to make a generalization about the poem. In selecting phrases from the infinite number of possible phrases available to him to make this particular poem, Stevens has done three distinct things, namely:

11 (i)   He has selected verbs which can under no circumstances take agents.

 (ii)   He has selected the nonagentive sense of verbs which can but need not take agents.

 (iii) In the two instances where he has selected the agentive sense of a verb, i.e. *impose* and *call for*, he has displayed the verbs in a syntactic construction which requires that the agent be deleted from the surface of the poem.

What all three items in (11) have in common, of course, is to remove from the poem's surface any agentive phrase. If we accept this intention as part of the poet's design—conscious or otherwise—we are essentially saying that stanza two of 'Death of a Soldier' is consistent with the poem as a whole in a way in which the following stanza would not be:

12 He does not become a three-day personage,
    Who imposes his separation,
    Who calls for pomp.

Note, in particular, that the hypothetical stanza (12) is metrically virtually identical to the corresponding one in the poem. In fact, in any other terms, save deletion of surface agents, the two stanzas seem identical. At this point we ask whether there is a relationship between the suppression of surface agency and the meaning of the poem? In

the world of the poem the death of a soldier in particular and of anyone, for that matter, is a natural event which is not to be associated
with an initiator any more than one looks for an initiator in the death
of a leaf that falls from a tree in autumn. In this world where things
happen without the intervention of an initiator, the apparent paradox
of the last stanza disappears:

13   When the wind stops and, over the heavens
      The clouds go, nevertheless,
      In their direction.

This would be a surprise only if one supposed the wind was the agent
of the clouds' motion. But in the world in which the *soldier falls*,
it is not.[4] The manipulation of syntax and semantics to remove all
vestiges of an agent from the surface of this poem corresponds to the
world of the poem in which there are no initiators.

Once this is established, however, we can understand yet another
aspect of the poem. The most obvious feature of the poem's tense
system is that all of the verbs are in the simple present. Were it not the
case that all agents are also suppressed, this would be a peculiar feature
of the poem, even a bizarre one. Recall that agents presuppose actions
and that actions develop through time. In English the means of expressing action developing through time is not the present tense but rather
the present progressive tense. For example, if there is a knock at the
door, one would say, 'Someone is knocking.' and not 'Someone knocks.'
The latter has an archaic tone which is absent from the poem. As a
consequence, the line *The soldier falls.* does not describe an ongoing
action. The absence of agents in the poem, therefore, is consistent with
the absence of the progressive aspect of the verbal system.

There is a morphological contrast in this connection employed by
Stevens which is worth noting. The *-ing* forms *imposing* and *calling for*
resemble present progressive forms; e.g. 'The king is imposing his will
at this very moment.' Stevens could have chosen another construction
at this point; for example, the infinitival *to impose* or *to call for* which
might appear in the hypothetical 'He does not become a three-days
personage come to impose his separation/to call for pomp.' Rather he
has chosen that construction which resembles the present progressive
and which, by its presence in the poem, calls attention to the present
progressive's absence. This use of the design possibilities inherent in
the syntax of English is even more apparent in what follows.

Having established the rationale for the absence of the present
progressive tense in the poem, let us consider the function of the tense
which does appear in the poem, namely, the simple present. The first
line of the second stanza *He does not become a three-days personage*
introduces a notion of transitoriness. This is emphasized by the brief
time span explicit in the phrase *three-days personage* who engages in

the transitory actions of *imposing separation* and *calling for 'pomp,* and by the nonfinite verbs themselves, whose forms resemble the transitory present progressive tense. This stanza contrasts with all the others in focussing on persons and actions which take place in time. In contrast to this, the present tense in the first line of the third stanza, *Death is absolute*, expresses a truth which is outside of time. The use of the present tense here is like that in such sentences as 'Two and two is four.' or 'The set of all prime numbers is infinite.' This use of the simple present expresses general truths which, because they are always so, are timeless. The simple present adds this force to all of the verbs in the poem, importing to each the sense that its action is lawlike rather than transitory.

Two independent syntactic and semantic features converge in the poem. First, agency is suppressed. This requires a nonprogressive form of all verbs. Second, consistent with this requirement, the simple present tense is chosen. This imparts timelessness to the actions described in the poem. Both syntactico-semantic choices delimit a special world; namely, a timeless world without agency, a world in which events are inevitable and human agency is absent. Such a world is, from a human standpoint, absolute. It is both free from and impervious to human intervention. Death is like this world and Stevens has ordered the syntactic and semantic parameters described above so as to make the form of his poem reflect its content, which is, ultimately, that death is inevitable and timeless; in a word, absolute.

Poetry Is a Destructive Force

Poetry Is a Destructive Force

That's what misery is,
Nothing to have at heart.
It is to have or nothing.

It is a thing to have,
A lion, an ox in his breast,
To feel it breathing there.

Corazon, stout dog,
Young ox, bow-legged bear,
He tastes its blood, not spit.

He is like a man
In the body of a violent beast.
Its muscles are his own . . .

The lion sleeps in the sun.
Its nose is on its paws.
It can kill a man.

In this rather strange poem the syntactic chiasmus or reversal of the second, third and fourth lines stands out quite clearly. We can represent it diagrammatically as follows:

Nothing to have (at heart)
          to have (or)   nothing
                    (It is a)   thing to have

In other words, using the words *nothing* and *have* he constructs these lines so that the second is a reversal of the first and the third is a reversal of the second.

What is perhaps not so obvious is that this same device of reversal, albeit on a phonological scale, appears much later in the poem. Consider the first line of the fourth stanza and the last line of the fifth stanza:

He is like a man
It can kill a man.

The fact that *like* and *kill* are phonological reverses (1-k, k-1) is no accident and is merely the device of reversal seen in the first two stanzas, though now worked at a different level.

We shall assume that the principal formal device which characterizes this poem is chiasmus at the morphological and phonological levels. Now let us turn to the meaning of the poem.

The first two lines state that misery is to have nothing at heart. The third line of the first stanza expands this definition of misery, saying that it is both to have and it is nothing. The logic of the first two sentences is one of reversal, matching the formal chiasmus.

The next two stanzas appear to continue this consistency with respect to form and meaning. The first line of the second stanza continues the device of chiasmus, reversing the pattern of the last line of the first stanza and repeating, in particular, that misery is a thing to have. The poem then goes on to characterize this thing. It is to have a lion and, by extrapolation from the first stanza, it is to have a lion in one's heart. If the phrase *ox in his breast* is taken in parallel with *lion* and if, further, *his* refers to an unnamed poet implied through the title of the poem, then the second stanza may be paraphrased as follows:

Misery for the poet is to have a thing at heart,
For example, to have a lion in his heart or an ox in his breast
And to feel it breathing there.

Given this paraphrase, the series of names that follows in the third stanza, *corazon, stout dog, young ox, bow-legged bear*, are all appropriate epithets for someone with a thing in his heart. That is, they are all names that might be given to someone to represent that the person so named has within him the spirit of the animal or object contained in the name. The next line states that he (the poet) tastes the blood of the animal contained in his breast and not spit. The implication of this is that the poet is someone possessed by something violent in his breast and therefore tastes its blood as opposed to the unpossessed person who tastes spit.

Up to this point, then, the poem seems to be saying that the poet is like someone with a beast inside him. When we come to the next stanza, however, we find that this image is dramatically reversed so that now we are told that a poet with a beast inside him is like a man inside a violent beast. This sudden reversal of the dramatic image that has been developed up to this point corresponds in an obvious fashion to the devices of reversal seen in the chiasmus linking the first two stanzas and in the phonological chiasmus of *like* and *kill* linking the last two stanzas.

The final stanza is now clear. The lion is presented as a destructive force outside of the poet who can kill a man (and a poet, of course). Simultaneously, it symbolizes the destructive force inside the poet which makes him a poet, and, of course, it represents the poet himself. Thus phonological, morphological, and imagistic chiasmus all converge relating form and content in an integral fashion.

Anecdote of the Jar

Anecdote of the Jar

I placed a jar in Tennessee,
And round it was, upon a hill.
It made the slovenly wilderness
Surround that hill.

The wilderness rose up to it,
And sprawled around, no longer wild.
The jar was round upon the ground
And tall and of a port in air.

It took dominion everywhere.
The jar was gray and bare.
It did not give of bird or bush,
Like nothing else in Tennessee.

The immediate impression one receives upon reading this poem is that it is akin in some way to a painting. The juxtaposition of objects in an incongruous and unexpected way and the ways in which the juxtaposed objects influence one another is common to much surrealistic art and to this poem. It would be useful to see if there is some deeper reason for this impression.

The most obvious feature of the poem is the unnatural word order of the first line. Were it to be paraphrased naturally the first sentence would be:

> I placed a jar upon a hill
> In Tennessee, and it was round.

or perhaps:

> I placed a jar, and it was round,
> Upon a hill in Tennessee.

By inverting the order as he has done, Stevens has constructed a second line of the form:

> And round it was, upon a hill

And this line is paralleled by the fourth line of the first stanza:

> Surround that hill

where the obvious repetition of the nouns and verbs appears, though with the variation of the prefix *sur*-added to the verb

```
        round it was, upon a hill
  (sur)round    that        hill
```

The second line of the stanza continues the variation on *round* by prefixing *a-* to it:

```
            round it was, upon a hill
      (sur)round    that        hill
sprawled  (a)round  no longer  wild
```

And the third line of the stanza completes the variation by returning to *round* itself but this time with internal rhyme:

```
            round it was, upon a hill
      (sur)round    that        hill
sprawled  (a)round  no longer  wild
The jar was    round
  upon the  (g)round
```

Thus one formal device made use of in this poem through the first two stanzas is simple variation on the syllable *round*.

Between the second and third stanzas the introduction of rhyme words takes over where variation on *round* stops so that the last line of the second stanza ending in *air* rhymes with *everywhere* and *bare* of the first two lines of the last stanza. Then, in the third line of the last stanza, alliteration picks up where rhyme ends off. This appears in the alliteration of /b/ in *bird* and *bush*. Finally, in the last line a repetition of the ending of the very first line, *in Tennessee*, concludes the poem.

There is, then, a nonoverlapping succession of rhyming devices which appear in a serial fashion in this poem beginning with variations on *-round*, moving to end-rhyme, then to alliteration and terminating with identical rhyme between the first and last lines. This by no means exhausts the devices in the poem, for example, the heavy repetition of liquid and nasal consonants, but these devices are certainly the central ones.

In Winters (1937) the poem is explicated in a way which takes issue with certain previous explications. For Winters the central point of the poem is that the juxtaposition of a jar in a wilderness makes the wilderness slovenly in the poet's eyes, and, taking dominion everywhere, dominates the wilderness to its detriment. The jar is described as *gray* and *bare*, a barren object. Being barren, then, it is like nothing else in Tennessee. It is lifeless and therefore objectionable. The clash of the artificial in the jar and the natural in the wilderness to the detriment of the latter is the point of the anecdote.

Winters presents this explanation to counter an opposing interpretation whereby the placing of the jar acts not to the detriment of the wilderness but to its benefit. According to this view, the jar lends an order to the wilderness which it did not possess before.

In favor of Winters's view is the sense it makes of the phrase *sprawled around*. The notion of *sprawling* is, according to Winters, best viewed as a negative attribute imposed on the wilderness by the jar. Moreover, any interpretation which treats the placing of the jar as beneficial to the wilderness must be embarrassed not only by the phrase *sprawled around*, but also by the obviously negative properties of the jar cited later; namely, *The jar was gray and bare*. On the other hand, Winters's own interpretation requires a special view of the phrase *slovenly wilderness* which appears in the first stanza. Thus he wants to argue that the jar makes the wilderness slovenly; however, the use of slovenly as an adjective implies that it was already slovenly prior to the placing of the jar. This is certainly the most natural reading of the first stanza, and any other reading requires a special dispensation on the part of the reader.

Neither reading; (1) that which views the jar as beneficial to the wilderness, or (2) that which views the jar as detrimental to the wilderness is without difficulty. If, however, there exists a relationship between form and meaning in this poem, it should be possible for us to find an interpretation congenial to the structure that we have already established for *Anecdote of the Jar*, i.e. the successive nonoverlapping series of rhyming devices.

There is no apparent relationship between either reading and the structure we have discerned. There is, however, a third interpretation of the poem. This interpretation avoids viewing the placing of the jar as detrimental or beneficial. Rather it takes a more distant view and notes that the placing of the jar in Tennessee changes the perception of the wilderness. That is to say prior to the introduction of the jar, there was a wilderness. After the introduction of the jar, there was a new object: namely, a wilderness containing a jar. It is quite literally as if Stevens were creating a still-life painting in words (cf. Buttel 1967, p. 166).

This still life is seen in terms of the properties of the new element introduced. The jar possesses three properties which are germane: (1) it is round; (2) it is tall and of a port in air, i.e. imposing; (3) it is gray and bare, i.e. barren. These properties have a specific effect on the environment in which they are introduced. Consider the property 'round'. Placing the jar on the hill causes several things to happen. The jar makes the wilderness, already slovenly according to the poem, appear to surround the hill on which the jar is placed. Further, the jar makes the wilderness sprawl around, where here the word *around* is meant in its directional sense; i.e. the wilderness literally sprawled circularly around the hill on which the jar stands, whereas before, without the focal point of the jar, it simply sprawled without direction. Now it sprawls *no longer wild*.

Notice that the apparent contradiction between slovenly wilderness in the first stanza and sprawling wilderness in the second stanza now disappears. In both stanzas the wilderness is slovenly and sprawling; moreover, in both stanzas the placing of the jar on the hill has had the same effect, i.e. it has given direction to the slovenly and sprawling wilderness by making it seem to surround and sprawl around the hill. The jar has tamed the wilderness by imposing upon it a certain order.

The second property of the jar is described in the phrase *tall and of a port in air*. This means that the jar is of an imposing bearing. The wilderness appears to be diminished since, because of this property, the jar *takes dominion everywhere*. The final property, described in the phrase *gray and bare*, contrasts with the wilderness. The jar appears as a barren object that does not offer life, that does *not give of bird or bush*. In this respect the jar is like nothing else in Tennessee.

In summary, then, the poem is structured in a very simple fashion. A property of the jar is mentioned and the relationship of the property to the environment is specified. With respect to the property 'round,' the jar made the wilderness surround the hill. With respect to the property 'tall and of a port in air,' the jar dominated the wilderness. With respect to the property 'gray and bare,' the jar contrasted its own barrenness to the implied life of the wilderness.

We can now relate the structural properties of the poem to the semantic properties just discussed in an attempt to integrate form and content. We have seen that the first structural device of the poem concerns the syllable *round*. The poem begins with variations of this syllable, starting with *surround*, moving through *around* and *round* to *ground*. The actual phonological shape of the property of the jar which, in English, takes the form of the word *round* imposes an order on the poem just as the semantic property 'round,' which the jar possesses, imposes an order on the wilderness. Using the shape of the word *round* to impose an order on the poem parallels using the actual shape of the object to impose an order on the wilderness.

This relationship exists with respect to the second property, namely *tall and of a port in air*. Once again the physical shape of a word used to describe the property, i.e. *air*, imposes a new rhyming order on the poem (*air:everywhere:bare*) and this parallels the imposition of a new perception on the wilderness by the semantic content of the phrase of which the word is part, i.e. *tall and of a port in air* takes dominion everywhere.

Finally, a new property appears, *gray and bare*. This property contains the word *bare*, which begins with the sound /b/, and it is this sound which participates in the alliteration of the following line. (Indeed, the assumption that the physical shape of the word imposes order explains why the alliteration in the next line is on /b/ and not some other sound.) In this case too the physical shape of a word imposes an order on the poem just as the meaning of the property which takes that physical shape imposes an order on the wilderness. That is, the jar imparts a sense of contrast between its barren self and the life of the wilderness. And the closing line, *like nothing else in Tennessee*, indicates the uniqueness of the object described, the wilderness with jar.

The apparent order of this poem is consistent with its affinity to a still-life painting. The latter is a highly ordered form of visual art with great emphasis placed on the structure of conjoined objects in a single field. Indeed, the apparent framing of this poem between the repeated phrases *in Tennessee* which appear in the opening and the closing lines of the poem provides a verbal counterpart of a frame to the still life in words.[5] However, there appears to be yet another level of meaning which can be imposed on this poem, especially in view of the analysis which has gone before.

It is possible to view the poem as follows. Placing a jar in a wilderness becomes, like juxtaposing objects in a still life, an artistic act.

The chief characteristic of this act is that it imposes an order where none was before. The poem, then, becomes an allegory of what it is about. The wilderness is language. The jar is the poetic form which orders that wilderness. The placing of the jar in the wilderness is the act of poetic creation which imposes form on disorder. The poem is an allegory because Stevens has constructed *Anecdote* so that as each property imposes order on the wilderness, it also imposes an order on the form of the poem. The poem is in form what it is about in content.

The Snow Man

The final poem to be analyzed in this discussion is also from *Harmonium*. This poem is considered to be not only one of Stevens's best, but one of the best short poems of the twentieth century:

The Snow Man

14   One must have a mind of winter
         To regard the frost and the boughs
         Of the pine-trees crusted with snow;

         And have been cold a long time
         To behold the junipers shagged with ice,
         The spruces rough in the distant glitter

         Of the January sun; and not to think
         Of any misery in the sound of the wind
         In the sound of a few leaves,

         Which is the sound of the land
         Full of the same wind
         That is blowing in the same bare place

         For the listener, who listens in the snow
         And, nothing himself, beholds
         Nothing that is not there and the nothing that is.

The opening stanza constitutes what appears at first sight to be a complete sentence and, for all intents and purposes, simply the first of a series of coordinate statements which make up the poem. If we were to diagram its syntax, we would obtain the following schematic representation (where S means that the sequence of words connected to *S* by lines forms a sentence):

15

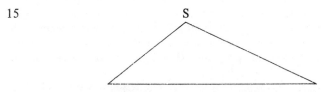

One must have a mind of winter
To regard the frost and the boughs
Of the pine-trees crusted with snow;

What is rather striking about this stanza, however, is that while it at first glance appears to stand alone as a complete syntactic structure, the beginning of the next stanza requires that the reader reassess the syntactic analysis in a very special way. The beginning of the next stanza indicates that an ellipsis has occurred and that the sentence which apparently terminated at the end of the first stanza is, in fact, the first member of a co-ordinate sentence. The ellipsis is with the phrase 'one must' and reinserting it, we represent in (16) the diagram of the first stanza and the new syntactic material which extends over the second stanza and ends at the semicolon in the middle of the first line of the third stanza:

16

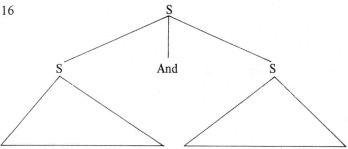

One must have a mind of winter
To regard the frost and the boughs
Of the pine-trees crusted with snow;

(one must) have been cold a long time
To hold the junipers shagged with ice,
The spruces rough in the distant glitter
Of the January sun;

At this point the almost perfect symmetry between each member of the co-ordinate pair which spans stanzas one and two becomes apparent. In (15) there is a main clause *one must have a mind of winter* and a subordinate clause introduced by the truncated subordinate conjunction (*in order*) *to*. The subordinate clause is *to regard the frost and the boughs of the pine-trees crusted with snow.* Notice that it contains a verb *regard* and a compound object; namely, *frost and the boughs* . . . . When we come to the second member of the co-ordinate sentence, we find that it is structured in precisely the same way. There is a main clause (*one must*) *have been cold a long time*, a subordinate clause introduced by the same subordinate conjunction (*in order*) *to*, the subordinate clause contains a verb *behold* and a compound object; namely, *junipers* (*and*) *spruces rough* . . . .

This near perfect symmetry cannot but reassure the reader of the correctness of the reanalysis occasioned by the ellipsis at the beginning of the second stanza. It is for this reason that the ellipsis which appears in the middle of the first line of the third stanza is especially striking. For this new ellipsis shows that once again we have been mistaken in our syntactic analysis, and we must now go back and reanalyze.

The occurrence of *and* before the phrase *not to think* indicates that we have to do with yet another co-ordinate phrase and if we backtrack, we find that it must be taken as co-ordinate with *behold* syntactically and semantically. We find, then, that to reanalyze the structure through the third stanza, we have the schematic representation, shown by the diagram in (17).

17

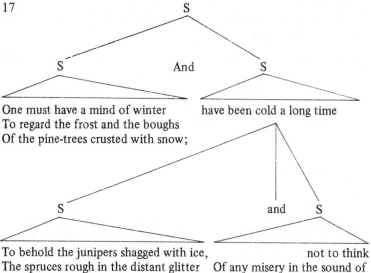

One must have a mind of winter
To regard the frost and the boughs
Of the pine-trees crusted with snow;

To behold the junipers shagged with ice,
The spruces rough in the distant glitter
Of the January sun;

have been cold a long time

not to think
Of any misery in the sound of
the wind,
In the sound of a few leaves,

The results of our analysis up to (17) have been as follows. The second stanza proved to be the second conjunct of two co-ordinate sentences which are, in addition, perfectly symmetrical. However, the third stanza proved to be precisely the same thing, namely the second conjunct of two co-ordinate sentences which are perfectly parallel, only at a deeper level of embedding than the first and the second stanzas. This literal syntactic design is possible only because the second stanza, in particular the phrase:

18   To behold the junipers shagged with ice,
                  The spruces rough in the distant glitter
                  Of the January sun;

plays a double role. It mirrors the structure of the phrase beginning *to regard* . . . in the first stanza and is itself mirrored in the third stanza in the phrase beginning *and not to think* . . .

This maintenance of syntactic parallelism while deepening the level of embedding and at the same time requiring the reader to take an active part in determining through reassessment the syntactic structure of the poem constitutes something of a virtuoso performance in manipulation of syntactic form. We shall see below that this formal structure is closely related to its semantic content. At this point we must continue to explore the formal structure itself.

The fourth stanza of the poem consists of a deepening of levels of embedding. The diagram in (17) contains in its rightmost S the noun phrase (NP) *the sound of a few leaves*, which we schematically represent as:

19   NP

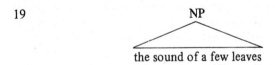

                        the sound of a few leaves

Picking up the syntax at this point we find we must extend the diagram in (17) by adding a series of relative clauses attached to the NP in (19) which is, itself, part of the overall diagram (17). We do this as follows:

20

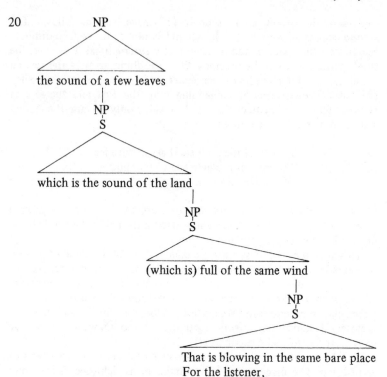

The three relative clauses descending from the NP *the sound of a few leaves* comprise the fourth stanza of the poem. Syntactically this stanza consists of a repetition of the same syntactic structure, a relative clause, three times. This recalls the earlier repetition of the same syntactic structure, conjunction, which also occurs three times [cf. (17) above].

Along with this repetition there is the obvious repetition of certain words. Thus, in the second line of the third stanza *sound* and *wind* appear in a noun phrase. The next line echoes the word *sound*. The same word appears in the relative clause which begins the fourth stanza. The second relative clause contains the word *wind* repeated from the third stanza. It also contains the word *same* and this is repeated in the third relative clause in the phrase *same bare place*. Finally, on the even narrower level of alliteration, it is noteworthy that from the noun phrase *in the sound of the wind* in the third stanza all the way through each relative clause to the last (i.e. to *For the listener*) alliteration of *s*-occurs. Since the subject of this entire construct is the sound of the wind, /s/ alliteration is undoubtedly sound symbolic.

The mark of a great poet is his ability to juggle many interesting balls at once. The brief passage we have been analyzing illustrates

Stevens's ability to perform syntactic, lexical, and phonological repetitions simultaneously, and in part this virtuosity has been perceived by the critics and praised by them.

We now come to what is perhaps the most striking syntactic manipulation of all. The third relative clause represented in (20) ends with the phrase *For the listener*. It is followed by these lines:

21   who listens in the snow,
        And, nothing himself, beholds
        Nothing that is not there and the nothing that is.

The most obvious aspect of (21) is that it too, is a relative clause. It begins with the relative pronoun *who* and it obviously modifies the NP *the listener*. The structure of this stanza is represented in the diagram (22) without attempting to relate it to the previous diagrams.

22

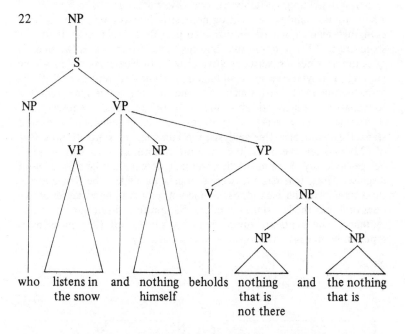

Note: In the above diagram the symbols VP abbreviate *verb phrase* and V abbreviates *verb*. The symbols NP (*noun phrase*) and S (*sentence*) have appeared earlier.

The most obvious fact about the structure in (22) is that it contains all of the properties which we have seen earlier in the poem. Thus (22) contains a compound VP just as (17) contains a compound S. Moreover, the second conjunct of the compound VP contains a compound NP just as the second conjunct of the compound S in (17) itself contains a compound S. Thus (22) is very close to being a structural repetition of all of the structure that has gone before.

There are two possible ways to relate (22) to the structure elaborated thus far. The first is simply to treat (22) as yet another relative clause attached to the NP *the listener*. In other words, the diagram in (20) would have one more relative clause extending downward; namely, the relative clause in (22).

There is, however, an alternative proposal. It has long been observed that there is a similarity between nonrestrictive relative clauses and co-ordinate clauses. The following paraphrases of one another are illustrative:

23 (a) John will come, and he is certainly trustworthy.

(b) John—and he is certainly trustworthy—will come.

(c) John, who is certainly trustworthy, will come.

Assuming the validity of treating nonrestrictives as being derived from conjoined clauses, we are now able to provide another analysis for the structure in (22). (Notice that Stevens himself punctuates the lines in question as a nonrestrictive relative clause.) In particular, we may now view (22) as yet another conjunct of a conjoined sentence. With its introduction in the last stanza, we find ourselves once again required to reanalyze the syntactic structure of the poem just as we were required to do upon encountering the syntactic material in the second and third stanzas. If we accept this analysis, the fact that the syntactic structure of (22) parallels the preceding structure is nothing more than the same device used by Stevens earlier, though now in a slightly different disguise. Thus, whereas the second stanza paralleled the first and the third paralleled the second, each time within a conjoined sentence, we now find that the last stanza parallels the first four, itself in a conjoined sentence. The syntactic unity that this analysis of (22) provides is represented in (24), once again very schematically:

24

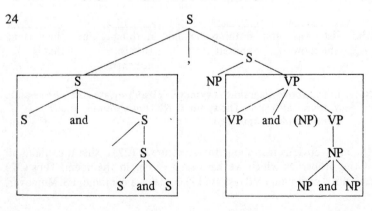

Note: The sections of this schematic tree which are parallel are enclosed in the superimposed boxes. The diagram has been simplified to emphasize the structural parallel between the first part of the poem and the last stanza. In particular, the parenthetical NP *nothing himself* has been placed in parentheses in (24). The , extending below the highest S indicates the use of the nonrestrictive relative clause in its conjunctional sense.

The reason for adopting the analysis in (24) is precisely that the resultant structure is consistent with a poem requiring reanalysis at several key points in the reader's progress through the poem. The poem demands that we analyze and then reanalyze yet again as we pass linearly and in time from one point to another in the structure.

At this point let us look at the relationship between the formal device described above and the meaning of the poem. Frank Kermode talks, in part, of its meaning as follows:

> Out of 'The Snow Man' grows the recurring metaphor of winter
> as a pure abstracted reality, a bare icy outline purged clean of all
> the accretions brought by the human mind to make it possible
> for us to conceive of reality and live our lives. So purged, reality
> has no human meaning, nor has a man; he is
>
> . . . the listener, who listens in the snow,
> And, nothing himself, beholds
> Nothing that is not there and the nothing that is.
> In winter, things are seen as they are. (1960, 34).

In contrast to Kermode's interpretation of 'The Snow Man' we have Wallace Stevens's own explanation which he gives in a letter to Hi Simons, dated 18 April, 1944: 'I shall explain the Snow Man as an example of the necessity of identifying oneself with reality in order to understand it and enjoy it.' Now while the interpretations differ in the value assigned to having a mind of winter (i.e. Stevens speaks of it as being a state in which to enjoy reality while Kermode speaks of it as a state in which enjoyment is absent, indeed in which no human meaning is present), there is a clear common core of meaning. Both Kermode and Stevens speak of the need to perceive reality in a clear fashion.

Now if we return for a moment to the development of the poem, we find that in the. implied regimen needed to move toward a clear perception of reality there is a constant change of perspective. Thus Stevens observes that to begin with one must have a mind of winter, i.e. a particular state of mind in order to regard the frost. However, this state of mind is not in itself reliable for one must have had it for a long time in order to behold the junipers shagged with ice and not think of misery. In other words, a mind of winter will enable perception of winter but will not separate the perception of winter from the misery it entails. However, if one has a mind of winter for a long time, one will be able to see the winter without thinking of the misery.

At this point one becomes, according to the poem, a listener who is now able to behold 'nothing that is not there and the nothing that is.' In this ultimate state of mind one sees clearly, i.e. one sees no thing that is not there and in seeing only those things which are there one will finally perceive the nothing that is really there. This final change of perspective is one in which the ultimate realization is that in seeing what is really there one sees that what is really there is nothing. It is this perception which is underscored by describing the listener as being nothing himself and presumably able to perceive nothing.

It seems quite reasonable then to view the semantic thrust of the poem as the need to constantly change perspective in order to achieve a real understanding of reality. But now let us return to the formal structure of the poem. We saw that in an extremely intricate fashion the poem consists of a syntactic pattern whose main characteristic is that its structure at any one time seems clear but which, at the next moment, requires a complete reanalysis. What seemed clear earlier turns out to be an illusion. This designed need to change syntactic perspective cannot more closely parallel the sense of the poem which is to change one's outward perspective in order to more accurately understand reality. The poem is in its structure precisely what it talks about in its content. It demands of readers that they reanalyze in order to see the truth of its syntax and this is what Stevens claims one must do with respect to one's perception of the world in order to perceive the truth of the world's reality. There can be no more direct relationship between a poem's form and its content than that exhibited by 'The Snow Man.' Indeed, making the poem's syntax a virtual allegory of its content constitutes a brilliant poetic achievement.[6]

Conclusion

In each of the four poems analyzed above a formal structural feature was isolated. An attempt was then made to show how this feature is related to what the poem is about; in a word, how form and content correlate. Since it is logically possible for the formal structure encountered in a poem to bear no relation to that poem's content, it seems significant that in these four poems such a correlation can be drawn. The question immediately arises, to what extent can similar correlations be found in other poems and other poets? An attractive and obvious conclusion that one might ultimately wish to draw is that the aesthetic worth of a poem in part depends on the existence of such correlations. The worth of this conclusion must await a much more comprehensive body of studies of which the present study is, hopefully, one.[7]

NOTES

1 I would like to acknowledge the debt I owe those students who participated in a poetry seminar in the spring of 1971 at Brandeis University whose insights contributed significantly to this essay: Louise Arthur, Janet Stojak Kaplan, Ann Reed, Kim Weeks, Suzanne Spadola and Julia Waldman. In addition, I would like to thank Noam Chomsky, Morris Halle, and Eleanor Young for their insightful comments on an earlier version of this paper, as well as Mr Dan Wallace for his valuable suggestions for presenting this material schematically. An earlier version of this article appeared in French translation in *Change 16–17*, Seghers/Laffont, Paris, 1974. This work was in part sponsored by NSF Grant No. GS 3179 to Brandeis University and in part by a NSF Grant No. GS 35283 to the University of Massachusetts at Amherst.

2 Sentences like:
   (a) The robot washed the dishes.
   (b) The wind opened the door.
   suggest that some other category beside that of agent, or perhaps in addition to agent, is required (cf Huddleston 1970). In particular, it may be that a category like Causer must be set up and subdivided into agentive Causer, like *John* in (3a,c) and nonagentive Causer like *robot* and *wind* above. But even so the point to be made below will still go through though with the category Causer, animate or otherwise, substituted for agency.

3 That *expect* can be considered as a verb which can take an agent is based upon some observations in Huddleston (1970, 508):
   (i) Don't expect any mercy from John.
   (ii) Expect me when you see me.
   These sentences involve clear commands and commands are limited to actions which the hearer is assumed to have some control over. This sense of *expect* does not appear in the poem. But notice that even if one supposed that it did, the agent of the action of *expect* would still be suppressed from the surface. And this, as will be seen, is what is really crucial to the analysis.

4 The separation of *wind* (the causer) from *clouds go* (the effect) is underlined by the phrase *in their direction*. That is to say, the clouds have a direction that they are going in and they continue in that direction irrespective of the wind.

5 For a discussion of the relationship between poetry and painting in the work of William Blake, Henri Rousseau and Paul Klee, see Jakobson (1970).

6 It is noteworthy that the last line of the poem contains within itself

precisely the kind of syntactic change of perspective which characterizes everything that has gone before. Thus, in the line *Nothing
that is not there and the nothing that is*, the first occurrence of
nothing constitutes a noun phrase composed of a determiner and a
noun and can be represented as:

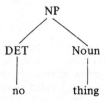

The second occurrence, however, contains *nothing* now as a noun
within the noun phrase *the nothing* and can be represented as:

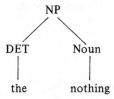

Thus, the syntactic shift from *nothing* to *the nothing* parallels the
shift whereby the listener, beholding what is there beholds the
nothing there.

    It has been pointed out to me by Morris Halle that the shifting
of syntactic perspective in 'The Snow Man' is quite parallel to the
building of several perspectives into a single plane in the work of
the Cubists. This parallel between a poetic device in Stevens and a
painter's device in say Picasso or Braque is quite striking and has
not gone unnoticed: 'In a more serious vein, "Metaphors of a Mag-
nifico" (1918), Stevens seems to have the Cubists' ability to see
different perspectives of an object simultaneously . . . . One must
assimilate the multiplicity here just as the viewer of Duchamp's
painting must assimilate the fragmentation and multiplicity of the
nude descending the staircase' (Buttel 1967, pp. 164, 165).

    For a discussion of the relationship between poetic and visual
forms see Jakobson (1970).
7 Two recent studies which attempt to draw the same kinds of correlation between form and content are Freeman (1975 and 1978).

REFERENCES

Buttell, R. (1967), *Wallace Stevens: The Making of Harmonium*
(Princeton, New Jersey, Princeton University Press).

Freeman, D. C. (1975), 'The Strategy of Fusion: Dylan Thomas'
Syntax', in *Style and Structure in Literature*, ed. R. Fowler
(Oxford: Basil Blackwell).

Freeman, D. C. (1978), 'Keats's "To Autumn": Poetry as Pattern and
Process', *Language and Style*, xi, pp. 3-17.

Huddleston, R. (1970), 'Some Remarks on Case Grammar', *Linguistic
Inquiry 1.4*, pp. 501-11.

Jakobson, R. (1970), 'The Verbal Art of William Blake and Other
Poet Painters', *Linguistic Inquiry 1.1*, pp. 1-23, Edinburgh.

Kermode, F. (1960), *Wallace Stevens* (Edinburgh: Oliver & Boyd).

Stevens, H. (1965), *The Letters of Wallace Stevens* (London: Faber
& Faber).

Stevens, W.(1955), *The Collected Poems of Wallace Stevens* (London:
Faber & Faber).

Winters, Y. (1937), *In Defense of Reason* (Denver: University of
Denver Press).

Style as tension between meaning and form

CHAPTER FIFTEEN

Topicalization as a stylistic mechanism

*Shivendra K. Verma**

[Verma's paper is divided into three sections. In the first he provides a new definition of style. Verma sees style as neither completely inseparable from nor completely separable from meaning, but as a different kind of meaning, different, that is, from propositional meaning, resulting from the tension created by the various factors—message, medium, tradition, and personality (of the writer)—in the communication process. Thus, he does not effect an artificial disjunction between style and content, yet he offers a means of conceptualizing their distinction and, thus, their reaction. In his second section Verma briefly outlines the communication process and asserts that linguistics is no general panacea which can offer full explanation of literary texts, but rather a useful adjunct which can do a great deal to help the literary critic by 'offering tools of considerable precision for describing and explaining topically and contextually significant varieties of language.' Verma's third section illustrates this precision. Here he offers a formal analysis of topicalization transformations which can serve as a tool to explain the stylistic variations which may be produced by the various factors in the communication process. In particular, he shows the effect of the message on stylistic variation by introducing the theme-rheme theory of M. A. K. Halliday, and the effect of medium by examining topicalization for prosodic purposes in poetry.]

This paper[†] falls into three parts: first, a discussion of literature as a 'hypersemanticized' use of language; second, a review of the relevance of linguistic analysis to our understanding of 'how the language of literature works'; and third, an examination of topicalization as a stylistic mechanism.

*First published in *Poetics* (1976), pp. 23–33.
†This is a revised and enlarged version of a paper presented at the seminar on stylistics organized by the Central Institute of English and Foreign Languages, Hyderabad, from 28 January to 1 February 1974.

1

All literature may be said to be an exploration of experience. In processing and sieving human experiences literary artists exploit the 'meaning potential' of language. Language and personality, which embody multidimensional features, get coupled as twin forces in this complex process of exploitation and exploration. Language as a mediator between man and his experience uses a network of inter-related systems—phonological, syntactic, and lexico-semantic. Each system represents a network of choices—choices are triggered off and also restrained by a host of linguistic and extra-linguistic features. The choice of the passive, for example, depends on the choice of a transitive verb and also on the contextual requirement to highlight the object by subjectivizing it. The coupling of language and personality (already referred to) necessitates a re-examination of the notion 'personality in language'. Every person is a bundle of *personae*, a bundle of roles—each role having its socio-culturally determined lines. If he does not know his lines, he has no value in the play (Firth 1957: 184). In selecting his lines he is influenced by a number of socio-idiolectal factors: socio-cultural setting, topic of discourse, participants involved and his own indexical and idiosyncratic traits. On the one hand there is 'nurture'/'tradition' (literary, linguistic, and cultural) and on the other individual 'nature'/'talent' (innovation and creation). Every time an individual speaks/writes, he recreates patterns by weaving 'nurture' into 'nature'. This recreation is always an outcome of 'tension', of an interaction between 'tradition' and 'individual talent'. In fact, it is a complex tension: the forces involved are message, medium, tradition, and personality. An individual's style is, in fact, generated by this tension. There are different degrees of tension and hence different levels of style.'The artist's "intuition", to use Croce's term, is immediately fashioned out of a generalized human experience—thought and feeling—of which his own individual experience is a highly personalized selection' (Sapir 1949: 224). The evidence of 'style as tension' is in the individual's performance—in how he explores the expressive resources of his medium and welds together 'idea' and 'form', 'meaning' and 'structure'. Style markers—i.e. phonological, graphological, syntactic, and lexical patterns (including patterns of metaphor and selection of literary conventions such as particular 'forms' of poetry, novel, drama etc.)—are all surface manifestations of underlying tension, of how creative artists pair off sound and meaning, of how they externalize their ways of thinking and feeling in their medium. This does not mean that languages have tension-specific style markers. 'Literature moves in language as a medium, but that medium comprises two layers, the latent content of language—our intuitive record of experience—and the particular conformation of a given language—the specific *how* of our record of experience' (Sapir 1949: 223). No one uses all the resources of a language: everyone selects and organizes. Style is the structuring of choices (choice of types of sentences, clauses, phrases, words, morphemes, tunes, images, and graphological markers) made within the framework of a language and of literary forms (Gleason 1965: 428). In this process of structuring, the language used in a literary text becomes, as it were, 'hypersemanticized' (Weinreich 1963: 147).

2

When we speak of linguistic analysis, we refer to a general framework of universal linguistic principles and particular frameworks peculiar to individual languages in terms of which we try to understand how language works and how individual languages work. By 'how a language works' we mean how that language uses a network of mutually defining and interlocking systems to mediate, in a highly complex way, between the universe of meaning and the universe of sound. On the one hand we have 'some message(s) to transmit', and on the other we produce 'sounds' which, under ordinary circumstances, convey these messages to a listener or listeners. The path which leads from 'clusters of meaning' to 'clusters of sound' is often remarkably circuitous. The primary goal of linguistic analysis is to describe and explain the organization of sounds, words, and sentences (and also suprasentential units) and thereby help us (listeners/readers) retrace our path to meaning. In order to do this effectively we have to examine the structural, systemic, and transformational mechanisms used by languages to externalize meaning. 'The most challenging theoretical problem in linguistics is that of discovering the principles of universal grammar that interweave with the rules of particular grammars to provide explanations for phenomena that appear arbitrary and chaotic' (Chomsky 1968: 40). These explanations are provided on the basis of linguistic mechanism used. There is, however, no one-to-one correspondence between linguistic mechanisms used and meaning(s) expressed. Embeddings, for example, may be used to convey the richness and complexity of a piece of experience or to gloss triviality and vacuity.

The function of linguistic analysis is not the same as that of literary analysis. No linguist worth his salt would claim that this aim is to replace the literary critic. Why a critic responds to a text the way he does is a question which is at the moment beyond the domain of linguistic analysis. A critic's hunch does not come out of the air as such; it is prompted by a number of factors—such as his own sensibility and the tradition behind him, and also the forces underlying the text. Some of the things that he looks for to confirm his hunches are stylistic markers—linguistically significant features of the text. There is, in fact, a subtle 'trading relation' between 'hunches' and 'markers'. It is in this area that we can hope to have a meaningful dialogue between linguists and literary critics—linguistics offering tools of considerable precision for describing and explaining topically and contextually significant varieties of language. The current centre of interest in linguistics is not the organization of texts so much as the nature of the organizing power which is capable of handling such texts.

In order to understand notions such as 'grammatical' and 'ungrammatical', 'normal' and 'non-normal', we have to study them not only in terms of a grammatical framework but also in terms of the framework of the texts in which they occur. Expressions like *the tree married the girl* are deviant in terms of the syntax of general English but non-deviant in the language of fairy tales. Deviance is of two types—unmotivated, random deviance such as *sky the rainbow a behold I* and motivated, context-governed deviance like *a grief ago*.

> There are circumstances in which the use of grammatically deviant sentences is very much in place. Consider, for example, such phrases as Dylan Thomas' 'a grief ago' or Veblen's ironic 'perform leisure'. In such cases, and innumerable others, a striking effect is achieved precisely by means of a departure from a grammatical regularity (Chomsky 1964: 187).

And interpretations are imposed on them by virtue of analogies that they bear to non-deviant sentences. There is no single universally relevant norm, no set of expectancies to which all instances may be referred. What is a departure or a deviance may be perfectly normal in the context of a restricted text.

3

Word-order or the order in which the constituents of a sentence are organized may be said to be an external manifestation of the organization of constituents of experience. One must, however, note that there is no one-to-one correspondence between the organization of experience and its externalization in terms of word-order. Consider the following:

> *He had his tea after he had unpacked*
> *and arranged his books.*

In terms of factual sequence, he unpacked and arranged his books and then had his tea. In terms of linguistic sequence the principal clause *he had his tea* precedes the subordinate clause *after he had unpacked and arranged his books.*

The point to examine here is: is this arrangement 'random' or 'motivated'? No two arrangements of the same set of constituents in any human language mean exactly the same thing. Languages have their own language-specific rules to permit non-normal scrambling of constituents. Languages like Latin and Sanskrit in which grammatical functions are marked inflectionally permit greater freedom in the positioning of elements, whereas languages like English where grammatical functions are defined positionally impose constraints on the shuffling of word-order. The communicative function of word-order and the different formal means available in different languages of achieving a distribution of content in keeping with the communicative intention have been investigated in a number of studies by Prague linguists. In every language (and in every registral variety of a language) one can identify the normal or unmarked order of words. This may be said to be that order which is statistically the most frequent and matches the native speaker's intuitive 'feeling' for normal word-order. Once the normal patterns are established, the non-normal arrangements can be easily highlighted for purposes of analysis (Verma 1970a: 29). 'The *normal* W.–O. is formed by grammatically set constructions and normal patterns (cliches). The *special* W.–O. is constituted by functional variants of the normal sentence patterns (cliches)' (Simko 1957: 7). In English what occurs first in clause structure is the 'topic' of discourse, i.e. 'What I am talking about' and the remainder is the 'comment'. In registrally unmarked declarative sentences the subject is also the topic—this may be labelled 'unmarked topic'. This tendency of many languages to put the known first and the unknown or unexpected last is called 'sentence perspective'. It is generally thought that 'subject' and 'topic' are identical, but in fact this is not always true 'for though there is often correspondence, a linguistic *subject* may not be the topic of a sentence, nor the topic be expressed by the linguistic subject' (Strang, 1962: 71). One of the stylistic mechanisms by which an element is fronted for thematic prominence is called topicalization or thematization. Topicalization may now be defined as a syntactic device which isolates one of the constituents of a sentence as 'topic' and shifts it to the sentence-initial position (cf. Chomsky 1964: 221). We approach an English sentence with certain expectations conditioned by our long acquaintance with the basic, non-transformed sentence patterns. We come expecting a subject first and only then a predicate. When we find something non-normal contrary to our expectations, we at once realize that the speaker/writer has pulled certain features into the foreground or relegated them to the background to produce certain effects (cf. Jespersen 1969a; 99). Consider the following:

	S	P			
'Topicalization'		V	O	A	'Extra-position'

S(ubject) P(redicate) represent the normal order of the constituents in a sentence. Within P(redicate) the normal order is: V(erb) O(bject) A(djunct). Two types of non-normal, stylistic shiftings are possible— S may be shifted from its normal, initial position to the end-position to delay the introduction of the main theme, that is, to keep the readers/listeners in a state of suspense. One of the distinguishing features of this S(ubject)-shifting is that it leaves a trace behind either in the form of a dummy *it/there* or in the shape of some other pro-form. This shifting is called extraposition. O(bject) too, when backshifted, may leave a trace behind in the form of 'it'.

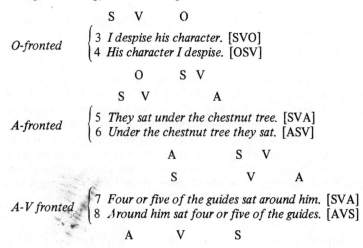

        S   V   C

1 *To play with explosives is dangerous.* [SVC]
2 *It is dangerous to play with explosives.* [SVCS]

  S V   C   S

In fact, sentence (2) is marked by the presence of two subjects—a dummy subject *it* and the real subject *to play with explosives* in *extraposition*. Sentences (1) and (2) are stylistically variant forms of the same set of basic constituents: they are allosentences (Verma 1970b: 4). The subject of sentence (1) and its topic are the same: *to play with explosives*, but by using the mechanism of extraposition the speaker separates these two rules in (2): he introduces a dummy as the grammatical subject and puts his listeners in an anticipative mood for the delayed topic which appears at the end of the sentence. The other type of shifting mentioned earlier on is front-shifting—shifting an item from its normal, non-initial position to the initial position, for example, O-fronting, V-fronting, and A-fronting.

              S   V   O

O-fronted   3 *I despise his character.* [SVO]
              4 *His character I despise.* [OSV]

              O   S V

              S   V   A

A-fronted   5 *They sat under the chestnut tree.* [SVA]
              6 *Under the chestnut tree they sat.* [ASV]

              A   S   V

              S   V   A

A-V fronted   7 *Four or five of the guides sat around him.* [SVA]
              8 *Around him sat four or five of the guides.* [AVS]

              A   V   S

It is interesting to note that V-shifting is always preceded by A-fronting or C-fronting. These are all examples of marked topic or of topicalization which represents a foregrounding of the speaker's point of departure and has a contrastive meaning. The *topic* of a sentence is the element that the sentence is 'about'. The rest of the sentence labelled the *comment* contributes new information about the topic.

> Communication becomes effective if the speaker assumes that something is already known to the listener and organizes his speech in such a way as to make it clear which element of the utterance conveys the new piece of information. A sentence is, therefore, divided into two parts: (1) the part that expressed something that is assumed to be already known both to the listener and the speaker, and (2) the part that contains information proper. These two parts of a speech event are called the theme and the rheme respectively (Drazdauskas and Mikael'an 1973: 13).

Halliday makes a distinction between theme–rheme structure and given –new structure. According to him given–new is a structure not of the clause but of the information unit, and is realized not by sequence but by intonation, theme–rheme on the other hand is a structure of the clause, and is realized by the sequence of elements: the theme comes first. The meaning of theme is not the same as that of given, although the two functions are often realized by the same element. 'First position (and note that this does mean first position in the clause, and not in the information unit) expresses the function of "theme". What the speaker puts first is the theme of the clause, the remainder being the "rheme" ' (Halliday 1970: 356). Halliday emphasizes the point that the given is nearer-oriented and context-bound, whereas the theme is speaker-oriented and context-free.

> The difference can perhaps be best summarized by the observation that, while 'given' means 'What you were talking about' (or 'What I was talking about before'), 'theme' means 'What I am talking about' (or 'What I am talking about now'); and, as any student of rhetoric knows, the two do not necessarily coincide (Halliday 1967: 212).

Creative artists exploit the possibilities of this mechanism of non-normal front-shifting to highlight certain features, whereby some feature of the language of a text stands out in some way and contributes to the writer's total meaning. Consider the following sentence in its linguistic and extralinguistic context and see how Dickens has effectively exploited the mechanism of object-topicalization to bring into focus some of the significant traits of the character of Mr. Micawber.

9 *Talent, Mr. Micawber has: capital Mr. Micawber has not.*

Consider also the following:

10 *Like a comet through flames she moves entranced.* (Stephen
    Spender, 'The Express')
11 *A poor life this if full of care.*
    We have no time to stand and stare. (W. H. Davies, 'Leisure')
12 *A neat little luncheon*
    Of sandwiches is brought to each on a tray,
    Nourishment they are able
    To take with one hand without looking up

    From papers a couple
    Of secretaries are needed to file,
    From problems no smiling
    Can dismiss; . . . (W. H. Auden, 'The managers')

The items topicalized are *like a comet through flames* in (10), *a poor
life* in (11) and *nourishment* in (12). In the process of describing the
journey of the Express through familiar towns and crowded cities into
the wide open country beyond, Stephen Spender brings into focus
the significant features of her movement by front-shifting them. This
shifting, it may be said, has also been motivated by the metrical structure of the poem. Instead of saying—*She leaves the station, gliding
like a queen; There lies the open country beyond the town; She moves
entranced like a comet through flames*—Spender topicalizes his key
constituents: *gliding like a queen, she leaves the station; beyond the
town there lies the open country; like a comet through flames she
moves entranced.*

Notice the contrast between *A poor life this if full of care* and
What is life, if full of care. By using the mechanism of topicalization
and the deletion of the verb *be* in *a poor life this* (instead of *this is a
poor life*), the poet heightens the effect of the question with which the
poem begins and pinpoints the thematic focus of the poem: *A poor
life this, if full of care.*

All languages possess some means of carrying out topicalization.
In fact, languages offer a number of devices for identifying or high-
lighting or delaying the topic. Some of these devices are:
  (i)   Passivization
  (ii) Pseudo-cleft transformation
  (iii) Cleft transformation
  (iv) Extraposition
The choice between these is not always entirely free; it is context-
governed and topic-oriented. Passivization, for example, is a special
type of topicalization which moves the 'noun phrase' that is the centre
of interest at the moment to the subject position and marks it 'thematic'.

13 *The town was occupied, the defender defeated, and the war finished.*

Passivization allows the actor either to be a constituent of the 'rheme' with unmarked focus or not to be specified at all. 'The difference between the active and the passive (a structure in which the normal subject is acted upon) is mainly one of emphasis . . . . By putting a sentence into the passive, prominence is secured for the object rather than the subject; and the passive should therefore be regarded as a useful stylistic device, not intended only to dispense with subject personal pronouns, as in modern officialese' (Partridge 1969: 134). The pseudo-cleft transformation nominalizes a sentence (i.e., converts a sentence into a noun phrase) using *Wh*-mechanisms and produces an equative-type of sentence in which one of the components is identified as the carrier of the main unit of information. Compare the following:

Non-identifying

14 *Mohan saw the play*

Identifying

15 *What Mohan saw was the play.*

Here the topic is *What Mohan saw* and *the play (and nothing else)* is the exclusive goal of Mohan's perception as far as the communication situation is concerned. This is a highly favoured clause type in modern English. 'It is not surprising that the London brewer's slogan *We want Watney's*, which envisaged the possibility that we might want other things as well, was very early replaced by the identifying form *What we want is Watney's*' (Halliday 1967: 224).

Related to 15 is 16:

16 *The thing that Mohan saw was the play*

Here *the thing that* is an expanded form of *what*. The topic of the sentence therefore is *the thing that Mohan saw*. This pattern presupposes the question: 'What is the thing that Mohan saw?' It is more specific than the *what*-pattern: it clearly states that *the thing was the play*.

Another type of cleft mechanism makes use of *it/there + be + NP + S*(entence). It is a powerful stylistic device, for it combines the mechanisms of predication and topicalization. It serves as a deictic category to draw the attention of the hearer to one particular part of the sentence. The topicalized constituent is preceded by predication: *it + be* and followed by S(entence). *It* and *there* are syntactic devices for anticipating the topic of discourse.

       17 *You could try Mohan.*

With cleft 18 *It's Mohan you should try.*

       19 *There's Mohan you could try.*

In both the types—*it* and *there*—extraposition of the relative clause is obligatory. *There*-type means: 'One person—there may be others—you could try is Mohan'; *it*-type means: 'The person you should try is Mohan (Mohan and nobody else)'. *It* refers to 'Mohan and no others'; *there* refers to 'Mohan, possibly among others'. 'With *it* the theme is defined (uniquely specified), with *there* it is described (non-uniquely specified)' (Halliday 1967: 238). The mechanism of cleft construction can be used to predicate and topicalize any of the constituents: subject, object, adjunct.

Subject   20 *It was* Mohan *who presented a paper yesterday.*
Object   21 *It was* a paper *that Mohan presented yesterday.*
Adjunct   22 *It was* yesterday *that Mohan presented a paper.*

Discussing cleft sentences Jespersen says that this construction may be considered one of the means by which the disadvantages of having a comparatively rigid grammatical word order (SVO) can be obviated. This explains why it is that similar constructions are not found, or are not used extensively, in languages in which the word-order is considerably less rigid than in English (Jespersen 1969b: 76). In the following extract adapted from Virginia Woolf (*To the Lighthouse*) the introducers *it* and *there* have been used effectively as two kinds of run-in towards the communicative core:

23 *The children were not asleep. It was most annoying. It was obvious that something had upset them. There was James wide awake and Mildred out of bed in her bare feet, and it was almost eleven, and they were all talking. What was the matter? It was that horrid skull again. There was not much use doing anything about it now. It was foolish of her really to bother. She should not have put the skull there; well, it was no use crying over spilt milk; after all, there are more ways of killing a cat than choking it with cream.*

The way *it* has been used here shows that there is yet another type of mechanism by which the subject slot is filled by a dummy *it* or a pronoun and the real topic is relegated to the end of the sentence. We have already examined this device in the context of back-shifting. This mechanism enables writers to delay the introduction of the real theme/topic. When the listener hears a structure of predication such as *It is . . . ,* his anticipation is aroused by the dummy *it* and he expects a completion of thought.

24 *It is true that he is arriving today.*
25 *They don't seem to match, these colours.*
26 *He is a nice guy, this journalist.*

In all these sentences we have two subjects—an anticipatory subject and the extra-posed subject. This extraposition of the topic necessitates the use of a cataphoric pronominal filler in the subject position. Topicalization, however, shifts the real topic to the subject position and deletes the pronominal fillers. The sentences that we get are:

27 *That he is arriving today is true.*
28 *These colours don't seem to match.*
29 *This journalist is a nice guy.*

Thus, what a creative writer has at his disposal is a repertoire of mechanisms for externalizing different degrees of topicalization and a variety of other features. He makes choices keeping in view topical, cotextual, and contextual requirements. These choices get organized into layers of patterns which represent external manifestations of inner style. Style, as detailed earlier on, is the patterning of choices made within the framework of the conventions of the language and of the literary form. Modern linguistics can help literary critics get a deeper insight into the working of the language of literature, can offer them a powerful methodology and a rigorous set of technical terms to capture and explicate their generalizations. Linguistic and literary scholarship should be complementary and mutually reinforcing. Linguistics can illuminate stylistic problems and stylistic problems can draw linguistics out of its shell. As readers and hearers we react to the whole of a writer's creative use of 'meaning potential'.

REFERENCES

Chomsky, Noam (1964), 'Some methodological remarks on generative grammar', in H. B. Allen (ed.), *Readings in applied English linguistics* (New York: Appleton-Century-Crofts).

Chomsky, Noam (1968), *Language and mind* (New York: Harcourt, Brace).

Drazdauskas A. and G. Mikael'an (1973), *An outline of English syntax*, Olga Akhmaniva (ed.) (Moscow: Moscow State University).

Firth, J. R. (1957), 'Personality and language in society' in *Papers in linguistics 1934-1951* (London: Oxford University Press).

Gleason, H. A. (1965), *Linguistics and English grammar* (New York: Holt, Rinehart & Winston).

Halliday M. A. K. (1967), 'Notes on transitivity and theme in English, Part 2', *Journal of linguistics 3*; pp. 199-244.

Halliday, M. A. K. (1970), 'Functional diversity in language as seen from a consideration of modality and mood in English', *Foundations of Language 6*, pp. 322-61.

Jespersen O. (1969a), *Essentials of English grammar* (London: Allen & Unwin).

Jespersen, O. (1969b), *Analytic syntax* (New York: Holt, Rinehart & Winston).

Partridge, A. C. (1969), *Tudor to Augustan English* (London: Andre Deutsch).

Sapir, E. (1949), *Language* (New York: Harcourt Brace; first published in 1921).

Simko, Jan (1957), *Word Order* (Halle: Max Niemeyer).

Strang, Barbara M. H. (1962), *Modern English structure* (London: Edward Arnold).

Verma, S. K. (1970a), 'Word order in Hindi', *Archiv orientalni* 38: pp. 28–32.

Verma, S. K. (1970b), 'Allosentence: a study in universals of linguistic theory', *Indogermanische Forschungen 75*.

Weinreich, U. (1963), 'On the semantic structure of language' in Joseph H. Greenberg (ed.), *Universals of language* (Cambridge, Mass.: M.I.T. Press).

CHAPTER SIXTEEN

Understanding poetic speech acts

Michael Hancher *

[Hancher argues that, in part because of the lack of suprasegmental elements, the risk of misunderstanding illocutionary force in literature is great enough to merit precaution. He discusses two poems (Shakespeare's 'Sonnet 19' and Frost's 'Spring Pools'), showing that the failure to understand 'what is being done in what is being said' can lead to a misinterpretation of the poems. In 'Sonnet 19,' Hancher sees a tension between the imperative words and the speech act being performed by these words. In order to perceive this tension, the reader must realize that, in spite of his language, the speaker, not having the requisite status to issue an order, is performing an illocutionary act of conceding. This tension is central to the poem's meaning as evidenced by the final couplet's clash between this concession and the poet's boast that he will immortalize his love. Illocutionary force is also central to 'Spring Pools.' The reader who fails to interpret the last four lines as an indirect warning misses the poem's 'If summer comes, can winter be far behind' motif.]

The thesis of this paper[1] is simple, perhaps unexceptionable. I propose that in understanding 'literary' or 'poetic' discourse, as in understanding ordinary spoken or written discourse, we should and do regularly take into account what it is that the author or dramatic speaker is doing *in* the act of uttering a given piece of discourse.

Deliberate attention to such matters is common enough in ordinary speech. A mother says to her son, 'It's time for you to clean up your room'; she may then go on to specify that in uttering those words she is *ordering* him to clean up his room (and not *suggesting* that he do so) by adding, '—that's an *order.*' A diner says to a short-order cook, 'This chili's hot'; the cook may ask, 'Is that a *compliment* or a *complaint?*' When we (as speakers) do *not* deliberately specify the force of our utterances, nor (as hearers) raise such questions about the force of what we have just heard, it isn't because such niceties don't matter. We

*First published in *College English*, 36 (1975), pp. 632–9. Copyright © 1975 by the National Council of Teachers of English. Reprinted by permission of the publisher and the author.

assume that they are patent and don't need to be specified

What is true of ordinary discourse in this respect is true also of 'literary' or 'poetic' discourse—regardless of whether that discourse is as *bona fide* as ordinary discourse (as in the case of *Areopagitica*) or whether it merely mimics some of the rhetorical conventions of ordinary discourse ('My Last Duchess,' for example). Some literary texts are evidently utterances of the author *in propria persona*; others are utterances not of the author but of a *dramatic persona*: in understanding both kinds of literary discourse the reader needs to register correctly what it is that the speaker is doing in uttering the words he speaks. There is some uncertainty whether the first poem that I shall examine in this paper was meant to be taken as the utterance of the author, or as that of a dramatic *persona*; that uncertainty does not affect the point about it that I wish to make.[2] The poem is Shakespeare's Sonnet 19:

> Deuouring time blunt thou the Lyons pawes,
> And make the earth deuoure her owne sweet brood,
> Plucke the keene teeth from the fierce Tygers jawes,
> And burne the long liu'd Phænix in her blood,
> Make glad and sorry seasons as thou fleet'st,
> And do what ere thou wilt swift-footed time
> To the wide world and all her fading sweets:
> But I forbid thee one most hainous crime,
> O carue not with thy howers my loues faire brow,
> Nor draw noe lines there with thine antique pen,
> Him in they course vntainted doe allow,
> For beauties patterne to succeding men.
>   Yet doe thy worst ould Time dispight thy wrong,
>   My loue shall in my verse euer liue young.[3]

This startling poem seems not to have attracted much comment. What comment it has attracted is misleading in that it ignores what the speaker is doing at various points of the poem, uttering the words he does.

In the middle of the last century Ignatius Donnelly remarked of the first four lines, 'I know of no quatrain in Englis[h] poetry more heroic, more swelling, more original or more climactically finished.'[4] Part of such an impression would stem from such powerful nouns as 'Lyon,' 'Tiger,' 'teeth,' 'blood'; but much of the 'heroism' might plausibly seem to lodge in the imperative verbs: '*blunt* thou the Lyons pawes,' '*make* the earth deuoure . . .,' '*Plucke* the keene teeth,' '*burne* the long liu'd Phænix . . . .' This imperative syntax hammers on into the next quatrain: '*Make* . . . ,' '*do* . . . .' Stephen Booth, noticing (I suppose) these features among others, characterizes the octave of Sonnet 19 as 'affirmative,' and therefore 'set off against a third quatrain in which the verb is governed by *not*' ('O carue not with thy howers my loues faire brow').[5] But despite the bold diction and the even bolder grammar, it won't do to call either the first quatrain or the whole octave 'heroic' or 'affirmative' in any unqualified sense. If there is heroism here it is only of a special kind; and in a strict sense there is no affirmation in the octave at all.

For in uttering lines 1–8 the speaker does not *affirm*; nor, despite the boldly imperative verbs, does he *command*; rather, he *concedes*. His utterances are not *affirmations*, nor *commands*, but *concessions*. They bespeak not his strength and authority, but his weakness and incapacity.

Some part of this actual state of affairs should be clear from the start. The reader should early recognize that an apparent order issued to Time to exercise his power over the creation cannot be quite what it seems: that is, it cannot really be an *order*. For a mortal has no authority to issue genuine *orders* or *commands* to Time; and no *order* or *command* is genuine unless the speaker has the appropriate authority over the hearer.[6] (I cannot issue a *bona fide* order to the President of my university to dye his hair; for that matter, he cannot issue a *bona fide* order to me to cancel my subscription to *College English*. We may *advise* each other to do such things; but at present we each lack the appropriate authority to issue such an *order* to such an effect.) Furthermore, even if Shakespeare's speaker *did* have the social authority over Time that an authentic *command* would presuppose, he could not without anomaly pretend to *command* Time to do a thing that Time in any case could not help but do. (An absolute monarch may say to his slave, 'Metabolize your blood sugar!'; but in so speaking he issues no genuine *order*.[7] Conversely, no parent can genuinely *order* his child to speak in Urdu unless he knows that that child *can* speak in Urdu.) Despite appearances, in addressing his many imperatives to Time the speaker is not *ordering* or *commanding* Time to do anything: we recognize this—or ought to—because we sense intuitively that these imperatives fail to satisfy at least two rules or preconditions that partly constitute the speech act of *ordering* or *commanding*. Despite their considerable syntactical power the speaker's many imperatives do not, as uttered, exert the power of *command*.

What the speaker *is* doing in uttering these imperatives is obvious in the last clause of the series: '. . . do what ere thou wilt . . . .' Despite the imperative grammar, the speaker of this utterance is not commanding Time to do anything, but rather is *conceding* to Time the power to neglect the speaker's wishes. So, in uttering all his imperative clauses, the speaker does not *command* Time, but *concedes* to Time certain powers that the speaker regrets but does not dispute.

As Donnelly and Booth suggest, there is great power in the octave of Sonnet 19. Much of that power takes the form of a tension between the dynamic, imperative grammar of what the speaker says, and the passive, concessive acts that the speaker performs in the saying.

The speaker's long introductory series of concessions ends abruptly with an utterance that is patently not a concession: 'But I forbid thee one most hainous crime . . . .' The verb in this case makes explicit what the speaker would do in saying these words: in saying them he would *forbid*, he would *prohibit*, he would *enjoin*.

To find out *what* the speaker would forbid Time to do, the reader must go on to the next line:

> But I forbid thee one most hainous crime,
> O carue not with thy howers my loues faire brow . . . .

G. Wilson Knight comments on these two lines in a way that catches something of the force of the first, if not of the second: 'He [the speaker] can even assume authority greater than death's.' Knight then questions the sanity of such an assumption of authority: 'Is this just rant? Or do we respond to anything deeper? Is there any point at all in talking like this? That is our problem.'[8]

In a recent book on the *Sonnets* Philip Martin repeats Knight's question, 'Is there any point at all in talking like this?'—and decides that there is no point: 'For the command is plainly absurd, as the speaker himself must recognize . . . .' (Martin goes on to reject the final couplet as 'facile' and 'unsatisfactory.')[9]

Knight's misgivings, and Martin's impatience, are both partly based on a misimpression—a misimpression shared by J. Dover Wilson, who paraphrases: '. . . the Poet . . . boldly forbids the tyrant to lay a finger on his beloved's brow.'[10] Knight, Martin, and Wilson all take line 9 as extending and specifying the prohibition announced in line 8. But there is a difference between the two lines.

Though in uttering line 8 the speaker begins overtly to *forbid*, in line 9 he does not forbid at all; rather, he *pleads*, or *petitions*, or *entreats*. The force of line 9 as an *entreaty* is marked by the inter-jection 'O'—a locution recorded by the *O. E. D.* A more explicit lexical marker would be the word 'please': the speaker is in effect saying, 'O *please* do not carve with thy hours my love's fair brow.' The metrical reasons are obvious for doing without the word 'please' here; and there is this additional reason: it is to the speaker's advantage not to make explicit the speech act of *pleading* or *entreating* that he carries out in uttering line 9. For if he were to make that act explicit it would clash impossibly with the act of *forbidding* that he has explicitly undertaken in the preceding line. Professor Martin's objection to lines 8 and 9— that the command is 'plainly absurd, as the speaker himself must recognize'—nears the mark, but misses it. The command *is* absurd, and the speaker himself does sense that; but the command or prohibition occurs in line 8 only. By line 9 the speaker has already abandoned that kind of verbal enterprise as insupportable on its face.

The absurdity, the insupportability of *forbidding* Time to have his way with the speaker's love, is corollary to the absurdity and insupportability of *commanding* Time to have his way with other creatures: in both cases the speaker lacks authority over Time to issue such a prohibition or command, and in both cases Time lacks the requisite power to bind and loose. Line 8 begins boldly enough; the speaker is momentarily 'heroic' and 'affirmative'; but the bravado can't be sustained. Therefore in line 9 the speaker reduces his *prohibition* to a *plea*.

The speaker completes his adjustment of speech to reality at the start of the final couplet, with a massive concession: '. . . doe thy worst ould Time . . . .' This brings to a climax the concessions that began in a limited way in line 1; the speaker has now surrendered everything to Time, including his beloved. But he counterbalances all these concessions in uttering the final words: 'Yet . . . dispight thy wrong, / My loue shall in my verse euer liue young.' This last speech act engages the full affirmative power of Shakespeare's poem. It is not a *statement*, nor even a *prediction* or *prophecy*: it is a *boast*; and concentrated into it is the equal of all the power that the speaker has reluctantly *conceded* to Time. With this authoritative *boast* of his power as a poet to immortalize his beloved, the speaker all but reduces 'deuouring time' to the impotent condition of a senile beast.[11]

(An afterthought may be in order. I once thought, as in the general mode of Booth's *Essay on Shakespeare's Sonnets*,[12] that the reader of Sonnet 19 undergoes a shifting of perceptions while reading the poem roughly like the shift undertaken during the course of the speaker's speech acts. I still think that some such account is true of the second half of the poem, particularly of the shift from *prohibition* to *plea* in lines 8 and 9. But I doubt that the normal tendency to misread the early verbs by mistaking *concessions* for *commands* is in itself meant to be significant. That is, not too much should be made of the fact that the reader doesn't really know how to 'take' the early lines until late in a first reading of the poem. If the initial misreadings were in some sense 'required,' and were meant to be meaningful, the reader would have to be thought slow to notice the speech-act rule violations that infect any supposed *order* issued to Time. Maybe competent readers and hearers *are* slow to register such phenomena; in that case attention to the reader's changing response might be justified. But that justification would hold only if Sonnet 19 were meant to be encountered exclusively in written or printed form. The confusions that beset the reader of a text are greater than any that beset the *listener* to a proper saying of the text aloud. The listener has more information available to help his understanding; the suprasegmental phonemes of live speech [stress, pitch, juncture] work to disambiguate speech-act performances, as well as aspects of syntax and semantics, which would seem unresolvably ambiguous in cold print. In the case of Sonnet 19, a rise in pitch in the articulation of such words as 'blunt,' 'pawes,' 'make,' and 'broad,' can make explicit what the speech-act conventions would otherwise suggest—i.e., that these opening lines are not *commands*, but *concessions*. Unless one holds that Sonnet 19 is meant to depend upon the spare ambiguities of the printed page only, it is safest to call the reader's misreadings of the early lines just that—misreadings.[13])

There is a brief poem by Robert Frost that, like Sonnet 19, rewards close attention to its speech acts, for it is easily misunderstood unless the reader listens to what the speaker is doing in saying what he says:

Spring Pools

> These pools that, though in forests, still reflect
> The total sky almost without defect,
> And like the flowers beside them, chill and shiver,
> Will like the flowers beside them soon be gone,
> And yet not out by any brook or river,
> But up by roots to bring dark foliage on.
>
> The trees that have it in their pent-up buds
> To darken nature and be summer woods—
> Let them think twice before they use their powers
> To blot out and drink up and sweep away
> These flowery waters and these watery flowers
> From snow that melted only yesterday.[14]

Discussion of this poem with students has shown that they often miss the point of the final stanza. They suppose the speaker to be merely expressing a private wish or desire that the trees might hold off a bit before they destroy the fragile and lovely spring pools. Such a reading pays little attention either to the emphatically accented word 'snow' in the last line, or to the odd adverbial phrase that closes the poem. The last line is understood to have something to do with the spring pools, but not much to do with the trees.

Such readers take the final stanza as a *wish* (to give it the name of a speech act) probably because of the effect of the optative or subjunctive mood governing the phrase, 'Let them think . . .' ('Let' often introduces a *wish* or a *prayer*—'Let the garden flourish; let there be peace in the land.') Perhaps, too, readers expect to find wistfulness and sentimentality in Frost's poems. In any case, it helps to turn a reader's attention to the phrase 'think twice,' and to its ordinary uses. 'You'd better think twice before going to New York'; 'He should think twice before buying that house': such sentences are typically used to enact not an *order* or a *wish*, but a *threat* or a *warning*—whether directly (in the first or second persons), or obliquely (in the third person, as in 'Spring Pools'). In saying what he says Frost's speaker does not *order* the trees to stop doing something, on the one hand, nor *wish* that they would stop, on the other; rather, he indirectly *warns* the trees about the consequences of their actions. He *warns* them that there will be a quick return of the snow and the season of death—from which they have escaped 'only yesterday'—if they do not halt their destruction of the present moment and their mindless rush into the future. Frost varies this Wordsworthian topic in 'Nothing Gold Can Stay,' 'The Oven Bird,' 'West-Running Brook,' 'Reluctance,' and other poems. If summer comes, can winter be far behind? The major irony of 'Spring Pools' is the fact that the speaker knows that the trees are literally mindless and cannot act on his warning (which is one reason why the warning is oblique and not direct); like Shakespeare's Time, they cannot do otherwise than as they do.

I suggest that deliberate identification of speech acts, as in the examples given above, can be helpful in discussing some poetic texts—helpful, at least, in correcting misunderstandings like those cited. No doubt most texts don't need such an explicit analysis: for them we will have already grasped the force of the speech acts in the act of understanding the texts. That is because the conventions governing what we do in what we say are a natural part of language, as important as the conventions that govern syntax and semantics.[15] This aspect of language has engaged the attention of many linguists and philosophers of language, and several literary critics. Two comments will relate what I have said here to what has already been written on the subject.

First, the systematic study of speech acts undertaken recently by philosophers and linguists, preeminently J. L. Austin and John Searle, should prove useful in clarifying the interpretation of literary texts.[16] But I don't think that the projected audience for any such interpretation should be expected to master speech-act theory first. Successful analysis of language only codifies conventions that are already part of our knowledge of how to use and understand language. An instance of such a convention should be recognized as such by any competent speaker if it is pointed out to him. You don't have to be a philosopher of language to tell a *warning* from a *wish*. Nonetheless, explicitness and even jargon have their value, and I'd welcome, for practical purposes, any detailed and reliable taxonomy of what Austin calls 'illocutionary acts'—the center of a cluster of verbal acts that Searle calls, collectively, 'speech acts.' (In this paper the acts referred to as 'speech acts' have all in fact been, more narrowly, 'illocutionary acts.')

Second, applications of speech-act theory to literary criticism have so far concentrated on either metacritical or stylistic concerns. The metacritical applications usually involve efforts to distinguish the concept of literature from that of ordinary discourse. The stylistic applications often involve characterizing an author's 'style' in terms of the speech acts that he tends to engage in, and the presuppositions that lie behind those acts.[17] I think that a third, more narrowly interpretive kind of application, like that attempted in this paper, also holds promise. Understanding the meant meaning of any piece of discourse involves understanding what Austin calls its 'illocutionary force' as well as its 'locutionary meaning' (which involves 'sense' and 'reference'). The risk of misunderstanding illocutionary force is frequent enough in literature to require some precaution. Illocutionary ambiguity is as common in spoken and written language as are syntactical ambiguity and semantic ambiguity. Most sentences can be used to execute many different speech acts. Fortunately, the information contained in the context of a live utterance goes a long way towards disambiguating all three kinds of ambiguity. But, because the context available for understanding a *written* utterance is narrower, ambiguities can persist. In the normal course of events we may manage to muddle through such complexities without having to think about them. But there are times, in literature as in life, when we must deliberately study what it is that is being done *in* what is being said, or else run the risk of missing the illocutionary point altogether. Sonnet 19 and 'Spring Pools' are two such occasions.

NOTES

1 This paper has been improved—if not approved—by Paul Alkon, Thomas Clayton, Donald Ross, and Martin Steinmann.

2 For an account of the kinship of dramatic and non-dramatic texts, see Marcia Eaton, 'Good and Correct Interpretations of Literature,' *Journal of Aesthetics and Art Criticism*, 29 (1970), 227–33, esp. 231–2; and Michael Hancher, 'Three Kinds of Intention,' *Modern Language Notes*, 87 (1972), 827–51, esp. 847–8.

3 William Shakespeare, *Sonnets, 1609: A Scolar Press Facsimile* (Menston, England: Scolar Press, 1970). I have adopted the standard emendation of 'yawes' to 'jawes' in line 3.

4 Ignatius Donnelly, *The Sonnets of Shakespeare* (St. Paul: G. W. Moore, 1859), p. 14; cited in *A Variorum Edition of Shakespeare: The Sonnets*, ed. H. E. Rollins (Philadelphia: Lippincott, 1944), I, 53. A quarter-century later, Donnelly launched the notorious theory that there are Baconian ciphers embedded in the text of Shakespeare's plays.

5 Stephen Booth, *An Essay on Shakespeare's Sonnets* (New Haven: Yale University Press, 1969), p. 43.

6 The discussion here of speech-act anomalies assumes the prior interpretation and discounting of a more basic anomaly involved in

addressing *any* remarks to a non-human entity ('time'–also printed as 'Time'). Simply to talk to time at all is to violate what Noam Chomsky calls a selectional restriction rule of grammar (*Aspects of the Theory of Syntax* [Cambridge, Mass.: M. I. T. Press, 1965], p. 95). In this case the governing rule would be: the object of direct address must be human, or animate and human-like. To violate this rule by addressing an inanimate entity as if it were a person, is to invent an instance of personification–which is the figure of speech basic to Sonnet 19. That figure 'explains away,' as it were, the anomaly involved in talking-to-time *per se*. What remains to be explained, after one grants the personification, is the anomaly involved in *giving orders* to such a person or personification *without the proper authority*.

7 This varies an example invented by Bruce Fraser, 'On Accounting for Illocutionary Forces,' *A Festschrift for Morris Halle*, ed. S. A. Anderson (New York: Holt, 1973); cited by Katherine Hammer, 'Searle's Conditions and the Determination of Illocutionary Force,' *Centrum*, 1:2 (1973), p. 146. The example of 'This chili's hot,' in my second paragraph, is adapted from Hammer's remarks on p. 137.

8 G. Wilson Knight, *The Mutual Flame* (London: Methuen, 1955), p. 76. Knight here identifies death with time.

9 Philip Martin, *Shakespeare's Sonnets: Self, Love and Art* (Cambridge University Press, 1972), p. 160.

10 John Dover Wilson, ed., *The Sonnets* (Cambridge University Press, 1969), p. 116.

11 In the introduction to her edition of the *Sonnets* (New York: New York University Press, 1969), p. 29, Barbara Herrnstein Smith describes in passing the phrase, 'Yet do thy worst, old Time,' as a 'challenge.' Perhaps it is the combination of the *concession* in line 13 with the *boast* in line 14 that makes a *challenge* of the couplet as a whole. While this essay was in press I discovered Thomas Tyler's compact summary, which nicely coincides with the present account: 'In this Sonnet Time is first *implored* to restrain his power; and then he is *defied*' (*Shakespeare's Sonnets*, ed. Thomas Tyler [London: David Nutt, 1890], p. 176; italics added).

12 Cited in note 5. See also the program proposed by Stanley Fish in 'Literature in the Reader: Affective Stylistics,' *New Literary History: A Journal of Theory and Interpretation*, 2 (1970), 123–62; reprinted as an appendix to Fish's *Self-Consuming Artifacts* (Berkeley: University of California Press, 1973). Neither Booth nor Fish incorporates speech-act analysis into his critical method, but the possibility of doing so remains open.

13 Those who hold that a poem is by definition 'a structure in which ambiguity is a constitutive device,' and who favor readings of poems that nurture ambiguity, may defend such 'misreadings' along the lines of Samuel R. Levin's argument in 'Suprasegmentals and the Performance of Poetry,' *Quarterly Journal of Speech*, 48 (1962), 366–72; Booth's *Essay* offers another kind of support. (Levin's essay was published in 1962, and therefore does not go into the

question of speech acts; but suprasegmentals can 'flag' speech acts as well as syntactical constructions and lexical meaning.)

14 *The Poetry of Robert Frost*, ed. E. C. Lathem (New York: Holt, 1969), p. 245.

15 For a recent explanation and application of this line of reasoning, see Martin Steinmann, 'Figurative Language and the Two-Code Hypothesis,' in Fasold, Ralph W. and Roger W. Shuy, eds, *Analyzing Variation in Language: Papers from the Second Colloquium on New Ways of Analyzing Variation* (Washington, D.C., Georgetown University Press, 1975), pp. 220-7.

16 J. L. Austin, *How to Do Things with Words* (New York: Oxford University Press, 1965 [rpt. of 1962 ed.]); John R. Searle, *Speech Acts* (Cambridge, England: Cambridge University Press, 1969). Marcia Eaton's extensive checklist of publications in speech-act theory will appear in *Centrum* 2:2 (Fall 1974).

17 Examples of metacritical applications are Monroe C. Beardsley's argument in *The Possibility of Criticism* (Detroit: Wayne State University Press, 1970), 49-61, revised in his essay 'The Concept of Literature,' *Literary Theory and Structure*, ed. Frank Brady (New Haven: Yale University Press, 1973), 23-39; and Richard Ohmann's discussion in 'Speech Acts and the Definition of Literature,' *Philosophy and Rhetoric*, 4 (1971), 1-19. Stylistic applications are exemplified in Ohmann's two essays, 'Speech, Action, and Style,' *Literary Style: A Symposium*, ed. Seymour Chatman (New York: Oxford University Press, 1971), 241-54; and 'Speech, Literature and the Space Between,' *NLH*, 4 (1972), 47-63, esp. p. 54.

CHAPTER SEVENTEEN

Toward a general typology of the pun

L.G. Heller *

[This article suggests a basis for a general typology of the pun.[1] Heller begins by pointing out and labeling the differences between the following puns:

1   The doctor fell into the well
                     And broke his collar bone.
                     He should have tended to the sick
                     And left the *well* alone

2 Come *forth*, Lazarus! And he came fifth and lost the job.

Heller labels the first pun a Type 1 and calls it a RETENTIONAL NON-DISAMBIGUATIONAL PUN because the double meaning is present at first glance and is retained. The second, he labels a Type 2 and calls a NONRETENTIONAL DISAMBIGUATIONAL PUN because the double meaning is not present at first (i.e., in perceiving the pun the original correlation between word and meaning is not retained) and because the double meaning is not present in the final context (i.e., the ambiguity between *forth* and *fourth* is resolved in favor of *fourth*). Heller goes on to construct a system for categorizing puns in eleven classes with the following terminology:

1 The correlation(s) between the manifesting mark and the function(s).
2 The retention versus the nonretention of the original correlations between manifesting mark and the function.
3 The disambiguation versus the nondisambiguation of the correlational possibilities.
4 The medium (or the media) of the manifesting mark.
5 The full versus the partial identity of the manifesting mark correlated with the functions.
6 The intra-versus the interlinguistic basis of the manifesting-mark identity.
7 The functional normality versus the functional shift of the units

*First published in *Language and Style*, 7 (1974), pp. 271–82.

used to accomplish the identity of the manifesting units, and a
specification of the type.

8 The discreteness versus the neutralization of the manifesting identity.

9 The hierarchal level, monolectic versus polylectic or both, of the
manifesting units.

10 The quantification of the pun-structures (single, double, etc.).

11 The immediate versus the displaced (duplex) correlation of the
functions.]

Down through the ages the pun has served as the object of disparaging
remarks and 'Oh-no-how-could-you' comments, but this fact has done
little to discourage its use, and indeed, many of the greatest writers
of all time (e.g., William Shakespeare) have employed the pun with
great relish. At its finest, the pun constitutes art of the highest order,
yet lack of formal analysis has long obscured the central insight that the
basic structure of the pun is identical at a deep level with a number of
more respectable literary genres, including the allegory, the mystery,
and the detective story, as well as with various other types of narrative
and poetic discourse which thus far lack specific nomenclature, since
their fundamental organization has gone unrecognized. Furthermore,
the structure of the pun holds implications basic to an understanding
of many psychological problems, and a knowledge of its dynamic processes offers important insights into the nature of reasoning itself. This
article, however, restricts itself to elucidating the structure and suggesting a basis for a general typology of the pun.

What has largely gone unrecognized, thus far, is the fact that the
'pun' represents not just one pattern but rather an entire class of different patterns which all share the following structural characteristic:
namely, that a single manifesting mark signals more than one conceptual
function. Consider, for example, the following (rather archaic) verse,
which ends with a pun:

> The doctor fell into the well
> And broke his collar bone.
> He should have tended to the sick
> And left the *well* alone.

Here the word *well*—a manifesting mark—stands simultaneously for two
concepts: (1) 'a place for collecting water' and (2) 'people who are
healthy.' This pattern may be charted as follows:

Function 1: place for collecting water ———— Manifesting Mark: *well*

Function 2: people who are healthy

The foregoing represents only one fundamental type of pun among many. By way of contrast, consider the following quotation from James Joyce:

'Come forth, Lazarus! And he came fifth and lost the job.'[2]

Here the word *forth* (phonologically identical with *fourth*) normally signals only one function according to the traditional orthographic correlation which identifies *forth* as the word signifying direction (as in *back* and *forth*), not sequence (as in *third, fourth*, and *fifth*). Yet the introduction of the word *fifth* into the context immediately suggests a *re*interpretation of the phonological /fɔrθ/ as 'fourth,' the indicator of sequence, not direction. Thus the structure may be mapped as follows:

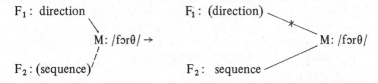

F_1: direction

  M: /fɔrθ/ →

F_2: (sequence)

F_1': (direction)

  M: /fɔrθ/

F_2: sequence

Had the spelling been identical for both functions, the *initial* structure would have been the simultaneously-signaled pattern seen in the 'well' example. Thus one may differentiate subvarieties of the pun: (1) on the basis of the correlation(s) between function and manifesting mark in the initial structure (that is, are two or more correlations perceived or is only one correlation identified, etc.) and (2) on the basis of the retention versus the nonretention of this initial structure. In the 'should-have-left-the-*well*-alone' type of pun, the word *well* is seen simultaneously in both correlations, and no change of structure ensues. Thus for convenience one may call this variety a TYPE 1 or RETENTIONAL, NONDISAMBIGUATIONAL PUN and rechart it, as part of a general typology, as follows:

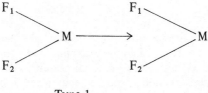

F_1

  M ⟶ M

F_2

Type 1

The 'Lazarus-come-forth' type of pun contrasts with the Type 1 in two ways: (1) the initial correlation between the manifesting mark (/fɔrθ/) and in one function (F_2, the sequential one) is not seen and (2) the structure of the correlational set changes. One may call this kind of pun a TYPE 2 or a NONRETENTIONAL, DISAMBIGUATIONAL PUN (*disambiguational* because, although both potential meanings of /fɔrθ/ are eventually seen, one of them is rejected by virtue of the context) and chart it as follows:

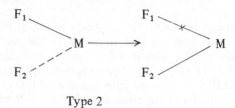

Type 2

In line with this classificational scheme, then, one may likewise recognize two other types predicated on the basis of the same two choices—(1) the complete versus the incomplete identification of potential correlations and (2) the retention versus the nonretention of this structure—and chart them as Types 3 and 4:

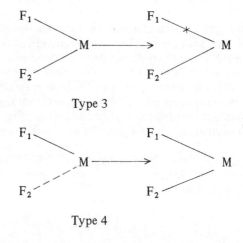

Type 3

Type 4

The Type 3 is disambiguational, since it eliminates all possible correlations (here only one, F_1-to-M) except one (F_2-to-M). It is nonretentional since it does not retain its initial correlational structure. The Type 4 is nondisambiguational, since it ends up with more than one possible correlation. It is also nonretentional, since it changes its initial correlational structure.

Not all of the four types have been illustrated yet, since the main emphasis here is the nature of the structural range, not simply its enumeration. All four types, however, enter into a more complex classification scheme, and unillustrated variants will appear later.

The foregoing classificational grouping rested on the relationships of the functions and the manifesting marks. Another basis for categorization—and one which crosscuts the foregoing—is the nature of the manifesting mark itself; that is, whether the signal is phonic, orthographic, or kinesic (gestural). In theory, it can be *anything* perceptible. The puns already illustrated depended on phonological identity. The gestural analogue of this pattern has not traditionally been classified as a pun at all; but whatever label may be used, the fundamental similarity of structure (differing only at the manifesting level) ought to be recognized and brought into the typology. Thus, for instance, one may consider the type of situation comedy familiar through countless variations of cinema and stage presentation in which a young man, on seeing a pretty girl, tries to make her acquaintance. He therefore follows her into a large auditorium where, unknown to him, an auction is taking place. He waves to the young lady with a friendly gesture designed to show his interest. *She* ignores the gesture, but the auctioneer interprets the motion as a bid on the item being displayed. Again the young man waves. Again the auctioneer perceives the gesture as a bid. After about five minutes of this gestural discourse, actually intended to establish a social relationship, not to acquire a possession, the hero finds that somehow—unexplicably—he has purchased a Rembrandt for some enormous amount of money. The pattern is the following:

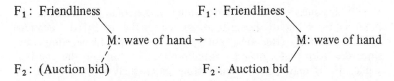

F_1: Friendliness $\qquad\qquad$ F_1: Friendliness

$\qquad\qquad$ M: wave of hand $\to$ $\qquad\qquad$ M: wave of hand

F_2: (Auction bid) $\qquad\qquad$ F_2: Auction bid

From the point of view of the previous *sub*typology, this 'pun' is a **Type 4** or nonretentional, nondisambiguational variety:

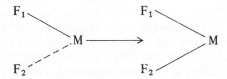

It differs from all four varieties of the foregoing classificational scheme by virtue of the medium of the manifesting mark, this one being kinesic rather than phonological. Thus one might catalog this variety (subject to additional expansion according to criteria yet to be discussed) as a KINESIC TYPE 4 (or KINESIC NONRETENTIONAL, NONDIS-AMBIGUATIONAL, if one combines the typological lables). All four structural possibilities exist for each communicational medium. Hence one may have orthographic, kinesic, phonic, and other varieties of the same set of correlational types.

Some potential puns *cannot* be transmitted through a different medium. Consider, for instance, the following:

> The medieval schoolmaster was determined to tame his unruly pupil. Therefore he threatened to flog the youth within an inch of his young life if he didn't measure up and do his work properly. He added, 'Thou hast better study thy lesson, Master Jonathan, or else methinks thou wouldst do well to get a weapon and defend thyself.' He bowed stiffly and prepared to leave. Then the pupil made a *bow*.

Here, of course, the *written* form, *bow*, correlated each of two functions, F_1 and F_2 below:

$$F_1: \text{'weapon to shoot arrows'}$$
$$\diagdown$$
$$M: bow$$
$$\diagup$$
$$F_2: \text{'bending from the waist'}$$

Yet, if this anecdote were spoken aloud, rather than read silently, the potentiality of one of the correlations—either that of F_1 (the weapon) with M or of F_2 (the social amenity) with M—would be eliminated, since the word that signals F_1 is phonologically /bo/ and the one that signals F_2 is /baU/. Some manifesting units, such as the *well* of the Type-1 pun given before, can be transmitted in different media, with each manifestation, e.g., the orthographic *well* or the phonological (/wεl/) preserving the structure-based ambiguity. Other manifesting units, such as the word *bow* above, would lose this ambiguity if transposed to a different medium. Thus one may further typologize on the basis of the potentialities of the avenues of transmission.

An additional and extremely important crosscutting criterion from the point of view of audience reaction is that of absolute versus only partial identity of the manifesting units correlated with the functions. Most communicational schemes carry a certain amount of inbuilt redundancy of signaling. Consequently, in appropriate contexts, even a partial rather than complete identity of manifesting units suffices to suggest correlations with functions normally associated with slightly different manifestations. Consider, for example, the following:

> The patient took a turn for the *nurse*.
> She was too beautiful for *wards*.

The word *nurse* in place of the anticipated word *worse* shares a partial phonological identity with the latter, but differs by a single phoneme, /n/ rather than /w/. The context, 'took a turn for the ———,' which precedes the word, however, assures the double correlation. Likewise the visual change of one grapheme (the *a* of *wards* for the *o* of *words*) or, alternatively, the sound change of one phoneme (/ɔ/ for / ɜ /) still fails to preclude the correlation of the manifesting unit (*wards*) with both potential functions (that of F_1: the conceptualization behind the words *wards*, and also that of F_2: the conceptualization behind the word *words*) since both the context—'too beautiful for ———'—*and* the partial identity of the manifesting mark (either the orthographic or the phonological) point to the second correlational possibility ('words' as well as 'wards'). This partial divergence within a framework of similarity is a unique type of foregrounding device that regularly produces the oh-no-how-could-you reaction, referred to, that has unfortunately brought other types of pun into disrepute. Whenever this structural deviation occurs, the audience *predictably* chuckles, then groans. Sometimes the chuckle is omitted, but the groan—or some equivalent—is inevitable whenever precisely this type of structural pattern appears.

Additional bases for the classification of the pun may rest on the structural means by which the manifesting units correlated with each of the different functions become identical (in whole or in part). For example, one may have a manifesting deviation which is structurally interpretable as an absolute identity because of *neutralization*—'the cancellation in some context of the differential function of a feature which is demarcative in some other context.' Consider, for instance, the following:[3]

> The Japanese farmer had just mastered the game of chess and the
> intricacies of movement of the pawns, the bishops, the knights, and
> so on. One day, his good wife came out and caught him playing
> when he should have been taking in his crops. After he had listened
> to her tirade, he said, 'One minute, honorable wife,' and made one
> more move with his rook. 'Everyone know, honorable wife-san, that
> one should rook before one reaps.'

Here the neutralization is the cross-linguistic one between Japanese and English whereby the Japanese speaker regularly produces /l/ as /r/, whence the articulation of both *rook* and *look* as *rook*, and of *reap* and *leap* as *reap*. Note, of course, that the presentation of the pun must contain any contextual clues necessary for the recognition of the neutralization. That is, here the anecdote specifies that the speaker is Japanese. Had the farmer been identified as Italian rather than Japanese, the same punch line would have produced bewilderment rather than the intended effect, since Italian does not neutralize an /l/-/r/ contrast.

The subvarieties of neutralization are numerous, but a general typology might first subdivide the entire range into *inter*linguistic versus *intra*linguistic at the initial level of classification. Thus the *rook-before-one-reaps* type would, in addition to being a phonology-based nondisambiguational retentional (Type 1) variety, be further classified as an *inter*linguistic neutralizational type. Of course, any type of interlinguistic neutralization is structurally predictable on the basis of a simple comparison of the relevant levels (here the phonological) of the languages involved. Hence a German–English neutralization could rest on a substitution of /v/ for /w/ or, in word-final position, of any voiceless stop for a voiced one (e.g., of /t/ for /d/, as occurs in German, both *Bund* 'bundle' and *bunt* 'colored' being articulated with a final /t/). A Spanish–English neutralization might include a substitution of medial /ð/ for /d/ (e.g., *lather* for *ladder*) since Spanish has no medial /d/.

A special subcategory of the *inter*linguistic might be an *intra*linguistic pathological type such as lisping, baby-talk neutralization, and so on. For example, consider the following, which has appeared in a variety of versions:

The young man, having wined and dined his date, especially the former, asked her if she wanted anything else.

'I want to get weighed,' she said.

He thought the request peculiar but complied, taking her over to a scale and dropping in a penny.

Later he again asked her if she wanted anything.

Again she said, 'I want to get weighed.'

He complied, but began to wonder what sort of lunatic he had taken out. Several times more this took place, each time the young lady replying, 'I want to get weighed.'

Finally, growing exasperated, he took her home. When her mother saw her come in the door, she asked 'How did you enjoy yourself?'

'Wousy!' came the reply.

Here the neutralization is interlinguistic to the extent that an /l/-/w/ neutralization is not indigenous to normal English, and the particular pathological variant constitutes a different system from that norm. The neutralization, however, can rest on an *intra*linguistic structuring. Thus in English there is a phonological rule which precludes the gemination of homorganic consonants belonging to the same articulatory class. Hence any juxtaposition of words which would place a final consonant of one word in close juncture with a word-initial consonant of its own set-class (according to the particular rule) would effectively neutralize one or the other of the two, as in the following:

> Patrick Doyle was justly renowned for his drinking habits. He could down whole gallons of alcoholic stimulants at a sitting.
>
> One day he choked on a pretzel, and as he gasped for breath, the spectators hollered, 'Give the man a glass of water.'
>
> 'Water,' roared Doyle, regaining himself. 'Everyone knows that water and Doyle don't mix.'

This type of neutralization may be considered a deletional neutralization, since one of the potential interpretations of (functions associated with) the phonological correlate of the orthographic manifesting structure 'and Doyle' is 'and oil,' which involves the apparent dropping of a phoneme (here /d/). The *reap/leap* type may be classified (in addition to its *inter*linguistic categorization) as a substitutional or replacement neutralization.

An *intra*linguistic substitutional type is the following, which rests on the neutralization of the voiceless/voiced contrast directly after a sibilant:

> Dawn Kleppermeyer's new beau was as handsome a youth as ever had been seen, and she was wild about him. Yet he drove her frantic with his strange habits. Every evening before he kissed her good night he would insist on eating a can of tuna. Night after night this practice went on until, almost in tears, she cried, 'It's always Star Kist before Dawn.'

Here the word *darkest* (not given explicitly but which is implicit in the sequence *It's always ——— before dawn*) and the *–tar Kist* (from *Star Kist*, the brand name of the tuna) become phonologically identical because of a *double* neutralization; (1) the /s/ of *Star Kist* is neutralized (a deletion neutralization) in close-juncture with the sibilant of *always* and (2) the nonaspiration of the /t/ following the sibilant renders this /t/ functionally indistinguishable from /d/. Phonologically, *Dawn* and *dawn* are identical. If the pun is spoken, no manifesting level distinction is perceptible between the /dɔn/ correlated with the conceptual function 'time of sunrise' and that correlated with the girl's name. When read, the distinction is noted, but the written form still calls to mind the phonological sequence, which in turn suggests both correlations, not just one. Although there is no neutralization here of the orthographic elements, it *is* quite possible to have orthographic neutralization. Neutralization may take place in any medium of communication. Here, for example, is an orthography-based neutralization, which rests on three structural facts:

1 English spelling differentiates proper nouns from common nouns by capitalizing the first letter of the former but not that of the latter.
2 English spelling marks the start of a sentence by capitalizing the first letter of the first word in the sentence, and
3 a potential neutralization of the proper-noun-versus-common-noun capitalization contrast takes place in sentence-initial position where even a common noun would be capitalized by virtue of the sentence-onset marking rule.

This is the age of dissent, protest, and unionization. The teachers had organized, the firemen had organized, and the hospital employees had organized—all in a growing determination to get their rights and improve their living standards. At long last even the race horses at Hialeah went on strike for more hay and shorter hours. Not too surprisingly they won their demands immediately, since the track season was in full swing. The union leader, being a bit greedy, however, directed the horses to stage an extra slowdown so that they might also get some additional pension rights.

One old stallion named Lightning talked them out of the action, but said that he himself would comply with the union's request when he got to Santa Anita.

The union leader, a bit puzzled, asked why the old horse would comply with this request at Santa Anita but not at Hialeah. The answer came, 'Lightning never strikes twice in the same place.'

Here, as seen, the distinction between *Lightning* (with a capital *L*) and *lightning* (with a lower-case *l*) disappears (is neutralized) in the appropriate context. As this example also shows, however, the principle of neutralization is operative regardless of the communicative medium, whence one must again recognize the medium as a crosscutting basis for classification in the total typology of the pun.

Another consideration in such a scheme is the phenomenon of functional shift, whose potentialities differ from language to language. English regularly employs this grammatical device for a number of categories, particularly in the shifting of nouns to verbal use, as in the word *man*, which appears in both functions in *Man the pumps, man.* Since English already has so many examples of words with the same form used in both nominal and verbal capacities, the native speaker of the language readily recognizes any innovations which first extend the use of some noun to a verbal function, even if the specific noun in question should never have been so used before. Hence writers may, for one or another reason, utilize this recognitional ability when they need to have a new verb corresponding to a particular noun. In most such instances, the 'normal' use of the language would employ some circumlocution, which would retain the noun as a noun. Nevertheless, since the structural potentiality does exist, one may base puns on this functional shift, as in the following:

> Ephraim's son Willie was a hot-rod enthusiast. He spent every moment of his leisure time—and many hours of what should have been his study time—tinkering, adjusting, or otherwise monkeying with the unlikely heap that shone in the garage. Ephraim's patience grew shorter and shorter as Willie's schoolwork suffered.
>
> One day Willie, satisfied at last that his auto was ready, needed only a few spare tires to allow him to enter the annual hot-rod contest. His father adamantly refused to contribute even a single penny, saying, 'Spare the rod and spoil the child.'

As seen, the word *spare*, originally an adjective, later used as a noun according to a regular rule (not described here), which still governs such shifts, is employed now for the first time as a verb meaning 'to provide one or more spare tires.' Any typology of the pun might appropriately specify any special devices, such as functional shift, in the nomenclature. Of greater consequence, perhaps, is the fact that all special devices, including but not only functional shift, utilized in the production of noncasual discourse of any kind *must rest on regular processes indigenous to the language*. English does use this particular kind of functional shift wherein both the noun and the verb have exactly the same form, and the marking of the specific function (nominal or verbal) of that form in any given instance rests on its position with respect to other words of the sentence. Latin also had devices for extending the lexicon, but since Latin was a highly inflected language and did not employ word-order as a first-level signal as English does, *this* kind of device, not inherent in the Latin grammatical structure, was precluded from use in Latin puns. Romans could and did innovate for stylistic effect, but the nature of the innovations was confined to the indigenous patterns of Latin. English can innovate with *this* kind of functional shift because the structural model already exists in the language. The mere fact that such a model does occur makes the innovation both possible and comprehensible to the audience; but it does not, of course, necessarily make it socially or stylistically acceptable for all forms of discourse: formal usage, for instance, generally eschews neologism.

The *spare-the-rod* example further illustrates an additional consideration for setting up a typology: singularity versus multiplicity of pun structures in the patterning. Here not only does the word *spare* have a double functional correlation, but the word *rod* does too (with one function—the conceptualization meaning 'a wooden switch employed in punishment'—and with another—the conceptualization meaning 'a special type of automobile'). Hence this *spare-the-rod* pattern constitutes a double rather than a single pun, as does 'It's

always Star Kist before Dawn,' given earlier. In theory one may have
any number of puns embedded in the same utterance. In one recent
book,[3] the late Bennett Cerf included a quintuple pun, but this type,
although possible, occurs rarely in practice. Most English pun-structures
are of the single variety. Some languages, however, have other tradi-
tions. For instance, the great number of Chinese words borrowed
by Vietnamese had led to so many homophones in that language
that the double pun has now become a fundamental art form there.

Still another typological consideration is the hierarchal level or
levels which the manifesting marks employ. Consider, for example, the
following double pun which rests on a number of different devices,
only one of which is the focus of consideration at the moment:

> The spectators watching the roulette wheel scratched their heads
> in astonishment. Every time the little man placed his money on a
> number he roared like a lion. 'Five dollars on number 23, grrr!'
> 'Ten dollars on 17, grrr,' and so on. After winning steadily for
> half an hour, he pocketed his money and turned to go.
>   Observing the faces of the crowd, he commented, 'What's so
> strange? As you make your bet, so must you lion it.'

The first pun—the dysphonic *bet* for both 'bet' and 'bed'—causes much
of the oh-no-how-could-you reaction referred to earlier, but, as indicated,
may be ignored here. The use of *lion*, however, illustrates several
analytic points of interest. At one level, of course, it represents functional shift of a noun to a verbal use in the sense 'act like a lion' ('roar').
At another level, however, it illustrates a cross-syntactic structuring,
that of *lion*, a monolectic (single-word) unit, homophonous with *lie
on*, a polylectic (many word—here, two-word) phrase. Hence one may
characterize this part of the pattern as 'monolectic-polylectic,' since
the manifesting unit stands for both possibilities simultaneously. If
one employs the total range of classification illustrated thus far, the as-
you-make-your-bet-so-must-you-lion-it type then is a double pun, part
one being a dysphonic retentional, nondisambiguational type and part
two being a phonological, monolectic-polylectic manifestation with one
functional shift (the monolectic part) of a retentional nondisambiguational type.

One additional structural possibility will be considered, namely that
between direct and displaced puns. All of the foregoing illustrations
utilized a manifesting mark which represented two functions (and which
in theory, could just as well have represented more). These are all *direct*
puns. Sometimes, however, the conceptualizations (functions) represented by the manifesting mark may themselves stand for manifesting
marks in a higher-level structure whose functions are sociocultural, and
which therefore must be analyzed in terms of this sociocultural

structuring. Consider, therefore, the following, which was originally called to the author's attention by a former student, Deborah Posner, but a slightly different variant of which has subsequently appeared in print:

> A sociology professor at the local college was fond of telling off-color jokes, a fact which embarrassed the young ladies in his class tremendously. (The college could not have been the City College of New York, where the author teaches.) Finally the girls got together and decided that at the next hint of an off-color joke they would get up en masse and leave the classroom. They sat there primly awaiting his next lecture. Sure enough, he began with the words, 'There is a terrible shortage of prostitutes in Singapore.'
> The girls looked at each other, rose, and started to leave. He called after them, 'Don't go now girls. The boat doesn't leave for Singapore until Friday.'

Here the *secondary* manifesting mark was the girls' rising and starting to walk out. At the primary level, the *linguistic* cues stand directly for a conceptualization, 'the act of walking out.' As a *sociocultural maneuver*, however, the act of walking from a room itself has two potential functional correlations:
1 a situation-avoidance activity (the correlation the girls had in mind) and
2 a goal-directed activity (the one the professor had in mind and which the audience missed until the professor's words—'The boat doesn't leave for Singapore until Friday'— explicitly call attention to it.)
Since this structural pattern is one of change from the initial single correlation to the later double correlation, it may be characterized as nonretentional nondisambiguational, the simple Type-4 structure; but since the functional interpretation, which is duplex, goes beyond the simple primary phase seen in all of the other examples, this pun may be called secondary or displaced (sociocultural).

At this point it may be useful to recapitulate the various criteria which may serve to suggest a general typology of the pun:

1 The correlation(s) between the manifesting mark and the function(s);
2 the retention versus the nonretention of the original correlation(s) between the manifesting mark and the function(s);
3 the disambiguation versus the nondisambiguation of the correlational possibilities;
4 the medium (or the media) of the manifesting mark;
5 the full versus the partial identity of the manifesting mark correlated

with the functions (i.e., iso- versus heterophonic, iso- versus hetero-
kinic, etc.)

6 the intra- versus the interlinguistic basis of the manifesting-mark
identity;

7 the functional normality versus the functional shift of the unit(s)
used to accomplish the identity of the manifesting units, and a
specification of the type;

8 the discreteness versus the neutralization of the manifesting device(s),
and if the latter, a specification of the resultant in terms of deletion
or change;

9 the hierarchal level, monolectic versus polylectic or both, of the
manifesting units:

10 the quantification of the pun-structures (single, double, etc.); and

11 the immediate versus the displaced (duplex) correlation of the
functions.

Undoubtedly other criteria will come to light as more examples of
puns are examined against the framework of the general classificational
scheme suggested here. This article may be considered, then, as a simple
prolegomenon to the analysis of a very large, complex, and important
family of communicative structures.

NOTES

1 A brief treatment of the relationships between different types of
puns and some other literary genres appears in L. G. Heller and
James Macris, *Toward a Structural Theory of Literary Analysis*
(Worcester: Institute for Systems Analysis, 1970), pp. 34–41 and
passim, and in the same authors' monograph *Multilateral Allo-
variance* (London: International Linguistic Association, 1972),
pp. 19–22, the latter of which also explores some of the non-
literary varieties of this general family of more-than-one-function-
to-one-manifesting-mark structures.

2 James Joyce, *Ulysses* (New York: The Modern Library, reset ed.
1961), p. 105, cited also in Heller and Macris, *Parametric Linguistics* (Paris and The Hague: Mouton, 1967), pp. 26–7.

3 *A Treasury of Atrocious Puns* (New York: Dell Publishing Co.,
1970), p. 28.

CHAPTER EIGHTEEN

Interpreting meaningful nonsense

Marvin K.L. Ching

[Responses to an open-ended questionnaire demonstrate that readers use fairly defined methods to interpret oxymora of the adjective noun construction. Certain of these oxymora can be explicated through case grammar although the interpretations may widely differ or even conflict. The readers' interpretations of oxymora where the adjective functions more like a noun can be explicated through case grammar. The headword, the head noun, acts as the central word and case relations are assigned to the adjective, which also functions like a noun.

This explication of readers' responses goes beyond Stockwell, Schachter, and Partee's treatment of noun phrases showing case relations to the head noun in complex noun phrases in *The major syntactic structures of English* (1973), because a study of readers' responses to oxymora shows that adjectives can also be considered as nouns and show case relations to the head noun. Only after case relations are assigned, do these nouns take the syntactic marker of an adjective.

The oxymora *friendly terror* (from Joyce Carol Oates's poem 'Family') and *evil innocence* (from Thomas Wolfe's short story 'The child by tiger') are used not only to illustrate a variety of readers' responses through case relations, but also to show how the multiguous meanings, some of which are even contradictory, may be reconciled to give a virtual world, a semblance of the paradoxically and complex nature of human experience.]

Two oxymora—*friendly terror* and *evil innocence*—are semantically interpreted by readers not merely as a coexistence of the contradictory characteristics named. That is, *friendly terror* does not mean merely the notions of *friendliness* and *terror* added together; *evil innocence* on many readings means more than a neat balance of the antithetical ideas of *evil* and *innocence*. Readers seem to interpret each adjective-noun construction in fairly defined semantic relations that can be explained by case grammar through extending the concept of complex noun phrases of Stockwell, Schachter, and Partee (1973, pp. 1–31), where surrounding noun phrases of the head noun are related to their headword through case relations or meanings.

Stockwell, Schachter, and Partee's interpretation of complex noun phrases through case relations already provides a tool for interpreting noun-preposition-*of*-noun phrases like *Shame of Nobleness* (from Emily Dickinson, '#551' [1955, p. 442]), which already shows in the surface structure two nouns: *Shame*, the central noun, and *Nobleness*, a noun that is the object of the preposition:

> There is a *Shame of Nobleness*—[1]
> Confronting Sudden Pelf—
> A finer Shame of Extasy—
> Convicted of Itself—
>
> A best Disgrace—a Brave Man feels—
> Acknowledged—of the Brave—
> One More—'Ye Blessed' to be told—
> But that's—Behind the Grave

There is a shaming of *Nobleness*, the recipient for the action named by the first noun of the oxymoron. As a kind of animate direct object that is personified, Nobleness shows the case of *patient* to indicate that Nobleness receives the shame, because the *patient* case indicates an animate being as recipient of an action. We may also pose an *agent* or *causer* for the action, a shaming of Nobleness by something or someone. In the context of the poem we can see that Nobleness has done nothing to merit shame.

Far from having some fault, the perfection of Nobleness is revealed by her reaction to that which makes her feel ashamed. What makes her feel guilty and uncomfortable only points out how magnificent Nobleness really is: the agent or causer of her shame is Pelf—riches. Nobleness has good values because she feels uncomfortable and embarrassed when confronted by sudden riches. She is not motivated by wealth, neither is she dependent upon its resources; her very nature makes her uneasy in the presence of Pelf.

But evidence from readers' responses definitely indicate that not only oxymora of the noun-preposition *of*-noun construction like *Shame of Nobleness* can be interpreted by case grammar. A number of oxymora of the adjective-noun construction can also be interpreted by case grammar when the modifier functions like a noun in its semantic relation to the head noun. Two such oxymora are *friendly terror* and *evil innocence*.

Because readers' responses on an open-ended questionnaire reveal that the adjectives of some adjective-noun oxymora like *friendly terror* and *evil innocence* are semantically interpreted more like nouns, the adjectives *friendly* and *evil* may be treated as nouns on the level of meaning—the deep structure—and thus they possess case relations to their head nouns *terror* and *innocence*. The words *friendly* and *evil* later surface syntactically as adjectives for the sense of seeming contradiction inherent in all oxymora.

Appearing in strategic portions of a poem and a short story, the two oxymora named above are not merely contradictory nor semantically anomalous. Each phrase succinctly and aptly summarizes the main ideas of its literary selection. For example, in Joyce Carol Oates's poem 'Family' (1973, p. 43) *friendly terror* recapitulates with epigrammatic precision the situation of the 'family' in the poem:

Family

What are we doing here jumbled
smelling of dust in a potato
sack? What is this dance we perform
sitting down? Tell me what our faces
meant to declare, mashed together nose
against nose in *friendly terror*?[2]

What is that word stamped faintly
on your forehead?—reversed blue ink
of an A & P melon? Oh in this crowd
it's a chore to breathe to thrust a fist
through the bag to the dark
quiet cupboard—

Do we need so many elbows? so many
eyes crossing? Names leaping from mouths?
Why is it necessary to embrace
to make room? necessary to flatten
      the face
of stubborn signs? Why is the dance
      a jumble
of buttocks and calves
fingertips and eyelashes and stinging
      molecules
of sweat?

What are we doing here jumbled
for decades sharing the ache
of our dark back teeth? What is
the purpose of the dance? How
      does this
cupboard door unlock? Who has tied us
in here together and walked away?

And the pressure of the context of *evil innocence*—the concluding paragraph of Thomas Wolfe's 'The child by tiger' and the preceding elements of the short story—also guides readers to produce readings which reveal more than a combination of the two qualities named in the oxymoron. The reason is that the elements of the whole story— the characters, the plot, and the title itself—force readers into thinking how the savagery which erupted from the protagonist—the Negro Dick Prosser—is related to his innocence. The emphasis is on the protagonist's being overpowered by evil, and the narrator's shock at the evil which resided in a tender, talented, and good man. Readers also wonder about the relation between the white society's evil and its innocence. The last paragraph reads:

> He came from darkness. He came out of the heart of darkness, from the dark heart of the secret and undiscovered South. He came by night, just as he passed by night. He was night's child and partner, a token of the wonder and the mystery, the other side of man's dark soul, his nighttime partner, and his nighttime foal, a symbol of those things that pass by darkness and that still remain, a symbol of man's *evil innocence*,[3] and the token of his mystery, a projection of his own unfathomed quality, a friend, a brother and a mortal enemy, an unknown demon,—our loving friend, our mortal enemy, two worlds together—a tiger and a child.
>
> (Wolfe, 1939, p. 156)

In both selections a number of readers see a cause and effect relationship with the adjective acting as a noun, an animate *agent* or an inanimate *causer* of the head noun. For example, many readers' responses reveal that they interpret the word *friendly* more like a noun. They consider the word to mean 'friendliness', or 'the characteristics of friendliness', that is, intimacy, warmth, comfort or cheer; or they interpret the word as 'friends' or 'people who act like friends'. Thus it was friends or friendliness that caused the terror. These case relations of agent or causer also appear when the meaning of friends or friendliness is ironically interpreted.

These concepts of the physical proximity of friends or the psychological intimacy of friendship producing feelings of claustrophobia are evident in readers' responses to the meaning of *friendly terror*:

> Forced into relationships but afraid of these relationships. Forced to be close but fearful of exposing ourselves.

> *Friendly*—part of the loss of freedom or *imprisonment* described in the poem is caused by the bonds of *affection* between the family members; another aspect is the familiarity from close

association. *Terror*—revulsion felt at times from too close association.

Friendly is used ironically to describe the closeness of the faces. Obviously, the situation is not a friendly one.

Friendly is purely ironic, referring only to the proximity of these people which in other circumstances would denote concord. *Terror* is their real condition.

In the interpretation of *evil innocence*, some readers also consider the adjective as the causer of the innocence. That is, the white society, in its social code, made the black Dick Prosser innocent or naive. He had to address all the young boys as 'Mister' or 'Cap'n'; though bruised and bleeding when struck by a white man who was drunk, he had to maintain his temper and not retaliate even though he was struck when defending his employer; Prosser could not own a gun. He had to play the role of a black man—an innocent. The evil dictates of society, which made him suffer all these injustices without manifesting his emotions, also led him to think naively and erroneously that he could maintain emotional and psychological control over his situation. However, his rage eventually burst forth in a grand madness.

But the reverse causal relationship also occurs in the interpretations of both oxymora. Many readers feel the adjective of the oxymora is the result rather than the agent or the cause of the action. In readers' responses to *friendly terror*, many take the oxymoron to mean that the terror produced friends or a friendliness among people, a comraderie, a shared terror which united the people:

Because the terror is shared by all the occupants, it is *friendly*. It implies a comraderie of fear.

. . . The terror seems to be a *community* feeling which results from adversity within the group. *Friendly terror* is terror a group feels, tries to huddle against, and attempts to console one another about.

A collective, therefore *friendly*, terror of some common enemy, outside force, etc.

. . . because it is a *shared terror*. The speaker is not alone in it.

Not only is the causal relation reversed in relation to the head noun *terror* so that *friendly* is assigned the case of *result*, but *friendly* can also be considered as exhibiting the case meaning of *patient*, which indicates the animate being that receives the action of the verb. Thus, the case of *patient* is assigned if *friendly* refers to the recipients of the terror as friends or those who became friends. The case of *neutral* may be assigned to _friendly_ if the word shows that the thing which was produced by the terror was friendliness. The _neutral_ case is the case associated most closely with the headword itself and is least interpretable independently of the headword; it is often used to explain the semantic relationship between the headword and a noun phrase when the noun phrase is not animate. It can be defined negatively as the semantic relationship indicated when no other case relationship is applicable. Because the word _friendly_ also reveals with whom the terror is shared, with friends, it may be designated as being in the _commutative_ case. Finally, _friendly_ functions as the case of _manner_ as well as the cases of _result_ and _patient_ and the _neutral_ and the _commutative_ cases. That is, the persons affected by the terror responded in a friendly way as reflected in this reader's response:

> Civility, the learned politeness we have devised in order to make waiting in the cupboard easier—as if it is too horrendous or potentially destructive to let go and cry out the terror.

Of these cases just cited, readers' intuitive responses to _evil innocence_ can be explained by the _neutral_ case and the cases of _result_ and _manner_. Many readers consider _evil innocence_ to mean Dick Prosser's innocence, unawareness, or naivete of the evil around him and within him. The relation of evil to innocence in this interpretation shows the _neutral_ case: Prosser was innocent of the evil. Many readers, for example, cannot hold Prosser responsible when he went berserk and indiscriminately shot down the townspeople because he had lost his sanity: 'He did not know what he was doing,' readers say. The protagonist was also innocent of the knowledge that the hatred he suppressed would one day unleash itself in an evil, uncontrollable fury: he did not know that the irrational cannot be subdued by the rational. His passion for order and perfection as seen in his immaculate housekeeping and his daily activities could not suppress the inevitable eruption of the tiger within him. Moreover, he was naive to think that his belief in God as manifested in his quotation of verses from the Bible and his meditation of the Twenty-Third Psalm could save his soul from the society that kept him playing the subservient role of a Negro.

Readers' responses also indicate that the relationship of evil to innocence meaning 'innocence of evil' can be extended to the narrator and the white society. The narrator, a young boy, was at first ignorant of the evil within Dick, who seemed 'a friend, a brother' (Wolfe, 1939; p. 156). The narrator was also initiated into the knowledge of evil in all men—not only the evil in Prosser. The white society, in its gleeful triumph over riddling Prosser's body with bullets, indicated the basic savagery in man. But the white society was innocent of evil in the sense that it was unaware that its actions were evil. Besides these 'innocent of evil' interpretations—semantic relations which can be explained by the *neutral* case—the relationship of the modifier to the noun can be that of *result*.

Like all of the preceding interpretations using case relations, the modifier is interpreted like a noun in the response showing the case of *result*. The *evil* which occurred was a result of the *innocence*—the *naivete* or unawareness—of the protagonist and also of the white society. The adjective *evil* can also be treated as a noun in these readers' responses which show the case of *manner*: 'Evil was the outward manifestation of Prosser's innocence' and 'The evil was the way the innocence showed itself.' These readers think that Prosser, the tiger of the title of the story, was innocent, but his manner of behavior was interpreted as evil. He was like a beast that instinctively kills those that threaten its self-preservation or an animal that naturally destroys its victims for food. His actions were, of course, not really motivated by evil. The beast does not pounce upon its prey with malice. It is we human beings who attribute this quality of evil in our description of what occurs. The interpretation of the evil in the tiger's mode of behavior is a projection of anthropomorphic qualities of intention upon the tiger. Another interpretation exhibiting the case of *manner* is that the townspeople thought that their vengeance was morally defensible—innocent—but actually their extreme acts of vengeance and their taking the law into their own hands proved that their innocence manifested itself in an evil manner.

For both oxymora, then, the modifiers *friendly* and *evil* can be assigned a variety of cases, depending upon the semantic meaning that is placed upon the relationship between each modifier and noun. The adjectives function more like nouns in the base component of the grammar, where case relations are assigned to these noun phrases to show their relationship to the head noun. Both *friendly* and *evil*, according to readers' interpretations of the oxymora *friendly terror* and *evil innocence*, possess the case relations of *causer, result,* and *manner* and the *neutral* case. The modifier *friendly*, in addition, shows the case relations of *agent* and *patient* and the *commutative* case.[4]

Case grammar rather than the syntactically based grammar of the standard and the extended standard theory explains the readers' responses on the questionnaire. Because cases are assigned by semantic considerations of the constituents in questions and the final syntactic shape of the constituents are derived later through transformational rules from the case relations, case grammar can assign different cases to constituents having identical syntactic appearance in the surface structure—the level of pronunciation—but different semantic functions in the deep structure—the level of meaning. In *friendly terror* and *evil innocence*, readers thought of each adjective and headword as two nouns, and their intuitions divided evenly on the causal relationship between the two constituents of each construction: the causal relation between *friends* or *friendliness* and *terror*, and the causal relation between *evil* and *innocence*. The divided intuitions of readers' responses indicate that the semantic relationship between the head noun and its modifying noun are part of the deep structure, the level of meaning. These relationships are expressed as case meanings. It is the deep structure of case grammar that reveals which word is to be considered the head and which constituent is to be viewed as the one which shows different semantic relationships to the head. Later, through trans-formational rules the modifying noun and the head are expressed as *friendly terror* or *evil innocence* in the surface structure, the level of pronunciation. The modifying nouns take on the syntactic form of an adjective on the surface, but are really nouns in the deep structure.

But what is the significance of the multiple interpretations which unfold in an oxymoron, some which are contradictory to each other and some of which may be produced without authorial intention? The context of the poem may not only legitimatize individual readers' responses, but it may also reveal how the contradictions in interpreta-tion may be reconciled so that they produce the sense of the true nature of life—the enigmatic contradictions of human experience and the complexity of reality. The diverse interpretations thus produce the illusion of life, a mimesis of the psychological reality of a situation, experience, or event which is described by the oxymoron. Rather than one idea or feeling, the whole set of interpretations for an oxymoron may produce for readers the illusion of an integral picture of life through the simultaneity of ideas produced by the multiple readings of an oxymoron. The oxymoron thus becomes a vehicle for expressing the intricacy of life where all the different ways of viewing it may be given. Thus, in *evil innocence*, we have seen how the innocence of a black man may cause an evil end because naivete is unequipped to cope with malignant forces, but also how the evil of the white society can cause innocence by stifling the black man's growth and maturity, reducing him to a child. In *friendly terror*, perhaps the good and the bad interpretations of friendship do produce this paradoxical truth: terror produces a camaraderie or friendliness among people against a common alarming situation, but friendliness or intimacy may also be frightening in this situation because it stifles individuality and pre-cludes individual privacy. The contradiction or nonsense of an oxymoron thus becomes meaningful, and readers interpret this meaningful nonsense.

NOTES

1 Italics, my own.
2 Italics, my own.

3 Italics, my own.
4 In the analysis the terminology for the different cases comes from several sources, because in the evolution of case grammar there has not been general agreement as to the actual number and types of cases needed. I also devised the term *causer* to name an abstract quality, idea, or characteristic that causes an action as compared to the case of *agent*, which indicates an animate being that causes an action.

REFERENCES

Stockwell, Robert, Paul Schachter, and Barbara Hall Partee, 1973. *The major syntactic structures of English*. New York: Holt, Rinehart & Winston.

Index